THE GENTLE WAY III

MASTER YOUR LIFE

A SELF-HELP GUIDE FOR THOSE WHO BELIEVE IN ANGELS

TOM T. MOORE

Other Books by
Tom T. Moore

The Gentle Way

The Gentle Way II

First Contact: Conversations with an ET

THE GENTLE WAY III

MASTER YOUR LIFE

A SELF-HELP GUIDE FOR THOSE WHO BELIEVE IN ANGELS

TOM T. MOORE

ISBN: 978-1-62233-005-8

PO Box 3540
Flagstaff, AZ 86003
1-800-450-0985
1-928-526-1345
www.LightTechnology.com

Contents

Foreword

Almost three years have passed since *The Gentle Way II* was published. Yet as many success stories as that book contained, I have continued to receive truly unique stories from people all over the world requesting most benevolent outcomes (MBOs) and asking for benevolent prayers (BPs) for their families, friends, other people, and other beings. It just proves that there are no limits to this modality, which is becoming a gentle movement as people discover how much better their lives are with these simple yet powerful requests.

MBOs Work Perfectly

When I began requesting MBOs about sixteen years ago, I had no idea how many extra benefits there were in making these requests. I just knew they worked *perfectly*, and I had never been able to say that about any other modality I had tried over the past thirty years. But I eventually discovered that this process was raising my vibrational level, which some people also term "ascension." This allowed me to begin communicating with my own guardian angel (GA), Theo, in 2005, as well as many other beings.

My angel communicated to me in my "active meditations," as I call them, that requesting MBOs is the first and easiest way to raise your vibrational level a little at a time. He said you can read all the articles and books and listen to all the programs, but until you start implementing communication with Spirit, you'll remain on a plateau of sorts. And it does take a lot of the stress and fear out of our lives, as you'll read over and over again in this book. This includes even dangerous situations in which people found themselves in perilous circumstances.

For those of you attracted to this book for the first time, you simply say,

> "*I request a most benevolent outcome for* _____. *Thank you!*"

This is the language to use when the request is specifically for you. For other people, you change it to say a benevolent prayer:

> *"I ask any and all beings to _____. Thank you!"*

As an example, here is one I've been testing out over the past couple of years. I record my dreams each morning, since dreams are messages from our souls and can inform us of something good about to happen in our lives or challenges that are coming up. When I feel as if I've had a dream about an upcoming challenge, on awakening I'll say,

> *"I request a most benevolent outcome for anything that will occur in my physical world that this dream may have referred to. Thank you!"*

It makes me feel better knowing I'm getting a jump on the challenge the dream symbology referred to.

Some Common Questions I Get

One of the common questions I am asked is, "Should I say the request once, or can I say it multiple times?" My guardian angel tells me just one time works, but those golden lightbeings we call guardian angels understand that we live stressful and fearful lives, so you may say the request as many times as you wish. My angel tells me that we are not penalized for repeating our requests.

Another question I get often is, "Should I address a particular archangel? Or God or Jesus? Or whom? If you notice, there is no deity mentioned in the request, which I believe I was inspired to word that way. Just keep the request simple. If you wish to believe, however, that your request goes to a particular deity such as God, Jesus, Mohammad, Allah, Buddha, Vishnu, or any others I have not mentioned, that's fine, because these golden lightbeings we call our guardian angels are tremendously powerful souls. I use the analogy of my own angel being able to handle two million requests for a parking space at one time without breaking a sweat!

Another question I receive is, "Why don't my MBOs always work?" I explain that if you make a specific request, such as for a particular job or a particular love interest, that job or love interest may not be in your best short-term or long-term interests. You'll find several months or even a year or two later that a better job or love interest was on the way.

Taking the Most Benevolent Path

Another benefit I did not realize when I began requesting MBOs is that this practice keeps you on your soul path, or "soul contract," as my guardian angel calls it. People really have a lot of misconceptions about soul contracts, so let me explain them according to what my angel has told me. A soul contract simply means you chose the most perfect life you could for learning, challenges, successes, and so on. My angel explained it more fully when I conveyed this question to him from one of my newsletter subscribers: "How much leeway does one typically have on a soul contract?"

"As we have discussed many times, Tom, you do have the freedom to choose other paths during your time on Earth," my angel responded. "But when you begin requesting MBOs, it does keep you on that path. Let's say the path does allow you to wander just a bit — but not too far. Requesting MBOs does keep you on a path to meet those people you're supposed to encounter and interact with and to meet those challenges set up for the maximum growth of your soul. So missing minor influences in your life can be okay, as others can be shuffled in to perform the same tasks for you, but it is so much better to request MBOs so that no shuffling takes place. Everything happens as it's supposed to in your life, and when you finish this life and review it, you will be quite pleased with the results. It's an almost perfect life from the viewpoint of a rearview mirror, shall we say? Again, you do have free choice, but taking the most benevolent path will get you to your destination much faster than wandering through the woods."

Enjoy the many inspiring stories in the pages of this book, and if you have not tried requesting MBOs in your life before, please do so. It will be the best thing you have ever done for the rest of your life!

01

How MBOs Work

Guidelines for Requesting MBOs

Tom says: I have found that requesting an MBO for a situation is more effective than the law of attraction. I received an email recently asking if "declaring a thing" is the same as requesting an MBO. I asked my guardian angel in meditation, and he replied, "No, Tom, and I'll explain why. A declaration is just that — a demand for some action. This is more than the law of attraction, and it's not cocreating with Spirit. It's taking into consideration whether it is good for you and for all those in the demand. It's saying, 'Do this no matter the consequences.'"

❋ ❋ ❋

Here are some things to keep in mind when you are requesting MBOs:

- You must request the assistance, as your guardian angel — or whoever else you believe is assisting you — is otherwise not allowed to assist.
- It must be benevolent for all those connected with the request.
- It must be a request for you specifically.
- It must be said aloud or put down in writing to create the energy.
- There is no limit on the number of MBOs you can request.
- Trust in the process by starting with mundane requests.

❋ ❋ ❋

Consider what begins to happen when you request MBOs in your life:

- You become more aware.
- Your stress and fear levels decrease.
- You get back on your soul path or contract.
- Your vibrational level increases.
- You take the first major step to cocreate with Spirit.
- Your spirituality increases.

The Radiant Effect

Annette writes: "I want to thank you for the wonderful advice you have given on requesting MBOs. I have learned that the more I request benevolent outcomes and living prayers, the more in touch with my guardian angel I become and the faster the answers, blessings, and lessons come to me and flow to others. Yes, I feel that happening."

Tom responds: I've been remiss about reminding everyone of the radiant effect requesting MBOs has on other people. When you request an MBO for your drive to work or to a restaurant, those who are riding with you are in what I call the "bubble effect." Not only that, but the cars that are in front, behind, or beside you most likely will also be in the bubble of energy that you create.

Think of all the other times you have requested MBOs for relations with others in business and your personal life. They're also affected by these requests. You're bringing just a bit of peace to the world every time you request MBOs. That's how powerful this simple little spiritual tool is. The more you use it, the more you'll grow and the higher the vibrations you'll cocreate.

I have also noticed that a number of people just say "MBO" in their benevolent requests, so I thought I should ask my guardian angel about whether or not it makes a difference when people just say "MBOs" and not "most benevolent outcomes." My guardian angel replied, "Just a little, Tom, but actually not much. You see, the intent is there, and that's what matters to us. We understand what that person is requesting and honor it, although it is slightly better to say it completely. So allow, Tom, and don't demand. We are thrilled to have these people request assistance."

Whom Do You Address?

Sandy writes: "Hello, Tom, and thank you so much for your information on benevolent outcomes. I think I've been using this process for many years, but I never used the specific words 'request' and 'benevolent.'

"Anyway, I would like to ask a question: When beginning the request, whom do you address? I seem to get in the way of myself, using angels, the universe, God, All That Is, higher self, energy, and so on. It seems, from what I can tell from your articles, that there is no direction for addressing one entity and that our request just starts out as,

> **Most Benevolent Outcome Request**
> *"I request a most benevolent outcome for _____."*

"Is this correct? Does All That Is know who we're speaking to? Then, when I say thanks, it seems I want to thank the universe. Will you please comment on this? Thanks so much for your uplifting advice. I've shared this with my family. It is so positive and loving to use."

Tom responds: I've been told that addressing angels, Creator, God, archangels, and so on just gets in the way and can even limit your request. When you request an MBO, keep in mind that your guardian angel is monitoring you every minute of the day, as he or she has great capabilities far beyond even my understanding (and I've been asking questions for four years now). When you say, "I request _____," that immediately tells your guardian angel that you're requesting an MBO. Even though he or she knows your thoughts in advance, you have to say it out loud and with emotion, if possible.

You don't have to thank your guardian angel at the end of the request, but I always do. That's just showing your love and respect for what this beautiful being volunteered for millions of years ago in Earth time: to be of service to us, as we have these hard, challenging lives, completely veiled from knowing who we really are. And when my MBO is granted, I thank my guardian angel three times. Again, this is my way of acknowledging and recognizing the assistance I received.

Requesting MBOs Verbally

Shirley writes: "Doreen Virtue [the author of many books on angels] says you don't have to pray out loud, that you can indeed say prayers in silence because your guardian angel will still hear them. But you mention they can only hear them if you say the words out loud or write them down, due to the fact that we are in the physical world.

"This just seems contradictory to me, that's all. Who is right? Or are some of us evolving to where our thoughts are heard by the angels anyway? I had to write to ask because it is causing me distress, as I have read a lot of books by Doreen Virtue, and I often feel more comfortable talking to angels, God, or whatever it is in silence."

Tom responds: For Shirley and everyone, I never said that you would not be heard if you make your request in silence, but that it's simply much better to say the MBO and BP requests out loud.

As you may have read elsewhere in my writings, guardian angels and prayer angels can read your thoughts, but a comment from Lois J. Wetzel might clarify the issue a little further. She wrote to me: "I woke up at 2:30AM thinking I need to tell you this: When you request an MBO verbally, as I mentioned, you are vibrating the throat chakra and creating sound. Sound is the creative force of the universe. In many major religions, sound is what creates everything, from the Om of Hinduism to the ideas expressed in the first lines of the Gospel of John: 'In the beginning was the Word, and the Word was with God, and the Word was God' (John 1:1, KJV). The word is a vibration, and everything that is has a frequency. Everything is energy vibrating, so everything has a sound or hertz frequency — whether it is in the human auditory range or not."

What synchronicity! Again, this is, I think, another validation for the benefit of requesting benevolent outcomes out loud. The conversation Lois references, by the way, was an interview with me on her Blog Talk Radio show on November 13, and you can listen to this interview and to the November 18 interview on Dick Sutphen's Metaphysical World show by going to my website, clicking on the "appearances" tab and scrolling down to those respective dates.

Requesting MBOs in Dreams

Daphnee writes: "I only wanted to let you know a funny and short thing that happened to me. After I started reading your book, I had a dream one night. I cannot remember the dream, but I do remember that during the dream, I was requesting an MBO for something. I was amazed that I was still able to request one while dreaming. I cannot explain it, and I was wondering if you ever heard of such a situation."

Tom responds: Yes, I have dreamed of requesting MBOs as well, and I think that you were being reminded in the dream to do that also.

If You Stumble While Requesting an MBO

Rick writes: "I have a quick question. I sometimes stumble through an MBO. Does that affect the outcome? If so, is it best to repeat it until I get it right? Thanks."

Tom responds: "I asked my guardian angel in meditation whether you need to start over again if you stumble while requesting an MBO, and he responded: "No, Tom, you do not need to repeat it. Your friendly guardian angel accepts your request even if you stumble, as you call it, verbally. BPs are virtually the same. We can naturally read your thoughts as you say these prayers. It matters not to the 'prayer angels,' we shall call them, or your friendly guardian angels, as the intent is there, you see? Yes, some channels say to start over, but that's your choice. If you wish to start over, that's fine. And no, you don't have to wait some specified time. You can still say the prayer or MBO request, and we will respond, as there is no time here."

MBOs for All Things Big and Small

Tammy writes: "I use MBO requests and am so excited when I get one like a parking spot or something small like that. My question is this: Can we have blocks against MBOs working for us when we ask for bigger things than the little MBOs for things like parking spots? I wonder, because I use them and love them and am thankful for them, but they don't seem to work for larger requests. Thank you."

Tom responds: For Tammy and anyone requesting MBOs, the reason I suggest that you start with the smaller requests is that the larger ones — for jobs, homes, mates, and so on — can take a lot longer. I've told many stories about how things have taken longer to manifest than I would have preferred, but they do manifest eventually, unless it's not in my soul contract to go down a particular life path. Requesting MBOs keeps you on your soul path — or "soul contract," as my guardian angel calls it. So trust in your own guardian angel to provide what you asked for at the most benevolent time, according to the path you're taking in this life.

Answers to Spoken MBOs

Dori writes: "Thank you for your magnificent work. I own and have read many different books about many angels and their various specialties. I read your books to guide me in my continued work and requests with angels. Asking for benevolent outcomes from my guardian angels is the fastest way to accomplish my desires and goals. My modes for serving feel near to being revealed.

"You are a blessed one, my friend. Though I've long known the power of the spoken word, I was not speaking my requests out loud often enough. This was mostly due to needing an MBO when in public. Now I think further ahead. My results are excellent for large and small requests for myself. Currently I am clarifying and listening to my guidance for greater understanding of my soul contract."

Not Worthy to Request MBOs?

Marie writes: "I want to know if angels can help you only if you're on the right path. My friend Sandra says that she can't really ask for help from the angels at this point because she hasn't done her part."

Tom responds: Anyone who has doubts about being worthy enough to request MBOs should pay particular attention to this answer from my guardian angel in meditation. My angel told me, "These people, Tom, are being limited by their beliefs. We guardian angels stand ready to assist you at whatever point in time you wish to call on us. When you request MBOs, as we have repeatedly said, this puts you on a more benevolent path instead of the more difficult one. So believing that you must perform some service or work before requesting assistance yourselves is simply an outmoded religious belief. Everyone should be requesting assistance from us every day — no exceptions! It will put you on the right path and will keep you on that path with less stress and fear."

Can Two People Share the Same Guardian Angel?

Kathy writes: "Is it possible for two people who are involved in an intimate relationship to have the same guardian angel?"

Tom responds: I asked my guardian angel whether two people in an intimate relationship can have the same guardian angel, and he responded: "Quite so, Tom. It happens all the time. Remember that there are soul fragments of the same soul that can have lives together at the same time. These are typically intense relationships, and they can sometimes be too much in the long run for those people to remain together. There can also be two soul fragments from similar soul groups that a guardian angel is tuned to assist from their very first lives on Earth as they meet over and over again — male and female lovers or just family and friends. So it is not so unusual, but not necessarily the norm either. Each circumstance is different. As I mentioned before, most guardian angels, as you call us, take care of the soul fragments of at least 6,000 or more whole souls, and most of us handle a number far larger than that. It really all depends on how well we vibrate in relation to the souls."

Requesting Multiple MBOs

Diane writes: "Can you please clear something up for me when it comes to MBO requests? Would it be confusing to my angels if I requested a few things right after each other? For example, I might request an MBO for a good, calm, happy day, and then after that, I could request an MBO for a good rate for getting my car fixed as soon as possible. Then I might request an MBO for my husband to calm down and be happy. Is that okay, or should I just stick with one MBO request, say, within an hour?

"I'm not sure about this, but I do know that my MBO requests work in the short term or the long term? And then there are some I am still waiting on! About two weeks ago, I requested to find the lens for my camera, and every time I would think about it, I would request it again, but then I'd forget about it. Nevertheless, my lens showed itself the other day, so I do know that some MBOs just take a little longer than others."

Tom responds: For Diane and everyone else: Keep in mind that there is no time "on the other side," so your guardian angel can handle any number of MBO requests you make and literally a million others from his or her other "clients," all at the same time.

My guardian angel reminds us that humans are very impatient; you have to give MBO requests time to manifest. My daughter couldn't find her backup contact lens last week and was leaving for Indianapolis on a business trip. She said she had requested an MBO to find it, but there was still no lens. When she returned, she found them in a pocket in her camera bag. At least she found them!

A Matter of Phrasing

Brian writes: "How do your MBO requests differ from Robert Shapiro's benevolent magic requests? I find Shapiro's method hard to remember and easily craft into a sentence, but I know that he quotes you and you also quote him. Is it really the same mechanism?

Tom responds: As I related in my first book, it was in an article by Robert Shapiro and then in a book of his where I first read that you could "request benevolent outcomes in your life." This is not his real focus, as he's a full trance channel with many books in many series, so I started experimenting with that gem of an idea and have made it much easier for people to request MBOs, as I call them — and now benevolent prayers, which he originally called living prayers.

Are "Any and All Beings" Always Well-Intentioned?

Sandra writes: "I would like to suggest that when requesting MBOs, you use the words 'any and all spiritual beings.' Just saying 'any and all beings' could include some not-so-beneficial entities. Thanks for all you do!"

Tom responds: For Sandra and anyone who has this question: We don't want to limit the prayer to just spiritual beings. As an example, if we say a BP for aid to come to people trapped in an earthquake, that aid might come from men and women searching the wreckage, or it may come from a search dog, a cat, a child, a bird, or even a guardian angel who manifests physically to render aid. My guardian angel has said that when you say this prayer, only beings "from the light" will respond.

Past MBO Requests Working Now

Rick writes: "Some things, it seems, are coming to fruition for me, and I feel that MBO requests are the reason. I've obtained a provisional patent for a weightlifting device that will increase user safety. I have a broker working with me who believes it will fetch a lot of money. In addition, my broker has completed a patent search on two other products he believes are moneymakers.

"I believe this is the answer to the following MBO that I said in the past:

> **Most Benevolent Outcome Request**
> " *I request a most benevolent outcome for obtaining more money than I will need for the rest of my life. Thak you.*"

"This was said not with the intent that I would retire to an American colony in Costa Rica, but that it would give me the financial freedom to do anything I want, including financing my own movies. Secondly, the MBO for the perfect producer you provide in your book may have occurred too. I have one producer in North Carolina who likes my wrestling screenplay and another in San Francisco who wants to produce my screenplay on the first openly gay baseball player.

"I feel the MBO for the money and the MBO for the producers are interlinked. Now I am saying living prayers to all the players here to guide them to the best results. I am visualizing what I want as if it is already here as it suggests, but it is difficult to temper that with the reality that the money is not yet in the bank. That's a dicey one to balance."

Tom responds: Sometimes it takes a while for MBO requests to manifest, as they are just starting to now for Rick. Here's another piece of advice I gave him that I came across recently: Imagine that you already received the money in the past — not in the present. Say something like, "Gosh, it was great that I received that huge check for _____ last month!"

You Need to Ask for Angelic Help

Angel writes: "I have been using benevolent angel requests for months and months now, and I have to say that if you have not tried them, you must! They are amazing, wonderful blessings to incorporate into your life. The angels want so much to help us but cannot without us asking for help. I have had amazing experiences with their help, and I hope more people will give these a try as well!"

Tom responds: Angel makes a good point here: You have to request the assistance, or the only time they are allowed to assist you is if your life is in danger and your soul contract calls for you to continue to live.

How Do MBOs Differ from Other Prayers?

Anonymous writes: "All over the world, there are millions of people who pray every day, but most of them don't get results. How are MBOs different? They are also prayers, so why should the guardian angel hear an MBO more clearly than another prayer?"

Tom responds: My guardian angel told me that this is the first major step in cocreating with Spirit. And it's something so simple that anyone can do it, no matter if you are just being introduced to spiritual concepts or you have spent the past thirty or forty years reading everything you can get your hands on and experimenting with all sorts of modalities.

By requesting an MBO, you are not demanding a specific outcome — just the best one that is benevolent not only for you and your soul contract but for all those connected with the request. As you may have noticed, most prayers say "give me this" or "I want you to do this." MBO requests say, "I'm asking for this, but I'm relying on your knowledge to know if this is best for me and for everyone else."

So you may request an MBO to win the lottery, but that is probably not in your soul contract. The benevolent outcome will be for the person who has a soul contract to experience sudden great wealth to win, and then you have to learn how to handle this. The template is the same for the person who inherits great wealth, finds a vein of gold, or comes into wealth some other way.

Note how simple these requests are. There are no deities mentioned, which allows everyone to use these requests, and whether you believe your request is going to God, Allah, Vishnu, Jesus, Mohammad, or a guardian angel, that's okay.

Requesting MBOs in Dreams

Teresa writes: "Twice I have been dreaming of something unwanted happening to me but was lucid enough in the dream state to request an MBO. It happened last night — I dreamed I was losing my balance and falling a good distance, but I said this MBO and never fell. In fact, the dream shifted to another dream with people I remembered clearly within my dream world but have never actually met in this lifetime. I wonder if that was some sort of bleed-through from one of the other timelines. Anyway, I just wonder what happens when we request an MBO in the dream state."

Tom responds: I asked my guardian angel about this during my active meditation: What happens and why when people request MBOs in the dream state? He responded, "Yes, Tom, part of it is review and reinforcing the importance of requesting MBOs. Another part may be that you are teaching others either in a class or simply doing one-on-one teaching. There are other people on Earth this person perhaps thinks about and to whom she wishes to explain what MBOs are and how they can be beneficial to their lives."

MBOs Raise Your Vibrational Level

Dan writes: "Maybe this is just a simple question, but here it goes. You've made it clear that being in touch with our guardian angels and using MBOs helps to raise our vibrational levels. In a practical way, I suppose I can even feel that. When I'm connected, I literally feel lighter and in a more relaxed place, while when I'm not using MBOs, I feel disconnected and perhaps even in a darker place, if that makes sense.

"What I'm wondering is just exactly how that works. Do our MBOs elevate us and speed up our vibration, or does that happen through the interaction with our guardian angels? It's kind of a 'chicken or egg' question."

Tom responds: When I began experimenting with requesting MBOs fourteen or fifteen years ago, I had no idea that this would begin to raise my vibrational level — what some people call ascension. I just knew it worked perfectly. Anyone can do this no matter where they think they are on their path in life. Two guardian angels work together in conjunction with your own soul to give you the MBO.

Time Limits on MBOs?

Kendra writes: "Hi, I finished reading your book and had a question that wasn't covered: Can you put time limits on your benevolent outcomes? For example, can I say something like,

> **Most Benevolent Outcome Request**
> *"I request a most benevolent outcome to find a competent and good new physician by tomorrow"*?

I asked my guardian angel this question in meditation: Can you put time limits on MBO requests, and if so, how effective can they be? He responded as follows: "As you guessed, Tom, it all depends on the MBO request, the soul contract, and what is being requested. If it is assistance that may well be needed immediately, then certainly the guardian angel will pull strings for that MBO request. If it is something general like the perfect job, home, or mate, then it will take as long as it will so that it will fulfill the request of the person who requested it. We must not forget soul contracts either, as there are times when someone wishes for something to happen, yet the soul contract calls for that person to experience something as a lesson. The MBO request does not prevent the event from happening — it only affects the severity of the event. So you see, Tom, one MBO request is treated perhaps much differently from another. If there is truly a time limit on the request, it is looked at most carefully."

Three Questions on MBOs

Deleah writes: "Tom, I am anxiously awaiting the arrival of your e-books for my Nook; however, I am finding myself at a time in my life when I need MBOs more than ever, so I hope you will not mind if I ask you these three questions I have had for a long time now.

"First of all, should you say an MBO request and then forget about it and release it to the angels, or should you keep saying the MBO request until something happens? Secondly, will MBO requests work if you write them in a journal? I saw this somewhere and thought it was a neat idea, but do they need to be said out loud too? Thirdly, do you need to direct the MBO request to the angels in general, or does this cover the angels, archangels, spirit guides, and so on?"

Tom responds: You only have to say an MBO request once, my guardian angel says, but he also says humans are a little fearful — or a lot — and if it makes you feel better to say the MBO request multiple times, that's okay. The same goes with writing it down. When you say it out loud, though, you are cocreating with Spirit.

I was inspired to create just the simple saying you use, which anyone with any belief system can say. You can limit yourself somewhat if you direct your request to a specific angel, so just make the request and know it instantly reaches where it's supposed to go.

Requesting MBOs Out Loud vs. Writing Them Down

Anonymous writes: "Last year in November, I moved in with my fiancé ahead of our wedding in December. Around December, our washing machine started making weird sounds and would at times not complete a wash cycle.

"Seeing that we might need to get it fixed or buy a new one altogether, I said an MBO request and wrote it down in my MBO journal a few days later — sometimes when I feel my words won't be or are not effective enough to bring about an MBO quickly, I write it down as well for backup. My request was that we would be able to get the washing machine fixed at a cheap price or be able to somehow afford a new washing machine, not knowing where the money would come from since we had spent a lot of our savings on our wedding — which was to come in a few weeks — and just didn't have any spare cash.

"Well, a day or two after writing the MBO request, we received a $250 check in the mail from my fiancé's grandparents as an early wedding present. I remember being a little confused when we received the check, as it was sent before I wrote down the MBO request and it was the exact amount we needed to buy a new washing machine, plus delivery charges. I guess the MBO I had requested out loud earlier on still worked, despite me not having any feeling or strong belief that it would come about. It was once I had written it down that I was more confident it would be taken care of by the angels.

"So my question to you, Tom, is does it really matter if you believe the MBO requested would be taken care of for it to work? In my case, I said the MBO but didn't put much faith in it till I wrote it down. But I wouldn't know how to explain the check being written and sent a day or two before writing my MBO down unless it was all a coincidence!"

Tom responds: You just have to say the request. When I began requesting MBOs, I had no idea if it would work and was probably a little skeptical, as I had tried many modalities that did not work. But I discovered they worked perfectly, and with each one I requested, I became more confident.

Have Patience for Your Big MBOs to Manifest

Daphnee writes: "I wanted to tell you that I have been using many MBOs lately and, wow, they are working so well — for a good flight, for smooth traffic, for parking spaces, for quick solutions, and more. The other day I had to bring my daughter to the hospital, and I asked for an MBO, and within forty-five minutes all was done: registration, exam, x-ray, and getting her foot into a cast. That's very fast, since you can wait for hours at a hospital here. For quick stuff, MBOs are working perfectly, but for bigger things it seems to take a very long time, which is quite frustrating. Do you have any good advice on how to deal with waiting for them to happen? Maybe an MBO for more patience?"

Tom responds: That's why I recommend requesting MBOs for everything in your life, even the most mundane things such as your drive to and from work, a seat on a bus or train, work meetings, and all the other normal things that occur in your life. This builds up your confidence that requesting MBOs does work, so that when you ask for something important — the perfect mate, job, home, etc. — you have enough trust to know that things are conspiring in your favor, even if it does take months or even a year or so. You develop a certainty that everything will work out!

My guardian angel says that you can request MBOs multiple times if that makes you feel good. You will not be penalized. And yes, you can even request an MBO to be more patient in your life.

The Importance of Saying MBOs Out Loud

Madeleine writes: "I have a question about MBOs. Very often when I am in a meeting, with others, or in a public spot, I confess that I do not say the MBO out loud. How much does intent have to do with this process of prayer?"

Tom responds: For Madeleine and anyone else who feels strange when saying an MBO request, you can whisper it, even turning your head away from people for just a second. My guardian angel says that it needs to be said physically and not mentally, as this is a physical world and you're creating an energy — you're cocreating with Spirit.

You can also just address the person and say, "Well, I'll request an MBO for us working this out." They won't know what you're really saying and might just think you're saying you're hopeful the two of you can come to an agreement. I do this all the time.

Any and All Beings to the Nth Power

Johnny writes: "I think a lot of people may be put off by this whole concept of talking to their guardian angels or guides. It is strange at first, but the more you do it, the more natural it becomes. I think it's of the utmost importance that you be yourself when doing this. Although your requests should be clear and precise, you should use language that is comfortable for you and not get bogged down with being so formal. Some of these guys have been with us all our lives. So if we can't speak plainly with them, who can we be direct with?

"I've now gotten into the habit of speaking to them in the morning; I start by wishing them good morning and telling them about my dream interpretations. I then thank them and tell them how much I love them and appreciate all they've done and continue to do for me. I then move on to my MBOs and BPs. I know this may seem like a lot, but it really can benefit you. Only twenty minutes of this per day could drastically change your life for the better. It fills you with such a happy feeling once you get used to it that nothing could remotely spoil your day.

"I've also started combining MBOs and BPs with the law of attraction. As you ask for your MBO for a certain event or area of your life, picture in your mind's eye the result that you're asking for. You should also attach to your MBO request the emotion you imagine you will feel when it comes true. This takes some practice, but it is potentially very powerful.

"This is my latest BP. It hopefully will send out waves like a pebble dropped in a pond.

> **Benevolent Prayer**
> *"I ask any and all beings to help and assist any and all beings who are helping and assisting any and all beings in positive, productive, and benevolent ways. Thank you."*

"Thanks for reading this, and if this helps just one person, it will make me extremely happy."

Say Your MBOs with Feeling

Kate writes: "This is just a small one, but you could add it to tell people that it works to say MBOs with feeling. I have a CD player that always works for playing the radio but only sometimes works for playing CDs. Just now I really needed it to work for CD to amuse a fussy baby, and it wasn't working at all. I said an MBO request in my normal voice — no luck. Then I remembered to say it forcefully with a lot of feeling, and it worked right away!"

Some Thoughts on MBO and BP Phrasing

Robert writes: "I have been requesting benevolent outcomes for about a year now, and they have completely changed my life from anxiety and frustration to empowerment and joy. Thank you! Lately I have added more wording in keeping with my new self-perception, and I wanted to see what you think.

"My MBO suggestion to be said out loud is this:

> **Most Benevolent Outcome Request**
> *"As I now say this most benevolent outcome request with emotion, intent, and feeling, it has the multiplying energy, force, and effect of my having stated and intended it of nine times to the ninth power."*

"Since we are, as you say, cocreators in training, I rephrase my MBOs and BPs to ask for help in cocreating the thing I want rather than staying in the old paradigm of asking or praying to others to do something for me. For MBOs I say,

> **Most Benevolent Outcome Request**
> *"I request help in cocreating the most benevolent outcome for _____."*

"My benevolent prayer is,

> **Benevolent Prayer**
> " *I ask all beings, cocreators with me, to* _____."

I think it's the next step in development; what do you think?"

Tom responds: I asked my guardian angel about these suggestions on changing the wording of MBO and BP requests to say such things as "multiplying to the ninth power" and "cocreating." He replied, "Yes, Tom. For those who wish to change and experiment with requesting MBOs and BPs another way, allow or encourage them to make these requests in their own way and form, just as you did years ago.

"Regarding the suggestion about the ninth power, yes, for the person saying this, it does give energy to maximize the request and to give it the most energy possible, and it is the same for the language about cocreating. These requests are not set in stone but can be individualized as people wish. Their own guardian angels will receive and act on them. For the majority of the people, the actual act of requesting the MBOs or asking for a BP for someone is a great accomplishment. So, to use your vernacular, 'keep it simple' is my best advice.

"The advantages to keeping it simple are numerous. If people do not have to think about what they are saying, it becomes a simple habit. There is more thought that goes into expanding these requests over time, so unless they make it a habit by saying them over and over and over again, they will probably revert back to the more easily said request."

Yawning Means a Good MBO?

Jill writes: "I love the newsletters, and I have noticed that more and more people are actually stating what they have said in their MBOs word for word, as opposed to just giving a vague summary of what they said. This helps the other side of my brain!

"My question for your audience is: After you have said your MBO request or a BP, do you get a feeling of it being heard and that it is working, and if so, what do you feel? I let out a huge yawn when I feel as if my request has been heard. If I do not yawn, then I reword the statement until I receive one. Sometimes all I have to do is start to think of the statement and then I yawn.

"You can just imagine me reading page after page of MBOs, and I'm yawning so much that my eyes are tearing and I can hardly read anything. Someone explained why I do this, but I have forgotten. The bigger the yawn, the better the statement, I think. I have also noticed that if someone is taking my power or energy, like in a phone conversation, I will also yawn. It was explained to me that this yawning protects me.

"Before this was explained to me, I thought I could not feel anything. Maybe people get tickles in their noses, ears, or fingers, or maybe they have coughing, eye twitches, or hear voices, and so on. I think it would be great if we could read other people's feelings on 'feelings.'"

Tom responds: Well, this is the first time I've heard of someone yawning, but perhaps it happens more than I've been made aware of. I do think you've set this up on a subconscious level to make yourself more aware of what's being created when you request an MBO. I think the act of requesting MBOs will always affect the person asking, but how it affects you personally is left up to your physiology.

When I request an MBO with emotion, I sometimes feel a nice warm feeling in my solar plexus. You can actually work on this feeling, as is described in the appendix of my first book. So readers, what happens when you request an MBO, if anything?

02

Benevolent Outcomes at Home

Resolving a Family Dispute

Sky writes: "A female cousin of mine wanted to forcibly occupy the second floor of our two-story house and another vacant house of the estate in the same area. She presented a legal document — a deed of sale signed by her mother that she claims entitles her to use our property, along with four other legal heirs. The five heirs had already had an earlier meeting on how to operate the two houses. But my cousin — who had already been having a longtime squabble with her sisters on her father's side over property sharing — wanted to complicate matters and said she would file a lawsuit against her sisters if needed.

"I recited an MBO five times daily for three days:

Most Benevolent Outcome Request
"I request a most benevolent outcome that my cousin does not use the second floor of our house for her personal gain, and may this outcome be even better than I can hope for or expect."

"On the third day, the sisters had a meeting and my cousin reached a peaceful settlement with the administrator. She did not pursue her planned use of the two houses of the estate, thus relieving all concerned of legal troubles, costs, and hassles."

Benevolent Furnace Repair

Ken writes: "I had a new furnace put in about two years ago, and on one particular fall day, the temperature dropped thirty degrees. It was cold in the house when I got up Sunday morning. I was chatting with a friend, and she reminded me to ask Archangel Michael, who is good with electronics, for an MBO. I asked for help getting my furnace working.

"I called a friend who works on furnaces, but he wasn't sure he could get here till the next day. I said thanks and went to do some errands. When I got back, I opened up the furnace panels to see if I could fix it myself. It is all electronics and sensors, and I didn't see anything. I reset the power to see if that would fix it, but nothing changed. While I was looking at it, my friend called and said he had a few minutes because the rain had canceled some of his plans. He came over five minutes later and tested all the circuits with no results.

"I looked down and saw a blue wire that was hanging by the circuit board and asked what it did, and we figured it was to the main flame sensor. When we plugged it in, everything started working fine again. Thank goodness for our friends and angels! It is now cozy and warm in the house again."

Help Plowing My Driveway

Jan writes: "I was sick this winter and out of work. I requested an MBO for assistance on everything. I even asked for an MBO for people to plow my driveway, since I could not afford the plowman. Four or five different men noticed my driveway needed plowing over the winter and plowed it for free. A high school friend of mine whom I have not seen or spoken to in a few years happened to be doing a job nearby, and he plowed my drive quite a few times. A neighbor who lives down the road who I don't even know very well plowed for me as well.

"My children — fifteen and eighteen years old — and many of my friends now use MBOs. They have seen the amazing results that I have had using them."

Selling a Dining Room Set

Jackie writes: "I had a dining room set for sale for over a month. I advertised on craigslist.org and at work on our internal newsletter. It missed the July publication, and I was upset because I needed the money. Then a close friend, John L., forwarded your newsletter, and I thought I would try out an MBO. I only said one.

"My ad came out in the August newsletter at work, and in less than fifteen minutes, I got an email from a coworker in the IT department, and he came over that evening to buy the set. I paid four bills that were due with the money I made, and I even bought a new purse, since I had noticed the night before that the old one was beginning to tear at the zipper.

"Now I say the phrase about expecting great things every day. It really works when you get out of the way and have faith that your angels really will do the best for you. Thank you, thank you, thank you, Tom."

MBO for a Finicky Lock

Rick writes: "The lock to the laundry room door in our apartment complex has been balky lately. It seems as if I spend five minutes trying to get the key to unlock it every time I need to get in. I've used MBOs for it, and they've worked.

"The other day, I asked for one almost an hour before I went down there.

To my surprise, when I arrived, the door was wide open and a couple of people were already doing laundry, and I guess previous MBOs must have gone beyond my key working, as the property owner finally fixed the lock. It's now in perfect working order."

Tom responds: It's those little mundane MBOs that make life easier!

Benevolent Firewood Outcome

Jan writes: "A few weeks ago, I requested an MBO for the perfect wood to burn in my wood stove that ended, 'May it be better than I could hope for or expect.' It's starting to get cold here in Vermont, and I was thinking how nice it would be to have a cozy fire.

"Yesterday, I was doing the dishes and heard a car door shut out in my driveway. I looked out the window, and a neighbor of mine, Barb, had pulled her truck up to my garage where she was unloading a load of dry, beautiful firewood — cut to the perfect size for me. I now have enough wood to burn for at least a month. I appreciate the wood that I have, and I'm already feeling appreciation for the wood that will be coming!

"I have now put in a request for the perfect new wood stove. I'll keep you posted! Thank you, thank you, thank you!"

Tom responds: Don't forget to thank Barb's guardian angel for assisting your guardian with the MBO request too.

An MBO for Peace and Quiet

Denise writes: "A wonderful friend gave me your book for my birthday in April. I did not get around to reading it until July. As I sat on our swing on the front lawn reading, three young boys from the neighborhood began skateboarding on the street in front of the house, because the pavement is smoothest in front of our house. I found it distracting, but I told myself to be patient because it is a good thing that they are happy to play near home. After a few minutes, however, the swearing started and I became upset. I thought to myself that this would be the perfect opportunity to try this newfound technique.

"I requested an MBO about being allowed to read in peace. The boys immediately picked up their skateboards and moved down the street. I read for about a half-hour and then went back into the house. As I closed the front door, the skateboarders were walking back to the spot in front of the house. I said another thank you. Needless to say, MBOs are now a part of my daily life."

MBO for Smooth Repairs

Jason writes: "I had been putting together a shed in our backyard for days after work and was finally putting the roof on. Unfortunately, the screw holes didn't always line up perfectly, and one in particular was giving me a lot of trouble. After trying for fifteen minutes to get the screw lined up and put in, I was getting very frustrated. So I took a deep breath and said to my guardian angel,

> **Most Benevolent Outcome Request**
> *"Max, I request the most benevolent outcome to get this screw in quickly and easily so I can move on. Thank you!"*

"I took another deep breath, tried again with the screw, and it stayed lined up and went right in. I think my smile must have lasted an hour! I only wish I had thought to make the request sooner.

"The next night, the skies were ominous with threatening rain. I had just a few panels left to put on the roof and really didn't want the shed interior and wood floor to get soaked. So I requested an MBO from my guardian angel that I'd get the roof on before the rain started with results better than I could hope for or expect. I also asked Gaia to please hold off the rain just long enough for me to get the roof on the shed. I was close to being done but still had one panel to go when it started sprinkling. I grabbed the panel and put it in place, but I didn't have time to get any screws in because the skies opened up with pouring rain. I was stuck inside the shed, holding the panel in place — which was the only thing keeping the inside dry.

"My wife and daughters were watching me from the back door, just laughing and carrying on about my predicament, and texting me words of encouragement for the twenty minutes of the downpour. I realized afterward that the way it worked out actually was the MBO: I did get the roof on in time to keep the inside dry, and my family got a kick out of watching me holding the panel in place and had a great story to tell later. Perfect!"

Directed to a Better Home

Angel writes: "I want to share this MBO that happened to me. I've been looking for a cheaper place to live. A while back, I requested an MBO:

> **Most Benevolent Outcome Request**
> *"Guardian angel, I request an MBO that you help me find a bigger place with two bedrooms. Thank you."*

"Well, a few weeks ago, my friend was trying to purchase his third house, so he gave me the opportunity to live there and pay cheaper rent. I was happy.

"This week, however, my friend broke the bad news to me that he was no longer getting the house because the bank was taking too long processing the paperwork. Just yesterday a friend told me about the big apartments where she lives now; they are spacious and the rent is cheap. So now I am planning to move to an apartment! It will help me a lot, because where I live now, the main stores are thirty to forty-five minutes away, no matter what direction you're going. So I will save on gas!

"The weird thing is that I had a strong intuition that I was going to move very soon; I had already seen the signs. Sometimes when you request an MBO, be careful what you ask for. In a way, I appreciate what my guardian angel did for me — even though it wasn't the house that I expected to live in it, and it turned out to be an apartment. Our guardian angels know what's best for us!"

A Totally Benevolent Gym Outcome

Sara writes: "I have been enjoying and sharing your newsletter for a couple of years now. MBO requests are becoming a way of life for me. There have been so many that I now wish I had written them all down (I was a skeptic to begin with). However, I wanted to share this one, because I can't stop grinning when I think about it.

"I've had a gym membership for many years. We recently moved to a new area, and I had my membership transferred, but it is not convenient for me to get to the new facility. So I saw an ad for a Total Gym® and thought that would be something I could use at home, allowing me to cancel my gym membership. Not wanting to pay full price, I checked online for a used model. At that point, I requested an MBO for myself to acquire a Total Gym. I contacted a couple of people selling them online, but each one already had a buyer. I stayed confident that my MBO would work.

"That weekend, we had friends come to visit, and in the course of conversation, I mentioned to them that I would like to get one but didn't want to pay for a new one. Here it comes: My friend has one in her basement that she is looking to get rid of! I am grinning again as I type this. Thanks, Tom!"

The Best Possible Roommate

Ivy writes: "Aloha from Hawaii, Tom. My friend introduced me to your story and the concept of MBO requests, so I decided to try them after reviewing your videos. My roommate informed me that day that she was giving me a two-week notice. She is under contract for a forty-five-day notice. It had taken me four months to rent my other room, so I was very nervous and scared, as I cannot afford two rooms.

"I decided that afternoon to try requesting an MBO. I asked for an MBO for that day, the next day, and the rest of the week, and then said thank you. I then addressed my guardian angel and asked for a new roommate right away. I had just posted the ad on craigslist.org, and then I went to Blockbuster to return a video.

"When I was in the store, I got a phone call. It was from a woman who had called to look at the other room from three months ago! She had had a bad reaction to her blood pressure medicine at that time and never came to look at the other room when it was up for rent. She had not even seen the new ad posted. She asked me if the room was still available.

"I told her I had good news and bad news. The room she was interested in had been rented; that was the bad news. The good news was that I had another room that had just become available — a bigger room! She was so happy and wanted to see me right away. She came over an hour later, loved the room, and paid me a deposit. Two days ago, she came back and paid me the rest of the money for the room, and she will move in on September 1.

"I have never had anyone rent a room that fast who was agreeable with our household and would fit in. This really saved our household and peace of mind with the upcoming holidays. Your MBO requests are fantastic, and I practice the Gentle Way every day."

MBO for Water Main Break

Margaret writes: "Hello Tom, and thank you so much for the wonderful work you are doing! I've been using MBO requests for about two years and have had so many great outcomes. Here is my most amazing MBO story, and I hope you will consider sharing it with your readers.

"On the afternoon of Sunday, October 24, water burst through the pavement and began pouring down the roadway of my condo community. An inspector from the utilities department determined that a valve had broken and decided to leave things alone until Monday so that our residents would not be without water overnight. I asked for an MBO for the problem to be found and corrected quickly in order to avoid inconvenience to our residents as well as to avoid wasting water.

"Work began the next morning with several large, noisy, earth-moving machines and trucks, and soon they had created an enormous hole in order to reach the pipes nearly ten feet down. At 5:00PM one of our board members came by to report that the problem had not been located until an hour before (at 4:00PM), and the best time we could hope for the water to be turned on again was by midnight — if we were lucky.

"I went inside, thinking about how my neighbors would come home after a full day's work and find no water available. So I blessed the crews who were working so hard so that strangers could get the water service they were used to. I blessed the trucks and earth-movers that were making it possible to heal the broken pipes. I blessed the pavement that was being torn up and damaged by the heavy machines. And I blessed the pipes themselves and thanked them for their service.

"I blessed the earth, which was being assaulted and dug up; I blessed the soil that was being moved around and the new soil that was being trucked in. I blessed the water for its service and for reminding us how important it is to human life. All this took about ten minutes, and less than ten minutes later, the same board member returned, astonished to announce that water would be available again within half an hour!"

Benevolent Prayer Attracts Neighbors

Eleanor writes: "Some time ago, I moved into a new complex and experienced a great deal of stress as a result of not transitioning well and being affected by the negativity in my new surroundings. When I shared this with you, you kindly suggested a BP that I used. Here is what you suggested I say:

> **Benevolent Prayer**
> *"I ask that any and all beings help everyone in this complex come to love and respect all people of different races and beliefs, and that those who don't will move away and be replaced by others who vibrate at a higher level."*

"Over a rather short time, I began to notice fewer cars in the parking lot and the apparent — but unexpressed — stress of the manager. After checking, I found out there were an inordinate number of vacancies. At least a dozen, I think. When I checked again yesterday, I was informed with great glee by the office personnel that they had six people coming in today to sign new leases. I simply had to share this with you because it is just one more proof of the authenticity of what you teach — MBOs do work! Thank you, Tom."

MBO During a Home Invasion

Kanti writes: "First, I of course want to thank and bless you for the great insights and realizations that your wonderful newsletters bring to us every Friday. We wait anxiously for each edition! Now, for my recent MBO experience: the sixty-second robbery!

"Earlier this month, my fiancé and I settled in around 8:30PM to watch a movie — which I rarely do — on a new birthday-gift TV that my roommate had just installed in my bedroom minutes before. The roommate retired downstairs, and we turned on the set. Suddenly there was an enormous crash at my back door that sounded like a car rammed into the house. We looked at each other in total confusion and shock. There was another crash, then another, and we ran to the basement door, thinking that something terrible had happened to my roommate downstairs.

"The kitchen door flew open, revealing two gun-wielding men in ski masks and hoodies who came rushing in and found us trying to get out the front door. They ordered us on the floor, pistol-whipped my fiancé in the temple, and kicked my head because we tried to look up.

"I immediately said,

> **Most Benevolent Outcome Request**
> *"I request a most benevolent outcome for this situation."*

"I said it three times and began a prayer to the lord, but before I got several words into it, everything went silent. We were afraid to move. Then

I saw a shadow, and suddenly my roommate was standing there saying, "You can get up; they left!" He had sneaked upstairs, grabbed two knives from the kitchen drawer, and run outside in his skivvies and socks, even though it was 29 degrees outside. After waiting a second, he heard them in the house saying, "Get down! Get down!" to us, so he ran out the back gate, which has bells on it to call the police. No neighbors would let him in, since he looked pretty crazy in his underwear and socks, waving knives, but then he saw the two fellows leave and run down the street.

"We called the police, and very quickly there were at least twenty officers on the scene. The robbery detectives said that the guy must have had an iron leg to kick down my very solid and secure oak door and that we were very lucky to be relatively unharmed. They had never seen or heard of such a quick crime, and all the robbers got was an empty wallet carrying only an ID. The gun part was very scary, Tom!

"My fiancé was taken to the hospital for an MRI for his head, and I asked any and all beings to assist, comfort, and protect him from any serious injury. Later, my son picked him up at the hospital, and we found out that the only real damage he had received was huge shiners on both eyes.

"It was wonderful to have the MBO requests to say, and I am eternally grateful for the knowledge about them and for our wonderful, wonderful guardians. We love you and thank you from the core of our beings, Tom and our fantastic friends. MBOs are extremely powerful and cannot be underestimated — especially in a life-threatening emergency. Happy endings and thanks to you and the benevolent ones!"

Tom responds: I'm happy for Kanti and her family too!

Losing the Household Lush

Kylie writes: "My husband's best friend — let's call him Frank — was living with us and our two young children. He was one of the worst alcoholics I have ever met; his energy was being drained by entities. After a few months of him living with us, I knew he had to leave. I had to keep my children safe from this person.

"I was attending weekly spiritual development classes at the time, and we had learned about Reiki in class a couple of weeks earlier. Then this one particular class was about requesting MBOs. We did a guided meditation in which we visualized a situation we wanted an MBO for, followed by a burn and release after the meditation. The results were amazing.

"The day after the class, I cleansed the house and garage with sage. Frank had two vehicles that weren't running at all so I gave them Reiki, not even really knowing what I was doing at the time. The next evening — a Friday night — Frank was in the garage with a friend getting drunk, and I was out there chatting with them. All of a sudden, from out of nowhere, Frank got very violent toward me. His friend intervened and got him out of there. Then my husband evicted Frank for his behavior.

"I remember wondering how Frank was going to get these cars out of the garage. But he sold one car a few days later and the other car started the first time Frank tried it — wow! Frank and all of his belongings were out of our house within seven days of asking for an MBO that my children and I be kept safe. It was such an amazing outcome because I couldn't see how it was all going to work out.

"That particular MBO moment changed my life and has helped me become the person I am today. MBOs are by far the best way to deal with any situation. Thanks, Tom, for allowing me to share my story with you."

Tom responds: I had a small but important MBO occur just a day ago. My wife was trying to find a special recipe for cake icing and went through three pages of recipes on the Internet but couldn't find the right one. She gave up, so I requested an MBO to find the right recipe, turned the page, and found the one she had been searching for.

Does This MBO Have a Snooze Button?

Gemma writes: "I always request an MBO at night to wake up no later than such-and-such time the next day. It works perfectly without an alarm, as long as my body is not overly tired."

Tom responds: Waking up this way also has an added benefit. If you are recording your dreams each morning as I do, it's easier to remember them as you slowly awaken. So I never use an alarm clock either.

MBOs Help Get Rid of Annoying Neighbors

Janet writes: "Hello, dear Tom. I am so excited to tell you this MBO story! I live in a small co-op condo building, and I own my unit. In February, some young people moved into the apartment below me. They are renting from the young lady's mother (who doesn't live in the building). They like acid-rock type music played as loudly as possible. I recognize that we all have to make noise and that the personal choice of music is important, but my floors, furniture, and body were being vibrated with the intensity of the sound.

"As you can imagine, I've been complaining and asking the building management to control the situation since early February, but nothing has had a lasting effect. In the meantime, I've been making MBO requests every night for these young people's trauma to be healed. This has kept me somewhat even in my outlook toward them; you can't hate someone if you are praying for them to be healed. So this has been a huge benefit for me all these months. I will continue to pray for their healing.

"Two days ago, a friend said he hoped that these people would move out, which planted the idea for a very different MBO request. So I asked for an

MBO for them to move out of the apartment. I never would have expected a very quick response to this. First of all, I was awakened yesterday at 5AM by very loud music, so I called the police. They were here quickly, telling my neighbors to turn the music off. Shortly after they left, the music started up again, so I called the police again. They came back. When the music started up a third time, I called the police one more time, but the music stopped after five minutes, so that call went unanswered.

"I was quite surprised when I got home around 6PM yesterday to find the place was rocking once again, and this time the music was nonstop. Once again I was being vibrated by the intensity of the sound. Our anti-noise bylaw doesn't kick in until 11PM, but at 9PM I'd had much more than enough, so I called the police again. I was surprised that they came without an argument.

"The police came upstairs to talk to me afterward. They told me that the tenant had been charged a hefty fine in the morning and also last night. They asked how long this had been going on and said that the next time, they would press criminal charges and take the tenant to court if I would be the witness for them. I responded that I definitely would. The music stopped after they had come, and the silence in here has been rather deafening by contrast — and ever so delightful!

"Later on, I realized that all these events with the police were the answer to my MBO. While I try to pray for positive outcomes for all people, I had no idea that — when justified — an MBO to relieve my difficult situation would be so effective. I thank you so much, Tom; I can't tell you what a blessing this turn of events has been in my life! I don't know what I would have had to do to get an outcome even close to this one. I don't think the saga is over, and I may actually have to appear in court later, but I now have a deeper understanding of the protection offered by my guardian angels."

MBO Saves Our Granddaughter's Graduation Party

David writes: "I use MBO requests daily. My son-in-law was fretting over an air conditioning unit in his home because the blower had stopped working, and our granddaughter's graduation party was the next day with temperatures expected to be in the nineties. The technician didn't have the part needed to repair the unit and couldn't get it, so he called around and found one. After installing it, it still didn't work, and he frantically called at least three other services who all said they would try to make it before the day was out. My wife and I joined hands and asked for an MBO. While the tech was on the phone, the blower finally came on. The graduation party was saved! Thank you, Saint Tom T. Moore."

Fixing a Water Leak

Carol writes: "Last week I noticed one side of my brick-paved driveway was damp like a sprinkler had sprayed it, but there is no sprinkler nearby. However, my main water and sewer lines run underneath the driveway. When the dampness didn't go away after a few days, I knew I had a leak and needed to call a plumber. So before I called, I said to my guardian angel, Anthony,

Most Benevolent Outcome Request
"I request an MBO that when the plumber arrives, whatever is causing this will be an inexpensive fix."

"After my plumber came out and tested the water and sewer lines and found no leaks, he tested the sprinkler system and noticed the one in the backyard — quite far from the leak — was actually running down and going underneath the driveway, which was an easy fix! Thank you, my guardian angel Anthony!"

Tom responds: Want to find out the name you can use to address your own guardian angel? Just say out loud, "Guardian angel, what name shall I call you?" You may receive an immediate whisper in your ear, or it may take a few days, as it did for me. Keep in mind our vocal cords are not made to pronounce angelic names, so you'll receive a name that is comfortable for you to use.

Sticky Situation Averted

Lucy writes: "MBOs are triumphant! My daughter called last week with the news that her bedroom was taking on water, probably because they had had a lot of snow and then rain on top of the snow. She had contacted the manager, and his crew showed up eight hours later and pulled the carpet up and set up heaters to dry the area. They then painted it with a sealant and came to put down new carpet while the floor was still seeping.

"My daughter did not think they understood the problem, so I suggested she talk to the owner and express the thought that he needed to get someone with some expertise in flood restoration, because if this was not taken care of, the place would be uninhabitable due to mold, mildew, and mushrooms growing in the bedroom. She emailed him; soon the corporate troubleshooter called and she was able to express her concerns to that person.

"I told my daughter we needed to get the angels involved. We both asked any and all beings who knew what they were doing to aid in bringing in people to take care of the situation and that it be sooner than we could imagine and less stress-filled than we could dream. Early the next morning, she texted that she had a flood restoration crew on site. It would take three or four days, but at least the fix was being done correctly. They are also going to compensate her for the hassles involved and put in new carpeting. I told her, 'Those any and all being guys are really good!' A lot of her MBOs seem to involve calling Mom!"

MBOs Unblock British Toilet

Helena writes: "My loo keeps blocking. I have not put anything down it to cause it to block. I was getting really mad, because no matter what I did, the loo would not unblock. I poured bleach down it, thinking that would unblock it; I kept flushing it, because the water was going down slowly, but it just would not unblock. Every time I flushed the loo, the water and loo paper kept coming right up to the top — nearly pouring out the top. I just kept getting angry and frustrated, and I couldn't think what to do.

"I had to go to work, so I left the house, and when I got back home, the loo was still full. I was getting really mad. I poured more bleach down it, and I was getting worried because I needed to use the loo. I threw a tantrum. I put on rubber gloves and got a metal coat hanger and forced it down the loo, trying to unblock it, but it would not unblock!

"I was talking to myself, saying 'Please loo, please empty.' After a couple more hours of frustration, it suddenly dawned on me to say an MBO request. I said with force,

Most Benevolent Outcome Request
"I request an MBO for my toilet to unblock itself right now! Thank you!"

"You will never guess what happened, Tom. The loo made a loud gurgling, rumbling sound like it had bad indigestion, and then — presto! — the whole lot went down, just like that. I then flushed the loo, and it was working as normal. Guess what, Tom? I just laughed my head off. If only I had requested an MBO earlier. I was amazed! I said thank you three times!"

Benevolent Board Members

Lisa writes: "The most amazing thing has happened. Here in my condo complex, we have had a majority board of directors who were landlords, not owners living onsite. Because of this, their decisions tended to be unpleasant for those of us who are owners and who do live onsite, even though we are in the majority of members. The board was dominated by these landlords, who consistently voted themselves back into office. The way they do this is a bit complicated and involves a mistake in the bylaws long ago.

"I said an MBO request and a BP for this to change for the better and for our amazing co-owner, Vic, who is really too busy to be on the board, to step up for a while and be on the three-member board in order for us to oust the one nasty man, Rob, who was making the most trouble for all of us. We all suspected that Rob had a kickback scheme going with the hired property-management company, costing us all a lot of money. The woman who dealt with us from the property-management company treated us all like we were naughty school children, and she was the principal. Why? Because she always knew she could not be ousted as long as Rob was on the board.

"There was an annual board meeting last night, and this morning I got an email stating that for the first time in twelve years, Rob would not be on the board any longer. The other two members got together and voted him off. One of those was a newly elected member, and the other landlord owner actually sided with her, which was beyond a miracle. This board had been dominated by off-site landlords for many years, but now we have a majority of owners who live on the premises on the board for the first time in at least twelve years!"

MBO for an Old Lawn Mower

Dave writes: "It had been a week since it started raining, and it was cold. The lawn was getting out of control, but there was a slight break in the weather on Sunday, so I broke out the lawn mower. It would not start. The engine kicked over but would immediately die, so I requested an MBO. I pulled the cord twenty times and requested an MBO. I replaced the gas and requested an MBO. Then I got a blister on my finger after forty-five pulls and finally gave up. I went out to buy a new lawn mower and found Home Depot had one just like my twelve-year-old version at less than half the price. I was determined to get a new one the next day.

"For some reason, that morning I decided to call my lawn mower guy. No answer! Joe is eighty years old and has been fixing lawn mowers forever and has developed a very independent attitude. After five tries and five MBOs, I got my neighbor to help me load the mower into my van — yes, I tried to start it again first — and we were off to the service store.

"I was fuming and a bit frustrated, to say the least. I pulled up to the store and saw fifty mowers out in front, but it looked as if nobody was there. Joe was just inside and said, 'Hey, welcome back.' I hadn't been in there for a couple of years, but he apparently remembered me. He helped me unload the mower as I explained the problem. He primed the engine, took off the air filter, and put his thumb over the opening, and told me to crank it up. It started right away, but the engine seemed to struggle, revving up and down. He walked over, picked up a ball-peen hammer, and struck the side of the engine three times in a strategic place, and the motor smoothed right out. Apparently, the combination of the cold air and some dirt in the gas tank caused the problem.

"I thanked him profusely and told him I was actually planning on replacing the mower with a new Lawn Boy and wondered if I could buy one from him. 'Sorry, Dave, they don't make Lawn Boys anymore,' Joe said.

"'What about the ones I saw online?' I asked.

"'Oh, those are knockoffs from China. The twelve-year-old original you have here would probably outlive any new one of those you could buy!'

"'Wow,' I thought, 'Not only did I get my mower fixed better than new, but I avoided a costly purchase.' I am still confused as to why I drove to get a mower fixed that I had already decided to replace, but the lesson for me is pretty clear: If the MBO hasn't seemed to happen yet, be patient. The best is yet to come."

MBO Fixes Garbage Disposal

Maria writes: "This story is quite astonishing. I dropped a piece of a tin can down my garbage disposal, and it just quit and would not work. My husband had all he could stand and went to get his tools to fix it, but he told me it was so bad that we would have to buy a new one. So I asked for an MBO, and when he came back inside the house, I said, 'Let's try it again.'

"He said, 'Don't bother. It's done.' Well, I tried it, and guess what? It made a strange sound and started working! We just looked at each other in amazement, and I sent thanks up to my angels. They came through again! My husband could not believe it.

"I must say, Tom, you have made a huge difference in my life. I use MBOs each and every day of my life, and it's been like the biggest Christmas present ever! I truly believe in this and have extended your books to my family and friends. You were sent from above as a gift to us all from the Holy One. Thank you from the bottom of my heart."

03

Benevolent Outcomes around Town

Meeting the Most Benevolent People

Jeremy writes: "Today I requested an MBO to meet only those people who are here for my highest good — in other words, people who are directly related to furthering my path. While I was sitting in the food court at our local plaza, my old kung fu and tai chi sifu instructor walked right past me. Just the night previously, I had looked up a website to find sessions again. I have been thinking of doing tai chi for ages, and it seems like my guardian angels think it's a good idea too.

"I also asked for an MBO to find the best anatomy book for me to learn from so that I can continue my path down healing. I ended up buying two, and they are even better than I could have ever expected or anticipated. Thank you for this gift!"

Smooth Visit to the Hospital

Lee writes: "My husband was in the hospital again, and I needed to stop on my way to work to drop something off for him. So I requested MBOs for the drive, a good parking space, and to get to work on time. Well, traffic was slow, crowded, and just awful. Then when I got to the hospital, parking was out in the lot far from the front door. I thought, 'Wow, those MBOs didn't work.' I parked and got out of my car, turned, and there was the most delightful gentleman driving a courtesy golf cart, and he asked if I wanted a ride! I never use them, as I prefer to walk, but today I accepted. He drove me right to the front door.

"I had to ask at the desk for directions to my husband's room, as they had moved him, and a nice woman took me right to his door. The best thing was it was on the first floor and not too far from the lobby, so I got to spend a few minutes with my husband instead of traveling through the hospital just to get to his room. Soon I had to leave to go to work, so I headed for the exit. And who was sitting there but the same delightful gentleman! He said, 'That was quick,' and offered me a ride, which I gratefully accepted. I told him I wasn't sure where I was parked, as I hadn't made a note when I got out of my car earlier. He said it was no problem because he remembered where I was parked and promptly drove me right to my car. I thanked him profusely and told him he was my guardian angel. I made it to work on time.

"The universe gave me such a beautiful gift this morning with how my request unfolded. I regret that I was frustrated that it wasn't working out as I had requested, but I am so happy that it worked out the way it did. The gentleman truly was delightful, and I am sorry I didn't get his name to write a letter telling his boss what a gem he has on his staff. This experience made my day. And even better, my husband was able to come home this afternoon! Thank you for MBOs."

MBO Proof

Helena writes: "When I first started doing my MBOs, I was trying too hard, and I got fed up with wanting results. One day I was walking through our local park, muttering away to myself, and I said,

> **Most Benevolent Outcome Request**
> *"I request an MBO for a robin to show me its big fat breast as proof to me that my MBOs are working for me."*

"I laughed and thought to myself, 'This will not work for me,' as I was trying too hard and being quite negative. Well, nothing happened!

"On my way back through the park I requested the MBO again for the robin to appear. I carried on walking, and you will never guess what happened! Out of the bushes shot this robin. It puffed itself up like a fluffy ball and tipped its head to the right as if it was looking at me. I just stood still, as I had full shopping bags in each hand. When this robin appeared, I just got the shock of my life. I just stood there laughing my head off and could not stop. It just happened so quickly, and then it shot back into the bushes. I waited to see if it would come back out, but it didn't. This robin only appeared for about thirty or forty seconds, but it did seem longer. It was just so funny, Tom. I remember every detail like it happened yesterday.

"Well I most certainly got my proof that my MBOs are working for me. And I most certainly said, 'Thank you, thank you, thank you!'"

Across a Crowded Grocery Store

Marie writes: "Hi, Tom. I have an MBO. My friend and I went grocery shopping, and we lost track of each other. The store is so huge, there's no way I could find him, so I requested an MBO. I said,

> **Most Benevolent Outcome Request**
> *"Guardian angel, I request an MBO that I find my friend ASAP. Thank you!"*

"Guess what? Not even five minutes later, I found my friend heading toward the checkout line. Thank you, angels."

Benevolent Swing Dance Lessons

Nancy writes: "I always say an MBO request for Tim and myself as we travel Thursday nights to our dance class and to do our errands later. We are taking West Coast swing and ballroom dancing. Swing is a lot harder than ballroom for us, so I always say an MBO request for having fun and learning our new steps.

"Well, during our last class, Tim was having trouble with a new move we were learning and was getting really frustrated. I thought he was going to blow a gasket! We are not dance wizards, and sometimes the steps are hard. The move involved a double-spin for me, and it kept throwing me off balance. Somehow Tim didn't explode, but he was unhappy that he hadn't learned the move. I reminded him of how hard the hustle was for us initially and how now it's one of our better dances, and I told him he'd get it tomorrow.

"Meanwhile, I started trying to reverse-engineer the move in my mind. When we practiced the next day, I was able to help him continue to move me past him as he spun me, and he got it. He had been reversing my motion, which was what was throwing me off. It was wonderful to see him get it and feel better about the dance. No, he didn't get the move during the class, but one day later is pretty good!"

Benevolent Outcome at the Library

Ann writes: "I am trying to give away books to someone who can use them, and most of them are on the subject of grief. I had one about the suicide of a young man. I prayed for an MBO to find someone to give it to and then went to the library to see if they would want it. Just as I was explaining the book's contents, a young woman asked if she could have the book; she had just come from a young man's funeral — he'd committed suicide — and had overheard me. Wow, what a God wink! A big thanks for what was very much a most benevolent outcome. Every day I ask and pray for MBOs for my life and others."

Tom responds: That was a nice, thoughtful gesture — one that our readers might consider doing with books they have no room for anymore.

A Whopper of an MBO

Marie writes: "I've had many MBO experiences lately that keep me believing that the MBOs I request for my son's safety will truly keep him safe. I had my son visit during Thanksgiving, and as we were out shopping, we decided to stop at my favorite fast food place. The whole day, I was asking for MBOs, even though my family does not believe in them.

"We stopped to get my favorite Whopper at Burger King. After we ordered, I decided to request an MBO out loud as I placed a quarter in the 'Win a Whopper Meal' container. I felt good about the quarter landing on the pedestal, and so it did! Thanking the angels, I requested another MBO for the quarter to land on the pedestal again, and once again, it did! My son wanted me to try a third time, but I felt it wouldn't happen, and it didn't. Since my son was not able to use the free meal, I gave one to a homeless man, and I'm holding on to the other one for an opportunity to give it to another person."

Benevolent Blood Donation

DeLeah writes: "I have been a long-time donor of blood to the Red Cross because I believe in giving back, and this is an easy way for me to do so. However, being born with rolling and collapsing veins makes this difficult. For the past six months, I have been saying,

Most Benevolent Outcome Request
"I request a most benevolent outcome that I am received by a wonderful technician who is able to hit my veins on the first try with no issues and with results even better than I could expect or hope for."

"And every time I have done that, it has been a breeze donating! Thank you, angels!"

UPS MBO

Shannon writes: "I request MBOs every day for almost everything, and as things usually work out, I assume they are working, but I wanted to share one from last night. I had a package that needed to be mailed UPS, and I totally forgot that it needed to be at the UPS office by 4:45PM. I decided to start catching up on reading my email and forgot about the time — I was actually reading your latest newsletter — and when I finally noticed the package on my desk, it was 5:15PM.

"I called the UPS store to see if they could still take it, and the customer service representative said it was past time, so then I called some stores near my home to see how late they could take it, but I couldn't get there by their cut-off times, so I just said, 'Okay, I'll have to contact the customer tomorrow, but I'll go ahead and take it by the UPS store,' all the while requesting an MBO for the package to be delivered on time.

"When I got to the UPS store, the driver was just there picking up the packages and said he would take care of it. I said thank you prayers all the way home! When I checked on the package this morning, it was out for delivery. Thank you so much for sharing this wonderful tool! I tell all my Reiki students and clients about it. It's so easy — and free!"

Tom responds: The same thing has happened for me many times when I'm running late to drop off a package; I'll request an MBO and catch them before they leave or before the truck is out of the parking lot or stopped on a street nearby.

MBO for Jury Duty

Cynthia writes: "I have a great MBO for you. I had jury duty last week and really had too much to do to sit on a jury right now. I requested an MBO that I would be let go early and not be on a jury. The day of the jury duty we all waited for two hours. Then the court officials came and let us all go at 10:30 in the morning. There were no panels that day, so we all left. The MBO worked for everyone, whether they knew it or not! Thanks so much."

Tom responds: In my first book, I noted that when other people benefit from your MBO request, I term it the "radiant effect." You'll find a whole chapter devoted to this in *The Gentle Way*.

Post Office Provisions

Sandy writes: "Yesterday, income taxes were due. I have a fear of math logic — or should I say, I have an absence of math logic? — but push came to shove, and I had to do my taxes myself this year. Since Monday, April 12, I've been saying one or two MBO requests daily, telling myself it was perfectly fine to break up the tasks so that I didn't overwhelm myself. All the requests worked, of course.

"The neatest outcome out of that experience was yesterday, when I had to take one of the state returns to the post office to be mailed. Things had been going so well that I got brave and thought I'd add some more details to this request. So I said,

> ### Most Benevolent Outcome Request
> "*I request a most benevolent outcome for getting all the documents together that are needed. May I go to the post office during a window of time when traffic will be almost nothing, and may the post office have relatively few customers at the time I need to go.*" This is where I decided to add the detail, so I continued, "*as a matter of fact, I would like to request that there be no more than five people in front of me in whichever line I choose — the counter or the automated postal kiosk. Thank you very much.*"

"I decided to leave the house at a few minutes after 1:00PM. It's a very short drive to the post office, and there was hardly any traffic on the road. I hit all green lights, turned in to the parking lot and noted that there were quite a few parking spaces for April 15. So I pulled into a space, got my envelope, and proceeded to walk toward the building.

"At that moment, I caught sight of a woman about fifteen feet ahead of me carrying a toddler. The thought came to me that I was going to amend my MBO. I made sure to slow my pace so that this woman with her child could go ahead of me, and I requested silently that '*if this woman makes it six people instead of five, then that was as it should be. Thank you.*' Do you even need to guess how many people were standing in line when I got inside the post office? In case you do, it was six.

"That was surely the most wonderful, stress-free tax season I've had yet. Nothing better could have happened in terms of actions to remind me that requesting MBOs daily would be the best thing that could happen to me. Thank you once again for all your gifts — they are very welcomed!"

A Benevolently Broken Water Main

Tom says: A couple of weeks ago, an old friend of ours came back to Dallas to visit friends, as she and her husband had moved to San Diego to be close to their children and grandchild. She loves Tex-Mex food, and California does not have this style of Mexican cuisine, so we decided to meet at a Mexican restaurant on one of the main arteries through Dallas. Naturally, I requested an MBO for the drive and an MBO for our dinner to be "even better than we can hope for or expect. Thank you!"

When we arrived at the Mexican restaurant, we noticed water gushing out into the street, and I commented that I hoped a water main had not broken. While we were eating our dinner, we noticed that there were fewer and fewer people in the restaurant, and we all commented that the economy must have really hit the restaurants hard.

As we paid our bill, I overheard the host turning people away at the door. It seems that we were some of the last people to be seated that night, because thirty minutes or less into our dinner, the water department cut off the water to the broken pipe, preventing the restaurant from accepting anyone else for dinner. As we walked outside, I said, "Now that was an MBO!" And it was. We had a pleasant dinner with our friend and could easily carry on a conversation, as there were few people seated at the nearby tables.

Senior Citizen Benevolently Breaks Up a Brawl

Carl writes: "I was walking down the street the other day through a crosswalk, and I could see a bus shelter ahead where several young men were waiting for a bus. Two young men in their late teens came across the intersection on their bikes, moved on to the sidewalk behind me, and then quickly passed me as I approached the bus shelter.

"Suddenly, they dumped their bikes ten feet in front of me and ran into the bus shelter swinging and cursing. A real brawl was starting right before my eyes. In my mind, I called out to my spirit guides: 'Guys, I really need your help down here. Please give these guys the grace to ...' and just then, the words 'cool it!' shouted out of me. I was just as startled as they were. I was right in front of the shelter, and everyone stopped the fracas. They just stared at me in total silence. I turned and continued walking down the street. The silence was deafening.

"In the next few seconds, I was thanking my spirit guides for their intercession as the two young men whizzed by me on their bikes and turned down the next street out of sight. I suddenly realized that all those guys could have made mincemeat out of me and I would have been helpless to stop it — I am seventy-four years old. This was one of the strangest experiences I have ever had. All I can say is that everything stopped as quickly as it had started, and it was all over in a matter of seconds. Please ask you readers to never underestimate the power of their guardian angels and spirit guides."

Tales from the DMV

Tina writes: "I used your MBO request this morning when I had to take my daughter to the Motor Vehicle Division to get her learner's permit. We were both dreading it because the lines are tremendous and the service is not too great. Generally you will wait in line for forty-five minutes just to get a number to be directed to the correct desk. You cannot get in and out in less than two or three hours. After listening to your webinar last night, I thought I would put what I learned from it to the test. So I suggested to my daughter that we use the MBO request prior to walking in, and I said it out loud, fully expecting a great outcome.

"Well, guess what? We walked in, and the lady at the check-in desk greeted us, smiled, and asked if she could help us. Wow! That has never happened. She processed my daughter's eye exam, and we were given the next number in line for a photo. Once that was done, we waited only ten minutes — unheard of! — and were processed by another friendly staff member and put in line for the test. Unbelievably, it worked and was so easy! Thank you."

✳   ✳   ✳

Lee writes: "I have an MBO story. I had to renew my driver's license with all the required paperwork back in May. Due to some unforeseen circumstances, I didn't get to the renewal office until June 3. After waiting in line for about fifteen minutes, I got up to the worker who goes over your paperwork first to make sure everything is in order. I had one paper missing, so they gave me a temporary license and a new date of expiration. Everything else was in order, they said. I just had to contact an office in another state to get a copy of a marriage license from over forty years ago! Almost $50 and seven weeks later, I got the required document.

"Today I headed back to get my license with all the paperwork in order. I said an MBO request for everything to run smoothly and for the line to be short, even though it is the beginning of the month. I got to the office, and there were about a dozen people ahead of me and about another dozen people waiting. It was not looking too benevolent!

"When it was my turn, the person was taking a long time looking at all my documentation. When I asked what the problem was, he said a different piece of paper was not the proper one. At this point, I was not happy and let him know that the last time I was there they didn't tell me that. He checked with someone else, and they said I would have to come back again with a new certificate that was going to cost me another $50. Boy, was I trying my best to stay calm, but I wasn't too successful.

"I said a quick MBO request for this to work out for the best, and then I sat and waited for my number to be called. An hour later, it was my turn. When I got to the window, I let the man know how unhappy I was as calmly as I could at the time. I explained the 'paper trail' and how one document was fine two months ago but now was not. He left and came back a few minutes later and asked me some questions, and then he told me to stand in front of the blue screen and smile. I finally was able to renew my driver's license! I didn't get the MBO I hoped for in the way I had hoped, but I did get it! Thank you, Tom. These MBOs are awesome!"

04

Benevolent Outcomes for Vehicles

A Most Benevolent Automobile Sale

Veronica writes: "I have waited to share a story that I was absolutely sure was the result of an MBO. Ever since I read about requesting MBOs, there has always been a parking space ready for me. And there were other little things too, like traffic that was moving, short waiting times, or someone lending me a book that I have always wanted to read. The list goes on.

"But just today, the realization of an MBO said and forgotten many months back finally came through. My brother has a very old car — twenty-two years old to be exact — that got into a fender bender and has not been repaired. The car was beginning to rust here and there. He had kept it in tiptop condition, but since he had to work abroad, no one was left to drive it around. So it just gathered dust in the garage.

"It was finally decided that it would be best to sell the car. But the real hitch was that the car was registered to my auntie because, at that time, she had a good deal with the car's financing, and we were the ones who made all the payments. Somehow we never got around to transferring the ownership from my auntie to my brother.

"I requested an MBO for a buyer who would be willing to pay the amount we wanted and would be okay with the documents to be prepared after the sale. I had forgotten about this MBO. I didn't even remember this MBO when another interested buyer came and haggled us to a much lower price. He had promised to come back with cold cash in some effort to entice us into agreeing to his price. But his son needed to go to the hospital, so that blew his budget.

"Then just today, someone came along, looked at the car, checked out the engine, agreed to pay the amount we wanted, left to get money, came back to us, handed us the money, and we handed him the keys. He was also okay with waiting for my auntie to sign the deed of sale. He didn't flinch when we said it might take a few days because my auntie lives abroad. As I was waving goodbye to this buyer, it finally dawned on me that this was my MBO!"

An Automotive Miracle

Penny writes: "I am writing to tell you of a benevolent outcome we experienced. Our minivan was acting up terribly when we drove it one rainy day last week. After we got past a few blocks, the trouble stopped. My husband was on vacation, so he had the time to get the car checked out. He then told me it had been acting up for several months, but not that badly. We left it at the shop the night before it was to be worked on, and I asked for a benevolent outcome for the mechanic to be able to know exactly what was wrong with it and for us to be able to afford to fix it within our means.

"The shop had a new mechanic who was very good. As soon as my husband told him that it acts up when the weather is wet, he said "I know what it is!" and went right to the distributor cap and spark plug wires. Once he looked at them, however, he couldn't believe his eyes. He said he did not know how our car could have even been running at all — the pieces were so worn and melted. I know why it was still running: Because they had to keep our car running until my husband was on vacation and he had time to fix it. And the bill? We had figured we didn't have more than $250.00 to spend, and the bill was $256.00. Our car runs much better now, and I told my husband what I had requested."

Car Repossession Averted

Melissa writes: "Peace and blessings to you, Tom. This morning, I heard a whisper in my ear that said, 'benevolence.' This word has been on my mind very strongly lately, and while I have always considered myself spiritual, I wasn't sure what it meant. I have a full-time job and am also a Reiki master who offers service to clients in the Detroit area. The past year has been a challenge for me, financially and physically. I have continued to ask for divine assistance in my affairs, but the help would always seem to be not what I fully needed. So when I heard the word 'benevolence' whispered in my ear this morning, I didn't know what to think.

"I happened upon your website through a link on a blog, and the results have already been benevolent. I am two months behind on my car note, and I requested an MBO that the bank accept my payment terms with kindness, and that's what happened! The representative who helped me said that she had been just about to turn my case over to be repossessed and that I had called 'just in time.' She accepted my payment arrangements, and of course I immediately said an MBO for my car payments to be paid in full by the due date.

"I know that you receive letters like this all the time and you probably won't even read this letter, but if you do, thank you Mr. Moore! I will keep you up to date on how my MBOs are answered."

Tom responds: Notice that Melissa was listening to that whisper in her ear, as each of you should concentrate on doing each day. For anyone not familiar with the situation in Detroit, they have a 25 percent unemployment rate and 45 percent of the population is not employed full time. Send lots of white light to Melissa — I know she'll receive it — and to everyone in that area.

Do MBOs Always Work?

Deborah writes: "I requested an MBO to have a safe trip and that our camper would be safe. When we went up this hill, it ripped our jack off and bent our camper's steps. So this tells me an MBO can't always help you, right?"

Tom responds: Well, it could have rolled back onto another car, or into a ditch, or you could have hit a pole or tree or what have you. Or it could have come off in the middle of the highway and flipped the camper. However, your camper remained safe, and I bet steps are easy to replace. You have to count your blessings when you have a mechanical failure like that!

My guardian angel explained to me that requesting MBOs does not rid you of all challenges; it just makes them easier. He described it like this: When you're not requesting MBOs, suddenly there's a wall you have to climb over on the path, and requesting MBOs turns it into just a big speed bump.

Benevolent Car Inspection

Jan writes: "I was due to get my car licensed at the end of June, which includes a safety inspection requirement. Two years ago when I had to do that, the technician at the garage doing my inspection almost didn't pass it because my horn was too quiet. It works, but it isn't nearly as loud as it is supposed to be. After quite a bit of arguing and my insistence that he allow me to have a highway patrol officer come and gauge the actual loudness in decibels, he had finally agreed to let it pass with a notation that they recommended it be replaced.

"This year on my way to get the inspection and license tags renewed, I said an MBO request that my car pass the safety inspection with flying colors and that my licensing process be quick. It worked! The garage passed my car's inspection without any mention of the quiet horn I had not done anything about from the previous two years. On top of that, I was in and out of the Department of Motor Vehicles in less than ten minutes! Thanks, Tom!"

Keep On Truckin'

Louise writes: "I had a wonderful outcome for an MBO! I went on an eight-hour round trip. I was driving a truck and pulling a trailer with a horse in it. On the way home, I had also picked up two monster bales of hay weighing 800 pounds each. This was all in the back of the truck — quite a load for a little sixty-four-year-old lady to be in charge of!

"My truck began making some weird sounds just before I got the hay. I always say an MBO before leaving to go anywhere, but because of my new concern about my vehicle, I asked for any and all guardian angels to help get me and my horse home safely. I couldn't see anything out of the ordinary when I stopped and looked under and around the motor. I made it home safely and then got my horse and the hay unloaded with no problem.

"Then when I took the truck to the service man, he asked me what on earth I had been doing with my truck and how I had managed to drive it to him. I can only say that it was with the help of my guardian angel that I managed to get back home! Thank you, thank you, thank you!"

Louise writes back later: "Further addition to my MBO: After talking to the mechanic, I asked any and all guardian angels to help the truck's condition so that there wouldn't be a huge outlay of funds from my husband's hard work, but whatever would be best for the highest good. The mechanic phoned a day later. With trepidation, I asked the outcome of his further investigation. He said that some bolts had been really loose in the torque converter but as soon as they were tightened, everything appeared fine. Again, thank you, thank you, thank you!"

Congratulations on Your Car Wreck

Lois writes: "Tom, one of my students called me after having a horrific accident on the freeway in which she was rear-ended by two vehicles, including an eighteen-wheeler. She hit the car in front of her, and her car was totaled. I talked her into going to the hospital and getting checked out, and I said a BP for her and the others involved in the crash. Later that day, I called her again. At the hospital, they said she was just fine; they gave her some pills for pain. She had muscle soreness.

"She then began to tell me that her dad had financed the car, and it was being paid for in full by insurance, plus more than she owed. So her father is keeping all that money, but he is deeding to her the title to another car he owns free and clear. It is a miracle. Her kids were not with her, she is not hurt, she is now disentangled from her father, and she has a new car without a car payment.

"I paused a minute and said, 'Sweetie, did you ask for an MBO for a new car and add, "May the outcome be better than anything I could have hoped for or expected?"'

"She gasped and said, 'Oh, yes I did!'

"I replied, 'Well, in that case, congratulations on your car wreck.' We both laughed."

Inexpensive Auto Repair

Patsy writes: "Until my eighty-year-old friend Vera gave me a copy of your book, I thought that asking for things from our angels should only be reserved for important or spiritual things. Reading your books changed my thinking on that, and I have begun requesting MBOs for just about everything. These past few months have been nothing short of amazing. I could write a book!

"This week, though, I feel especially blessed and grateful. I've been worried about my car. It needs some major repairs, but I was hoping I could hold out for a couple more months till my friend who is a mechanic came to town. While I was on my way home from work this week, my car started sputtering, and I just prayed for an MBO to get to my neighborhood gas station. I held my breath at each stoplight and prayed. I felt momentary relief when I pulled into the station. They were busy and would have to keep it overnight. I'd get the estimate in the morning. They did say it was going to cost a minimum of $72 just to diagnose it, and that this money could not be put toward any repairs. I was literally sick to my stomach all night, trying to figure out how I'd get to work, where the money would come from, and so on. Finally, I just released my problem to the angels.

"I got the sweetest-sounding phone call the next morning. They tightened a couple belts, changed the oil, and only charged me $56. With the diagnosis, they assured me it was okay for a couple more months. Thank you, thank you, thank you! And thank you, Tom, for facilitating all these wonderful stories."

Found Money and Benevolent Vehicle Costs

Diana writes: "I truly appreciate the work that you are doing and want to offer a fabulous testimonial for requesting MBOs. A couple of months ago, I said an MBO request for unexpected income in an amount greater than I could hope for or imagine. In my mind, the purpose of the income request was that my husband drives a car that is, shall we say, on its last leg. It is actually not a safe vehicle, and the expense to repair it would cost more than the car is worth. I did not want to go into debt. I figured that I might be able to find a decent, gently used vehicle, and I wanted to start accumulating money.

"By the end of that month, I had received an unexpected check in the amount of $4,000! We decided we should be able to get something workable for that amount. While traveling from Canada back to Seattle just a week later, my husband and I were talking about MBO requests. I felt compelled to say an MBO request out loud and I said,

Most Benevolent Outcome Request

"I request a most benevolent outcome that we cross paths with someone who has a good used vehicle to sell that we can afford, that is safe, and that will provide my husband with a reliable vehicle to get to work safely. Thank you!"

"The next weekend, we went to visit my husband's youngest brother, whom we had not seen since last fall. He had a camping trailer that he wanted to sell, and my husband wanted to upgrade from our pop-up tent trailer. We liked the trailer, and then his brother said, 'I'm also going to sell my truck too, because I just don't use it.' I asked him how much, and he said $4,000. I asked if he would take $3,500 for it, and he said yes. It had some brake issues and the estimate for the brake work was between $1,700 and $2,500, based on the calls the owner made to automotive repair shops. We agreed to buy the truck for $3,500 and pay for the brake repairs, and we bought the camping trailer too. My brother-in-law was thrilled because he did not have the money for the brake work, but he needed to sell the truck and trailer so that he would have the money to buy an old van to start his mobile janitorial service.

"We delivered the truck to a brake-repair shop. The next day, I was riding in my car with my son and I said this MBO request out loud:

Most Benevolent Outcome Request
"I request a most benevolent outcome that the brake repair expense be $500 or less. Thank you."

"I said that amount to keep the vehicle expense within the amount of money that I had available to buy my husband this truck without having a debt tied to it. Within five seconds — yes, five seconds! — I got a call from the brake repairman, who said the break fix would run between $500 and $800, depending on what things looked like when they got in there and whether or not a master cylinder had to be replaced. I said another MBO request that it would not need a master cylinder replacement, and in the end, the brake fix cost $560 and did not need a new master cylinder.

"So I was able to get a 2000 Chevrolet 1500 Silverado LT with 115,000 miles on it — in beautiful condition with a king cab — and a heavy duty towing package for the trailer for $3,500, plus $560 for brake work. Along with that, I got an awesome twenty-foot camping trailer for another $3,500, and my husband is paying for that. The cool thing is also the benevolent part that my brother-in-law did not have to come up with money to fix the truck so that he could sell it and that he sold it to us and was then able to find the van he wanted to create his mobile janitorial service. This all came together within nine days after driving home from Canada and saying an MBO request to find a great vehicle for a price that I could afford. Yahoo! Thank you, angels and Tom!"

Benevolent Auto Accident Results

Tosca writes: "Every time I get in my car, I say an MBO request for myself, my car, and for every driver, every passenger, and every vehicle on the road. It has been working wonderfully. This week, I was coming home from work and wanted to go to the gym. My ride from work is twenty-six miles and at times is tiresome. I was looking forward to getting rid of stress at the gym and was looking for a good parking spot.

"Suddenly a large SUV was in front of me. My car is a small four-cylinder Toyota. As I hit the other vehicle, I said a prayer for my angels to be with both vehicles and drivers. The crash sound was deafening! But when the other driver and I got out to inspect the damage, there was no damage to either vehicle. Onlookers in the area, together with the other driver, her two passengers, and I were totally amazed, knowing what the consequence could have been. God bless you, Tom, for spreading the word about the wonders of MBOs."

Angelic Auto Repair

Silvia writes: "Here's a story of MBOs and angels. Saturday, my son Ryan and I drove to the Hobby Lobby store on a little outing. When we got back out of the store, we looked at a car and its license plate said 'ANGEL.' We got into our own car, but it would not budge. We could not make it work.

"Out of the blue came a car with a man and a woman in it. The man asked if he could help, so we tried several times to get our car jump-started, but it did not work. The man said sorry and I thanked him and told him how much I appreciated their help. He then gave me his card; he was a minister.

"There was a garage nearby, so Ryan and I walked over there and talked to a nice man. He drove over to see if he could jump-start the car. The car did not move, and the man said it looked like the starter was out. 'I can get you one for tomorrow,' he said, 'or maybe today.' We left the garage for a walk, and I kept praying to the angels and saying MBOs. We went back to the garage. The man there said he could get a starter that same day for a large amount of money. I told him I could not do that, as I needed to watch my finances. 'Let's get it tomorrow,' I said.

"In the meantime, I called the only person I knew and asked if he could pick us up; he did just that. We ate and then were on way back to where we live — about an hour's drive away. Ten minutes before we arrived at the house, my phone rang. The garage had fixed the car; it turned out that the problem was not the starter, but with the battery and a broken cable. These were replaced, and the garage gave us new windshield wipers too. The total price was much lower than it would've been for a new starter. We drove right back and I got my car. Incredible, huh?

"Well, my point of view about all this is the angel prepared me to see that when it is the right time for anything I'm waiting for, it will happen quickly, smoothly, and easily. Thank you, angels! Thank you, universe!"

Angels and Auto Mechanics

Gisel writes: "Some months ago, my car broke down. I requested an MBO and took it to the mechanic. The results were awful — they had my car for twenty days and gave it back with the same malfunction plus other bad things it didn't have before I took it in. Of course, I took my car to another mechanic and again requested an MBO for the best result. I got my car back in perfect condition this time. I wondered why my first MBO did not have the desired effect.

"The answer I heard — or think I heard — was that I had to learn something about this situation. Of course I had to meditate on that. Am I hearing it right? Have you heard the same thing from other people? Do other people request things and not get desired results right away but later? Maybe the time isn't right, or perhaps we have to learn something?

"Another question: I seem to have better insights when I'm doing something mechanical like washing dishes, driving, or cleaning than when I'm meditating. Is this common? Or am I just hearing myself? Finally, can people have more than one guardian angel? I sense two by my side — maybe my guides or my oversoul?"

Jeannine writes: "I have been told I am very protected with lots of angels, guides, and spirit animals. If this is true, how many angels and spirit animals are around me?"

Tom responds: This answer is for both Jeannine and Gisel — and perhaps everyone else too, as I've received similar answers to these types of questions from my guardian angel before. He says, "Gisel has several guides, with two of them from her soul cluster being very prominent. The others are there to assist her in her daily work, but the two are there and on-call twenty-four hours a day. They have been together with her physically in a large number of lives. That is why she feels their presence so easily."

I then asked my angel why the repairs on Gisel's car did not work the first time she requested MBOs, but then did work the second time. Here is his response: "Her soul contract called for her to experience the first time for her learning, Tom. The MBO result was that she was able to take it to another mechanic who successfully took care of or fixed the problem. Had she not requested the first MBO, this situation would have been worse."

MBO for Abandoned Vehicle

Louise writes: "I just had to report an amazing MBO! Over the weekend we received a code violation for an abandoned, deteriorated vehicle on a vacant lot that we have for sale. Due to the Memorial Day weekend, I couldn't get a hold of the person who was in charge of the lot; I couldn't even find his phone number. Needless to say, with trepidation, I have been requesting MBOs that the vehicle would be removed without any cost to us — dealing with the county regarding code violations is a real challenge here — and I had my friend do the same.

"This morning I called a towing company and they informed me that I had to have clearance from the police for the vehicle to be removed. I arranged for someone from the police department to investigate. I spoke to a deputy sheriff who went to look at the vehicle and said that the VIN number plate had been removed. He gave me a case number and said to proceed to get someone to pick it up. I told him that the neighbor who lived across the street had permission to park his vehicles there overnight and maybe he would have some info. The deputy said he would check it out.

"Many phone calls and 'no ma'ams' later, I found someone who would go look at the vehicle to see if they could tow it. He phoned me back and said that he was at the lot and there was no vehicle there. Wow, was I gobsmacked! I didn't even have to go to the lot — which is about an hour away — to sign a release or anything. My guardian angel clearly asked the junk fairies to get involved here. Yay!"

MBO for Flat Tire

Dorothea writes: "Every morning I have been saying your daily affirmation and requesting benevolent outcomes whenever I can. I want to tell you of a very benevolent outcome I experienced the other day.

"I purchased a used car last November and knew that I would need new tires soon. Then I forgot about it. The other day I came out of the store to find that one of the tires was almost flat and had what looked like a tear. I made it to the tire store and was told that there was a plug in the sidewall — not a good thing — and that the tires were actually too small for my car.

"New tires were installed. I consider this a very benevolent outcome due to the fact that I am on the freeway a lot driving 70 miles per hour. Thank you for spreading the word about this technique; it works perfectly. And in addition, I have reconnected with my three angels."

MBOs Fixed It!

Pam writes: "Yesterday, I requested an MBO. I was driving my car in New Hampshire and heard a clunking noise under the car. I thought it was a flat. It was nighttime and rainy, and I was alone. At first I was in denial that there was a problem, but the noise intensified and it was clear that it wasn't an ignorable situation. I called in my guardian angels and asked for an MBO for this problem. I was concerned that I would be stranded at night in the rain on a dark country road thirty miles from home.

"First, I got home safely without incident. In the morning, I had to figure out how I would work the problem through. Again, I asked for an MBO. I found a car repair shop that was closed, but an employee said that if I dropped my car off, they would leave a loaner there waiting for me with a key in it. I called AAA and they towed the car free of charge. I met a very nice driver along the way who was really helpful. I now have a temporary car to drive, and my vehicle is safe and waiting for a mechanic on Monday morning. A huge thank you to my guardian angels for this gift. And thank you, Tom, for sharing the MBO practice. Wishing you the best and many blessings!"

MBO for Returning a Leased Car

Diane writes: "I wanted to share an MBO that just happened — when it's time, it's time! I have had four Nissan vehicles. They were all great, and I leased all of them. I decided I wanted to try something new. In order to do that, I had to complete the lease and turn the vehicle in — something I have never done before. I said an MBO a few months back:

> **Most Benevolent Outcome Request**
> *"I am asking for an MBO for everything to turn out perfectly when I turn in my leased car from Nissan. I ask that the transaction goes quickly and smoothly, that the salesperson will be kind to me, that I will not owe any other extra money, and that it will be better than I would hope for or expect. Thank you."*

"I made an appointment to turn in the leased Nissan. The salesperson I dealt with was the manager of the department, and he was kind and nice to me. I quickly signed all the papers to turn in the lease, and I did not owe any extra money at all. I was in and out of the dealership within twenty minutes, and on top of that, they provided me with the appropriate papers that released me from the lease.

"I asked to use their phone to make a call to get a ride home and the salesperson said, 'You don't have to do that. Your son Jeff is outside waiting for you. I just spoke to him when I went out to check the car!' I had told my son I was going to turn in my car and that I had no idea how long it would be, so he shouldn't worry about waiting around for me. But he is very intuitive, and when I met him outside, he said he felt I might need a ride. So I got in the car and we went to have some coffee, and then he drove me home. So on top of the transaction going so quickly, smoothly, and perfectly, the bonus was my son helping me out when I had never asked him to do so.

"Thank you for the MBOs, Tom. They are so helpful."

Benevolent Tire Replacement

Marie writes: "Hello, Tom. I have an MBO to share with you. This past week on Friday, I had my tires changed. The very next day, one of the new tires blew out, so I had to put on a spare. I knew I had to go back to the tire shop on Monday and tell them what happened, so I requested an MBO that they give me another tire at no charge. To my surprise, the man at the tire shop did! I was a very happy customer. After I left the tire shop, I thanked my guardian angel(s).

Tom responds: As I keep telling everyone, requesting benevolent outcomes for all the more mundane things in life makes your life less stressful and much more enjoyable!

Working Up to the Big Stuff

Sharon writes: "Ever since I came across your books, Tom, my life has taken a different turn and somewhat improved that much more. I have always believed in affirmations and did do them — but not regularly enough. Coming across your books has put a whole new perspective on things, and it is so easy! I am so excited to the point that I share this concept with everyone I come across — if they are willing to listen to me. If they don't, then it's their loss, I guess, but I explain and share the message: What have you got to lose? Just try.

"Here is the story of a very recent big MBO involving my car. After all the small MBOs, I thought I'd test it out on something bigger, so I requested an MBO that 'any and all beings help to find out the problems with my car, that it did not cost me too much, and that it is a most benevolent outcome.' As it turned out, after much frustration in dealing with the mechanics, in the end I stopped myself, took a step back, and took out my emotion from the situation of dealing with the mechanics, leaving it up to the universe.

"I ended up with a nice result: All of the problems would be taken care of under warranty. I had started complaining about the problems that I was having back in 2010, so it seems when they checked my car history, and pretty much each service since then, it was decided to cover the transmission and fuel pump all under the full warranty instead of the extended warranty, under which I would have only got $1,000 off the whole price of fixing, which I can only imagine was a lot of money. So I consider myself very thankful. It is all down to trust! Thank you to you, Tom, and to universe. I'm sure now that my guides and other beings are smiling, knowing that they were able to help, are continuing to help, and are finally working instead of sitting around watching."

A Blessed Visit to an Amusement Park

Marie writes: "I can go on and on with my MBO stories, but I don't want to bore you. Let me just tell you my most significant and profound MBO story about when my car started to smoke because of leaking water when we pulled in at Universal Studios parking lot. We were at the parking-lot ticket window and our car started smoking everywhere. All the people in the other cars in line were looking at us, wondering if we were about to blow up.

"Before we left the house, the car's warning signal had come on and my husband had determined it needed water, so he filled it up and off we went. We happily drove one and a half hours on a busy LA freeway on Christmas Eve with no traffic at all, not knowing that something dangerous was lurking under the hood. It was a pleasant drive, and we were excited to get to the park. Of course, I requested a bunch of MBOs related to this activity.

"Then voilà, as soon as we pulled in to the parking lot, the car started to smoke everywhere. My husband was worried all day about how we were going to get back home on Christmas Eve, and he could not enjoy the fun stuff at Universal Studios. I was having a good time, because I knew in my heart that my guardian angel would take care of everything. I felt this very strongly. It was about midday when I decided to call AAA and let them know our situation. They said only two people could have a ride. There were four of us with our two sons — one visiting from Texas for Christmas to see us.

"So we finished our day, and when it was time to leave the park, my husband decided to ask Universal Studios customer service for help. They put us in a room complete with a phone and all kinds of directories — and some snacks too. My husband called the bus line, but there was nothing on Christmas Eve. He called shuttle services — nothing. His last resort was for us to take a taxi for a two-hour drive, and I didn't even want to know how much that was going to cost. So I finally told him to stop doing that and let me call AAA again. I told him not to worry.

"I called AAA and they said yes, that they had a truck available with seats in the back to fit four people. When the truck arrived at the parking lot, the driver checked the leaking water problem in the exhaust system. He started pouring water into the radiator, but it kept coming back out as fast as he poured it in. The radiator pipe had a large hole! I pointed out to my husband that the entire hour and a half we were on the freeway, we must have been driving without water in the exhaust system, and the engine did not blow up on us! As we pulled into the parking lot that morning, my guardian angel was really telling us, 'Here you go — you made it to the park. Enjoy your day and let me take care of everything else that needs to be done.'"

05

Benevolent Outcomes for Everyday Transportation

Request MBOs Before Driving

Tom says: I'll begin with an MBO story of my own. I *never* get in a car without requesting an MBO for the drive to wherever I'm headed — even if someone else is driving. In my first book, I told the story of renting a car to drive from the airport in Nice, France, to Cannes with my trunks for a world TV market. Naturally, I requested an MBO for my drive to Cannes. I had driven less than five minutes on the highway when a little French car just in front of me lost control, slid into the median rail divider, and popped out right in front of me. Had I been five seconds sooner I would have hit him, but instead I easily avoided it by going all the way to the right side of the roadway and slowly passing by.

This time, after requesting an MBO for my drive back to the grocery store near where I live, I took the North Dallas Tollway and exited at Legacy Drive, for those of you who know the area. A large black pickup truck turned onto Legacy in front of me and was on the outside of the three lanes, so I took the middle in order to not be right behind him. As we both approached the signal light for the entrance to the Shops at Legacy, I could see a car in the left-turn lane and could just barely see a smaller black SUV in the opposite turn lane.

Suddenly the black SUV started to turn; obviously, the driver had not seen the black pickup in front of me, as her vision was blocked by the other car in the opposite turn lane. I'm sure my eyes became as wide as saucers, as I saw there was no way the pickup truck traveling at about forty to forty-five miles per hour could stop. The truck slammed into the SUV and literally lifted it off the pavement. I came to a stop about five feet or so from the SUV, which had been turned 180 degrees after the collision.

So I remind you to request an MBO wherever you go, even if it's just to the local supermarket. I did say a BP for both drivers.

A Guardian Angel Takes the Wheel

Daphnee writes: "I happened to read the part of your newsletter regarding the guardian angels embodying in the third dimension to save someone's life. A few years ago while living in Cyprus, I was driving very fast in the fast lane and overtook two cars in the middle lane. There was a third car ahead in the slow lane. I was about to overtake this car and was slightly ahead of it already when, suddenly, invisible hands grabbed the wheel and I found myself slowing down and dropping behind the car I had nearly overtaken.

"In the same moment, a car came from the opposite direction toward me in the lane I had just been in. I don't know how you say this in English, but in German we call that a 'ghost rider.' I don't know what happened, but I knew it was not me. 'Daphnee' would never have slowed down and moved over to the slow lane, especially as I had nearly passed the other car. I thought, 'Oh, was that my guardian angel?'

"This is the event in my life when I started to believe in angels and dared talking to mine. For years, I have not been sure: Did I have only one or many? My feeling is that its a plural form of angel, but I am not sure. Maybe you can shed some light on that?"

Tom responds: There is only one golden lightbeing you call your guardian angel; this is who oversees you every minute of the day and night. We do have one or two main guides, as well as several who come and go depending on what we're doing at that time in life.

Freeway MBO

Linda writes: "Yesterday, before leaving to go to a friend's house, I requested an MBO for a safe return home. While driving down the I-75 local freeway, I realized I was going 55 miles per hour. I thought to myself, 'That's ridiculous,' and decided to speed up. At that moment, as we went into a curve, a black SUV with Georgia plates came into my lane and completed the whole curve halfway in my lane. Had I been driving at my normal speed, she would have taken me out.

"As I regained my composure, I dutifully thanked my guardian angel. I watched this person take an exit off the freeway, and I sent love to her in her oblivion of what had almost changed our lives. Funny how we affect others without even realizing it! Thank you."

Tom responds: That's also an example of the radiant effect in which your MBO requests affect others: The other driver was kept safe too.

Avoiding a Costly Traffic Ticket

Kathy writes: "I have an MBO experience to share. A couple of months ago, I moved back to my small hometown in East Texas from the Dallas area. It has been a challenge to slow down and adjust to the way it is in small towns and how everyone moves at a leisurely pace.

"One morning on my way to do errands, I was stopped by a train — a very, very long train. I immediately recognized that this was a message from the universe to slow down. I turned off my car ignition, and while waiting, I recalled childhood memories of waiting for this train, which was quite relaxing, or so I thought. At the first sign of the last car in the train, I started my ignition and zoomed across the tracks while the red lights at the railroad stop were still flashing.

"As I crossed the tracks, I saw a police car waiting on the opposite side, and remembered that I'm supposed to wait for the flashing lights to cease before crossing. The police officer immediately turned on his lights and did a U-turn, and I pulled over. When the officer approached my car, I had registration and insurance papers in hand and immediately apologized, stating that I was wrong and hadn't waited for the lights to go off. I also added that it had been decades since I had had to wait for a train.

"As he went to his car to run a check on me, I began thinking about how I did not have the money to pay for a ticket, so I said the following request for an MBO:

Most Benevolent Outcome Request

"I request a most benevolent outcome in this situation. May it be that I only receive a warning ticket or even be granted an outcome better than I could ever expect or imagine. Thank you, thank you, thank you."

"The officer came to the car and said, 'I'm going to give you a warning, but I don't have my warning book with me. This ticket would cost you $300 or more. You need to learn to slow down and take it easy, okay?' 'Yes, officer. I will,' I replied. And then I said thank you to my guardian angel."

Benevolent Van Pool Outcome

Sue writes:

"Hi, Tom. I have a great MBO story for you today! I work at a large university and participate in their van pool program to help our environment and save a lot of money on gas as well as wear and tear on my own vehicle. In this program, you cannot get a van pool vehicle until you have five additional people who work full time and are committed to riding with you on a daily basis. I left my other van pool in January, as their working start and stop times really didn't match with mine, and I had to stay an extra thirty minutes each day to catch a ride home with them.

"I decided to try to start up my own van pool with myself as the primary driver, finding five others who live near me and have my work hours. I immediately started out by saying a request for an MBO involving people who would be good matches for me and my alternate driver's personalities, so that we would be able to have a good group riding together for the two-hour commute we drive every workday. It took me a long time — seven months — to get all of the people together, but finally, after much frustration on my part and wondering why it was taking so long, I found my fifth person and applied for the van.

"This organization requires that every newly forming van pool attends a formation meeting with the university's alternative transportation coordinator and the representative for the van pool company. During this meeting, I was told that we would not get the customary brand new van, but would instead get the only van available, which was a used van. I was a bit disappointed, but having said requests for MBOs all along this journey of getting my van pool group started, I figured that there was a reason for all of these hurdles. I was assured that the used van was safe and trustworthy and, because I trusted in my MBO requests, I said that it was fine and that I would take whatever they gave me.

"This meeting was two weeks ago, and last Thursday, the company representative emailed me and asked if I would be available to meet her and get my van the next Monday, which was yesterday. Of course I said yes, double-checked the day and time with her, and made arrangements for it yesterday. Well, when we showed up for the meeting — for which we had taken time off of work and were driven several miles across town by my coworker — we were told that the representative had made a mistake in telling me the day and that the delivery was going to be the following Tuesday — today, as I write this — instead.

"I was very disappointed but tried my best to be polite and positive to the coordinator, even as I was wondering why this had happened and what was going on. Of course, I quickly remembered that I had said MBO requests for everything I could think of surrounding this whole event and thought that there must be a reason or two for the misunderstanding.

"So now we come to today — the real van delivery day. Once again, we show up at our meeting time, wondering what our used van will be like. The company representative shows up and takes us outside, saying, 'I felt so horrible about the mix-up before that I decided to give you a brand new van and not the older one!' Wow, talk about a fantastic MBO!

"Thanks, Tom, for your wonderful work and your efforts to get the word out about MBOs. Many blessings to you and your family!"

Parking Synchronicity

Pili writes: "My daughter and I met at the mall, and I was looking for a parking spot. The one that grabbed my attention wasn't very close to the door, but it looked like a good one; however, I didn't take it. When we left, we were carrying big bags, so I followed her to her car, and I was surprised when I saw her car right in front of the empty spot I looked at first. Now I know when we request an MBO we have to trust in what we ask for. I love your book, Tom."

Tom responds: I've had times when I requested an MBO for a parking space close to the front door of a restaurant or mall and took one that was fairly close, only to see one right next to the entrance as I continued on.

Bridge-Crossing MBO

Kathy writes: "The great results from using MBOs just keep rolling in! Here's the latest: My husband's commute to work and back takes him over the Hood Canal Floating Bridge. This bridge opens and closes to let marine traffic through, which causes quite a backup in traffic and usually a delay of half an hour to forty-five minutes. Yesterday my husband called me on his cell phone to let me know he was stuck in 'bridge traffic' and would be delayed. He called again a few minutes later to tell me that he'd found out the bridge was stuck open and no one knew when it would be open again. He was considering driving around Hood Canal, which would take him about two hours. I told him to wait about half an hour.

"As soon as we hung up, I requested an MBO that the bridge become unstuck and close within fifteen minutes. He called me again about ten minutes later and said the bridge had closed and traffic was moving. Fast results! Thank you, Tom, and thank you, guardian angels."

Passing an Irish Driving Test

Eileen writes: "I am here in Ireland and came across an old magazine I had at home called and liked your column on benevolent outcomes. I have a driving test tomorrow and was wondering what benevolent outcome prayer I could say to pass the driving test. I'm looking forward to hearing from you."

Tom responds: For anyone about to take almost any kind of test, you can say:

> **Most Benevolent Outcome Request**
> "I request a most benevolent outcome for my test today and that I remain calm. May the results be even better than I can hope for or expect. Thank you!"

Eileen writes back: "Tom, I passed my driving test on Tuesday, and I am so happy!"

MBO Prevents Horrible Auto Accident

Katriana writes: "I've been saying MBOs daily for some months now, ever since my friend gave me the link to your website. From the first one, I have absolutely loved MBOs and always feel uplifted when I say them. I have shared them with many people and forwarded your email to spread the good word. Thank you so much, Tom, for sharing the MBOs and for your generosity in sharing other information, such as news from Gaia.

"Here's a recent MBO result for me. I always start my day with the 'great things' mantra and also an MBO for 'for every moment of this day,' as well as more specific MBOs. Last weekend, as I headed to my car to take care of errands, I said a couple of MBOs for safe travel and so on. Not far from home, I approached an intersection and prepared to make a right turn. After checking traffic, I slowly proceeded when suddenly two young women decided to push their baby strollers into the road in front of me against the traffic light. I immediately stopped, and I heard brakes behind me.

"Somehow — thank you, guardian angels! — the SUV behind me missed my little Sidekick by a couple of inches, and the young women crossed safely. Had the SUV hit my vehicle, it would have been pushed directly into the mothers and babies. I know that MBOs are heard, and this wasn't the first example of quick response I've had, but it's certainly one for which I was most grateful."

MBOs for Japanese Traffic

Billy writes: "I've been continuing to use your MBO requests with great results. Thanks to them, I can pass through intersections that normally clog up for one and a half kilometers at rush hour, smoothly escape or avoid traffic blocking situations, and get where I need to be safely. I use your prayer method to ask for great days and solutions to problems for those dear to me, and they seem to work wonderfully too. Like others, I've found that the MBO request sometimes takes a turn that seems strange at the time, but if you 'go with the flow,' the reason often becomes obvious.

"A few months ago, I made my usual request for an MBO for 'a safe drive in little or no traffic to karate practice' at the elementary school where I teach karate. This usually works, and I get a nice relaxing drive in very little or no traffic, arriving at the school right on time. On this one occasion, I found myself in very fast-flowing traffic. I remember thinking to myself that I'd be arriving at the school more than ten minutes early at the speed I was driving. About two kilometers from the school, I suddenly hit a spot where traffic was backed up due to a four-car accident. Needless to say, it took me just about the amount of time I'd gained in the fast traffic to clear the accident scene. I arrived at the school exactly at my usual time."

Driving In Fog

Marie writes: "I want to share an MBO that happened this morning. I had to drive to the city, and the fog was so dense that I couldn't see the car in front of me. I got worried, but I have full faith in my guardian angels. So I said,

Most Benevolent Outcome Request
"Guardian angel, I request an MBO for the fog to disappear so that the other drivers and I can see the road better than we expect. Thank you!"

Not even ten minutes later, the fog dissipated and I was able to see the road clearly. I even added a BP:

> **Benevolent Prayer**
> *"I ask that any and all beings drive safely, and may they have a perfect day. Thank you!"*

Punctuality Counts

Joe writes: "I had a great result from an MBO request today. There was a staff meeting scheduled first thing this morning, and walking in late is always embarrassing. I encountered a major traffic jam a couple miles out from the office, and I asked my guardian angel for an MBO in getting to the office before the meeting began. I ended it with 'and may the outcome be better than I could hope for or expect.' I've learned to attach that final tag line to all of my MBOs, as I really do think it makes a difference!

"I started to stress about the situation since the cars were moving so slowly, but then I realized it wasn't worth it. I was going to be late for sure and I couldn't change that. I hoped that even though I'd have to walk into the meeting late, there would still somehow be a benevolent outcome. I popped in a CD from one of my favorite bands and jammed to the entire sixteen-minute-long first track, which put me in a great mood. I finally arrived at the office and walked in to see an empty conference room. It turned out that my boss had been caught in the same traffic jam and had called ahead to cancel the staff meeting."

Safe Traffic Conditions and Perfect Timing

Laurie writes: "Here's a recent MBO success story for you. I agreed to pick up a friend at the airport. I was worried about meeting her on time since her plane was delayed by bad weather. I tracked the flight on the airline's website, and the arrival time got later and later into the night. I said some BPs, and at last the schedule firmed up. My friend was in the air and on her way.

"Unfortunately for me, I now had to drive on I-95 very late at night. I'm really uncomfortable driving in the dark, and even more nervous about driving on I-95, which has gotten to be an extremely congested highway even at the best of times. I must have said about twenty MBO requests for safe driving conditions. All of them were granted. Traffic was light, there were very few cars around me as I drove to and from the airport, and there was only one nutty speed demon who came out of nowhere and swerved around me. Whew!

"I also requested another set of MBOs to meet my friend on time at the airport. We had agreed that she would come out to the curb at the arrivals area. I didn't want to be too early or too late, so I requested an MBO to coordinate meeting her perfectly. Well, you can guess what happened! She came out of the door no more than thirty seconds after I pulled up at the curb. She said, 'Wow, that's perfect timing.' I replied, 'Thank the angels!'"

MBOs for Safe Daily Drives to Work and Back

Sussana writes: "I've been meaning to write about my MBOs. I do the one about driving daily:

> **Most Benevolent Outcome Request**
> *"I request a most benevolent outcome for a smooth and safe drive home (or to work) and any stops in between. Thank you!"*

"I immediately take a deep breath and feel the gratitude. One day last year on my way home on a three-lane highway, a Pontiac passed me going at least ten miles over the speed limit, weaving in and out of the traffic. I sent up a quick thank you as he went on his crazy way. About ten miles after that incident, I came upon the Pontiac and another vehicle in an accident! I sent up another thank you for keeping me safe.

"I like doing this simple daily request because it keeps me in practice. Once I reach my destination, I say, 'Thank you for getting me here safe.' I love this idea of MBOs — it puts me into a fantastic, pleasant vibration."

MBO Avoiding Wreck

Anne-Marie writes: "I say a BP every time I get into the car. I was driving home from work one evening on a relatively light-traffic highway. A car ahead of me decided to change lanes without checking, and he overcorrected when he noticed a car in the lane he was attempting to enter. His car then spun out of control, hitting the vehicle he had been attempting to avoid. Both cars spun across five lanes of highway — without hitting other vehicles — before crashing into the median wall.

"One driver got out of a vehicle, but I do not know what happened to the other driver. I said BPs for all involved. The fact that no other cars were involved in this accident was nothing short of a miracle, and I can only credit the ambient effect of the BP for that."

Smooth MBO-Enhanced Drive Keeps Getting Smoother

Billy writes: "I've noticed an interesting trend in the MBOs I request for smooth driving. I drive on the same very congested routes during rush hour every week. When I first started requesting MBOs, the traffic lightened miraculously, and I got to my destinations smoothly. As the weeks went on, each week it seemed to get lighter and lighter. At intersections where the rush-hour traffic is normally backed up to almost a standstill for close to two kilometers, I've been getting through with no waiting at all.

"Do the folks taking care of these MBOs get better and faster when they are asked for the same thing repeatedly — as in smooth driving for my routine driving routes? My experience with the traffic seems to suggest they do, but is it only a coincidence?"

Tom responds: When I last consulted my guardian angel in meditation, I asked about Billy's question: "When you constantly request MBOs for your driving, is there a cumulative effect, or is it just that you become used to traveling at a tuned-in time, shall we say?"

Here's what my angel said: "Good question, Tom. Yes, there is a cumulative effect, as you do start tuning in when you should depart — the exact instant, I might add. And of course the other drivers pick up on their own guardian angels whispering in their ears as to when to depart on their own journeys. The tuning in on the best time to depart, however, comes down more to the individuals who request the MBOs than the guardian angels whispering in their ears. So there is a give and flow for an MBO that is requested each time that goes beyond the normal MBO request. A simple way of thinking about it would be, 'The more you use it, the easier it gets.' That applies not only to remembering to request MBOs but also the continued use of them."

MBO Saves Driver from Horrible Guilt

Diana writes: "I was driving at night, and I hardly ever drive, much less at night. All of a sudden, I saw a man standing in the road wearing a white robe. I stepped on the brakes to avoid hitting him. As soon as my car came to a stop, I heard a horrible crash. 'Oh ,' I said, 'Someone hit that poor man,' and I turned around to see. But there was no man in a white robe anywhere. It must have been a vision or an angel.

"What I saw was the car in the next lane hit and kill a man on a motorcycle! Oh my, if I hadn't seen that man in the white robe, I wouldn't have stopped, and I would have hit and killed the man on the motorcycle. He came out on my left side and I never saw him; he must have had his lights off and then run the red light. I know that if I had killed that man I would have not been able to live with myself."

Tom responds: I think this is a good example of how your guardian angel can step in to prevent something from happening that is not on your soul contract.

MBO for Flat Tire on the Freeway

Ellyn writes: "I had an amazing result for an MBO request last year that I've wanted to report for some time now. I was on my way to my brother's house, driving fairly fast — 65 miles per hour — in the far left lane of the Washington Beltway, when I heard what sounded like a helicopter about to land on my car! It took me a moment to realize it was the sound of a blown-out tire whacking on the pavement. As I looked at all the traffic in the two lanes between me and the shoulder of the road, I said an abbreviated MBO request, something like, 'I need an MBO for this now, please!'

"Fortunately, the car was not wobbling at all, and I was able to steer it with no trouble. As I started to change lanes, the traffic miraculously thinned out, and I was easily able to cross the two lanes and come to a stop on the side of the road. Of course, that was just the beginning; I still had to get help with the car. As I called my brother to tell him what happened, I looked in the rearview mirror and saw a tow truck appear behind me. I hung up the phone, and the wonderful gentleman in the tow truck secured my car and drove me to a service station near my home. He truly was my knight in shining armor, appearing out of nowhere to rescue me, and I told him so, much to his delight. My guardian angels came through in a miraculous way for me, as they always do. I didn't even have to sit on the side of the road for five minutes waiting for help. It simply arrived the moment I needed it!

"As you say, Tom, our guardian angels are happy to help us in miraculous ways at all times. The challenge is to remember to ask!"

Benevolent University Visit

Abby writes: "Yesterday I went to Virginia Tech for the memorial services and accidentally left my university map at home. There's nothing quite like taking on a university in a strange town without knowing where you are going! After a really heartfelt MBO request — I needed all the help I could get — I found a quick and easy parking space, walked all over the university, and returned to my car afterward without skipping a beat. This is a miracle for me! Don't you love how this works?"

Speeding Ticket Averted

Jason writes: "This morning I was driving to work and was running a little late, so I was going faster than I should have been. As I usually do on the way to work, I spoke to my guardian angel, who I've named Max, since he gets me maximum results. I said,

> **Most Benevolent Outcome Request**
> *"Good morning, Max. I'm expecting great things today, great things tomorrow, and great things all weekend long. Thank you!"*

"I spotted a police car pretty far down the road facing the opposite direction, so I jammed on the brakes to bring my speed down to the speed limit. But as I passed the car, the officer flipped on her lights and made a U-turn to get behind me. My stomach just dropped. This is not what I needed today!

"I immediately pulled over into a parking lot, dropped my window, and pulled out my license. She came to the window and introduced herself, then told me she clocked me going 48 in a 35. I said, 'Wow, I didn't realize I was going that fast!' in a very sincere way. She asked me if I was on my way to work, then asked me for my license and told me to stay in the car. She walked back to her car, and then a minute later she approached my open window again. I'll never forget these beautiful words: 'I'm going to let you off with a warning. Please slow down. Have a good day.'

"I replied, 'Thank you very much, Officer. You have a great day too!' I drove away elated, thinking, 'Wow, what a great thing to get out of that ticket.' And then it hit me: That was a great thing, directly related to the statement I had made to my guardian angel just minutes earlier. I thanked Max profusely for coming through for me. This stuff really works!"

Finding the Right Bus

Ian writes: "Here is another successful result of my MBOs. I use them every day, but this one was so good and straightforward I had to tell you. I am visiting Sydney, Australia, at the moment. I think I asked for a safe, fast, comfortable bus ride to my destination on the evening I want to tell you about. It was a rainy Sydney rush hour, and I am not very familiar with the bus system, which is comprehensive and has lots of buses to many places, and thus many bus stands. Having bought a ticket, I went to more or less where I thought the bus I wanted departed from, and I was looking around to see if it was the right place when, within a few seconds, a huge queue appeared behind me.

"So now I was standing in a valuable spot, at the head of a queue, and I didn't want to move. A bus came and stopped in front of us, and its destination sign looked promising. I hopped on the bus, and the driver confirmed I could indeed alight at my destination. I also had my choice of seats, being first on the bus. Naturally I chose the left side of the bus so I could read the building numbers to choose the exact bus stop to get off. The bus quickly filled, soon departed, and seemed to cut through the traffic quickly. I could judge from the numbers where to get off, and, in fact, the bus stop was only a couple of minutes' walk from where I was meeting friends."

06

Benevolent Outcomes for Jobs, Careers, and the Workplace

Improving the Mood in My Workplace

Helena writes: "I have told you about my workplace previously — the bitchy reception staff and the stress in my job. Well, in addition to the MBOs that you suggested that I do daily, I have also been saying daily, 'I request an MBO for being safely protected from Emma, Sharron, Shirley, and Jenny throughout this day and may the benefits be even more than I expect or can anticipate.' And guess what, Tom? I don't seem to get picked on or moaned at as much as I did before. And now they all seem to stay out of the way; before they were always there moaning about something. And there used to be many tears!

"Things are really getting better. One of the staff asked me why I was always so cheerful and grinning to myself. I told her about requesting MBOs and asked her if she would like to read your book; she got all excited and asked me if it was like *The Secret,* and I told her no, it is better! Now she is reading your book and trying it out for herself. She will be passing your book on to another member of staff when she has finished. Bear in mind, Tom, that the two people I've just mentioned are members of the reception staff who have not been that nice to me in the past. But now things seem to be improving."

A Scheduling Miracle

Karen writes: Regarding MBOs, I wake up each day and request the MBO for my day, often without being very specific. You just never know the form the day will take. Yesterday I had clients scheduled for 4:30PM and 5:30PM and someplace to be by 7:00PM. Needless to say, I had forgotten I needed to pick up my daughter at 6:00PM — not after 6:30PM. Well, my 4:30PM appointment did not show, and when I called him, he said he had thought the time was 5:00PM so we rescheduled; I contacted my 5:30PM client who was en route and could arrive early. At this time it still had not dawned on me that I needed to leave the office by about 5:50PM to pick up my daughter on time. At

5:45PM as I was nearing completion of the session, it finally dawned on me that I needed to leave the office in five minutes — without the no-show, I would have had to cut the session for this client short, but as it turned out, she got a full session!

"I'm sure others have similar experiences in their daily lives, but since you asked, I thought I'd mention it anyway to acknowledge the angels who are always watching out for my good. I'm thankful and grateful for the angels who are always watching out for me and helping to orchestrate my day to serve the highest good of all concerned."

Most Benevolent Macedonian Work Trip

AG writes: "For my trip to Macedonia, I requested one of the best trips so far. The most impressive thing was the plane flights. To reach Skopje, the country's capital, I had to change planes three times. Each time there was someone going to the same plane who told me how to make the connection on time. On the last plane, I sat next to a man who instantly became my soul mate. We exchanged cards, and we'll see what this friendship will turn into.

"On the way home, the plane from Skopje to Prague was late, and I had only twenty minutes to connect in a big airport. However, two of my male colleagues were on the same flight. One of them ran as fast as he could to the counter to say that we were late. They had already canceled us from the flight, but once my colleague got there, they waited for us and we got back to France safely.

"During the whole trip, I had this feeling that people were happy to see me, and I felt protected. I exchanged cards with some people I met in the hotel. In addition, there was a lovely sauna and jacuzzi there. As I write this, I am smiling. I am looking forward to new opportunities to use MBOs."

Benevolent Writing Job

Laurie writes: "In February of 2009, I made a trip to New York City. I considered it my 'last gasp' attempt to drum up work in my writing career. I asked for an MBO for helpful people to be put in my path. As a result of that MBO, I was introduced to an editor who assigned me a small writing project: a short children's book. I completed that project.

"A year later, in February of 2010, I contacted the editor to find out when the book was going to be published. He told me the publication date and then, out of the blue, asked if I wanted to write two more books. I accepted, of course! I thought, 'Wow! My original MBO request for helpful people sure is continuing beyond the original request!' Well, it worked for those two extra books, and it has happened yet again. Once I turned in the last two books, the editor asked me to write two more books in the series. This will make a total of five books since my original MBO request. I want your readers to know that I'm a living example that asking for MBOs works long-term and medium-term too!"

MBOs to Help My Husband with His Job

Eileen writes: "Here I am, requesting MBOs again — this time for my husband. He wants to remain in his current position as cabin crew, but today there was a vote, and it was not what he wanted to see. All the cabin crew got to vote for their positions, and today did not result in a positive outcome. Now there are talks of compulsory redundancies within the company. What MBO prayer could we say? We are also expecting our third child this month, and I wish for a natural birth, free of pain-relief medication. What prayer could I say to help bring this about? Many thanks. I am always expecting great things."

Tom responds: Here are some requests for MBOs and a BP:

Most Benevolent Outcome Request
"I request a most benevolent outcome for my husband's job, and may the results be even better than we can hope for or expect. Thank you!"

Benevolent Prayer
"I ask any and all beings to assist my husband in his work for the perfect job for him, and may the results be even better than we can hope for or expect. Thank you!"

Most Benevolent Outcome Request
"I request a most benevolent outcome for an easy birth for my child, and may it be even easier and more pain free than I can hope for or expect. Thank you!"

Regarding your husband's job, soul contracts are at play here, so whatever happens when you request an MBO will be the best outcome.

MBOs for a New Job and a Way to Get to It

Marie writes: "Hello, Tom. I have some MBOs for you to share. I was looking for a job and I said,

Most Benevolent Outcome Request
"Guardian angel, I request an MBO for the perfect job for me, better than I expect and hope for. Please show me where to apply. Thank you!"

"Over the following two days, I felt guided to my old employer. I applied and was rehired on the spot. Those beloved beings sure help! Another MBO I said was,

> **Most Benevolent Outcome Request**
> *"Guardian angel, I request an MBO that I don't have to commute for my job and that I may ride along with someone else to save gas. Thank you!"*

"The first day, lo and behold, I didn't have to drive my own car, and I rode along with two people. I later asked,

> **Most Benevolent Outcome Request**
> *"Guardian angel, I request an MBO that when I commute in the morning, please clear my way so I may drive safely to work. Thank you!"*

"That morning, there was hardly any traffic, and my driving to work was less stressful!"

Actress Lands Big Role with MBO Help

Lois writes: I have a friend and client who I taught to use MBOs. She finally was able to quit her stressful job and go back into acting. She just opened this week in a major motion picture with a large role. If you are an actor or know one, you can suggest that he or she say the following before an audition:

> **Most Benevolent Outcome Request**
> *"I request a most benevolent outcome for this audition, and may the results be even better than I can hope for or expect. Thank you!"*

"You'll find that you are calmer, less stressed, and able to present yourself in your best light. Perhaps you won't be right for that particular role, but the producer and director will remember you for a future role or recommend you to another producer or director in another production."

Helping a Friend with her Job

Kevin writes: "I have a friend who is a florist and wedding decoration designer. She asked me if I would help her bring some flowers and equipment into New York City from New Jersey. So the first thing I did after agreeing to drive her in was say an MBO:

> **Most Benevolent Outcome Request**
> *"I request an MBO that we have a safe, swift trip into the city, back out again, and home — and a wonderful parking spot. And may the wedding and everything go smoothly."*

"I may have added, 'And may it better than I expected or imagined,' but I'm not sure.

"To start, we dropped off flowers for the bride and bridesmaids in New Jersey. We headed into the city via the Lincoln Tunnel, since we were closest to it. It turns out my friend is a bit claustrophobic, and just inside the tunnel was a bumper-to-bumper backup. She was getting a bit tense and stirred up, so I reached over and gently put my hand on her shoulder till we were out. I told her we would get through quickly. A big bus was in the next lane, roaring its engine as it ran neck and neck with us, making the tunnel seem even smaller. I looked over, and my friend had closed her eyes. I didn't say a word. Soon after, the cars ahead began to pick up speed and we moved through the tunnel in a few minutes. I could feel my friend's relief as we emerged into the open air of the other side of the tunnel.

"We then wandered down to the club building. The roads were packed with people and cars, and we didn't see any available parking anywhere along the way. We needed parking for two vans — the closer the better. We turned the corner to the venue, and there was a commercial truck-loading zone with just enough space for our vans. I thought this was great; we could unload our stuff and then go find a regular parking spot. After reading the signs about ten times, we figured out that since this was Saturday, we could stay all day. We were able to leisurely take stuff in and out all afternoon. The setup, wedding, party, and cleanup went great, and we were able to take the George Washington Bridge out of the city, since we live closer to it. So all in all, it went exceedingly well."

Keep Your MBOs Specific

Chrissy writes: "I have been saying MBO requests for several weeks because my time at the project I work at was coming to an end. Weeks ago I started requesting an MBO for a job closer to home, on the north side of the city, without having my pay reduced. Construction companies pay better for office staff than private enterprise does. Every so often, I will either add something to the MBO request that I think would be better, or I remove something I think I don't need. I know that we don't have to say our MBO requests more than once, but I get myself into a routine and they make me feel better when I say them on a regular basis.

"There is a job with a colleague with whom I used to work that I would like, and it is with the same company. Recently, I changed my MBO request to include this job. Of course, my angels had other ideas. Long story short, last Thursday I was offered an administration job still on the same project but in another area at another site office. I started this week and will take the place of someone who is leaving this week, and I will have to learn new software, but I find that a challenge.

"I have been thinking about my original MBO request and realize that the angels have given me what I initially asked for: a job on the north side of the city, closer to home, without a drop in pay. How could I doubt that they would come through? I got exactly what I asked for. What I now realize that I didn't include was permanency, as this job is only for another three months or slightly longer. It's amazing how they give us what we ask for. We just have to be specific — or in my case, more specific."

The Mirror Never Lies

DeLeah writes: "I've got another awesome MBO story to share. I had been telling my husband about the MBO way of thinking, and he thought it was a great concept. When he was recently placed in a different position at work, he needed to bring up the district average of a certain criteria of numbers. Without going into too many details, the company relies quite heavily on this set of numbers.

"I made him an MBO request statement and put it on the bathroom mirror so he could recite it each morning while getting ready for work. It was basically a request for an MBO for raising his district numbers and that the outcome would be more than he could ever expect.

"In one week's time, the average has risen several points from the lower average to an upper average, moving his district into the number-one position and making his boss very happy! He now will not let me take that sticky note down, as he wants it to stay there so he will remember to state his MBO every morning."

Benevolent Prayer for Employment

Angel writes: "In your recent newsletter, we offered a prayer for Jamaica, that the people wanting to work would find work and so on. It came to mind that the prayer would also be very appropriate for U.S. citizens who want to find work in their fields, and there are so many who do at this time."

Tom responds: I do think we should expand the BP as follows. Please say this out loud:

Most Benevolent Outcome Request
"I ask any and all beings to assist all those people who wish to work to be led to the perfect work for them. Thank you."

That should cover the whole world.

MBO Requests Work for the Perfect New Job

Annette writes: "My life has become very active, so to speak, and some days I am so busy that, as the saying goes, 'I don't know if I found a rope or lost a horse.' But it is all a blessing in so many ways that there is not enough time to tell you about it. You can share the following story with the use of my name, however; maybe it will help people to not become discouraged if things don't happen the way they think they will or in the way they think they want.

"All of our staff knew we were losing our funding and that our jobs would end several months ahead of time. I requested an MBO for finding a job and an MBO for finding a way to manage my finances so I could keep my home. They were as follows:

Most Benevolent Outcome Request

"I request a most benevolent outcome for finding the perfect job for me, and may the outcome be better than I could hope for or anticipate. Thank you," and *"I request a most benevolent outcome and guidance to ensure I have enough income to pay my mortgage and car payments until I can find a job. May the outcome be better than I could hope for or anticipate. Thank you."*

"When the last day came, I was the only one not upset, panicked, or freaking out, because I knew deep in my heart that my guardian angel had my back. Yes, I had been frustrated, as I had applied for over forty-four jobs at the university where I worked and had only gotten called for three interviews. With each job, I knew I was perfect, but I was not hired. But I had faith and knew I would be guided after all; I was able to set aside enough money to make certain we could pay the mortgage and our car payments for six months while we lived on my husband's pay and my unemployment checks.

"I was out of work for seventy-seven days, but I am now in the job I have prepared for all my life. My guardian angel guided me to the job for me, and the outcome has been better than I could have ever imagined, dreamed of, or hoped for — let alone anticipated! Things might not happen exactly the way we expect, but they do happen when we build that relationship with our guardian angels. Thank you for sharing the information in your books and newsletters."

A Benevolent Prayer for Jobs

Colleen writes: "Having learned about MBOs from your newsletter, which someone sent me, I decided to ask for one for my son who has been without a permanent job for over eighteen months. Within ten days of my request, he had a strong interview for a lucrative position that had sixty-three applicants. Within forty-eight hours, he was confirmed as the man for the job. Yes! Much gratitude for the affirmative way this works."

Tom responds: If you have a loved one looking for a job, you can say a BP, which is what you say when you wish a benevolent outcome for someone else. As an example, you can say,

Resolving Anger in the Workplace

Helena writes: "I must seek your advice about my job, Tom. I have been in another doctor's receptionist job for almost three months. It is awful, Tom — even though I only work thirty hours because that's all they would offer me.

It is an awful experience. The receptionist staff is usually angry, and the two bosses are always angry. There are a lot of problem patients, and it is in a problem area. I have come home crying quite a bit, and I hardly have enough to live on. I can't afford to make ends meet. I had to take this job, as I was forced to just take anything I could find. It is not a friendly place. I am suffering with stress so badly. There are 9,900 patients, and we have to work like mad. I have to work from 1:00PM to 7:00PM each day, and I come home each day completely drained.

"Today I took the day off, as I feel I have a weight on my shoulders, but that means I will lose my pay for the day. I can't leave this job, Tom, but as you are well aware, there aren't any jobs. And I will definitely lose my home if I have no job this time. I have no parents or other support, and this in itself is making me a nervous wreck. Please Tom, could you tell me the right words for an MBO request I could use to get away from this place and get a new job? What MBO request can I use to protect me from the angry, bossy staff and patients? Thank you, Tom, for all your help and advice."

Tom responds: There must be some lesson you're supposed to learn, as you have been hired in two jobs where the staff was overworked and in a bad disposition. So request an MBO for each day you work. You have to be the shining light at that place. Because the patients are all ill, you need to send out beautiful, rainbow-colored light to fill the whole waiting room each day when you come to work. Say:

Most Benevolent Outcome Request

"I request a most benevolent outcome for my work day, and may it be even better than I can hope for or expect. Thank you!"

Then send out the light and imagine it completely filling the room. You need to read about how to clear negativity from an area. But most importantly, you need to thank your guardian angel each day for giving you work. Then request an MBO for the *perfect* job for you! Remember, you did that before, however, and here you are in a similar situation. Again, there must be a reason. You just need to keep requesting MBOs every single day. Be that shining light in the office to the point that people will start complimenting you on what a nice person you are and how you handle every patient so well. People will notice, and you'll find your hours will increase.

I add for everyone that if you are having a problem with either a supervisor or colleague at work, be sure to request an MBO each time you must interact with them — assuming it's not every five minutes — and be sure to request the MBO mentioned above for your whole workday to be pleasant. Imagine surrounding yourself with white light or even pink light when you go to work each day.

Benevolently Obtained Dream Job

Christa writes: "For the past week or so, I have requested several MBOs for employment and have just received an offer for my dream job. This is stuff that blows the mind — expect amazing results!"

Tom responds: For those of you seeking employment, you might say,

Most Benevolent Outcome Request
"I request a most benevolent outcome for the perfect job for me. Thank you!"

Then before the job interview, you say,

Most Benevolent Outcome Request
"I request a most benevolent outcome for this interview, and may the results be even better than I now hope for or expect. Thank you!"

Benevolent Prayer Results in Bigger and Better Job

Diana writes: "I haven't sent you many of my MBO stories — of which there are many — but this one is quite amazing. It's about a BP for someone else. My father-in-law's job was looking glum back in April. He was helping to negotiate an increase in salary for his whole group, and instead, the workers turned on him and signed a petition about not wanting to work with him. So he lost his job. This is too sad; he tried to help and the people he tried to help turned on him. At that time, I started saying serious BPs for his situation at work as well as for his health, since I don't want him to suffer heartbreak.

"Barely two months passed, which he filled with house-fixing activities and one home purchase, and now he is back in another branch of the same company. We thought it was a blessing in disguise, because if he hadn't lost his job for those two months, he couldn't have done all the housebound activities like renovation and purchase. This was the first good result.

"Then we just found out yesterday that he has been promoted to the very top of the company. He is now in the headquarters office. So not only did he become the boss of the workers who signed the petition before about not wanting to work for him, but he has also now become one of the top employees in the company, overseeing many of its branches. I just think the BP is really, really amazing, and I think the turnaround of six months is really quick! Thank you, and I hope your work is spreading fast."

Finding a New Job

Brenadette writes: "Hi, Tom! Just to let you know, I've been using MBOs for about four years. Last year in April, you gave me an MBO for purchasing a home. Well, I have to say I am a happy homeowner since November of last year. Now I need an MBO to find a job. My employer has downsized, and what I am now making cannot pay my mortgage and other obligations. Thank you, as always."

Tom responds: You simply say,

Most Benevolent Outcome Request
"I request a most benevolent outcome for the perfect job for me. Thank you!"

Each time you interview, you can also request MBOs that the results will be even better than you can hope for or expect. And request an MBO to find a way to pay your bills each month.

A Great Performance Review

Liysa writes: "I just wanted to share an enlightening experience from a few weeks ago. I had a review coming up at my job. My first year had been quite rocky. For two days, I practiced an MBO that the review would surpass my expectations; it did. The review was glowing and the suggestion to discuss a new job title and new salary was welcomed. For the rocky year we had, this was very much a success! Thank you for allowing me to share."

MBO Requests Result in a Great Job

Robin writes: "I wrote you last summer regarding my attempts to find a new job. I had been out of the work force for a few years and had also worked with my ex for the last ten of those years. Needless to say, I was very unsure of myself and my situation. I knew I needed to create a job. You gave me great advice back then, suggesting I 'dumb down' my résumé to get my foot in the door. I took that advice, along with the suggestion to do daily MBO requests that described the perfect job and situation for me in detail.

"Having spent months sending résumés out every day with no success, one day I became inspired to do something a bit different. Every morning when dropping my three-year-old son off at daycare, I would stare up at the same office buildings that I had looked at for years. Then it struck me — with a nice nudge from my guardian angel, Martha — that it would be great if I could get a job in one of those buildings across the street from the daycare, less than ten minutes from home. That same morning I went online and found the company whose name was on top of the main office building.

"To make a long story short, I have now been working in the most amazing environment for about one year. I have made a new group of close friends, my confidence is returning, and I am happier than I have been in over decade. My hours work perfectly, the salary is more than I was hoping for, and the work-life balance allows me to be present as a single mother. Everything I asked for — and I'm talking about seriously specific requests — came to be and beyond.

"I get shivers just telling the story! Thank you, thank you, thank you. I have remarkable results every day, but this one sticks out the most for me and makes me smile when I think of all the tiny adjustments and mini miracles it took to make it all come together!"

Tom responds: One thing requesting MBOs does for you is make you more aware and receptive to those whispers in your ear from your own guardian angel. Robin was able to listen and then act on the inspiration, and it worked beautifully for her.

Also notice that she has named her guardian angel. My own guardian angel says that humans can't pronounce angelic names because of our limited vocal chords; we would only become frustrated if we tried. Plus, he says, they aren't too big on names on his side, so he told me I could call him "Tom, Dick, or Harry"— whatever was most comfortable for me. He also suggested later that anyone might say out loud, *"Guardian angel, what name should I call you?"* You may get an immediate response, or it might take a few days, as it did with me. For me, "Theo" just popped into my mind one day. Give it a try.

A Benevolent Evaluation

Nancy writes: "I had an amazing MBO experience this fall! I have taught for over thirty-five years in the field of early childhood, and it is sometimes difficult for me to just accept what a supervisor tells me when I have experience and information that contradicts what I'm being told. Last school year — the 2010–2011 year — I had a few serious disagreements with my supervisor and argued for what I truly thought was a better approach. She wasn't interested. Instead, she cut my teaching hours and responsibilities. I was not happy!

"Then I received what was the poorest evaluation of my teaching career. I couldn't deal with it, as my supervisor was gone, it was the last day of school, and I was having hip surgery the next day. I had planned to protest this because the faculty contract wasn't followed regarding the areas of improvement she requested. Then a friend pointed out to me that pursuing this line of thought was going to get me in even more trouble, and that it would be best for me to give it up.

"Although my supervisor was wrong, I thought about it and chose to forgive her and move on. I have done my best to work with her since then, and I was showing her a possible way that the school could qualify for free field trips to a local museum. Then, out of the blue, I added that I had been upset over my evaluation and that I would appreciate it if she could explain to me at some point why it had been so poor. She said okay and left, and I began to pack up my things.

"Then she returned to my classroom and said that she had wondered what I had meant. She had gone back to look at my evaluation, and there was something that she didn't click on that she should have. She handed me a new evaluation. In the new one, I had done a lot better and had no areas needing improvement. So I accepted her answer and thanked her for it, because I didn't want to look a gift horse in the mouth!

"The new evaluation was far better and removed me from any difficulties with the administration. I learned about MBO requests last summer, and as soon as I realized they were for real, I started asking for one for my relationship with my supervisor. However, I have never heard of anyone getting help like this. Fabulous doesn't begin to describe MBOs! Thank you for introducing me to them!"

Benevolent Assistance in the Job Search

Brenadette writes: "My husband is new to MBOs. He finally caved and took my advice while dealing with a horrible job. He would put himself to sleep at night by repeating,

Most Benevolent Outcomes
"I request a most benevolent outcome for the perfect job for me."

Less than a month later, which is really quick in his field, he has the job he was looking for. We're so happy. Thank you, Tom!"

Benevolent Help with Career-Related Exams

Kathy writes: "I have a good MBO story for your newsletter. I have to pass a number of difficult financial management courses and exams to be certified for my new job. These courses are very difficult for me because my background is not in finance, and I am not the best test-taker to begin with, especially with timed tests. In these courses, you have to achieve a specific score by the end of each day to be sure you aren't cut from the course before it's finished, and people are cut every day.

"So a few weeks ago, I took one of these courses, and by the third day, on the fourth exam that week, I had a serious panic attack. I have never experienced something like this before — I broke out in a sweat, my heart raced, and my mind froze. I couldn't understand a single word on the page. I asked my guardian angel to help me calm down enough to pass the exam and make it through to the end of the course. I made it through that day, but I had to get a perfect score the next day to pass. I was not sure I could do that, so I requested an MBO for a perfect score, and I got one! It was a miracle, and I was so relieved.

"I have two more courses to take and have been requesting MBOs to pass both of them on the first attempt and to make sure I never have a panic attack again. Thank you so much, Tom, for teaching me about MBOs. Getting to know my guardian angel is transforming my life in such a positive way."

Reversing an MBO for Time Off from Work

Ruth writes: "For the first time ever, I had to ask for an MBO reversal. I had asked that I have an MBO for my work because I was tired and had worked for two weeks in a row. Well, I then got a very peaceful week off of work — the answer to my MBO. However, I realized quite suddenly that I was not making any money because I work on commission. So then I asked again that I have an MBO for my work and my commissions. Actually, they both worked, and apparently the angels knew that I needed a break for a few days. Many thanks for introducing me to MBOs."

Successful Prayer for an Out-of-Work Friend

Kathy writes: "Hi, Tom. I have a great MBO story for you. About two months ago, my dear friend Eric suddenly lost his job after over twenty years with the same company. This was quite unexpected and a total shock. We posted a BP request for him on Facebook and sent it out through email, and within one month he was hired by another company doing the same work — mid-management in resurfacing work. Everyone was so amazed by how quickly Eric found another job within commuting distance. His sister told me they are all certain this is due to the BP request, and all I can say is thank you to the angels and to you, dear Tom, for sharing this wisdom that has touched so many in such amazing ways."

Tom responds: I've had many people relate stories about using MBO requests in their jobs, so I would like to give you more ideas by relating how I request MBOs in my business. My wife and I have been in international film and TV program distribution for many years. I have related in my books how I request MBOs while traveling, but when I'm in my office, I request MBOs all the time too.

As an example, I just sent out two email blasts the other day — one internationally and one domestically. For each one, I requested an MBO that the results of the email blast would be even better than I could hope for or expect. If you say these requests with emotion, it creates more energy for the request. Then, as I received responses to these emails, I requested MBOs to do business with the companies that responded.

When I phone someone to solicit business or follow up on previous calls or correspondence, I always request an MBO for the results of the call to be even better than I can hope for or expect. When I have a meeting with someone on business, I always request an MBO for the results of the meeting to be even better than I can hope for or expect. Naturally, each day I say the "expect great things" MBO request that my guardian angel says will bring things into your life you never thought to ask for. In my business, people will call out of the blue wanting to license films from us I never even knew existed. You can print out the "expect great things" MBO under the "signs" tab on the menu of my website. Have fun requesting!

Employment MBO for a Father-to-Be

Shirley writes: "I'm wondering what would be a really good MBO to help my partner find a good, full-time, well-paid job? We are starting our family soon. Well, the baby is due next May, and it would be great if he found good work."

Tom responds: Shirley can say a BP for her partner, which is what you say for other people.

> **Benevolent Prayer**
> "I ask any and all beings to assist my partner in finding the perfect job for him. Thank you!"

And you can say,

> **Most Benevolent Outcome Request**
> "I request an MBO for my partner's search for a job. And may the results be even better than we can hope for or expect. Thank you!"

As for the pregnancy, say,

> **Most Benevolent Outcome Request**
> "I request an MBO for my pregnancy that will be easy, with little or no discomfort. Thank you!"

Video Production Runs Smoothly, Thanks to MBO

Rick writes: "I have a couple of MBOs for you. As you know, I have written a screenplay that is in development. The producer is putting together a crowd funding video for the website Kickstarter.com in order to raise seed money, which in turn will give us financing to pursue fundraising through venture capital, private investors, and so on, as well as allow us to attend conventions to pitch our movie to studios and distributors.

"Last week, I needed to record two interviews from broadcasting professionals who I've worked with over the course of my career. One is a recognizable sportscaster on network television, and the other is a state legislator here in New Jersey who has done battle with our very controversial governor. The sportscaster lives within two miles of a state university with a baseball stadium that they share with a minor league baseball team. The professional and courteous thing to do is to contact the athletic director and ask for permission to use the facility, but she refused to let us in the ballpark — she even went so far as to say the team was practicing on the date and time we needed the stadium. (Keep in mind we only needed it for twenty minutes.)

"I was not deterred. I set the date and time anyway. The broadcaster and I had a backup plan in case the campus police kicked us off the campus. Prior to our ninety-mile trip to get to the campus, I said an MBO requesting that we be able to shoot the interview freely and willfully. While we did not enter the stadium, we found a nice spot outside the main gate. It took the sportscaster twenty minutes to get his interview to the point where he was comfortable with it, but we got it. The shot was nice. (I must pat myself on the back for that!)

"The best part was that nobody bothered us — no campus police, no curiosity seekers, nothing. What we both noticed, though, was that we never heard any indication that a practice was taking place in the ballpark. The athletic director simply didn't want to bother with us.

"It took me five months to get the legislator to sit down for his interview. He owns a sound stage near Philadelphia. I said an MBO request for a great interview in an ideal location. Since the sound stage was available, we did the interview there, even using some of the lighting that he rents out to production companies. (We got to use this lighting free of charge.) It was a great interview.

"I've had problems with my video camera in the past, so I always say an MBO request for it to function properly, and it does so impeccably. The producer is pleased with my work as a videographer/field producer."

BPs Bring Many Blessings to My Workplace

Constance writes: "Hi, Tom. You've changed my and my husband's lives! We use MBOs constantly. Thank you so much. I had the bright idea — inspired by my guardian angel, perhaps? — to write out a BP for me and two other girls to say in unison each day at work. I work for a general commercial contractor, and we managed to make it through the recession but really want to grow the business. I've worked there for fifteen years, and I've turned the other women I work with on to *The Gentle Way*.

"So we've been reciting this BP for (1) the success of the company, (2) the health and vitality of the employees, (3) the perfect people to become part of our family (we are hiring now), and (4) for us to figure out and grow to love the new accounting software we were using but having serious problems with, among other things.

"We have more work now and coming up than we have ever had, even in this economy. One of my coworkers, who has been chronically sick with migraines and other ailments in the past, hasn't missed any work in months and even said, 'Those MBOs must be working!'

"When I became a grandmother, I contacted someone who used to work with us but had relocated to the Southeast to be near his grandchildren. Turns out the company he was working for was declaring bankruptcy, his children had moved away with his grandchildren (they're in the military), and he was dying to come home to the Northwest. I told him we were looking for people, and he is now here working for us again. He's one of my favorite people too.

"Our CFO, in frustration with our accounting software, started looking into alternatives, even though we had spent considerable money on this new program. He found that the company that had bought out our old software company has a new product that offers everything we want in a recognizable and, I'm thinking, much easier format for us to learn and convert to. *And* they're willing to work with us on the price because they want us back as customers!

"One of the other things in my daily BP was financial abundance for everyone in the company, and I just found out yesterday that I'm getting a $1,600 bonus for attendance and all the overtime I've been putting in!

"Thank you, Tom, Gaia, the Sun, and Antura for all your insight and this beautiful, gentle way. It's made all the difference in our lives!"

Helping My Coworker Has Helped Me Too

Nancy writes: "I have repeatedly said MBOs to get along better with my supervisor at the school where I teach and to increase my income. My teaching hours were cut to two-thirds time this year from full time. Recently the third grade teacher, who is fairly new, has had to request a leave of absence due to a number of health issues. As one of the Faculty Association co-presidents, I have helped to get her authorized to use the sick-leave bank. She is a single mother and this has been hard on her, so I have also said BPs for her health. In the midst of all of this, I was also given her remedial teaching hours, and I am now temporarily teaching about six hours above three-fourths time. The temporary income has just started coming in, and it is a huge help. Thanks for all that you have taught me, Tom!"

07

Benevolent Outcomes for Personal Finance

Finally, a Credit Card

Patricia writes: "Since I last contacted you, I have had many wonderful MBO results. I do the affirmations and prayers you gave us on a regular basis. The latest results: I declared bankruptcy thirteen years ago, and since then have been turned down for credit on a regular basis, because I have no credit history. When I went to my bank last week to make a deposit, I asked for an MBO that I would not have too long to stand in the line, as I have osteoarthritis in my knees and cannot walk or stand for more than a few minutes. As always now, I don't even have to ask for a parking space at the door, as this automatically happens.

"The bank manager — a relatively new one — met me and asked if I would prefer to sit at one of the cubicles and have someone come to me. I thanked him, and he proceeded to serve me himself. During the course of the transaction, he asked me if I had a credit card. I said that I did not and told him of the bankruptcy and of my history of trying for credit. He then asked me if I would like a Visa. I immediately thought, 'Here we go again,' and not too enthusiastically said that it would be nice. His next words were, 'It is done; you will have your card in ten days, delivered to your door.' Well, it happened! I received a notice saying I was accepted, and then the card arrived. To me, this is a miracle, as I'm seventy-three years old and living on a government pension. I cannot thank you enough for the information on MBOs, and I will send one to Oprah. I have had so many come through for me on a daily basis."

A Check from Out of the Blue

Linda writes: "I've been very short on money recently due to being out on medical leave and receiving only one-third pay. I couldn't make rent, the car payment, or the insurance payment, which were all due the same day. I was thinking of how I could do all three and still have money for food for two weeks for us and the cats. So I requested an MBO for help. I asked for obstacles to be removed and for the proper tools to do what I had to do. Well, two days later, my union disability check arrived. It seems I was owed an extra week that I was never paid. I managed to pay all three bills, buy food, and still put aside a little. Now that was a great MBO!"

An Unexpected $100

Sue writes: "This month, my sister and one of my brothers both decided to turn in their older vans and get new vans. I had suggested that both of them go to the dealership near me that I really like. Well, it turned out that my brother decided to come to the dealership while my sister and I were there, and both of them bought vans that day. The salesperson was very appreciative and told me that she wanted to send me a gift in thanks for having my brother and sister work with her to buy their vans. I thought that was so sweet of her. While driving home that evening, I requested an MBO that the gift would be something that would really help me, like a free oil change or something even better than what I was thinking. Several days later, I received a check in the mail from the dealer for $100 as a finder's fee. What a great benevolent outcome!"

Most Benevolent Tenant

Sisi writes: "Here is my MBO story. My home in Bowral, Australia, still had not sold, so after deep thought, I came to the conclusion that it was not meant to be sold, but rather I should keep it as an investment property. So I requested an MBO for the perfect tenant, like a doctor, to rent it for one year and to pay the rent in advance so I could get out of arrears. My previous tenant had fallen behind with the rent and left the home and there was a fair bit to do. I also asked a good friend of mine, Theresa, to take a Saint Joseph statue there and do the special prayer for a house. At this stage, my home had been untenanted for nearly eight weeks.

"Within a week my agent had found a tenant. It was a doctor who had taken on the lease for a family member for a year and at the last minute decided to pay six months in advance. The agent did not even ask him — he chose to! I see how everything can change in the blink of an eye when we request the help via MBOs from any and all beings.

"And even better, my loan broker has now, because of this lump sum payment, been able to organize interest-only payments and has successfully sorted out the whole package. Plus yesterday, after writing a letter to my ancestor and requesting an MBO for a little lottery win, I won a ticket in the two-dollar lottery. I am expecting many more benevolent outcomes. Day after day, they are just rolling in! Thank you Tom, and bless you!"

MBOs Help Solve a Three-Pronged Financial Challenge

Renee writes: "I can't stop talking about my recent success with MBOs, and I just have to tell you about what happened recently. Last

October I got hit with three financial challenges all at once. The first one was my hours at work getting cut back from thirty to twenty hours per week. At the same time, our tenants next door gave notice that they would be out by the end of October. At this point, we wouldn't have enough to make the mortgage payment for November unless we could get the space rented before the payment was due.

"Last, but definitely not least, I have another rental property that is way upside down, meaning I owe twice as much as it is worth. The monthly mortgage payment was raised by over $350 starting in November, and I was in the process of working with the bank to get a modification on it — which, by the way, I tried to do over a year ago, and they denied it, saying it was an investment property and not a primary residence. After many phone conversations and faxing plenty of documents to them, I flat-out told them I did not have the money to make the payments. At this point, I did not make the November payment and was planning to just walk away from it all.

"Well, once again my MBOs came to the rescue. Here's what transpired: In the first week of November, and within less than twenty-four hours, we found the perfect tenants who needed to move in right away, and not only did they pay for November, but they paid through the end of December's rent too. And the next morning, I accepted another part-time job to supplement my existing one, which I started the following week. Yahoo!

"Now for the best part. By the last week of November, I had received a packet in the mail from the bank. When I opened it up, I could not believe what I was seeing. In short, they cut my monthly payment in half and they nearly cut the loan balance in half! They offered me a twenty-five-year fixed rate at 2 percent interest on the remainder loan balance with a balloon payment at the end. And if I choose to sell the property, they would receive only 25 percent of the appreciation. I was so shocked. I quickly signed the documents and made a payment as directed by December 1 to seal the deal. I shared this information with my friend and real estate agent, and his exact words were, 'This is the best news I have heard in three years!'

"One of the universal laws is the law of belief — to know beyond doubt. That is what an MBO means to me: to know beyond doubt that they work miracles for all who use them. Once again, Tom, thanks for giving me this very important tool in my toolbox."

Helping Friends with Home Sales and Mortgage Payments

Lorene writes: "Tom, thank you for the work you are doing. I have been requesting MBOs for about a year and a half now, and I appropriately assist others as well. I recently assisted a friend who had had her house on the market for twenty-two months, and within a week of requesting the MBO I suggested, she had a successful offer, which she wrote you about and you published in your newsletter.

"Another interesting assist was with my hairdresser who has two teenage daughters and has been trying for some time to renegotiate her loan as she was in danger of losing her home. As with many people who have been trying to renegotiate recently, she was not having much luck but was expecting a final call from her lender in the next day or two.

"I was at the salon when she explained this to me, and I wrote out an MBO request suggestion and told her that if she felt it was all right, she should go outside the salon immediately and say the MBO request out loud. She did this, and she called me two days later to say that the lender had called and had reduced her loan payments to within $100 of what she had asked for, and that this was doable for her."

Benevolent Paycheck Supplement

Wendy writes: "I'm facing a rather large pay cut through January 2013. Every day I have repeated,

> **Most Benevolent Outcome Request**
> *"I expect great things today, I expect great things tomorrow, and I expect great things the rest of this week."*

"Today I was provided with an opportunity to make back the money I'll be losing by the same company that is cutting my pay."

MBOs Help Settle Disputes

Wendy writes: "In January of 2009, I had a doctor appointment. On the day of my appointment, I gave them my insurance information and then paid my copayment. I didn't think much more about it until I received a bill of over $300 from the medical center for charges that my insurance did not cover. Well, I called them immediately and told them that, per my insurance coverage, all that I was required to pay was my copayment. This went back and forth for weeks with neither side budging. A couple of months later, I received a letter from a collection agency that my account had been sent to. I told the agency that I had no intention of ever paying it.

"Every few months or so I would receive another letter from them, and again, I would call them and refuse to pay it. So last month (April 2012) I said an MBO request and called them again. I left the customer service representative a message and asked him to please return my phone call. I received a call back within thirty minutes, and the representative said that he gave the medical center another call — the agency had called and talked to them numerous times in the past — and they agreed to take it back and write it off. This was after three years of fighting it! Thank you, Tom, for sharing your knowledge and wisdom."

"Every time I spoke with someone, they indicated there was no problem with my application, but that it just had not been processed yet and that only the person who worked it up at the SSA could process it — the same person who never returned my calls. And yes, I requested an MBO for the issue to be resolved quickly.

"I am not so good at listening to the small voices yet, but I finally thought to call a benefits counselor for military personnel with whom I had worked in the recent past. I called, explained the problem, and asked her, on the off chance she could help, if she had a contact in the office where I had submitted my claim, but she said she did not. However, she said she did have a contact in another office in the area and would call him immediately. She asked me to hold and called her contact, then conferenced me in so I could speak with him. He was most helpful and indicated that a supervisor from the office I applied in was in his office. Two days later, she called to say my paperwork had been processed. Good news, and a large thank you to my guardian angel!

"The downside, however, was that it would be four weeks until I would receive anything in writing from the SSA. In the meantime, my civilian health care provision through the military was being canceled, so I could not get any prescriptions filled or see my regular doctor. I would need to go through a military treatment facility, which meant I would need to start over with everything. So I requested an MBO to receive the letter of approval sooner than expected and as soon as possible.

"The paperwork was sent from the local SSA on October 5, and I received the approval letter on October 16, which is much less than four weeks — another big thank you to my guardian angel. Had I not requested the initial MBO for a quick resolution and then acted on my intuition, I could still be waiting for a result."

Tom responds: Yes, remember to listen for those whispers in your ear. They will supposedly become easier to hear after the year 2012.

Protection from Fraudulent Activity and Identity Theft

Linda writes: "Bonjour, Tom! I've been a devoted fan of yours for about two years. Whenever possible, I share the info about MBOs to everyone. Thanks to your newsletter and your first book, I've learned to tweak my MBOs.

"This was tested just a few days ago. I had opened a PayPal account a few months ago to pay for a metaphysical class but ended up never using it. Well, in my email I had a message from PayPal that there was suspicious activity on my account. Something told me this was not a bogus email. I logged into my bank account, and to my horror, yes indeed, my account showed that $1,400 was pending to be debited. I immediately said at least two to three different MBO variations and then contacted my bank. The bank said it looked like this transaction was reversed — that PayPal had stopped the transaction on their end. Nevertheless, on my bank account, it showed a deficit of about $1,700!

"Anyway, I then called PayPal, and they assured me that this fraudulent activity had been caught and that all the money was in the process of being refunded back to me. This refund could, however, take anywhere from three to thirty days. I said another MBO regarding the refund timing. To my amazement, $1,200.00 was refunded back into my bank account within hours. The remaining $200.00 was refunded within twenty-four hours.

"Oh my God! If I did not have faith in these MBOs, I would have totally lost it. And yes, my PayPal account has been closed out. Oh, and my new debit card with a new account number arrived the very next day — another way to block any other fraudulent activity. I thank you and honor you for helping all of us to learn about our divine right to request help from the angels. I especially thank my heavenly father for creating angels to help us. Tom, you are awesome! Merci beaucoup!"

Tom responds: This is a good reminder, everyone, that the first thing you should do in any crisis situation is request an MBO.

Jackie writes: "I am writing about MBOs for fraudulent activity. In one of your recent newsletters, I read about the woman Linda who had a problem with her PayPal account, and I am now wondering how to say an MBO for fraudulent activity — not just in relation to PayPal accounts, but also for credit cards, bank accounts, and any other accounts or funds. How do you say a BP to stop any fraudulent activity and have the money returned right back in its proper place? Thank you for your time, and I appreciate it. God bless you."

Tom responds: As I mentioned in my first book at the end of the tenth chapter, you can say out loud,

> **Most Benevolent Outcome Request**
> *"I request a most benevolent outcome that my personal, established identity in all of its forms be safe and secure from harm and from corruption by others. Thank you."*

You only have to say this once, but you can say it every so often if it makes you feel good.

Whispers in Your Ear

Melody writes: "I have enjoyed your column in the *Sedona Journal* and have been using MBOs. I said them maybe several times a week in the beginning, but now I use them all the time. I just ordered your book *The Gentle Way II* and have almost gotten it all read. I now use MBOs a lot more often. Have you ever heard an MBO story like this?

"On New Year's Eve, I woke up to the words 'most benevolent outcome.' I immediately wondered what I should be asking about. I waited for more instructions or information, but nothing more came. I forgot about it for the rest of the day. On New Year's Day, I woke up and was thinking about those words again, and after a few minutes it came to me: I was being told the morning before that an MBO was coming that day!

"Three months before, I had bought a water filter that will make a difference in people's lives, but there was also a business opportunity that went along with it. A client was interested in a water filter, and I had asked at one time for an MBO about it. She had decided to buy one, and then she backed out. But on the afternoon of the day I woke up to those words 'most benevolent outcome,' as I walked in the door from work, my phone was ringing. The client I previously mentioned had decided to buy a water machine! I think it was my angels giving me a heads up. I may not have associated it with an MBO, since I had asked for one so long before. What do you think?"

Tom responds: I do think it was Melody's guardian angel reminding her that an MBO was about to come to fruition. Perhaps her angel wants to assure her that her requests are being heard and acted on. And just a reminder, you can go to my website and print out the sign "Request Benevolent Outcomes Today!" to remind you to make this a habit, along with the "expect great things" mantra and two other signs.

Tax Refund MBO

Beth writes: "I cannot begin to express how incredible, inspiring, and reassuring your newsletter is. I am so grateful and look forward to each week's updates and stories. *The Gentle Way* books are amazing and will light the path for many. Since I started requesting benevolent outcomes, I have been blessed with many wonderful successes.

"Most recently, my tax refund increased by $250 from the time it was submitted and the time that I received it. This is most welcome, as the extra funds will be put to good use. You may have covered this question previously, but can you please ask your guardian angel what the most effective ways are to raise our personal vibrational levels? And how can we most effectively contribute to other beings in need, including Mother Earth?"

Tom responds: I have covered this before, but as a reminder for everyone, my guardian angel says that requesting MBOs is the best way to raise your vibrational level, as you become more aware and start seeing and understanding more.

As I have also mentioned before, send white light every day, if possible, or whenever you remember, to Mother Earth, or Gaia. When I meditate, I first send white light over the surface of our Earth and all the other ten timeline Earths, releasing it to go where it is most needed. Then I send this white light to the center of Earth and on to the soul of Gaia as best I can.

Lost ATM Card

Millicent writes: "I just came across your material and I decided to try your method of MBOs. Today is the second day, and I already have a success story. I lost my ATM card, and I was worried sick. I requested an MBO for the card, and I got a message to put off canceling the card for just one more day. I did, and I found the card last night behind a chair in my bedroom. Thank you for the information!

"I am very interested to know when your books will be available as audio books. I don't like reading, and I find that I absorb information so much better when I hear it. I also love, love, love listening to books on my commute to and from work instead of all the negative news and morning shock junk. Please tell me that you have efforts going toward this."

Tom responds: If enough people write Light Technology Publishing, my publisher, perhaps they will consider an audio edition.

Thrilled to Be in Escrow

Nancy writes: "A dear friend wrote me about requesting MBOs when she heard that my house was still on the market after having been for sale for almost two years. She helped me to formulate the wording for the MBO and suggested I say it for a few days, which I did. I have received guidance from angels through a divining rod, a pendulum, and other tools for many years, asking if something is in my optimal harmony and balance. I'm finding requesting MBOs to be in alignment with what I've already been doing.

"One week after requesting the MBO, I received an offer on my house! It was a lot less than my asking price, though I will still receive enough profit for it to be acceptable. I believe it is the most benevolent outcome for me and the buyers. I purchased the house at a very, very good price, and it feels great to pass on the good fortune yet still have enough to pursue my goals. In the end, my angels guided me to take the offer rather than to wait for one that was closer to my asking price. I'm thrilled to be in escrow and even more thrilled to have this new tool of MBO requests!"

MBO on Canceled Trip

Tom says: Here's an MBO of my own. Last April I paid over $1,200 for entrance to a world TV market in Cannes, France, held two times per year, and I had reserved my hotel. Naturally, I requested an MBO for my trip way in advance.

As time grew closer, I grew perplexed, as I was working on two large deals for my company, and the number of people signing up to attend was far lower than the previous year at that juncture, plus business had really slowed. I had really wanted to attend, but I finally decided to let a representative of mine in Europe handle my meetings while I stayed put to work on the larger deals. I was not happy about this at all.

The results were that I was glad I did not go. One of the deals I was working on did come through, but business continued to deteriorate through the spring and into the summer. In addition to this, the volcano in Iceland blew ash, and if you recall, many flights to and from Europe were canceled. Several of my friends had to stay in Cannes an extra week — I know it sounds good, but you do have to get back to your office — burdened with the extra expense of hotels and food before they were able to get a flight out.

Financial Darwinism

Phu Diep writes: "CNN reports that 700 banks may go under this year. How many will go under with the highest probability?"

Tom responds: "Good question. As you are able to guess, this is a very fluid number to nail down, shall we say, but the highest probability is that only a portion of those will go under — somewhere in the 20 percent range. This is higher than perhaps thought, but much lower than the potential. These banks will be absorbed into the system, allowing other banks with wise financial policies to grow and have multiple locations."

MBOs For Wealth?

AA writes: "I have a question about money-related MBOs. Is it kosher to ask MBOs for wealth, abundance, and prosperity, as opposed to those relating to paying the bills or for specific profits? I would think it would be, but MBOs are generally for specific things, and asking for wealth isn't terribly specific."

Tom responds: In my business, I ask for MBOs all the time. I was recently informed by my agent in Spain that a national TV station in Africa is trying to back out on an agreement for forty movies and TV series. I requested an MBO for the contract to go through. We'll see how it comes out, but that's just one example of many MBOs that I request for a phone call or email to result in business. I sent out an email blast to seventy-five pages of email addresses around the world and asked for an MBO to have better results than I could hope for or expect. As you see, those are specific MBOs, but the results are profits.

Have you started saying the "expect great things" mantra each morning as I do? My guardian angel says that opens the door for your own guardian angel to bring you things you never would have thought to ask for.

A DHL Delay Becomes an MBO for All

Jackie writes: "Friday, my day was completely destroyed when I learned that I had made a shipping mistake the previous week. I had to correct it immediately and get the shipment out for Australia by the end of the day so they'd have it Tuesday — their time — to process. This wasn't a lot of time, and as the day went on, I began to worry. As I got to the end of the day, I knew my file wouldn't complete copying to the disk until about 5:45PM. The DHL delivery man usually comes between 5:00PM and 6:00PM, and he had called around 5:30PM to alert shipping that he was on his way. I was racing the clock. So I asked — twice actually, using different wording — for the most benevolent outcome for this shipment.

"I ended up getting the disk down there at 5:50PM, just moments before the DHL man arrived, after agreeing to wait for this last shipment. The reason this all worked out? Right when I said my MBO request, the signal light the driver was at broke, and none of the other cars would let him through. He ended up sitting at that light for twenty minutes, giving me the time I needed to complete the shipment. Right after he left, the light was fixed, so no one else had to experience delays.

"On top of that, I learned that the driver went into overtime pay at this point, so he earned a little extra cash, which he very much needed but hadn't asked for. If I hadn't asked for my MBO, he wouldn't have gotten his overtime. So this was a super-benevolent outcome in my mind. On my way out of the office to rush home, I said a ton of thank yous. I felt so much relief having it all work out. If it hadn't, I would have been okay, but I am very appreciative for the help."

Tom responds: If you remember, another rule of MBO requests is that they have to be benevolent for everyone involved in the request. In this case, the delay was not only benevolent for Jackie but also for the DHL driver who was paid for overtime — a win-win for everyone, including the clients in Australia!

PayPal MBO

Marie writes: "I want to share an MBO that happened this morning. To make this story short, I was having trouble with PayPal dipping into my bank account. They charged me too much, and I got the problem solved. I said:

Most Benevolent Outcome Request
"Guardian angel, I request a most benevolent outcome that I get my refund back to my bank account in a manner better than I expect. Thank you!"

"When I went to my local branch, I showed them the letter that PayPal had sent me, and with no questions, they fixed my problem and got my money back! So I blocked PayPal from dipping into my account without my consent. After that, I thanked my guardian angel. That made my day a brilliant one!"

Safety from Identity Theft

Lynn writes: "Hola, Tom! I used to write you all the time about the many wonderful MBOs happening once my friends and I incorporated them into our lives. There have been so many that I just stopped thinking about sharing them. But I never stop being amazed! I have noticed that I do not have to ask for them anymore or even think of them. I feel like they happen all the time without asking. I have to share this one.

"A friend and I went up to Portland to a doctor's appointment. When we do that, we also do some shopping. This time we stopped at an arts and crafts store. I had not been there for a while and wanted to look for some specific things for my garden that I had gotten there before. I was surprised to find that they had none. My friend was thinking about some art supplies she needed, but she just couldn't get into it that day. We looked around, decided there was nothing, and left. I even commented what a shock it was that we both walked out without buying anything!

"A couple of days later, a newspaper article said that someone scammed the store and got all the credit card numbers used on the very day we were there! I met people who shopped that day and used their cards, and they reported that it was a mess to clean up. My friend and I both use MBOs daily and we are sure our angels watched over us that day. Thank you again, Tom, for bringing us this treasure!"

Tom responds: I think Lynn forgot that I have suggested that all my newsletter and blog readers request an MBO for safety from identity theft. Saying it one time is all you need. You can stop having any fear of identity theft by saying,

> **Most Benevolent Outcome Request**
> *"I request a most benevolent outcome for my identity in all forms to be protected now and for all time. Thank you."*

Most Benevolent Tax Return

Belinda writes: "I was so worried about my taxes because I had not worked for a year. I had not paid any taxes because of the little money I received each month, and I had sold my house on short sale. I was expecting to pay a lot of money because the short sale lawyer said I had to pay a percentage of the forgiven amount.

"I started asking for a benevolent outcome. I asked to pay what I could afford and then by the time April came around, I asked that I pay nothing on my taxes. Then I kept getting this message in my head that even though I don't live in Las Vegas anymore, I should use my previous CPA to do my taxes. I did use him, and despite the fact that I hardly had any deductions, I received over $9,000 on my tax return. Thanks, angels!"

Tom responds: Notice that Belinda listened to that little whisper in her ear to contact her old CPA. Pay attention to those messages and "feelings!"

MBO to Help with Medical Bills

Ron writes: "Two weeks ago, I was admitted to the hospital for five days. Even though I do have insurance, I know I am going to have to pay some pretty expensive medical bills. Can I ask my guardian angel for help in this issue? If so, what would be the best way to word my request?"

Tom responds: Anyone who has this challenge should say,

Most Benevolent Outcome Request
"I request a most benevolent outcome that my medical bills will be less than I expect and that the insurance will cover much more than I expect or hope for. Thank you!"

You can also say another MBO to be able to pay your medical bills easily.

Ron responds: "Tom, I did say an MBO for paying my medical bills as you suggested, and so far things are looking good. I am receiving statements from my insurance company saying that my bills are paid. I am amazed! Thank you, thank you, thank you."

Choosing the Best Career Path

Diane writes: "Tom, with regard to MBOs for my perfect career path, I asked and received numerous messages, and they all are good! So now I'm just wondering how to determine the highest path. All of the responses involve writing or presentations around health, wellness, and healing spirituality. Each position would require a learning curve to do creative work. I will need to carve out time without income flowing from a part-time or full-time job. Do you have any suggestions on how to ask for these next steps? Thank you! Have a blessed day."

Tom responds: I suggest you say:

Most Benevolent Outcome Request
"I request a most benevolent outcome to choose the best path for me to take for my learning and success and for funds to appear that I have no reason to expect. Thank you!"

MBO Manifests Abundance

Sisi writes: "I had another benevolent outcome happen yesterday. I was wondering how I might make the loan payment on my home this month. I had received a lump sum six months ago that happened because I had intended it and had also requested an MBO for it. However, as the home had been empty for a period of two months prior to receiving this lump sum, I knew I would need to manifest some abundance this month.

"So I rang the bank and happily discovered I was able to change the date that the payment needed to be paid by about two weeks. I had a hunch I would need a little extra time. Three days after that I discovered that another lump sum payment would be coming to me around the beginning of July in exactly the amount I required. I thought, 'Thank you, God!'

"Then last night I discovered another bonus was coming my way shortly, and I am so glad, because it means that my son Peter can now go to his overnight music excursion, which is part of his school electives. He is so talented; I just knew God would work it out for us. My daughter Alex can also go on her overnight excursion, and I can finally pay off Peter's glasses, finalize the winter clothes I had put on layaway, and pay all the school fees.

"The thing is to remember to intend it, to be grateful about it, and to request an MBO around it. It's like a ring of white light. Be aware of synchronicity; be in tune."

A Charitable Donation

Carol writes: "Recently I found and ordered your books. I have been practicing MBOs for about two weeks. Last Monday I received a call out of the blue from my art dealer. My great uncle's painting sold for $25,000. After deductions for restoration and a percentage of the sale, I will receive about $16,000. I was in shock! I had requested an MBO for some more money to be able to donate $1,400 to a charity I support. So that will happen for sure. I am convinced MBOs work because I asked my guardian angel to tell me his or her name in a dream two nights ago and I woke up with the name in my head."

Mortgage Paid Off and Sisters Reunited

Veronica writes: "I have been asking for a money miracle in my MBOs on and off for about two months. My teaching time has been cut in half this year, and my husband and I weren't sure how we were going to make ends meet. I have applied for other part-time jobs, but nothing has worked out yet. Yesterday my sister called and said that she and her husband, who are quite wealthy, would pay off our mortgage of $120,000! My husband got the call and gave me the news. I was skeptical, but I talked to her tonight and it seems it's for real! How is that for amazing?

"I haven't talked to my sister much in the past few years because she thought that I should quit my job and come help her help our parents, who were living in a retirement home. My husband and I are not financially in a position for me to do that, although I helped when I could. So that makes this even more amazing, and I do mean amazing! I won't have to substitute teach, which would involve driving all over the place in the snow and ice in the winter in a hurry, which is not a good idea. And now I will even have a little extra time to do some painting!"

Benevolently Closing the Deal on a New Home

Renee writes: "I have a great MBO story. We recently bought a new home. We made an offer that included the seller giving us $6,000 back to cover closing costs, but the seller insisted that she wanted a certain amount after closing costs. So we offered $2,000 above what she was asking. We had the inspections done and the house appraised, and the appraisal came back at $14,000 *less* than what she was asking and $16,000 less than what we offered. We really thought the deal was dead in the water, so I requested an MBO that the seller would accept the lower price and that we would be able to buy this house. We really didn't expect her to accept the lower offer, but she did! We closed on the house a day later and moved in three days after the closing.

"In addition to that MBO, the mortgage company kept saying they needed 'one more thing' from us before final approval. It was really getting on our nerves. I finally said to my husband, 'Repeat after me:

> **Most Benevolent Outcome Request**
> *"I request a most benevolent outcome that the underwriters now have all of the documents we need to close on this house."*

We got the call the following morning from the mortgage company telling us we were closing the next day."

MBO for Money to Move

Sandra writes: "Tom, thank you! Thank you so much for offering the means to a beautiful, serendipitous encounter when I was desperately trying to not panic. This was my situation: I had no money. I was due to move out of my old flat on Friday, and as of Wednesday morning, I still had no new flat to move in to. I was struggling to not let fear overwhelm me because the situation really didn't look very good from where I stood.

"It was then that I prayed for a way out, because up to that point, I had been using visualizations, saying affirmations, and doing switchwording and EFT tapping until I was blue in the face. Though there were mild changes, nothing significant was happening. And then I randomly came across MBOs on Steve Pavlina's old forum and the floodgates opened. Interestingly, at first not much happened, or rather not much that jumped out. But forty-eight hours later, I was lent some money to pay for my move and had signed a lease on a new place.

"I could not have even envisioned what happened and how things turned out, and now I know I'm never alone in any situation: All I have to do is ask for help. Most importantly, I am at peace. I know that once my prayer request is sent I don't need to worry about anything. So thank you! Thank you for not keeping this to yourself, and thank you because my life will never be the same."

MBO for a Massive Medical Bill

Lyn writes: "In early February, I experienced a spontaneous coronary artery dissection. I had previously had painful episodes resembling heartburn that had prompted me to go to the hospital, so when I went into ventricular fibrillation, the hospital staff was ready to bring me back.

"During all the commotion, I was given an overdose of Heparin. I wasn't hurt by this but could have been if I had been cut into for the angiogram they wanted to do right away. Luckily, the overdose was noticed and the angiogram had to wait awhile.

"I wrote customer service at the hospital that I thought my bill should be reduced due to the Heparin incident. I requested an MBO for the bill to be cheaper than I could hope or expect. I heard back from the hospital that the remainder of my bill would be waived after my insurance paid whatever it would pay. Yay! I was looking at a $32,000 bill at one point. It was so nice to see that zeroed-out balance!"

Fixing a Phone Charge

Laurie writes: "Today I had to call my phone company because of an incorrect charge. I requested an MBO to get the perfect representative to help me resolve the billing problem. The woman who helped me was one of the most cheerful people I've ever encountered in such a situation! She was able to correct the problem and credit my account in a jiffy, even though she kept apologizing for the delay. I had to laugh at that, because I could hear her typing at the speed of lightning."

Tom responds: So all in all, a most benevolent outcome!

08

Benevolent Outcomes for
Self-Owned Businesses

Kick-Starting My Husband's Business

Pat writes: "I requested that all of our needs be met easily from now on, and so on, and today something wonderful happened as a result. The potential has been there for several months — my husband sells several how-to DVDs, and he had an inquiry about bulk sales months ago, but nothing had come of it until now. After this, I'm going to be using MBOs much more often. Thank you, angels, and many thanks to you, Tom, for spreading the word about them!"

Benevolent Help with Reiki Studio

Leanne writes: "Lucky me — my newly built Reiki studio opens on February 4! I want to ask for an MBO for continual healing for my clients and for many clients to come and see me and so on, but what I want to know is whether I ask for an MBO for myself or whether I say a BP for my business, for the room, or for my future clients. I would like to know your thoughts, if you have time. Kind regards from sunny Oz." [Leanne lives in Australia.]

Tom responds: For Leanne and anyone else who has a healing business, I would request a benevolent outcome for the success of your business, and then each day, you can request an MBO as you assist others, and may the results be even better than you can hope for or expect. You can also say a BP for each client, such as,

> **Benevolent Prayer**
> *"I ask any and all beings to assist my client in continuing to heal in the most benevolent way, and may the results be even better than we can hope for or expect. Thank you!"*

It will become a habit, and I think that if you even say this in front of them, they will appreciate it, and it will reinforce your work on a subconscious level. May I remind everyone that BPs are for all faiths and beliefs? So you shouldn't be afraid of stepping on toes. I also recommend saying the "expect great things" mantra every day. You can print out a sign with this mantra on it from my website. My guardian angel says that it opens the door for your own guardian angel to bring in business that you may have never expected.

Help in the Business of Healing

Diane writes: "Tom, I am in transition and just started asking for MBOs. I have my own business providing addiction therapy and energy healing. Until recently, I had very few clients and a lot of doors that wouldn't open, even after ten years in the field. I asked for an MBO to receive messages and guidance for my mission and to make a difference in my career and ended the request with a thank you.

"I received information indicating that I should focus on healing and study shamanism. Two clients were referred to me within two days of asking for the MBO. And just yesterday I had a practitioner ask if I can teach Reiki and another message to study to teach! I hope this will support your need to see results."

Tom responds: Anyone who wishes to increase their business should also be saying the "expect great things" mantra on the "signs" page of my website. You will see a noticeable improvement within just a couple of weeks of saying that mantra each morning.

Successful MBO for New Client

Mallie writes: "I have another testimonial of the power of MBOs. I have been trying to manifest a new client for the past month, and despite using visualizations and affirmations for a week or so, I was having no luck. It was getting frustrating because I had a problem client that I wanted to get rid of and replace. On Friday I had just had it with this client! I said an MBO out loud, very forcefully. On Sunday I got a call from a wonderful new client I know I will be very happy with.

"If you are tired of the so-so results you get from doing affirmations, then I urge you to give MBOs a try. To me, affirmations are like driving a Pinto and MBOs are like driving a Ferrari — both cars get you to where you want to go, but you'll get there a lot faster driving the Ferrari."

Tom responds: I love that simile! You'll probably hear me repeat this on a radio interview or talk that I give.

Benevolent Meeting with Building Inspector

Nancy writes: "Thanks so much for the teleseminar last night. As always, you inspired me and reminded me how the spirit world is there to help us when we ask for it. During your talk, I asked for an MBO for my new business venture. Today I met with the building inspector, something I had been dreading because many people have told me horror stories about him.

"Well, the meeting couldn't have gone better. The inspector made a few simple suggestions and then said everything else looked fine. I told him he had made my day, and he replied that that was the nicest thing anyone had said to him in a long time. Thanks again, and I'm looking forward to hearing more from you."

MBO for New Karate Students

Billy writes: "I've gotten to the point that almost all of my MBOs get positive results in the best way possible. The percentage has been so high that when one doesn't seem to work the way I requested, it really stands out these days.

"The MBO that most surprised me recently was one that I requested for more karate students. The parents of two children brought them to the very next practice after my request. The parents also joined. Utterly amazed and satisfied that my MBO had been answered, I was even more pleased when the following practices also saw new students enroll. Ten new students in four weeks is nothing short of miraculous, considering the low population of children in the area where I have my classes!"

MBO for a Catering Job

GF writes: "Last week I received a menu request for a big catering job. At first I was intimidated by the magnitude of it all and decided it was out of my comfort zone to prepare food for such a big event. I had convinced myself it was just too big. I decided to call the company the next morning and went to bed.

"Before sleeping, I said an MBO and picked up *Happy for No Reason* and read awhile. I woke up the next morning as if something was urging me to get out of bed. I immediately said, 'I can do this job; expect great things!' I put the menu together and within twenty-four hours was called to confirm my availability.

"I have been saying MBOs for quite some time and realized I needed a shift in consciousness to accept that there are benevolent beings waiting to help me. Gosh, they must have grown tired of my complaining when all the while they were waiting to do good things. When I get up every morning I say your daily MBO and also expect great things!"

Tom responds: GF is referring to my daily BP and "expect great things" mantra, as my readers call it. You can find both by going to the website and clicking on the "signs" tab in the menu bar. You can print those out, plus copies of a sign that reads, "Request Benevolent Outcomes Today!" which you can put up in several places to remind you to make it a habit.

Dog-Walker's Dilemma Solved

Lyn writes: "Hi there, Tom! This just happened last night: I was wondering how to attract some new dog-sitting customers. Dog-sitting is something I really enjoy doing, and I really appreciate the extra cash, so I decided to offer up an MBO request.

"I was walking home from a church service and passed a woman walking two labs. She used to own the Curves I went to when I first moved back to the Chicago area, which was two years ago and about forty miles away. She now lives near me, has a dog sitting business, and is looking for someone to help her with some new clients.

"Now, you know how big Chicago is. What are the chances of being on the same street at the perfect time? Well, it wasn't chance; it was an MBO!"

Benevolent Settlement with Former Partner

Diana writes: "We recently experienced an MBO when my husband was requested to urgently meet a former business partner to 'finish an accounting matter.' In the past, the former partner had always hinted that we owed him money — which we did not — since he had pushed us out after business had become successful.

"Anyway, when he requested the meeting, we thought he was going to ask for that money again. I requested an MBO for the meeting. The morning of the meeting, the man forgot about it, but later in the day they met again, and my husband told me that the former partner handed him $2,000 in cash as a settlement of accounting. My jaw dropped. I like to think that my MBO request was helping in that situation.

"The second MBO I would like to share happened two nights ago. I requested an MBO for help in organizing our office space, as I have had some quarrels with my husband about that issue. I had almost instant insight about the situation, and my husband agreed that the idea was good on how to reorganize our space."

09

Benevolent Outcomes for Physical Health

MBOs for General Health

Brian writes: "Do you have a good MBO request wording for general healing and health optimization? I could use help with this, as health is not covered that well in your first book and I have struggled with the wording on this subject in the past."

Tom responds: There are several MBO requests to say for health, depending on your particular circumstances. You can request an MBO for healing energy to be sent to you by your guardian angel. You can request an MBO to be led to the best treatments for the particular condition you are experiencing. Or you can request MBOs for a successful operation, as I did when I experienced congestive heart failure in 2006. If the illness or condition is unknown, you can say,

> **Most Benevolent Outcome Request**
> *"I request a most benevolent outcome for this condition of my body, and may I be led to finding out what is wrong and how to correct it in a most benevolent manner. Thank you!"*

Pain-Free and Healed

Annique writes: "I would like to tell you of the benevolent outcome I experienced with my illness. Despite being a Reiki master and theta practitioner, I still could not heal my irritable bowel syndrome (IBS). I know you already gave me a link when I wrote you about this before, and I did check it out, but I was already doing everything in there, so I requested an MBO one day when the pain was so severe I actually cried; I could not take it anymore. Well, the pain stopped about ten minutes after I requested the MBO, and I now no longer have IBS. It is totally gone. Thank you, Tom and my guardian angel! It is totally awesome to be pain-free and not have to worry about the bathroom anymore. Many blessings to you, Tom, and keep up the good work. We appreciate you. Love and light."

Request for a Body Shield

Patricia writes:	"I am a 74-year-old, red-haired, very fair-skinned gal who has the job of weeding the flower beds on our property. This

requires covering up with the equivalent of a toxic chemical suit to keep from being eaten alive by mosquitoes, bees, and anything that bites or makes itches or red blotches, along with the addition of sunscreen for protection.

"Because a previous MBO request headed off a white tornado aimed right for the house, and because I now routinely use MBOs to shield our property during vociferous rain and wind storms — of which we have had many the past few years — a thought grew in my mind. If I can shield my house successfully, why can't I put a shield around my body that will allow me to work in peace and comfort?

"You can guess the ending. I asked for a shield around my body that would protect me from the elements, and then I gingerly stepped out the door, telling myself, 'Trust, trust, trust: It works on other things.' I was dressed in shorts and a short-sleeved T-shirt with bare arms and legs and no sunscreen.

"I showered after an hour and a half of weeding, grinning all the time and totally free of any bites, itches, red blotches, and so on. I have now had three more comfortable weeding sessions using the same MBO request and telling the story to the birds and deer who are watching. This story is much too good to keep to myself!"

A year later, Patricia writes back, "After such success last year using a 'body shield' for working in the garden, I get no bites, no sunburn, and no itches. It was a simple step to request an MBO for another shield from the allergy triggers of the spring:

Most Benevolent Outcome Request
"Please shield me from the mold and pollen that now leave me struggling with swollen sinuses, a stuffy nose, and an upset intestinal system."

"Eureka! After three days of weed-pulling and cleaning up the yard this spring, I experienced no aftereffects. I love living this way! Tom, thank you for all you do with *The Gentle Way*. I give the books away every chance I get."

MBO for Eyesight

Karen writes:	"I wanted to tell you some exciting news! I've been very good at getting the most convenient parking spots on a regu-

lar basis. After learning of your MBO process, I started requesting them, but I wanted to request something more significant than just an ideal parking spot. A few weeks ago, I requested an MBO for my eyesight. When I made this request, I could almost feel those in the angelic region breathe a sigh of relief that finally I was getting on board!

"Last week, I saw my eye doctor, and with deep gratitude I am happy to report that my vision has drastically improved — no more astigmatism and I can now wear soft contacts, when before I was told I could not wear them. Best of all, my vision was in the -13 and -15 range, and now I can wear 8.5 and 9.5 soft contacts and am able to see clearly at a distance better than I can ever recall seeing. I believe my eyes will continue to improve. I've never dared to request something so meaningful before. Thanks again for your amazing work. I only recently became familiar with it."

MBO for Restful Sleep

Eleanore writes: "Wow! My daughter, with whom I went to Disneyland, can sometimes be reticent to try or consider new ideas. I took *The Gentle Way* with me and said that maybe she'd care to read it on the plane back to New Jersey. I didn't hear anything from her for about two weeks, but when I did, she was really, really excited. She is spreading the word with much happiness and joy where she works. I suggested she might order a few of the books to give to her coworkers for Christmas, and she really likes that idea.

"Until now, she has suffered from a very painful medical condition that often prohibits restful sleep. Yesterday, however, I got a call from one mightily enthusiastic person who said she has had the most restful night's sleep she has experienced in years and knows it was a result of MBO requests. She loves the whole thing and already has one new person with whom she shared the book. I asked that she and her friend please buy their own and send mine back, and that is in progress."

Tom responds: I'm just so pleased when others, family or not, discover and use MBO requests, because doing so makes such a tremendous impact on everyone who does. Expect great things — oh, yes!

MBO Helps with Scar Removal

Mara writes: "I've been saying MBOs for just about everything these days. A while ago, I said one for the clearing of two pretty angry red scars on my face. I don't care to wear a comprehensive foundation. I like the little freckles I get on my cheeks when I get sun; they've always made me feel unique. I really just wanted my face to clear, specifically so that I could be more confident in my outward appearance.

"I thought I was imagining things the other day when the angry red went away, but now the scarring has actually decreased in size. The two super-deep red splotches on my cheek that were really noticeable have now dwindled to small areas of mild red. I have light skin that scars easily, so for these marks to begin to clear so soon after receiving them is absolutely phenomenal to me.

"To give an example of how easily I scar, I have a mark on my hand from a shallow cat bite from the summer still clearly visible and the remnants of a scar from when a friend accidentally hooked me with her fingernail when I was fourteen. I'm not as fair as freshly driven snow, but my body apparently enjoys holding on to past wounds quite a bit.

"This is totally incredible and I'm loving it, especially since I had such a hard time seeing any results from regular law-of-attraction methods. I would always sit back and say, 'Gosh, it is so easy for everyone else. Why can't I?' I feel truly empowered for the first time in my life and it's just delightful. I love it. I feel so incredibly grateful that MBOs have come into my life."

MBO for Skin Problem

Judi writes: "Thank you, Tom, for sharing MBOs. They have changed my life. Your articles in the *Sedona Journal of Emergence!* led me to you.

"For some time now, I have been saying MBOs with great results. In the past, I've had to go to a dermatologist to remove basal nonmelanoma skin cancer growths from my many years in the sun. But this time when one appeared, I said an MBO for natural healing. To my wonderful surprise, it disappeared. I was more than happy to not have to go to the dermatologist. This was just miraculous! I thank you and my guardian angel for this wonderful healing."

MBO for Energy, Strength, and Health

Marie writes: "Hello, Tom. Here is an MBO for you to share. This morning I was very tired, so I requested an MBO. I said,

Most Benevolent Outcome Request
"Guardian angel, I request an MBO that you give me energy, strength, and health, and that you take my tiredness away. Thank you!"

"When I got to the shop, I felt better. I felt energetic."

Help with Healthy Weight Loss

Frances writes: "I have struggled with being overweight all of my life. I ask for MBOs to help me with this, yet I feel that nothing much has happened, or nothing much that I can perceive. Could you help with a suggested MBO for healthy weight loss and good eating habits? Thanks."

Tom responds: For Frances and anyone else with this challenge, I'll give you some MBOs to request and then some practical suggestions. You can say,

Most Benevolent Outcome Request
"I request a most benevolent outcome for attaining the best weight for my health and happiness. Thank you!

"I request a most benevolent outcome for choosing the healthiest foods both at home and in restaurants. Thank you!

"I request a most benevolent outcome for being led to healthy, enjoyable exercises for me, thank you!"

Now, having had a weight problem myself in the past, and still having to continually watch myself (thanks are due to my wife for helping me with this), we both found that Weight Watchers worked the best of any program we ever tried. I lost twenty-five pounds.

The best thing that came out of the program was portion control. Most restaurants serve twice what you should consume. Therefore, my wife and I either split the entree or divide it into two halves and take the other half home and eat it in the next day or two. During our Sedona trip, for a week we did just that almost every dinner and for our lunches too. We did not have our first dessert until our fifth evening when we split a mousse.

Weight Watchers' Smart Ones and Lean Cuisine's prepared meals both list the Weight Watchers points, although we don't count anymore. It's best to not eat out of the container, but spread it out on a plate. They normally take up the whole plate, so visually you feel like you're eating a full meal.

As for exercise, start walking if you are not doing so already. Either early in the morning or evening, get out and walk for at least twenty minutes. It really does boost your metabolism. I hope I've been of some assistance!

A Long Road to Believing in MBOs

Pricilla writes: "Thank you so much for all the information you freely share on your websites. My life has truly been transformed since I learned about MBOs, BPs, the daily affirmation, and all the other wonderful information that you share. I'm fifty-eight years old and live in Summerfield, Florida. When the economy tanked, I lost my job, and I have been unemployed since that time. Life has been one long, hard bump in the road after another, but I have managed to keep a roof over my head and enough food on the table to keep from starving, so I am more fortunate than many other people.

"About a month ago, I started having pain in my lower back. With no job, health insurance, or money for medical bills, I did my best to tough it out. I was raised to believe that God would never put anything in my life that he is not willing to see me through, so I hung on to my faith and just kept trying to make the best of the worst years I have had to live through. A smart person would have sought medical attention and worried about how to pay the bills later, but I've never claimed to be smart. I will not run up a bill I know I cannot pay; to me it's just like stealing. So I just toughed it out.

"I prayed to God to ease the pain, but it only got worse with each passing day. I've always believed we all have angels that watch over us, but in these past six years I felt alone, abandoned by my angels. I kept asking them how could they just sit around and watch me go through such a hard and stressful time in my life and not help me. I asked, pleaded, and begged my angels to help me, to point me in the right direction, to get my life on the right path, but I got no answer, no inspiration, and no direction. I got nothing for six long years of trying every single type of information on contacting my angels that I could find.

"On August 25, the pain was more than I could bear. The slightest movement sent lightning bolts of pain through my body, and I just couldn't take it anymore. I do not know how I ended up on YouTube, but I found a video in which someone said, 'Ask your angels for undeniable proof that they are with you, and they will give it to you.' I told my angels I believed they had abandoned me, but if they were with me, I wanted them to give me undeniable proof. I didn't expect anything to happen, and I'm sorry to say that when I went to bed I asked God to just let me die in my sleep because I just couldn't take anymore. I had finally given up.

"At 2:00AM, the bedroom TV and surround-sound system came on. Both the TV and the surround-sound system are quite old and do not even have a timer function, and they have to be turned on separately. My fiancé, Bill, and I were the only ones in the house, and we were both sound asleep. The remotes were nowhere near us. Bill did not even know I had asked for proof. Of course, Bill looked at me like I had two heads when I told him it was my angels giving me proof that they were with me. My angels gave me the undeniable proof I asked for, so now I had to find out why they weren't listening to me.

"So on August 26 I started searching the web. I found your website, and I read and read and read. I Googled every piece of information I could find on Tom T. Moore and MBOs. I was skeptical, to say the least — just a few simple words followed by 'thank you,' and my angels would be more than happy to help me? I had nothing to lose, so I wrote and said three MBO requests:

Most Benevolent Outcome Request

"I request an MBO for me to live pain-free, and may the results be even better than I can hope for or expect. Thank you"

"I am asking for an MBO that the form of life generating this pain in my body mutate now into a benign form that will be gentle on my body and that the results be even better than I can hope for or expect. Thank you"

"I request an MBO to have a money miracle happen to me today, and may this outcome be even better than I could hope for or expect. Thank you."

"On August 27, I woke up dreading the pain I knew would come the moment I moved. I rolled over, but there was no pain. I sat on the side of the bed — no pain. I cannot explain how wonderful I felt, being able to move for the first time in a month and not be in pain. In that moment, I decided to start my day with the BP and the daily affirmation. When Bill came home, I smiled at him and touched my toes. His jaw dropped. I explained about MBOs and told him I had made an MBO request for the pain to go away. He looked at me like I had two heads.

"On August 28, Bill asked me if I had put two twenty-dollar bills in his wallet. I laughed, because where in the world would I get forty dollars to put in his wallet? Besides, I haven't been able to leave the house for a month. He rarely has cash in his wallet, never mind forty dollars. Then I told him I had said an MBO request for a money miracle so the money was put there by my angels. Bill rolled his eyes and said he must have gotten cash out of the bank and just forgot about it. Normally I do all the shopping and run all the errands, but since I had been unable to leave the house for the past month, Bill had to do it. So I went through our online bank statement for the past month, and there was not one transaction that would have put that money in his wallet. There is no one who even has access to his wallet except for him and me, so I knew it was my angels.

"The next day he finally admitted it must have been my angels. He smiled and asked that if I did that again to please ask for more than forty dollars. I asked him if I had his attention yet and if he wanted to do some MBO requests. He said I had half his attention but he didn't want to say any. Then the strangest thought popped into my head: 'Take twenty dollars, say an MBO request, and go to the store tomorrow and buy the first scratch-off ticket you see.' It was a strange thought for me, since money is not something I generally throw away like that, but I wrote and said another MBO request:

Most Benevolent Outcome Request
"I request an MBO for choosing a winning scratch ticket tomorrow at Publix, and may the results exceed my highest expectations. Thank you!"

"On August 29 I went to the store and bought a twenty-dollar scratch ticket out of the machine. I admit I stood in front of that machine for a few minutes with that twenty-dollar bill in my hand, not wanting to put it into that machine, but I did. I brought it home, told my fiancé it was a winner from my angels, and made him scratch it. That ticket won $100! Bill didn't look at me like I had two heads. He said, 'Okay, now you have my attention.' He still doesn't want to say any MBO requests, but that's okay; it's his free choice, and I'm not going to pressure him.

"Because I do not earn a reliable income, I normally will not buy myself anything. I have this thing about spending Bill's money on something that's only for me. But my angels had just given us unexpected money, so I went online and bought both your books. Delivery was supposed to take three to five days, but I got notification this morning that they will be delivered by UPS tomorrow. Two-day delivery — how cool is that? I can't wait to read them!

"Today I went outside to mow my lawn, but the riding mower wouldn't start. I turned the key three or four times, and it just barely turned over but would not start. I turned the key again, and it wouldn't even turn over. I started to get frustrated and angry, but then I caught myself and simply said an MBO request for the mower to start right now. I took a deep breath and turned the key one more time. It turned right over and ran like a charm while I mowed the lawn.

"Do MBOs work? I know with all my heart and soul that yes, they most definitely do work. Do they work for big things? Yes, my pain was a very big thing. All I can say to anyone who doesn't even give it a try is this: You are missing out on the most powerful knowledge that has ever been laid out in front of you."

Guardian Angel Performs Heimlich Maneuver

PH writes: "Lately I've been using MBOs for just about anything that comes up that troubles me in the slightest way. Just the other day, I was eating a bagel and started to choke, but only just a little bit. It was more of an annoying choking sensation — not really too bad — and I tried everything to stop it. Finally in desperation, I stopped and started to think what else I could do. I remembered to ask for an MBO to stop choking, and within five seconds it stopped; I started to laugh out loud because it worked so well.

"Now this is a really small thing, but dang, that choking was super-annoying! And to see it just stop within seconds of doing an MBO was just so great. I even used it again for choking about a week or so later, and the same thing happened — in just a few seconds, my choking stopped seemingly all by itself. Even though I knew my guardian angel stopped it, I could not tell how it happened since it was such a smooth transition. It almost seemed like magic.

"I use MBOs every day, several times a day now. I never go without them and use them from the biggest things to the smallest — even just walking into a store to buy some simple thing. If you do an MBO before you actually get in the store, all sorts of cool things happen.

"You even mentioned using them before bed to get a good night's sleep, so I've been doing that awhile now too. When I forget to ask for an MBO before sleep, I wake up feeling so-so and not so great, which is normal for me. But other times I remember to say an MBO:

Most Benevolent Outcome Request

"I now request the most benevolent outcome for a good night's sleep and to wake up in the morning refreshed and rejuvenated. Thank you."

"When I do this, I wake up feeling so great that it's amazing."

Fishing with My Father

Fredrick writes: "What could be a more benevolent outcome than coming back to Oklahoma thinking I would have to bury my father but instead end up taking him fishing? He is ninety-six years old, frail, and was in the hospital with pneumonia and end-stage kidney failure. We were ready to order the flowers. Many people were praying for him in their own ways, but my sister was using MBO requests. I had never heard of this, but I felt it was something I could do, so I chimed right in.

"Now, the physical therapist at his nursing center has organized a little fishing expedition for the two of us at a nearby lake for tomorrow. Dad has been my fishing buddy for the past fifty years. I don't think he likes to eat fish all that much, but fishing is a way for a father and son to spend time together. To go fishing with my father another time is a precious gift for us both. Thank you for teaching this great approach."

An MBO for Clear Vision

Marjeece writes: "I requested an MBO to find my glasses. I looked all over for them last night as I was trying to go out, but I couldn't find them. I really need to find my glasses."

Tom responds: I assured her she would find them. She responded to me, "Got the glasses. They were in the stroller in the back kitchen. I had looked there many times without finding them. Then my husband came home, and the first place he looked, he put his hands right on them." I have now recommended that she request an MBO to never lose her glasses again. I did that after misplacing my own glasses; I even had to go back to a restaurant to retrieve them. So far, so good.

Goodbye to Acid Reflux

Ann writes: Ann writes, "My MBO story happened this winter. After going to bed one evening, I woke with severe acid reflux. I was quite sick and very disturbed. Fortunately, I remembered to do an MBO. The moment I said thank you, the acid reflux was gone immediately. I wasn't surprised, but I was so thrilled that it had worked immediately. I asked to remain free of this acid reflux, and I have not experienced it again. Thank you for sharing this wonderful tool with us to make MBO requests. I do them all the time about everything, and not only do they work, but I feel so good about doing them. I have shared them with many people who hopefully will benefit from them also. I know some already have. Thanks again for all you share with us."

MBO for Clear Breathing

Jim writes: "I'm ninety-two years old. Tuesday evening I went into a chill that lasted over two hours, then came out of that with a temperature of 102°F and my blood pressure at 199. The immediate decision was that I had become dehydrated on the golf course, and that is what brought all of this on. The solution was to go on antibiotics, take some aspirin, and drink lots of fluids. The next day I felt much better but still far from normal.

"Now, here's the MBO part. We went to bed about 11:00 Wednesday night, but I kept my wife and I awake with the noise of my gurgling breathing. Leslie was about to leave the room when I suddenly thought to say an MBO to clear my breath. My very next breath was absolutely clear, and it has stayed that way ever since. It happened so fast, I was actually startled. Just wanted to tell you about it."

Tom responds: I love this story, because it does demonstrate that we're never too old to learn something new!

Combating Pink Eye in a Most Benevolent Way

Liamona writes: "Recently my daughter invited a new friend over for a play date. They went outside for a while, and when they came back in, the girl had noticeable redness around her left eye that was painful and itchy. She said she often got pink eye, or conjunctivitis. I have a lot of natural remedies that could've helped, but I didn't feel comfortable giving them to her, as I didn't know if her parents would like that. Instead, I went into the laundry room and said a BP for her. I figured if that didn't work, I'd just drive her home. After I got back, I gave them some snacks and they went outside again. Not fifteen minutes later, they came back in and all the redness was completely gone!"

Relieving My Mother's Dizziness

Sky writes: "I use a BP daily for my mother's sporadic dizziness, which gives her a lot of trouble whenever it occurs. This has worsened for a year now, so I said,

> **Benevolent Prayer**
> *"I ask that any and all beings assist my mother in curing her dizziness permanently."*

"After five days, there was a marked improvement in her condition, and she has stopped ingesting costly tablets twice a day or more. To my relief, she only takes a tablet sometimes, and there are days she doesn't take them at all. The quality of my sleep has also improved since I used an MBO for sleeping easily at night."

10

Benevolent Outcomes for Doctor Visits

Quick and Painless Doctor Visit

Rick writes: "I had a nice pair of MBOs happen earlier this afternoon that I'd like to share. I had a scheduled appointment to see a specialist at a local hospital. The medical group's office is attached to the parking garage, connected by a walkway on the third floor of the building and third level of the parking garage.

"I normally do not do MBOs for parking because I prefer to walk, so I don't care how far I'm parked from the front door; it's good exercise. But parking garages can be confusing, and this one is no different. Before I left home, I said two MBOs. The first was this:

Most Benevolent Outcome Request
"I request a most benevolent outcome for arriving safely at the hospital and for finding a parking space on the third level of the parking garage. Thank you!"

"The second MBO was to see the doctor immediately. The ramps to this parking garage are in the middle. They've got two lanes, so you utilize the same ramp for entering and exiting each level. When I got to level three, the only parking space I saw available was for the handicapped, and I never park there. So I turned and began to go up the ramp to the fourth level, but then I stopped and said, 'No, the MBO is for the third level.' I backed up off the ramp and made the right-hand turn that was just past the ramp. Sure enough, on the third spot in on the right was a parking space! I pulled right into the nice, easy spot and had no confusion in remembering where I parked.

"As for the MBO to see the doctor quickly, the time between signing in and being seen by the doctor couldn't have been ten minutes! I signed in at 1:35PM for a 1:45PM appointment and was out the door and back in my car by 2:05PM. Nice, quick, and painless. I said a double thank you to my guardian angel."

Tom responds: That's called trusting in the process!

Benevolent Dentist Visit

Liz writes: "I enjoy receiving your newsletters and have been saying MBO requests for over a year now. I find they give me a peace of mind and a confidence that I didn't have before. Although I believe that MBO requests really work, my logical side always says that it could be just coincidence.

"I have a story I would like to share. I broke a tooth and went to the dentist for a crown. Being deathly afraid of dentistry, I probably requested far more MBOs than was required, but hey, it kept me sane. Anyway, the actual work went very fast. The dentist was surprised and said repeatedly and with amazement that he remembered only one other time that he had been able to make just one dental impression, since he typically has to make two. I thanked my guardian angel all the way home and continue to now, whenever I think of it. Keep up the good work!"

MBO for Stabilized Eyesight

Rick writes: "I just got back from the eye doctor with a pleasant, money-saving MBO I'd like to share. I have worn glasses for eleven years now. Up until four years ago, I was told I could never get laser surgery because of my astigmatism. That problem can now be treated with laser surgery, so I went to a doctor in the Trenton, New Jersey, area — a thirty-five-mile ride for me each way. He diagnosed what no other ophthalmologist or optometrist could: a condition called keratoconus, which means that my cornea is oddly shaped. It's bad enough that contact lenses fall off my eye!

"The condition has stabilized over the past two years, but I usually have to get a new prescription for the lenses of my glasses. Because of financial hardships, I brought an old pair with me to insist they put the new lenses in some old frames. Before the trip, I asked for an MBO that they would accept this. As it turns out, my eyes are so stable right now, the doctor didn't even recommend a new pair, so I can keep the old ones. That MBO request saved me more money than I could have if I had switched to Geico!"

Benevolent Diagnostic Outcome

Roda writes: "Here's another MBO for you. I was having heart palpitations — enough for me to feel the pounding in my ears and neck. So I decided this is one time I'd better listen to my body, and I made an appointment with a cardiologist I had written a story about. On the way there this morning, after having read one of your fan's notes about how to request an MBO, I asked simply for an MBO for this doctor's visit that ended with 'and may it be even better than I can hope for or expect.' I am a very alternative person — sixty years old, only taking vitamins and minerals — and I was quite concerned about what these palpitations might mean. I couldn't figure out what the angels could do, but I gave it to them and trusted them.

"It turns out that I have, of all things, this electrical problem with my heart called Wolff-Parkinson-White syndrome. It doesn't call for any medication — at least not at this time — which is fabulous. The irony is that I can't take any natural thing to fix it. Oh, toot! But they really did give me the very best treatment: a specific answer. I thought they were going to brush me off and call it a day with no meds and without me being able to fix it myself. Now I've really got to give it to the universe. I am so grateful for MBO requests. I never would have figured it would turn out this wonderful. Yay, MBOs!"

Goodbye to Back Pain

Sue writes: "Just from reading your newsletter, I thought I would give MBOs and BPs a try. I started out simple with a smooth drive into the city. Well, I got green lights all the way through town. Parking spaces showed up!

"I even went so far as to request an MBO that my lower back wouldn't hurt so I could get the walls and windows washed. I had a spasm, so I asked for an MBO. To my ultimate surprise, I have to tell you my lower back did not hurt one iota! What I didn't consider, though, was muscle ache. I laughed for two days over it. Every muscle hurt, but by golly, I had absolutely no back pain. I am thrilled!

"This is fun to personally experience in a game with my angel. I just love it. Thank you over and over again, Tom. The Barnes and Noble nearest me has your book. Next run into the city, I'll be getting it. Blessings, hugs, and fun to you."

Benevolent Hospital Outcome

Lynn writes: "Hi, Tom. I just came home from having a great experience I thought might not be so great: I had an appointment for physical therapy at a local hospital here. I live in a very low-populated area on the Oregon coast. The hospital serves its purpose as a first stop for most, so you hear good and not-so-great things about it. I have to get physical therapy for my knee and have heard various things about the physical therapy department at the hospital — including several not-so-good things — so I was concerned. But I needed to get this done as close to home as possible. Other options meant a trip to Portland, an hour or more away.

"As I went this morning, I said an MBO request for the best possible outcome for my therapist and the best outcome for my knee. When I got there, it was National Physical Therapy Week, so they had all of their therapists' pictures posted on a nice bulletin board. As I waited, I looked at all fifteen of them and thought, 'Surely there are some good ones for me.' Then I got called in and met Amber, a wonderful young woman who, despite her youth, knew just what she was talking about, listened to me, and answered every question I had very well, giving me more information than I'd even asked for. I left feeling hopeful for a good recovery and relaxed about it all. Thank you very much, angels and Tom, for showing me about MBOs."

Tom responds: I've previously described the same situation when I was in the hospital. I requested my benevolent outcomes and then didn't worry.

MBO for Breast Cancer Exam

Prudence writes: "After a recent mammogram, I was called back to see the oncologist. I was told that they'd found some small calcium deposits in my breast. Because I'd had cancer five years earlier, he wanted me to have a biopsy.

"I wasn't looking forward to the biopsy, as I knew what I was letting myself in for. So before I went in, I asked the universe for an MBO. I trusted that the universe would know what this might be better than I would.

"I was told that the doctor would take a couple of samples and that I should allow forty-five minutes to be on the safe side. In any event, I stayed 'squashed' — as with a mammogram — with the chair pushed so close to the machine that I couldn't breathe easily for nearly an hour and a quarter. My head was also cocked in a most awkward position for the entire time, so it wasn't surprising that after about half an hour, I began to feel very faint.

"At this point in time, the only other person in the room with me was a nurse. As a Reiki healer myself, I felt moved to ask the nurse to put her hand on my neck to give me some energy, which she willingly did. She was absolutely amazed at how quickly that caused my color to return and my breathing to settle down. Very soon I was completely fine again. That was certainly an MBO, because now the nurse will be able to do that for so many other patients and she was thrilled to bits!

"The reason my session took so long was that the cells in question were so small that they kept moving away as the needle went in. The doctor must have taken at least eight samples before he felt he'd been successful. However, when these samples were x-rayed, none of them showed any calcium deposits, so another eight samples were taken!

"After such an ordeal, I was told that I would need to take painkillers and that I should expect serious bruising. But to my surprise and delight, I was never even aware of the anesthetic wearing off. I had no pain nor any bruising. I put this down to the fact that I had asked for an MBO and asked to be surrounded by angels. It is my feeling that I had to have so many samples taken in order to reiterate to me how much I'd been helped. If I'd only had a couple of samples taken, I might well have thought I'd just been lucky.

"I truly believe that I received an MBO, although it certainly wasn't quite as I had envisaged. It had also never occurred to me that I wouldn't be bruised or in pain. Bless them, what a bonus! I have since received the results of the biopsy, and I'm pleased to say that I was given the 'all clear.' What a relief!"

Assuring the Health of an Unborn Child

Rose writes: "A few nights ago, my pregnant daughter-in-law thought that she was having a miscarriage. Since she has had one before, she was having an emotional breakdown over this. My daughter, a nurse, convinced her to go to the hospital just to be sure. After they left, I requested any and all beings to help her and the baby in the best and highest way possible.

"My daughter-in-law is only about nine weeks along. They went to the hospital but had to go back the next morning so she could have an ultrasound test. They found out that the baby is fine, and my daughter-in-law was diagnosed with a type of hematoma. She has to take it slow and easy for a while, but so far so good."

Good Blood Test Results and Healthy Blood Pressure

Antonia writes: "I had to get routine blood work done on Tuesday for cholesterol and diabetes. I said an MBO for the best result as it was being drawn. Today my doctor said all of my scores were normal for the first time in many years, and my blood pressure was 112/74. Usually it is 147/87. Thank you for sharing this process with us.

"If you find you are a little nervous when going to the doctor while waiting in the examination room, put your two thumbs and forefingers together and breath in through your nose to a count of 8, hold for a count of 8, out through thinly parted lips for a count of 8, hold for a count of 4, and then repeat this slow breathing exercise. You'll find your blood pressure will drop — at least it works for me."

Successful Treatment of Knee Pain

Jackie writes: "For weeks my wife has had a knee problem where the swelling and pain just won't go away. Finally we reached a point where we needed a specialist fast or we'd have to go to the ER. I made an MBO request because I knew how unrealistic it is to find an orthopedic surgeon on a Friday. I went down the list of options in our insurance and started calling. The first one wasn't open, the second couldn't see my wife until the next week at the absolute earliest, but the third said, 'Come on down!'

"They worked us in on a Friday afternoon, staying late without any glaring looks or resentment. The doctor was remarkably gentle and gave my wife a cortisone shot so she could start getting relief, and then he showed her an exercise to start physical therapy. The doctor even diagnosed her other knee with a partial tear. Not only did we learn my wife's injured knee wasn't torn, but now we know what was really torn in her bad knee! She's been slowly improving and strengthening while we wait for the results from the MRI, just to be sure. This MBO result left us both so grateful! It renewed my hope."

MBO for Quick Medical Attention

Jackie writes: "My wife is changing her medication, which is always challenging. We suspected her levels were too low and unsafe after a day, so we went to the emergency room. Both of us asked for an MBO for it to go quickly. She was given a room within minutes, even though other people had been waiting longer, and my wife didn't appear to be an emergency at the time. So that was one appreciated MBO. I suspect our other requests weren't agreeable to the doctor. Most doctors have strong wills and aren't as easy to convince when they are asked to do more than the normal, but at least our MBO for quick service was answered!"

Big Doctor Bill Benevolently Covered

Lee writes: "I went to the doctors in April for a checkup. I said an MBO request for a good report and small copay. Because of an insurance change, they said to wait and see what was paid and they would send a bill for the balance. I got the bill and was surprised that it was $153.47. My insurance usually pays more.

"Today I went to get the results of my blood work — which were excellent — and to pay the bill. Before I left, I said an MBO for great results and a more manageable balance to pay. When I checked out, the receptionist said my balance was $34.67. I asked about the past balance, and she said that was the past balance. There was no charge today because my doctor checked that it was my yearly physical, and I get one free visit per year. Thank you, thank you, thank you for MBOs and for always sharing your knowledge with us."

Smooth and Easy Visit to the Clinic

Patricia writes: "I would like to take this time to wish you and yours all the best in the new year. I never miss your newsletters, and I am so very thankful for your dedication to bringing others to the light through MBOs. I have seen my guardian angels make a 200 percent effort to answer my requests; everything I have asked them has instantly taken form.

"I had to see the doctor, as my feet were badly swollen, but my doctor was away. So I went to the clinic, which is an extremely busy place, with never less than a full house — often with twenty-five to thirty patients — from early morning to closing. There is usually a two- to three-hour wait. I said an MBO request for parking at the door, and I got one right in front. Then I asked for an MBO for a short wait and outcome."

"When I opened the door, there was one person ahead of me, and I was admitted in less than five minutes. As soon as I was called, the place filled up.

Later I had to go for blood tests again, so I asked for an MBO for parking and a short wait then too. Once again, I found parking at the door, and there was only one person ahead of me. As soon as I was registered, the place filled up again immediately. My son had driven me and didn't say a word until we got back home, then he asked me, 'What just happened in there?'"

Tom responds: Thanks, Patricia, for your inspiring story and reminding everyone that requesting benevolent outcomes truly does make your life easier and less stressful.

MBO for Medical Bill

Ron writes: "Here's another MBO story for you, Tom. My wife had to go into the hospital for some testing, and we don't have insurance for her now, so we got a bill for $3,000. She called the hospital to get financial help and they told her that they would take her information, name, phone number, and address and get back in thirty days. After she talked with them, she made an MBO request to have the medical bill paid in full.

"Thirty days later, she got the bill again with a letter stating that the balance had been adjusted to $0. How does it get any better than this? Thanks, Tom, for teaching us how to make MBOs, and I know that they work too. By the way, my bingo players are having fun too making their MBOs to win playing bingo."

A Benevolent Visit to the Orthodontist

Kelly writes: "The other day, as I drove my son to his orthodontist, he remarked, 'I hope it's good news.' I asked what that would be for him, and he said, 'To not have to wear my retainers anymore.' I immediately told him he should request an MBO. He's used to me advising him to do this as well as witnessing me create them myself; it happens a lot. I then immediately sent off a BP for him regarding the matter, and he softly murmured his own MBO request.

"Then, as we were about a block away, I realized I hadn't requested an MBO for a parking place close to the door, and we were really cutting it close in terms of time. So I quickly formed an MBO request for that parking place and, wouldn't you know it, as we pulled up, one spot right by the door was vacant! This had happened twice before — one time, I stated the MBO less than a block away and as we pulled up, a car was pulling out. That time had really bought my son's faith in the value of MBO requests; his eyes nearly popped out of their sockets in amazement.

"Well, as he was examined, the orthodontist noticed his old upper retainer had two springs missing. A bit concerned that if it were a big deal, we'd need to pay for a replacement, I quickly mentioned that the issue had been known for some time now and that my son only wears it to bed anyway. Then the doctor said, 'You actually don't need this anymore. Do you want to stomp on it?'. My son was grinning from ear to ear, although he declined stomping on it, preferring to save it. Then he was told he can wear his lower retainer even less than previously. He was truly convinced that the MBO request and the BP had worked.

"I realize that these things might sound like little things, but they happen constantly with the use of MBO requests in my life. I just wanted to be sure to send a note to extend my gratitude to you again for educating us all about them. Thank you, thank you, thank you!"

Easy Transportation to the Doctor's Office

Sandy writes: "I don't have a car and cannot drive, so I am dependent on the free taxi service provided by my health insurance. These taxis are notorious for snafus that leave people waiting for hours, stranded at home. So every time I must go to a doctor appointment, I request an MBO that I will be picked up for the trip to and from my doctor's office on time and without snafus. So far, it has worked like a charm."

Big Break on Pharmacy Bill

Lee writes: "Today was a day to expect great things! As you know, Tom, my husband has been in and out of the hospital this year. He went to the doctor for the third time this week after a hospitalization last week. I said a BP that his visit would be better than we could expect and any added charges would be cheaper than we could ever hope for. It turns out that he needs to do a series of shots for the next ten days, and the total charge for this will be $500. My husband was shocked and said he couldn't do that; it was just too much. The pharmacist told him to wait a minute while he checked on something. He came back and said that the insurance would cover the shots, so there was no charge. I still can't believe it. Thank you, thank you, thank you!"

11

Benevolent Outcomes for Surgeries and Medical Emergencies

Successful Knee Surgery

Patricia writes: "Well, I've had knee surgery, and it turned out perfectly. The doctor had said that he wouldn't be able to straighten my leg, as it was too bent. Well, I said the MBO request and the BP that you told me to just before going to sleep on the operating table:

> **Most Benevolent Outcomes**
> *"I ask any and all benevolent beings to assist the doctors and nurses to do their jobs safely and properly, and may the results be even better than we expect or hope for."*

"I now have a perfectly straight leg and no pain. I am just waiting now to have the other one done. I am seventy-six years old, and to walk again with straight legs is a blessing from heaven. Thank you beyond measure, Tom."

MBO Prevents a Potentially Fatal Accident

Linda writes: "It is only recently that I discovered your amazing website through the Faeries and Angels social network, and I have been putting requests for MBOs into practice with much delight. I have been asking for MBOs for just about everything, including an increase in business and treatments in my holistic-esoteric shop as well as for my own personal protection, safety, and personal healing due to a recent accident.

"I experienced a bad accident four days ago when I fell backward into a glass coffee table in the center of my lounge. A ten-inch-long piece of glass shaped like a dagger pierced the back of my right thigh just below the buttock and made its way through to the front of my body, coming out just below the hip. I remember falling and hearing the breaking of glass, but it seemed as if everything happened in slow motion. I lay there for a few seconds thinking, 'Hey, I think I am all right,' when to my horror, I felt the glass sticking out of my leg. When I pulled it out, I stared at the length of it in disbelief! I started bleeding profusely.

"I remember asking for MBOs while I was lying on the carpet with blood everywhere. I knew I wouldn't die if I requested MBOs, and I am sure that is what kept me alive until I was rushed off to the doctor's rooms, where I was treated for shock and stitched and bandaged for one and a half hours!

"I am thankful that it was the leg that was injured and not any vital organs; that piece of glass could have entered my body anywhere, and I put my luck down to the requests for MBOs I continued to say throughout the horrible ordeal, even though I knew you had mentioned that it was only necessary to ask for them once. I am ever so grateful to my guardian angel who stood by me and came to my rescue because of the MBO of protection I had requested earlier that day."

Tom responds: Let's all say a BP for Linda right now. BPs are what you say for other people, as a whole different set of angels handle these requests. When forming your BPs, it is important that you say "ask" instead of "request." I asked my guardian angel about this in meditation, and he said, "Go read a dictionary." And yes, there is a difference. So say the following out loud, since you're creating energy here:

> **Benevolent Prayer**
> *"I ask any and all beings to assist and aid Linda in her recovery, and may she recover faster than any of us can hope for or expect. Thank you!"*

Linda responds: "I'd like to send out a big thank you to you and to everyone else for the BPs that are being said for me. I have made such wonderful progress and am recovering from the injuries I sustained two weeks ago with the shard of glass in my leg. The stitches are all out, there is practically no scarring, and I am slowly gaining the strength back in my upper thigh muscle. Walking is no longer painful for me. So I am pretty much back to normal, and I love practicing my MBOs. How simple and powerful they are! Thank you for mentioning my story so that others may be inspired to make MBOs a part of their everyday lives. Expect great things!"

Benevolent Prayers for a Dying Son

Randy writes: "My older son Benjamin has inoperable brain cancer and he had a seizure last night. He wasn't coming out of it very well, so I asked for a BP for him, visualizing his body being surrounded by white light. He became cognizant within five minutes of that prayer. For anyone who would like to ask for a BP for my son, please do! Thank you for informing me about BPs and MBOs."

Tom responds: Let's all say out loud right now this BP for Randy's son Benjamin:

> **Benevolent Prayer**
> *"I ask any and all beings to aid, comfort, and bring healing energy to Benjamin in the most benevolent way, and assist his parents in finding the best treatments for his condition. Thank you!"*

Sleep, Dreams, and Benevolent Surgery

Eva writes: "I am reading your newsletter and following you on Facebook. I don't have the money to purchase your book, as I am strictly living on social security, but whatever I have available, I do read. Let me tell you what is happening with me now. I am seventy-one years young. Despite all the health issues I have — high blood pressure, diabetes, arthritis, and so on — I decided to go into the hospital on January 31 for a total replacement of my left knee. I have been experiencing a lot of pain.

"For ten days before surgery, I am not allowed to take any supplements. My pain is usually worst at night. The last few nights I asked my angels for an MBO to be able to have a painless deep sleep throughout the night — and I got it! Last night I also asked to remember my dreams in the morning, and for the first time, I did remember them. I will ask the sweet angels for an MBO for a successful surgery and for the least painful and fastest possible recovery."

Tom responds: I have found that when I have requested MBOs for my surgeries — even heart procedures — I have been completely calm and stress-free prior to the surgeries and have been able to joke with the nurses and doctors.

The arthroscopic surgery on my knee to repair two tears went smoothly. Naturally, I requested MBOs for everything, starting with one for my surgery to be early in the day. I was told my doctor's first surgery was at 7:30AM, which would have been a slow trip down the freeway in morning rush hour on Friday, so to be at the surgical facility for the surgery at 10:00AM turned out to be best for me, as traffic was quite steady — another successful MBO request.

At the surgical building, it was an easy check-in and my wife and I watched the news for a little while. The doctor came out to speak to the wife of another patient, so I asked him if he was running on time and he said there would be a twenty-minute delay. Still, they took us back to a pre-op private room with a TV. I was so calm I wound up dozing off, and the doctor had to rattle his book to wake me up when he came in. The anesthesiologist came in and said hello. I said a BP that all the doctors and surgical nurses would perform a perfect operation, with results even better than I could hope for or expect.

They inserted an IV, and the anesthesiologist came and said he was giving me something to relax me. I asked if I would be cognizant in the operating room, and he said I would be until he put me under, but I might not remember anything after the relaxer. I had hoped to say another BP in the operating room — and might have — but the last thing I remember was being wheeled down the corridor.

I woke up in the recovery room after what I was told was only a twenty-five-minute surgery, and they gave me crackers and grape juice. I even serenaded the nurses with some oldie-but-goodie songs. There was one nurse who became interested in my books, and I explained requesting MBOs to her. She wrote down my website and said she would check it out. They moved me to the discharge room about thirty feet away and my wife came in. I dressed, and then they put me in a wheelchair and rolled me out to the front driveway. Naturally, I requested an MBO for the drive home.

I'm now doing rehab and was told on the first day I was "ahead of the curve," and that is thanks to a lot of benevolent prayers many of you said for me. Another MBO was that the most experienced and knowledgeable physical therapist was assigned to work with me. I'm making great progress.

Angelic Anesthesia

Frani writes: "I have been doing energy work for over seventeen years and your book *The Gentle Way* has taken me to another whole level of being with angels. A friend gifted me your book and I read it in one evening.

"I used it instantly while doing my preparation for a routine colonoscopy. It helped so much. When I went in for the procedure, I made my requests every step of the way. The nurse who was to put in my IV was suddenly called away, and another nurse who happened to be more experienced came in and easily inserted the IV.

"Then, while waiting for the procedure to begin, a calmness flowed through me — almost a drugged feeling — and I asked if I had been given anesthesia. The nurse said, 'Not yet.' Almost humorously, she started shaking me and asking me to respond, which I could barely do. I was wheeled into the procedure room and I heard the doctor say, 'We'll start before you give her the meds.' Afterward, the doctor did confirm what I had heard and said that the littlest amount of anesthesia was used. I knew the angels had intervened on my behalf because I am allergic to so many medications.

"I have been sharing your book with my clients, and the instant connection to the angelic realm has provided such incredible love and healing. Thank you, thank you, thank you for sharing your book with the world."

MBOs and BPs for Surgery

MS writes: "I've been saying MBOs for a few days since first checking out Tom's website. I'm not sure whether it has made much of a difference for me yet. I already had a great relationship with my guardian angels and the archangels as well, and I have had many instances when I felt I had angelic assistance. I have had some of my MBOs answered in the positive, but they are things I would have just generally had a chat with my angels about anyway. After I say an MBO, I still just chat to them normally out of habit.

"I have no doubt that it works, though; any relationship you have with your angels has got to be good. I've said MBOs for a couple of things that a normal chat with my angels has had no results on, so I'm waiting to see how they go. I'm particularly interested in physical symptoms. I have a disfigurement that I'd rather not go into specifics about. A surgeon told me he can operate on it, but it's a difficult surgery, and he has doubts whether the results will last. I talk to my angels a lot about this and have come to the conclusion that it must be something I have to go through because of a prior soul contract. I have requested an MBO for this situation, but I know it will not be changed if it is indeed in my soul's path.

"I will continue to say MBOs, particularly for spiritual development and prosperity. I think they are a lovely way to communicate with the angels."

Tom responds: When preparing for the surgery, say,

Most Benevolent Outcome Request
"I request a most benevolent outcome for this surgery and may the results be even better than I can hope for or expect. Thank you!"

And then say a benevolent prayer for the surgery staff:

Benevolent Prayer
"I ask any and all beings to assist the doctors and nurses for this surgery today to operate to their highest peak of knowledge and professionalism. Thank you."

You can change this to fit your circumstances. When I had congestive heart failure a few years ago, I requested MBOs each time before a procedure and had absolutely no fear. I knew the results would be for the best, and when the first procedure of shocking my heart did not work, I knew that an even better result would occur the next time. I was even able to joke with the nurses and staff.

The second procedure was successful, but I was on medications afterward that affected my memory. So they did a third procedure that was only supposed to be 80 percent successful. But I knew it would be a full success, and it was. I was able to get off all the heart medications I had to be on after the second operation.

You are cocreating when requesting MBOs. My guardian angel says this is the big step of learning to be junior creators in training.

MBO for Surgery on a Newborn

Michael writes: "On April 7, my daughter-in-law Jen had a healthy baby girl. They came home on April 10. On April 11, the baby was running a fever, which finally broke that night. My son Chris sent a text at 9:40PM that evening, which said he had to take his daughter to the emergency room, straight to surgery. Immediately after receiving that text, I requested an MBO for any guardian angels around her to assist in the surgery.

"It's now 10:08 here and I just got a text. The surgery went well and is over. The doctor told Chris that not all of the placenta had been removed at the delivery. She will stay at the hospital tonight and, if there are no complications, go home tomorrow. All doubt is gone, Tom. Amazing results! I send thanks to all who offered assistance. I couldn't wait to tell you."

A Medical Emergency MBO

Teresa writes: "I just wanted to send an email about the value of habitually saying MBOs. I say MBOs every time I get in the car, before I start projects, and for business. My husband had a medical emergency last month. He passed out and fell hard on the floor. He was unconscious but moaning horribly. It was early in the morning and I was asleep, but the noise woke me and I immediately ran into the living room. I saw him on the floor, bleeding from a gash on his head, still moaning and still unconscious.

"Probably because I am in the habit of saying MBOs, I had the presence of mind to say a short one. I really don't even remember exactly what I said. About thirty seconds later, I was getting ready to call 911 when my husband became conscious, sat up, was lucid, and said he was not in any pain.

"We went to the emergency room where a CAT scan showed that he had blood clots in both lungs. Several doctors have said that he is the luckiest guy in the world to have survived that event. This happened just three days before he was going on an international flight. High altitude and prolonged sitting can actually cause or worsen blood clots.

"My husband normally has excellent health, but he had a back disk issue and was unable to exercise for several months. He also sat at the computer for extended periods. We now know you should get up every twenty to thirty minutes and stretch. I believe the MBO request really made a difference and that my husband's guardian angel was working overtime to keep him safe. I also realize it must not have been in his soul contract to cross over yet."

BPs for a Sister with Multiple Medical Issues

Sharyn writes: "I have had several MBOs that have come through for me as well as BPs for others. My sister who had a kidney transplant about six weeks ago had some further chaos with her medical challenges. I kept saying BPs for her, and she is doing so much better now after getting a stint placed in her heart and having a bypass in her leg. She had quite a run for the goal of recuperating. I am so thankful I have ways of talking to guardian angels — which I learned from you, of course. MBOs work most of time for me, and when they are on hold, I wait patiently, knowing all will be well in time! Thank you, Tom, for your graciousness!"

MBO Secures Last Visit with Dying Friend

Melissa writes: "My best friend has cancer, and I got the message that she would leave us in one to three days. I also knew that I wouldn't be able to visit her, since only the family is allowed to. She is in a coma, but I wanted to at least say goodbye and tell her what she means to me. She was the only person who supported me when others left. So, yes, I am very, very sad.

"Yesterday I drove to the hospital in the early morning, and before I went in, I made my MBO request, and they let me in! They said that normally they wouldn't have but that they would make an exception for me. So I was allowed to at least see her one last time to talk to her and tell her that I am waiting for her with fresh coffee and that angels are watching over her. I guess that will be the last time I will see her alive, but I am thankful that my guardian angel helped me get through this. Even my friend wondered how I made it in to see her."

Successful Surgery

Keisha writes: "I had surgery on November 30. Everything went well, and I am now home recuperating. I used the MBO requests you suggested, and I'm sure they helped. Once again, thank you for your kindness and compassion. Please let me know if you are ever in Michigan speaking. I would love to meet you."

Tom responds: I'll be happy to come when some group there sponsors me!

Benevolent Prayers for Healing

Carol writes: "About a month ago I wrote you asking for a BP for a friend of mine who had a brain hemorrhage and required brain surgery. Not only did I use the prayer you suggested, but I posted it on my Facebook page for all my friends to say as well. The doctors originally did not know if my friend would be able to speak or walk again after the surgery.

"I am happy to report she just left the hospital last Sunday after a month there with some rehab, and not only can she walk and talk but much of her memory is coming back too! The doctors said when they discharged her they expected a full recovery. She still has some healing and therapy to complete, and that may take a bit, but her family, friends, and I can't be more pleased. Thank you for your help."

Tom responds: A typical BP you can say for a person in the hospital might be said as follows:

> **Benevolent Prayer**
> *"I ask any and all beings to send healing energy to _____, and may their recovery be even faster than we can hope for or expect. Thank you!"*

A Nasty Spill Leads to Positive Life Lessons

Annette writes: "I had a very stressful time when we were beginning work on writing our RFP (request for proposal) for our federal contract at work. I had left my second job to be available to work on this. Honestly, after sitting in a few meetings, I did not want to be involved — my gut told me we would lose a portion of our contract — but this was part of my job. My friends and family had been telling me that I needed a break after working two jobs for three years while dealing with my Dad's passing with my Mom 800 miles away, and the contract issues at work were just too stressful. My guardian angel kept telling me that I needed to get some rest, and I would often reply, 'I can't take a break right now; I'll take one when all this is over.'

"On December 24, at 7:45 in the morning, I fell and broke my ankle outside of a shopping center while getting a last-minute Christmas gift on my way to the office. It looked like something from a cartoon: I slipped on some ice, and one leg went one way and one went the other. I landed on my more-than-ample backside and slid down the ice. Since I was wearing boots with excellent tread, when my foot hit the pavement, my right leg twisted up behind me and I ended up with a nice spiral fracture, a dislocated foot and ankle, and a few other interesting but minor injuries. The first person to see me was an off-duty paramedic who came running to me, followed by an on-duty police officer.

"In the emergency room, I had to wear the new flannel pajamas I had picked up for myself as an impulse buy — they were only five dollars! — after they cut my jeans away. They reset the ankle but told me that I would need surgery on the leg and would have to wait a week to let all the swelling go down. As I lay in the emergency room for what ended up being ten hours, I heard my guardian angel say, *'You needed to take a break.'*

"I had a great pity party Christmas morning, as I was in some pain, and I had surgery a week later. My husband was such an angel! I was out of the office for eight weeks and in a wheelchair for twelve weeks. While I was out of the office, the person one of the managers wanted to write the RFP got to write it, and I worked some from home with our budget officer.

"Throughout this experience, I learned several lessons — some serious and some humorous — all of which made a big impact on me and facilitated changes that have been positive. Be careful what you ask for — in my case, not wanting to work on the RFP — and listen to your guardian angels when they are looking out for your health; they have your best interests at heart.

"I also learned that my guardian angel has a sense of humor even while taking care of me completely; from the off-duty paramedic and the police officer to the flannel pajamas, my guardian angel had everything ready. So sometimes what seems at first to be a negative thing can turn out to be a positive thing. Slow down and smell the roses, everyone!"

Miraculous Foot Recovery

Jackie writes: "We just returned home from urgent care with a good MBO result. Two days ago my wife fell down some stairs. She hurt the top of her foot, but we weren't too worried. Today she stepped down and had a lot more pain and much swelling, so we went to urgent care to get x-rays. While in the waiting area, we made an MBO request for the foot to not be broken and for the x-ray to be beneficial. Almost immediately my wife's foot started to tingle internally in the area of the most pain. A few minutes later they did the x-ray, and it was clear. No breaks!

"We believe the MBO healed her foot, though under normal circumstances this wouldn't be the case. But with all the other things my wife is facing, spontaneous healing was the most benevolent outcome for her. Woohoo! I was told by my wife's guides not to say that this happened for sure because it could cause people to avoid the doctor, thinking they could request an MBO and just be healed. But the guide said there were two fractures in her foot before we requested the MBO. We're very grateful."

An Injury in the Shower Takes a Benevolent Turn

Mary writes: "I would like to share my MBO story with you and your readers. I am a devout reader of your newsletter and blog. I had been doing MBO requests for approximately six months when one morning, still half asleep, I slipped and fell out of the shower tub. As I was falling, I had a thought to say, 'Guardian angel, help me!' I believe that saying that saved my left knee. As I was slipping, I could feel my knee twisting with all my weight on it. I thought for sure that I would end up in the hospital needing surgery on my knee.

"I did end up going to the ER; my blood pressure was sky high because of the pain. I got a pain shot and pills, along with orders for no weight bearing for one day and then to increase weight bearing with each passing day. I did say MBO requests to be seen at the ER quickly, to be correctly diagnosed, and to receive proper treatment. I also asked for pain relief and for healing energies to come to me. My ER visit was very quick and I was seen as soon as I signed up. As my visit came to an end, ambulances showed up with motor vehicle accident patients, so my timing was perfect.

"In the coming days and weeks, I used EFT (emotional freedom techniques) tapping for the pain, which helped a lot. I have two young children and a husband to take care of. Without MBOs and EFT, I would have been in so much miserable pain. I am thankful for these tools that empower us. Thank you, Tom, for the work you do to get MBOs out to as many people as possible."

A Difficult Night at the Hospital

Marie writes: "I apply MBO requests to my daily life and to my job as a nurse, telling my patients about it to help them heal. I deal with sickness and sometimes death with my job, and MBO requests help to lessen the physical and emotional exhaustion I deal with most of the time. What is the proper wording to request MBOs if you are a nurse? Thank you very much, from the bottom of my heart!"

Tom responds: Regarding working in a hospital, here are a couple of suggestions, both for MBO requests and BPs, for anyone working in a health facility:

Most Benevolent Outcome Requests

"I request a most benevolent outcome for my work day, and may it be even better than I can hope for or expect. Thank you!"

"I request a most benevolent outcome for bringing the best care and attention to my patients today. Thank you!"

Benevolent Prayer

"I ask any and all beings to bring healing and love to all the patients in this hospital today in the most benevolent manner possible. Thank you!"

Marie replies: "Thank you for the reply. I also had a patient who died just a few days ago. I requested an MBO for him, but I knew his death was inevitable, because his condition had severely deteriorated. He died on my shift, and his code status was DNR — that is, "Do Not Resuscitate." I was with the family members the whole night, helping them to get through the whole sad situation. I was extremely busy that night with a difficult patient load — one on suicide watch and one dying. It looked like I would have to work overtime to finish the paperwork, charting, and so on, and that I would end up getting home very late.

"I was emotionally drained. I rarely get dying patients on my assignments — this is the second one in my fifteen-year nursing career — so I'm not used to dealing with death. I like to see my patients get well and go home; I try to give the very best nursing care to each of my patients every night. I really love my job as a nurse and tremendously enjoy helping people to heal. I was born to be a healer.

"In any case, the family members were very appreciative of my caring and compassion. I told them, 'I should be the one who needs to be strong for you,' but I was a wreck. They were the ones comforting me. I was the one who was crying, so they cried too. They were of Iranian origin, and the sister — whom I became very close with — was on exactly the same wavelength as I was when

I talked about guardian angels and balancing past lives and soul contracts.

"After that long night, I actually finished early with paperwork, and I know my guardian angel helped me to handle the situation and overcome my fear of dying patients, allowing me to connect with another person who knew what I was talking about regarding guardian angels. Thank you for this nurse's MBOs!"

MBO at Emergency Ward

Lisa writes: "I've been following you for about eight months now and love reading your MBO stories, so I thought I'd let you know mine from last night. I work the night shift as a nurse and had just arrived at work when I got a phone call from my husband that our eleven-year-old son had been involved in an accident. He and his friends had been playing about on a gate, and he had jumped off. The gate, which was a very heavy metal farm gate, had then swung full speed into his face.

"I was horrified, and my husband sounded like he was in shock. He repeatedly said, 'It's really bad' and told me they were on their way to the emergency ward at another hospital. I knew I needed to go and be with them, but our hospital was very busy and understaffed, and I was the only trained nurse in my ward. However, I was given an hour or so of cover from another ward since it was an emergency, even though that left them dangerously short.

"I prayed all the way to the hospital and said my MBO and 'any and all beings' prayers frantically. I protect my son every day with the angels' help, so I felt confident they would be there with him. I arrived at the hospital at the same time as my husband and son, and yes, it did look bad! His wee face was distorted by swelling, and there was a lot of blood.

"When we arrived at the emergency ward, I was conscious that I would be torn between needing to be there for my son and knowing I had left the ward where I work short. However, without a doubt, my son's needs would be taking priority over my work! Well, we were taken almost straight away in the emergency ward by a nurse I knew, which was very comforting. My son was taken quickly on to see the doctor via triage. He was examined and sent straight away to get an x-ray, as the doctor quietly told us that he suspected a fracture or break to the bones in my son's face.

"I was praying the whole time, and as a Reiki master, I was also sending him Reiki to comfort and heal him. We were taken straight away to the x-ray area and then back to get the results. Amazingly, there were no breaks or fractures! It was only surface damage and swelling. Now how could a heavy metal farm gate hit an eleven-year-old child full in the face without leaving at least a broken nose?

"The angels were indeed present. My son was discharged and sent home. I went back to work and all in all was only gone from my ward for one hour and fifteen minutes. Now I call that a miracle! Thank you, angels, and thank you, Tom. We are blessed indeed!"

Benevolent Stroke Recovery

Bruce writes: "On Friday, October 7, I had a mini-stroke, unbeknownst to me, as my right arm became weak and then I lost control of it for a few minutes. The event lasted for about fifteen to thirty minutes. I rationalized the experience away and thought that I was just tired or had had too much caffeine. This happened two more times in the next few days while I continued to stay in denial about what was happening. Then on Tuesday, October 11, 2011, I was out on the patio sunning, and I dozed off. When I awoke, I couldn't talk correctly: My words were slurred, and I couldn't get the right words to come out.

"Instead of panicking, I simply observed the speech event as an outside observer. My speech began to return after about thirty minutes, so I called my life partner, Charlotte, who is a special education teacher, and she came home. We then went to the emergency room of the local hospital. Charlotte had written me a note that morning before she went to school that said, 'What new and magical experiences await us this day will be a wonderful discovery.' How prophetic that statement would prove to be for us!

"As an aside, I was led by Spirit to come to the small Texas shrimping village where we now live in March 2011, to be with my life partner, Charlotte, after reconnecting on Facebook through an MBO. We had been apart and out of touch for thirty-seven years. The tiny town we live in has a four-bed hospital with no doctors, but it has a great physician's assistant, RNs, and medical staff.

"I was, at that time, a month away from being covered by Medicare and had no other insurance. So the physician's assistant called around to all the hospitals and doctors, trying to find a bed for me, as the local hospital did not have a neurological or cardiovascular department. At this point, I requested an MBO that a hospital and doctor be found that would be for my best and highest good and that it would be better than I could imagine or expect. The emergency staff performed a CAT scan, and it was determined that I was in stress and was suffering mini-strokes. The PA and staff kept trying every hospital in the area for hours.

"In the middle of the night, a hospital with a doctor who would accept me was finally found. As it turned out, it was the most prestigious hospital in Texas; I feel that the doctor, who I had never met, accepted me at the direction of Spirit. I was driven there by ambulance, two hours away, by two very caring EMTs. The hospital is a luxury hospital located in Houston that specializes in heart, vascular, and neurological areas, and they treated me like I was a VIP.

"The staff's hospitality was amazing throughout my stay. They ran every test possible on me the next day, including an MRI and several ultrasounds on my heart and vascular system as well as EEGs and EKGs. My primary doctor informed me that I had not only had multiple mini-strokes but also a full-blown stroke as well, though with negligible effects. And I don't have any effects that can be seen by others.

"The staff performed a carotid endarterectomy on me on Thursday, October 13. The surgery went perfectly and was performed by one of the best and kindest surgeons in the hospital, and that fact was confirmed by many of the different departments and personnel I came in contact with. I spent two days in the ICU, where the staff were also amazing, and then I spent my last night with my life partner in a special private room that was specifically arranged for us.

"I can't begin to adequately relate all of the synchronicities and spiritual events that occurred while Charlotte and I were there, but it was indeed a blessed event full of wonderful discoveries, even considering the reason I was there. We both intuitively recognized many of the staff as reincarnationally significant to us, including the doctor and surgeon.

"The hospital administration asked me about the financial end of it on the first day and then never mentioned it again after I told them that I had no insurance — not even when I was discharged. The last thing that my primary doctor asked me to do as he left our room on Saturday morning, the day that we returned home, was that I personally thank the PA at our local hospital, who had gone out of his way to secure a doctor and hospital for me. Now that I am recovering, this will be done, as this is a very important piece of this particular MBO and its closure. The fact that this very busy and prestigious doctor would remember the PA in this small town is very significant as well. At no time did I ask 'Why me?' Instead, I accepted each moment with complete faith and trust in Spirit.

"All of this came about because I asked that one MBO of my guardian angel. I had been using a form of MBO requests intuitively for years, but I didn't really get the process down until I was led to Tom and *The Gentle Way* in 2008. After that, I had two significant visions that I related to Tom in 2009 and 2010, and he related them to his guardian angel. It was discovered that Tom and I had used MBO requests together in ancient Atlantis and Egypt. I had been Tom's understudy in the priesthood that led thousands of his flock — who all practiced MBO requests — from Atlantis before its fall to Egypt in a lifetime that occurred chronologically about 12,800 years ago.

"My suggestion is that all of you use MBOs daily as many times during the day as you want and for anything and everything, as they raise your vibrational frequency each time you use them. They may not always turn out exactly the way you envision them, but what will happen will always be most benevolent for all concerned."

Group MBOs Help in a Medical Emergency

Sue writes: "Here's an MBO story from the time when my sister was in the pre-operative area while waiting to go into the operating room. She had to arrive a little early for a test to be done before the surgery, and then the surgery before her took longer than they anticipated, so she ended up being in the pre-op area for several hours. My two sisters, our good friend Linda, and I all do Reiki and also regularly say MBOs, so between the three of us, we had asked Archangel Michael to remove all negative energy from the surgical center and flood it with divine energy. We also asked for thousands of angels to be present as well and MBOs for the surgeon's hands and so on. They normally allow only one person to be in pre-op with the patient, but since she was there so long, they let two of us be with her.

"While the two of us were giving her Reiki, one of us commented that the energy didn't feel good — not bad, but not good either, just heavy and hard to explain. My sister said that she had heard several of the staff commenting that they were all having a strange day — that equipment wasn't working properly, that they'd been having trouble hitting veins, and other things that normally did not happen to them. We also noticed that the staff in the area didn't look too happy. As I sat in her area next to her bed, I said,

Benevolent Prayer
"I request that any and all beings aid and comfort all of the staff in this pre-op area. Thank-you."

Then I thought to expand the request to include all of the staff in the surgical center and then all of the patients and families and friends. I figured that should cover everyone.

"Literally within minutes, my sister said, 'Listen!' and guess what we heard? Laughter from the staff! She said that she had not heard that in the three hours she had been there. You could just see the difference in everyone; it was so amazing, and it continued for the rest of the afternoon. Another wonderful, instant benevolent outcome!

"Something I have started doing with my brother, two sisters, and our friend is that when we are in a situation where we are together and want to request MBOs — such as in the pre-op area — I suggest we brainstorm what ways we can request the MBO. For my sister's surgery, I started by saying,

Most Benevolent Outcome Request
"I request an MBO to have all of the medical equipment working properly."

Our friend then said,

"And for all of the medicines to work properly."

My sister added a request:

'that she wake up easily and quickly in a benevolent way."

"We all three said 'thank you!' together. It was fun because we all thought of different things, and it just felt great to come up with the ideas together. It made us feel so much better, the way one suggestion led to another and another and so on. How's that for a benevolent outcome of feeling comfortable saying MBOs?"

Tom responds: That was great!

Mother's MBO Brings a Miraculous Recovery for Her Daughter

Susannah writes: "I requested two MBOs recently. My daughter Alexandra was admitted to our local hospital recently with worrisome symptoms. She had severe pain behind her eye and in the left side of her neck, stomach, and ankle. Prior to her admission, she had slowly been going downhill; there was a period of one week in which she was not able to walk properly and could not put any weight on her left side. Her vision and hearing were also being affected, and it looked rather grim.

"My daughter has a condition called neurofibromatosis type 1, and there were concerns that she had tumors in her brain and spinal cord. She had been given the all-clear some years ago, as there were no lisch nodules in her eyes. Academically, she is very bright, apart from some mild ADD symptoms that I believe simply need to be channeled into creative pursuits because she is very artistic.

"They decided to admit her to the hospital because they had looked in her eyes and run some eye tests and became very concerned, and so did I. The week she was in the hospital, I requested MBOs that she be healed; that when the MRI was done on her head and spine, it would be clear; and that whatever was causing these symptoms would dissipate and be gone for good. Lo and behold, the MRI results came in totally clear — no tumors anywhere! Alexandra is now home, walking and running, and all her symptoms are gone. It is a miracle, indeed!"

Benevolent Cancer Treatment

Gerry writes: "I use MBOs all the time for everyday things, but I thought I would tell you about a biggie. The week before Christmas, I had been feeling weak and short of breath, so I went to the emergency room. I thought I would get an antibiotic and be feeling good by Christmas; instead, they said I was extremely anemic and admitted me to find out where the blood was going.

"They did extensive tests and found a large, cancerous tumor in my colon and immediately scheduled blood transfusions and surgery. I requested MBOs for the surgeon to get it all so I would not have to have chemo, for no pain afterward, and for a fast healing. That's exactly what happened — no chemo, no pain, and a fast healing."

12

Benevolent Outcomes for Peace of Mind

MBO for Help Sleeping

Carell writes: "Here's an MBO story. I've been having challenges with sleep apnea and getting the proper resolutions to my issues of snoring, talking in my sleep — in French! — and my throat closing off at night. Sleep apnea gives you morning brain fog, headaches, and low energy. It also makes you put on the pounds.

"I recently requested an MBO for all of these issues, despite the fact that my doctor won't schedule my sleep study till August 6. Lo and behold, just five days ago, one of my healing arts colleagues sent me info on essential oils, noting that when applied to the pads of the big toes at bedtime, thyme oil treats the respiratory tract, reduces snoring, and alleviates the symptoms of apnea. Madame Doubting Thomas here thought, 'Fat chance,' but since I had some on hand, I tried it and it works!

"I've had four wonderful nights of sleep now — no snoring and no philosophizing in French. And I wake up early and feeling alive, instead of waking at noon and feeling groggy. Now my mornings are fine, and I'm getting my life back. Yay for MBOs!"

A Prayer for Protection and Calm

Kimberly writes: "Tom, you have requested that we share our MBOs and BPs with you, so here is a simple one I have begun to use daily as a mom new to the world of high school freshman football:

> **Benevolent Prayer**
> *"To any and all beings, please watch over, guide, and protect my son on the field and assist in keeping me from panicking over it. Thank you."*

"It is working for both of us! Much thanks for sharing and reminding us to rely on assistance."

Helping the Stressed and Depressed

Diane writes: "How do you say an MBO for a person you love who suffers from depression and is stressed out? It seems a lot of people get stressed out over things like bills, money, and so on. So how do we handle it ourselves to keep balanced, and how do we request that our angels help the other person? I need a little guidance here. Thank you. I'm always expecting great things!"

Tom responds: You can say this BP:

Benevolent Prayer
"I ask that any and all beings send massive amounts of loving energy and pink light to _____ , who is stressed and depressed, and assist them in feeling better about themselves and know they can contribute to society too. Thank you!"

There are other, different BPs you can make up yourself to say on other days that pertain to your loved one's specific situation.

A Sober Request

Clay writes: "As a forty-year member of AA, each night I have a little chat with my higher power, whom I choose to call God. I thank him for another sober day and sometimes ask for guidance and help for others. Rarely do I ask for anything for myself, except to maybe cut me some slack if I have had a minor screw-up.

"Now if I switch to the more formal ritual of the MBO request, it makes me uneasy — as if I am visiting with two bosses, if you will. I suspect this is not a problem that you are hearing for the first time. Could you please address this? Thanks again; I enjoy and learn from our weekly visit."

Tom responds: My guardian angel has told me that guardian angels are "servants of the Creator," or God, as you prefer. When you pray to God, your prayer is filtered through your own guardian angel according to your soul contract. You can believe it's going directly to God — that's okay, and I've said that many times. MBO requests work no matter what your belief is, and I've said you can believe the requests are going to God, Jesus, Allah, or some Hindu deity — it does not matter.

When you begin requesting MBOs for everything in your life, you have begun cocreating with Spirit — the first major step. So if you wish to, say the same prayer each night and then afterward say,

Most Benevolent Outcome Request
"I request a most benevolent outcome for staying sober all day tomorrow. Thank you."

Then you should feel you are covered. This MBO request will allow things to work for you so you are not put in front of alcohol in some way you cannot expect or know about before the day begins or into a situation in which you might feel you cannot handle the stress. My mother was a member of AA for many years. She's one of my guides now for all things feminine, as the majority of people who read my newsletter are women.

MBOs Can Ease Times of Sadness

Carell writes: "My dear white-yellow lab had to be put down last Monday, which meant another vet bill. So I made an MBO request and ended it with this:

Most Benevolent Outcome Request
"And may the vet bill be easy and effortless — way better than anything I've been expecting — and with results beyond my wildest imagination."

"As I left the vet's office, so bleary-eyed with tears that I could barely sign the consent form in the first place, the vet said I could leave by the side door and bypass the office. 'But I have to pay,' I said. She replied, 'No worries, dear. We'll send a bill at the end of the month.' That's exactly what I needed, as most of my income arrives in late September."

Benevolent Outcomes for Addictions

Brenda writes: "First off, I want to thank you for all that you do with the MBOs. Since I have been saying them, my life is definitely better. We are all truly blessed! I have a question: How would I ask for an MBO for an alcohol addiction? Thank you so much for your help!"

Tom responds: If you have an addiction to alcohol, or for that matter, any other addictions such as drugs, eating, and so forth, say,

Most Benevolent Outcome Request
"I request a most benevolent outcome to be sent healing energy for my addiction at this time and to be led to the best treatments for me. Thank you!"

For someone you know, you can say this BP:

Benevolent Prayer
"I ask any and all beings to send healing energy to _____ and to lead them to the best treatments for their addiction. Thank you!"

Slow Down and Listen to Your Guides

DeLeah writes: "Here is a story you can use. I requested an MBO to be guided to what steps I need to take in my life next with results even better than I could expect or hope for. A few days after I said this, I hurt my ankle badly. I have been on light duty for a week now. I am getting the message loud and clear to slow down, to take time to listen to my guides and angels, to realize there are endings coming for me career-wise, and to stop pushing and trying to control the situation. I know now I need to relax and let things come about in a divine way."

Special Hugs

Christa writes: "Yesterday I felt down about something and just couldn't shake my sadness. I also felt very lonely, so I requested an MBO asking the angels for a hug. I felt better immediately. I also asked for an MBO for a human hug, and later during the day, the cleaning lady at our company — a wonderful soul — spontaneously came over to my desk and hugged me. She has never done this before. Another colleague — she's also a friend — also gave me a huge bear hug out of the blue."

A Gentle Passing for My Father

Cary writes: "My father had a massive stroke, so I went to the hospital, asking for MBOs to get there safely. One driver almost side-swiped me in Houston, but I avoided that. I arrived at my father's side, and the neurologist gave us the rundown and pictures of my father's brain, which was fried, and his prognosis. I asked for MBOs for a gentle departure for him.

"The angels were there with me. I like to work with Michael, Ariel, Gabriel, Raphael, and Uriel. It was only five nights before I had a spell and called all angels into my room and placed Herkimer diamonds in the four corners of the room to increase the energy. I was in a trance state, sometimes laughing and sometimes crying. Six days later, my father experienced a gentle departure.

"I drove back to Houston to retrieve my son and asked for MBOs for each trip and received them. Today, I attended my father's memorial service south of Houston. I asked for MBOs of safe travel and received them. I have received benefits every day from the angels and MBO prayers. I plan to receive many, many more.

"When my father was in limbo with his body, I found myself digging through my desk. I found a copy of a poem he wrote not long after my mother passed in 2007. It is titled, 'My Wish.' I published it on my Facebook page and it was printed in the memorial pamphlet. It was an MBO that helped me to find that poem and share it with the world."

Benevolent Prayer for a Troubled Brother

Rodger writes: ""Here's a big one: My brother is very affected with dementia. He was so brilliant before. What sort of request should I use to help others I love? Is it different from a personal MBO?"

Tom responds: In my first book I called them living prayers, but for the second book I worked the request into more simplified wording and it became a benevolent prayer (BP). You could say,

Benevolent Prayers
"I ask any and all beings to assist my brother with coping with his dementia and to send lots of healing energy to him. Thank you!"

You can also say,

"I ask any and all beings to assist my brother to find the best treatments and caretakers for his condition. Thank you!"

MBO for Mother's Rest Home

Suzanne writes: "My mother's dementia was getting worse, and we wanted to get her into a good care home within the following few months. So my brothers and I looked around at a few, but none seemed quite right. So I requested an MBO for the best local care home to be found quickly and for the best bedroom in it to become available without any waiting lists.

"Presto! My brother and I found a great care home with lively and happy residents; we had our eye on a great bedroom with an in-suite toilet and an alcove for a small lounge area of its own, although the alcove housed another resident. The care home manager agreed to come and assess Mum the following week, at which point she said to me that an identical room to the one we wanted was likely to be free at the end of that week.

"By the Monday of the following week, mum was in that home. And unlike the room we first saw, my mum's room was on the ground floor straight outside the manager's office, opposite the bathroom, and next to the lounge and dining area. That means Mum has less chance of getting lost in the corridors or elsewhere. So we got the perfect care home, the perfect room for her, and her condition was spot on for the timing to be right. Thank you to the powers that be!"

MBO for Quiet Weekend

Cindy writes: "Here's kind of a different MBO. My husband was going away for the weekend to coach a high school baseball tournament. They had just hired a new coach who was going along too. So I thought I would be nice and ask his wife and daughter if they wanted to come over to spend some time in the pool.

"Well, after I asked and they accepted, I sort of wanted to just have a nice relaxing weekend alone. I actually requested an MBO that they would either have other plans or some reason for them not to come over would come up. About forty-five minutes before we were to connect by phone, the wife called to say her daughter wasn't really feeling well. So now I get my 'alone time' weekend. It's funny how all we have to do is ask!"

13

Benevolent Outcomes for Relationships

Forgiveness

Joan writes: "I need your help on a matter. I have a friend who has a hard time forgiving. I have forgiven him, but he still holds on to what happened in the past. Is there a way I could go about helping him — with the help of my guardian angels, of course — without him knowing it? I know he still loves me, and I still love him, but he won't let go of the past. If your guardian angel has any help to offer, please let me know."

Tom responds: My guardian angel always tells me that he can't tell me which road to take; we're supposed to make those decisions ourselves. I think trying to recover a relationship or moving on falls under that category. However, you or anyone else in similar circumstances can certainly say,

> **Most Benevolent Outcome Request**
> "I request a most benevolent outcome for my relationship to improve with _____, and may the results be even better than I can hope for or expect. Thank you!"

You can also say,

> **Benevolent Prayer**
> "I ask any and all beings to assist _____ in forgiving me so that we can be close again. Thank you!"

Finally, while you may not like this last one, I think it's necessary to say it in case your soul contract is to move on so that you can meet someone else:

> **Most Benevolent Outcome Request**
> *"I request a most benevolent outcome for all emotional energy cords that are not in my best interest to be severed. Thank you!"*

If the ties that bind you to this person are still in your best interest, they will not be cut.

A Request for Peace and Harmony

Diane writes: "When someone is angry with you, what is a good MBO request to use to quiet the situation and bring peace and harmony back?"

Tom responds: How about,

> **Most Benevolent Outcome Request**
> *"I request a most benevolent outcome for my relationship with _____. Thank you"?*

You can also send pink light to them; just imagine that they are being surrounded with beautiful, pink, loving light.

Repaired Relationship with Daughter-in-Law

Wendy writes: "My daughter-in-law decided years ago that she was not going to like me. I tried in every way I knew how to show her that I am a kind and loving person. It did not seem to work. She ignored me quite blatantly.

"Recently, my son brought his wife and kids to visit us in Costa Rica for a few weeks. This was the first time my grandkids came to visit and the first time in eight years my daughter-in-law had come. She completely ignored me for the first week in our mountain home. Then we headed to the beach where she continued ignoring me for a few more days.

"I finally broke down and told my son that I could not spend time around them any longer, as it hurt me to be treated this way and felt very abusive considering all I do for them and their kids. I then sat down with my son and daughter-in-law to express my sadness and my feelings. She refused to speak to me.

"So I left and went to my daughter's house and finally asked my guardian angel for an MBO with my daughter-in-law. I was ready to leave them with my other kids and head home to the mountains. My son came and asked me to go speak to his wife. I was unsure if this could finally be a change, since she has been this way toward me for nine years. But I am always willing to try, so I went and found her a completely different woman.

"We spoke for forty-five minutes and she was open with me, she was herself, and she was kind. It was totally amazing. We talked about all the things that had happened in the past and agreed to start fresh and forgive and love each other.

"Wow, the rest of their visit was great! We returned to the mountain together and my husband saw a completely different daughter-in-law. I know if it were not for my guardian angel, the visit would have ended sorrowfully. Instead it ended joyfully, and they want to come back next year. Thank you, thank you, thank you!"

A Tragedy Averted

Florence writes: "I really have to send my thanks to you this week for the gift of MBOs; it may have saved a life! I will try to condense my story as much as possible. A long-time friend has a son — let's call him John — who has been involved in a fairly turbulent and traumatic relationship. He and his partner have been together for over four years, and at their ages, that might as well be a lifetime! This relationship has caused serious problems in the past, including an argument ending in one of them being sent to the emergency room from a self-inflicted stab wound to the abdomen — that was my friend's son.

"To make a very long story short, they had recently broken up, but due to living and financial arrangements had spent the last week together at the apartment they share. Well, as many of us more experienced individuals know, this is a recipe for disaster. At 5:30AM on Tuesday morning, my phone rang, and I answered half asleep. It was John, barely coherent and in tears, begging for me to allow him to take a taxi to my house but to not call his mother. In my fogginess, I agreed after asking all the relevant questions. It was clear to me that he was intoxicated and very, very sad. Now, I do not live alone, and needless to say, this did not go over well with the other members of my household.

"Feeling frantic and anxious, I requested an MBO for my situation with John. I decided to call his mother, which I decided to do out of the blue, since I would have normally kept my word and kept his secret. She was aware of their fight, as it had been going on all night. I told her I was going to have him redirect his taxi to her place but to keep cool. I called John on his cell, and he was able to turn back toward his mom's place, albeit very reluctantly.

"To fast-forward, by 8:45AM John and his mom were in an ambulance on the way to the emergency room because John had taken a handful of pills! If he had come to my home, I would have allowed him to just have some space by himself and be alone, and I would have assumed he was sleeping. He had the pills with him and I am guessing he had every intention of using them. Thankfully, they were able to help him at the hospital, and he is now at home, although feeling embarrassed and sad. I must add that his mom also requested an MBO when deciding whether or not to call the ambulance, since she was not certain if he had taken pills or was still just drunk and tired.

"I have been spreading the word as much as possible, since I am convinced this has altered the course of my life. I now wake up upbeat and expecting great things! I use the affirmations and have added to them to make them more specific to my life and circumstances. So although words are not enough, I thank you from the deepest part of my soul."

Will Her Ex Return?

Linda writes: "Could you please ask your guardian angel or Gaia if Mario, my ex-husband, is the man I am to get back with, or is it a new man? Thank you again for all that you do."

Tom responds: My guardian angel always says that your guardian angel cannot tell you which path to take. That's why you request MBOs — in order to stay on your soul path or soul contract, as he calls it. So you should say,

> **Most Benevolent Outcome Request**
> *"I request a most benevolent outcome for the perfect man for me. Thank you!"*

That way, if your ex is that man, he'll get back together with you, and if not, you'll find someone else appearing in your life.

You can also say,

> **Most Benevolent Outcome Request**
> *"I request a most benevolent outcome for all energy cords that are no longer in my best interest to be severed at this time. Thank you!"*

This helps you get rid of any old ties to people not in your best interest, and if your ex is on that list, it will assist you in moving on. If he's not on the list, it will not affect anything. Only your guardian angel knows.

Confusing Relationship with an Old Friend

Clairese writes: "A friend from about twenty-eight or so years ago has come back into my life, and I have been trying to figure out why. During those years, we ran into each other maybe three times — that is, until the last time we ran into each other at a Walmart.

"After talking by phone, he told me his wife had died of heart failure on November _____, 2009. That happens to be my birthday. Is there any significance to this or to me running into him at the Walmart after so long a time? He's been so lonely and celibate — and so have I. This must mean something. I have been praying for the reason to be revealed to me. Can you shed any light on this whole scenario? Thank you for all you do and share."

Tom responds: For Clairese and anyone else meeting up with old friends or lovers, remember that life has many surprises for us. As my guardian angel says, we would be bored if we knew everything in advance! These surprises can be happy or sad. In this case, I think both of you are tuning into each other. But also keep in mind that it usually takes people about two years to go through the grieving process. You can be good friends now, and perhaps it will become even more interesting — only time will tell — but I do suggest you say the following MBO:

> **Most Benevolent Outcome Request**
> *"I request a most benevolent outcome for my relationship with _____, and may the results be even better than I hope for or expect. Thank you!"*

If it is in your soul contract, then the relationship will continue to blossom, and if not, you will remain good friends and perhaps drift apart again. That's the beauty of life. You have to live it. I do find it interesting that his wife passed on your birthday — perhaps that was her last gift to him?

A Lover in a Faraway Land

Norma writes: "I am fairly new to your blog and MBOs, but I love reading the newsletter every week. I practice my MBOs and have told friends and family about them. I have a question that I know may be difficult to answer, and I'm not good with getting out exactly what I want, so bear with me.

"There is a very special man in my life who works overseas as a contractor in Afghanistan. His purpose is to reach a large financial goal. He says he loves me and if he were here we'd be together, but since he isn't, he feels it isn't fair to me to wait on him — even though I am more than willing.

"I understand he may have his own soul contract things to do over there, as I have my own here. I truly feel in my heart we are meant for one another and I yearn for that true, deep love between us to come to fruition. What prayer can I say for this situation?

"I am a very spiritual woman, so I do have a deep understanding of things. I have days when I feel okay about me and him and other days when I want to give up but I'm afraid to. I guess you could say I'm very confused. I don't know if it would be appropriate to ask if your guardian angel could give me some insight."

Tom responds: Here's what I suggested to Norma and for anyone else in this situation to say:

> **Most Benevolent Outcome Request**
> *"I request a most benevolent outcome for the perfect man for me. Thank you!"*

That way, if the two of you are meant to be together, it will happen, and if you're supposed to meet someone else, then this allows your guardian angel to work to bring someone new into your life. Then just release and see what happens. It normally will not happen in a day, a week, or even a month, but try to open yourself up to all possibilities.

A Love Story of Two Ageless Soul Mates

Bruce writes: "First of all, my reconnection with the love of my life came as a direct result of my guardian angel working with me via an MBO that you suggested, Tom. I requested an MBO for my perfect mate and said thank you. I reconnected with my love one month later. We had been thinking about and searching for one another for thirty-seven years. My guardian angel led me to find her on Facebook. Although we had looked for one another on Facebook for the past year, it wasn't until I said that perfect mate MBO that we found one another.

"I used the same MBOs that we talked about for the trip to see her:

Most Benevolent Outcome Requests

"I request an MBO for choosing the perfect airport for the flight. Thank you."

"I request an MBO for going through security easily with no delays. Thank you."

"I request an MBO for my luggage arriving safely and first up on the baggage claim. Thank you."

"I request an MBO for the safety of my flight and to be seated next to someone interesting. Thank you."

"I request an MBO for my drive to the airport to be on time for my flight. Thank you."

"I was led to take a nonstop flight to Houston via Southwest Airlines from Los Angeles International Airport. But I was nervous about all the details of everything that would transpire during the course of that experience, because I hadn't flown since 1995.

"I had a shuttle pick me up at home. I was the last pickup, so we went directly to the airport. I was the first one who was let off in front of the Southwest terminal. As I checked my bags, a young Asian gentleman could see that I was perplexed, so he metaphorically took me by the hand and led me through the process and on to security, including the x-ray and so on. We were completely through security in five minutes while the security personnel smiled and kidded with me — a very pleasant experience.

"I was seated next to a twenty-year-old young man who was an accounting major in Florida. We hit it off immediately and talked about many things. We bonded and are now Facebook friends, exchanging emails as if we were long-lost friends.

"I arrived in Houston, and the love of my life — whom I hadn't seen for forty years — was waiting for me with a big smile as I emerged from the gate area. Needless to say, there were long minutes and minutes of kisses and hugs.

We stopped several times in the middle of the airport for more kisses and hugs too. And everywhere we were, the eyes of those around us were following our every move and smiling. We expected a standing ovation because the intensity of our joy and the joy of those watching was overwhelming!

"Thank you, Tom, for being there for your devoted understudy of ancient Egypt. It was one more act of your love and mentoring for me. By the way, it's now been four days, and our love for one another is growing exponentially every day. It's like we were never apart. Our love is based not only in the linear but also as a partnered spiritual journey. For those who are interested, I am sixty-four and she is fifty-eight, and both of us are ageless!"

MBO for True Friends

Martha writes: "Thank you so much for all that you do. I really appreciate it, and I know many, many other people do too. I made a discovery recently that caring and having concern for Earth, the animals, and our fellow humans is not the same as having an open heart and allowing people into your heart. Maybe this is well known to most people, but it was unknown to me, as I was very guarded with whom I would allow in.

"I do say your daily BP, but I was hoping you might have an affirmation MBO that is focused on opening one's heart fully while protecting it from injury or harm. I want to begin welcoming everyone into my heart, but I do want to make sure I'm not welcoming something or someone who might cause harm."

Tom responds: I think anyone wishing to attract true friends and lovers could start with this MBO request:

> **Most Benevolent Outcome Request**
> *"I request a most benevolent outcome for attracting people who vibrate on my level or above it — people who can become true friends and loved ones. Thank you!"*

It's Raining Men

Diane writes: "Here's an MBO you can decide if you want to use; I thought it had a good twist in regard to my higher purpose. I asked for an MBO that I would find the perfect mate to share my life with and that the results be better than I would hope for or expect. Since then, numerous men have appeared!

"Last Friday I had my second date with Guy A, we'll call him. The day before I went out on this date, I requested an MBO that it be a perfect date if and only if it was in my highest good to continue dating this guy. I also asked to receive a message at the end of the night and added a request that the results be better than I would hope for or expect, finishing with a thank you.

"Well, guess what? The date was perfect! We had dinner, went to a poetry presentation, and then visited a pub. At the end of the night, I got a message while saying goodnight that it was a perfect date but also that it was not in my higher good to see Guy A again. I asked for this, and I feel that the true message came, so I will not date him again. This was a perfect date but not the perfect mate. Next week I have a date with another guy, and the following week with a third guy. So the universe is providing the men!"

MBOs Save a Failing Marriage

Liamona writes: "I was having some really bad relationship problems with my husband that were coming to a head just when I began requesting MBOs. A couple of months ago, my husband got a job in another state and could only come home to visit once or twice a month. I was secretly very happy to get rid of him and told him we should use this opportunity to separate. He agreed and even said that he wanted to get a divorce.

"I was a bit taken aback although not really surprised, considering the simmering hostility I'd been feeling toward him for months. I requested some MBOs regarding the relationship — requests for releasing it and for finding someone better suited for me. I really thought that I would move on and be on my own for a while.

"Instead, last month my husband ended up getting a job back in town and was starting to act strangely nice toward me at times. But things still continued to be rocky. As I kept requesting MBOs, I started to notice some of my own negative behaviors and thoughts about the relationship that I hadn't wanted to face before. They were always lurking in the back of my mind, but instead of facing them, I had been making him the bad guy. So I began to request BPs for him every day — such as requesting safety for his drive to work and that he have good conditions at work — even if I was mad at him. He started to act nicer and nicer, which is really saying something, because he can be a real jerk.

"After a few dramatic encounters — I'll spare you the details — we decided that we really want to be together after all. After more than eleven years, it is like having a new relationship. I even feel attracted to him again, which I haven't felt in a long time. I had really wanted to be free of him, but I think requesting an MBO for the best relationship for me and being okay with separation freed up a lot of cleansing energy.

"I'm stunned at how the big MBO requests get answered. They truly are for the highest good of all and not just for us as individuals."

Tom responds: One of the benefits of requesting MBOs is that it keeps you on your soul path. From what I read above, I think everyone will agree that Liamona's soul path is with her mate.

A Long-Distance MBO Love Story

Kim writes: "I planned a trip recently during Mercury retrograde. I knew this was a bit risky but decided that I would use MBO requests to assist with any travel issues that could come up. I was a bit apprehensive with this trip because its purpose was to see a man I had met for a few hours during a conference the month prior. However, I really liked him and had not been able to get him out of my mind. Let's call him Frank.

"The morning I left, I said my MBO requests for a safe, easy trip and asked that the outcome be more wonderful than I could ever imagine. Everything went very smoothly in the airport. We even got on the plane and pulled out of the gate early. And then things started getting crazy. We were stopped on the runway because Air Force One was landing. I decided that perhaps this was something I should relax and enjoy, as it is not often one gets to see this sight. I watched as the president's plane landed and taxied to a stop, and I took a few front-row pictures as it sat there. Obama was apparently still deciding what to do regarding the shooting that had just taken place in Aurora, Colorado, the night before. Forty minutes later, we were released to go.

"After my flight landed, my plan was to go into the city to the place where Frank was working. As I hurried my way through the crowd, I saw my cell phone was at 10 percent battery power. I decided I should eat at the airport and get it charged up because I would really need it functioning while I was in the city. While I was eating, someone gave me advice on how to get into the city via the bus rather than the train — and it was cheaper! I paid my fare, climbed on board, and then I found out that it was going to take me an extra forty minutes, and it was raining at this point. I was seriously late now. I thought to myself, 'What is up with the MBOs? They always work, but this is turning into a disaster!'

"Frank and his friend ended up picking me up in the friend's work van, which had stressed him out because he knew I would be dressed nicely. When they arrived, I was so happy to see Frank — my nerves had gone much earlier with all my travel problems — that I leaped into his arms, kissed him, and jumped right into the back of the van, catapulting myself over the tools. Frank and his friend both looked at me, astonished, and began to apologize for the condition of the ride. I just smiled and said, 'My father is the best man I know, and he is in construction, so it's like home to me.'

"Long story short, Frank said at that moment he knew that I was the girl for him! We are happily dating now, and it was all because I added in the 'with the outcome to be more wonderful than I could ever imagine' part of the MBO request. Thanks so much, Tom!"

Repairing a Family Rift

Tom says: I've included this next note for anyone in a situation in which you aren't on speaking terms with someone in your family.

Joy writes: "I realize I should be able to work this out myself by using a request for an MBO. However, I guess I'm just not very patient. I had a serious misunderstanding with my daughter that involved my granddaughter. My daughter sent me a picture message of my granddaughter that was very frightening to me and I overreacted. Shortly after that, my daughter texted me to say that we should not talk to each other for a while. She is still not talking to me at this point, and it's been almost two months. I've sent emails and cards to her with no response.

"My question is: Should I continue to let this go and just wait for her to contact me? Or should I attempt to contact her? I feel so unhappy that this situation has driven such a large wedge between us. I'm heartsick over it. I would so appreciate it if you could help me get this situation worked out as soon as possible."

Tom responds: I cannot advise you whether to contact her or not. Let your feelings guide you. Perhaps try a few days of sending light before you do. If you've never sent anyone light before, I can assure you it works. Imagine sending white and then pink light from your heart to the person or persons you wish to send love to. Imagine this light completely surrounding them.

If you have been angry with someone, this does a lot of good for you. Many years ago I had a competitor in business who was so nasty that I said, "Someone's going to shoot that guy." On a trip to Mexico, he was shot by bandits and barely escaped with his life. I was afraid my thoughts contributed to this, so I started sending him white light. I was glad I did so, because his wife allegedly hired a hitman who shot and killed her husband, although she never went to trial for this. At least I didn't have it on my conscience.

If you do contact your daughter, be sure to say beforehand,

Most Benevolent Outcome Request
"I request a most benevolent outcome for my telephone call and that the results will be even better than I can hope for or expect. Thank you!"

And send her lots of love and white light and pink light.

MBO for Long-Distance Marriage

Helen writes: "I introduced my daughter-in-law to MBOs and BPs. Her husband, my son, is in Afghanistan. She was experiencing sadness and stress because whenever my son called her on the cell phone, she noticed that he was not the happy and optimistic person he used to be; there were no more laughter and jokes. She said he was feeling a lot of anger, unhappiness, and stress from the mission. So I sat down and wrote a BP based on what she told me. That night, we prayed together the BP I had written. The next day when he called, she was amazed at the change in his tone of voice;

they even got to laugh together. She was so happy and felt so blessed after their talk. It has been several weeks since then, though it seems like years. His attitude is now back to that of the husband she recognizes, and she is a true believer in the power of MBOs and BPs!

MBO for Long-Distance Relationship

DeLeah writes: "I have been saying MBOs lately to receive signs about my long-distance relationship, which will have been going on for three years at the end of August. I said,

> **Most Benevolent Outcome Request**
> *"I request a most benevolent outcome to be shown several signs that this relationship is for the highest good of all involved with results even better than I could expect or hope for. Thank you."*

"Last night while connecting to my boyfriend's energy, I saw a vision of a man in the bluest of waters, and I sensed it was around the time of early Atlantis. Only his face came up from beneath the water like he was resurfacing. He had a blue mask on the right side of his face covering one eye, half of his nose, and one cheek. The mask was blue and had a yin and yang symbol on it. I took this to mean that my boyfriend's healing is almost finished and that, yes, things are on track as they should be.

"The next morning, I was watching television, and the show *Charmed* was on and gave me yet another sign. It was the episode about men and women, and yin and yang were mentioned several times. Thank you, angels, for listening to my prayers."

14

Benevolent Outcomes for Children

Improving Son's Behavior

Eleanor writes: "I made an MBO request for a very smooth experience during a necessary two-week residency with my son, who has been very difficult in the past. The boy has been here one week now, and I don't know who stole my other son, but this one is a keeper! Thank you."

Tom responds: Requesting MBOs does indeed make life easier and less stressful!

Saving a Child's Life

Luzmarie writes: "I am a teacher in Houston, Texas, and I have been teaching for twenty-three years. One morning, I asked for an MBO that I would see the Creator's power in my life and that I would be a vessel for His work. It was a time when I really wished to feel close to the universe (as I do now).

"That day, I went to the office to make copies for my class and walked through the prekindergarten hallway — something I rarely do because my classroom is outside in a portable building. I stopped by the water fountain when I saw a teacher's aide running down the hallway. When I asked her what was wrong, she just kept shaking her hands and saying, 'Oh no, Ms. A, oh no.'

"For some reason, I ran into Ms. M's room and asked what was wrong. There were three adults in the room: the teacher, an aide, and an office secretary. They were crying and saying that they had tried everything. In the room was a three-year-old boy who was limp and turning blue. They said that he was not breathing.

"'Give him to me!' I said. I don't know how I did it, but I stood behind him, threw him in the air, and caught him on his way down. I was able to give him the Heimlich maneuver and he threw up his cereal. I don't know why, but I kept on doing the maneuver, and he finally threw up a large purple grape! At last, he could breathe!

"I felt so grateful and blessed, and I feel that I was chosen to be a vessel for the Creator's work and to see his power in my life. To this day I continue to ask for MBOs, and I truly believe that they work. Later that day, the principal came to my room and thanked me for saving Eli and for saving her from having to make the worst phone call someone could make to a parent.

"I hope that my testimonial about MBOs brings a smile to your face, as Eli's life was saved and he now attends kindergarten. I thank you, Tom, for *The Gentle Way*, for your guardian angel, and for the bond I now have with my own guardian angel!"

A Most Benevolent Night's Rest

Lori writes: "I have an MBO story. I have six kids, ages thirteen months to twelve years, and they have all been sick. The thirteen-month-old hasn't been sleeping well, so I've been one tired mommy. A few weeks ago, I thought I would request to sleep until 8:00AM. It worked! My baby didn't wake up until 8:05AM. Needless to say, I've requested it every night since, and my baby and I have never slept better. I know it's a little thing, but these little things sure help my faith in the bigger things. Thanks!"

Benevolent Childcare Opportunity

Janet writes: "I have a dear friend in Turkey. His wife is returning to work after giving birth to their son in April and had asked her niece to stay with them to be a nanny. The girl was unreliable and withdrew at the last minute. You can imagine how upset my friend was about the situation, so I talked him through an MBO request via Skype about finding a suitable and reliable person quickly.

"In only a few days, they have found a mature person who will look after their son competently so that they have no more worries. This may not sound like anything special, but at the time of the girl withdrawing, there were no prospects on the horizon. My friend's wife can start work on Monday as scheduled!"

Grandson Gets Life Lesson Thanks to MBO

Lee writes: "I have a beautiful MBO to share. My husband and I took our grandson to Busch Gardens for the day. The day before we left, I asked for an MBO for a fun-filled day and for an unforgettable experience with the animals. Well, we stopped at the animal care center just in time for them to bring in a pregnant female bongo — a type of antelope — in distress. They had her sedated and needed to remove a mass in the birth canal so she could deliver her baby. After removing the mass, the doctor delivered the baby himself. It was amazing to watch. Unfortunately, the baby did not survive, but the mother will be fine.

"It was an unforgettable moment, and my grandson was able to better understand the life process in a way that wasn't frightening to him. He asked a few questions during and after, and we said a little prayer for the baby bongo's guardian angel to keep her safe. It truly was an unforgettable experience."

Calling Any and All Beings for Help with Kids

Pat writes: "I use MBO requests with much success, but I am stumped regarding how to request one for my two-and-a-half-year-old grandson who doesn't want to settle down to sleep until ten or twelve at night. It's exhausting, as I often babysit him when his mother goes out of town, and I am seventy-four. He is like this all the time. Please help! Thank you."

Tom responds: For Pat and anyone who might have a similar problem, requesting MBOs is for you specifically. Asking for a benevolent outcome for someone else is called a benevolent prayer (BP), and you say these slightly differently, as a different set of whole souls we call angels handle these requests instantly. In this case you would say,

Benevolent Prayer
"I ask any and all beings to send calming energy to my grandson and assist in changing his sleeping pattern to earlier in the evening. Thank you!"

MBO for Time to Teach Child

Tamara writes: "The way this worked out is rather strange. I live in southern Mexico. I've been unhappy with the quality of teaching in the first grade at the school my little girl attends. The homework is way over all the kids' heads, and they are assigned so much that it does not leave time for moms to do the teaching that they need in order to be able to even understand the basics.

"I have been asking for an MBO so that I could have time to do some homeschooling. Here's the weird part about how the universe works: Local people have been protesting what appears to be rampant fraud in the most recent election for mayor. Last Friday, an angry group actually burned the mayoral office and other offices. School was canceled for this entire week as a result, and I've been able to teach my little girl the basics to prepare for reading, basic math, and the difference between right and left."

Benevolent Outcomes for Bullied Children

Despina writes: "I have both your books and I absolutely love them. I am getting better at the wording of MBOs. But I have a question: How do I help my children? My eleven-year-old boy has issues with being bullied."

Tom responds: Despina, let's start with a BP to say each day for your son:

Benevolent Prayer
"I ask any and all beings to protect my children from any bullying today in the most benevolent way possible. Thank you!"

Then you can say an MBO:

> **Most Benevolent Outcome Request**
> *"I request a most benevolent outcome for protection for my son today to and from school and during the whole school day. Thank you!"*

Most Benevolent Song

Rita writes: "Tom, I want to tell you about an MBO I requested. It was too funny! Two weeks ago, my daughter, her husband, and three grandkids headed to Schlitterbahn in Galveston, Texas, for a day of fun in the water. We had to take two cars because we had so much junk, and my sixteen-year-old grandson was in the car with me.

"I told him that just to be safe, I was going to ask for an MBO, and of course he wanted to know what it was, so I explained. My request was,

> **Most Benevolent Outcome Request**
> *"Angels, I would like to request a most benevolent outcome for our outing for the day. Thank you, angels."*

"As the word 'angels' came out of my mouth, my grandson added, *'And please give us some good music to listen to on the way.'* I just laughed. Then he began to tell me about how he loved old seventies and eighties music, so I asked him if he liked 'Evil Woman' by Santana. He is autistic and has a photographic memory, but as he reached for the button on the radio to change the station, his reply was, 'That song doesn't compute, Meemah.' And then there at the other radio button was the song. We laughed hysterically. Then he said, 'No wonder I couldn't remember the song; it was by Electric Light Orchestra.' And the song was indeed by the Electric Light Orchestra. Anyhow, I just thought I would share."

Mom Turns Kids into Believers

Kimberly writes: "Here is my MBO story from yesterday. I was in the car taking the kids to their soccer game. They started to complain that we were going to be late when I stopped for a red light that is known to take a long time. 'Let's do an MBO together,' I told all three boys in the car:

> **Most Benevolent Outcome Request**
> *"It is our most benevolent request that we will arrive exactly when we need to be at the field with ease and grace."*

" My two kids rolled their eyes and went with it, as they are used to the program. The third child in the car, my sons' friend, looked at me like I was nuts but repeated the words anyway.

"Then without speeding or hitting another red light, we arrived five minutes early. As my boys' friend was getting out of the car, he asked, 'Now what was the request thing again?' My youngest son told him and then said, 'It also works pretty good for tests.' When they shut the car door, I laughed until tears came. By the way, they won their game too!"

Twelve-Year-Old Has Success with MBO Requests

Lindsay writes: "This morning when we arrived at school, my twelve-year-old daughter, Carly, announced today that 'these MBOs really work.' Why? Last Saturday we went to select soccer tryouts along with hundreds of kids. When we got there, she started crying and didn't want to get out of the car. She said she had a stomachache, that her eyes stung from the sunscreen that had gotten in them, and that she was sure there was no way she would be chosen since there were so many kids. I said it was time for her to request an MBO to help her. She did and reluctantly got out of the car.

"After that tryout — the first of the required four tryouts — the coach came up to me, introduced himself, and told me that my daughter has everything he could want in a player. He talked about her leadership, her tenacity, her presentation, her maturity, and her respect for adults. He went on and on. After the tryout the next day, the same coach came up to me and told me Carly is his favorite and that he definitely wants her for his team. Carly's angels must have really gone to town on her behalf!

"To top it off, Carly won Lady Gaga tickets from our local radio station a couple of nights ago after her MBO request to win, and against all odds, today we got to school in three minutes — a major record. My other daughters are noticing this and want to know her secret! I'll make sure she shares."

Unruly Kids and Restless Children

Jean writes: "How would you ask for an MBO for a roomful of unruly sixth graders?"

Tom responds: Perhaps you could try a couple:

Most Benevolent Outcome Request
"I request a most benevolent outcome for my day at school to be even better than I can hope for or expect. Thank you!"

Benevolent Prayer
"I ask any and all beings to send calming energy to my students today so that they can learn in the most benevolent way possible. Thank you!"

Benevolent Daycare Assistance

Marie writes: "Here is an MBO story for you. Before I started working, I had to find a daycare for my kids. I had two days to find a good daycare, so I grabbed the phone book and started calling to see if there were any available. I called three or four of them, and they had no openings — no luck! I was worried, so I requested an MBO that I would find a reliable and dependable daycare for my kids. Then I grabbed the newspaper, and an ad caught my attention. I called right away and left a message. Not even five minutes later, the daycare provider called me back and told me that she had openings. I immediately went to her house and met her. She was grateful I called, and I was grateful I had found someone to help me in this situation. Could it have been more synchronized? I filled out all the paperwork and had no more worries. After I left her house, I thanked my guardian angel; my guardian angel must be a fast one to work with!"

The Power of Children's Prayers at Accident Scenes

Karen writes: "I have always told my children — now ages sixteen and twenty-six — and any child I'm transporting to send blessings for the best possible outcome for all parties involved whenever we have passed a car accident or an ambulance en route or on the scene. The kids' responses were always beautiful — and I know powerful! — earnest little faces sending blessings. It never occurred to me to try the same for any and all other circumstances, however. I am so delighted to learn your method to refine and expand our requests. Again, thank you so much!

"Accident scenes and wailing alarms are distressing. Child witnesses, since they are so open and sympathetic, leave feeling sad and helpless. I've seen many children send blessings to accident scenes, and along with the real help we know it is to others, it instantly makes them feel better too. I think it is not only that they know they contributed to helping others but also the love sent out that immediately returns and comforts them. How wonderful is that? 'Expect great things' is your next phrase I'll be passing on to our little teacher-healers."

Eight-Year-Old Requesting MBOs

Diane writes: "I just wanted to tell you two wonderful stories about my gorgeous eight-year-old niece Jessica and her MBO requests. You might remember Jessica, since you mentioned a parking MBO story from her in your second book. My brother and sister-in-law recently moved home, and Jessica was not allocated a place in the school at which her younger sister was accepted. Jess had to stay home for several weeks while the appeal process went through.

"Finally, the family was invited to attend an interview and an appeal panel, and Jess went along too. Later that day, Jess called me very excitedly to say that she had been very, very nervous but that her request for an MBO had worked and she had been allocated her place at the school. A week or so later, she gave her mommy a birthday card, wishing her a 'Very Happy Birthday and a million MBOs'! Jess has well and truly got the power of MBO requests!"

Tom responds: Bless her, and may she always continue to use them and never, ever forget! I am so delighted to see how the power of *The Gentle Way* has so successfully escalated. With so many people requesting MBOs, the world will soon become what it was always intended to be.

One Kid's Close Call

Candy writes: "Every morning, I say an MBO request for my son (seven years old), my niece (eight years old), and my nephew (eighteen years old) as they leave for school in the morning. I have done that consistently every day for more than two years now. Just last Monday, when my nephew was riding the train home from school, he noticed a hand in his pocket. When he felt his pocket, he realized that his new cell phone was gone. He had a feeling that the person who took it was behind him, so there was a commotion. The man standing at his back had two other companions with him. My nephew insisted that he give the cell phone back. The man denied having it and said that whoever took the phone already got off at the last stop. When my nephew was getting mad, he saw one of the men slide the phone on the floor and then say that my nephew never lost it and that it had been was on the floor the whole time.

"I consider this a miracle because no one who steals ever gives back what they stole, unless maybe the police are in front of them or they are being tortured. But most importantly, my nephew was not harmed at all. The men were much older than my nephew and there were three of them. I know for sure that these criminals don't steal without a weapon in hand. I am very thankful that my nephew didn't get even a scratch on him.

"Just a few days ago, a similar incident happened, but unfortunately, the owner of the cell phone was stabbed to death when he tried to get his cell phone back. Again, I give thanks because I know my nephew was saved because of my MBO requests."

15

Benevolent Outcomes in Education

Tom says: When school is back in session, be sure to request MBOs for your drive to school, whether it's for yourself as a student, a teacher, or a parent taking your kids to school. You'll find the drives much less stressful. And if you're in school, you can request MBOs just before exams. Many students have reported they scored higher than even the best students in the class, as they are calmer and can receive help from their guardian angels during the tests. You just say,

> **Most Benevolent Outcome Request**
> "I request a most benevolent outcome to do well on this exam, and may the results be even better than I can hope for or expect. Thank you!"

A Big Decision on a New Educational Path

Luzmarie writes: "I have read your book and have taught my seven-year-old son Daniel how to ask for MBOs. I have also shared your book with my friends — even the skeptics. Now I need your advice.

"I am a teacher of twenty years and have decided to apply to an educational diagnostics program within my school district. I would have to quit teaching, but if I am accepted, I would get paid as a teacher while I finish. With all of the educational budget cuts, I worry that the program may be cut midstream and I will not have any employment. I am a single parent and cannot afford to be out of work.

"My question is this: How should I word my request for an MBO? Your guardian angel has told us that angels cannot 'tell you what to do, nor can they make decisions for you,' but I really do want my angel to help me decide whether to take the leap or not. Please help me figure out what I should say in my request. I thought maybe it should sound something like this:

> **Most Benevolent Outcome Request**
> *"I request a most benevolent outcome that I will be accepted into this program only if I will be allowed to complete it and will make more money in order to provide financial stability for my son."*

"Would that be the right way to say it? I want to make sure I say it correctly.

"By the way, I sometimes say, '*I request a most benevolent outcome*' so I know my angel is listening. The full MBO I then say is:

> **Most Benevolent Outcome Request**
> *"I request a most benevolent outcome that I become closer to you and feel your presence in my life. I want to thank you for always being there for me. I love you. Thank you."*

Tom responds: I think your MBO request was as good or better than the one I was thinking of, which is,

> **Most Benevolent Outcome Request**
> *"I request a most benevolent outcome for being accepted in this educational program if this is the most benevolent path for me. Thank you!"*

I also like your other MBO request. You should get a "comfy" feeling when you say that.

MBO for Engineering Exam

Richard writes: "I am sixty-eight years old and I work for an engineering company. From time to time, we take classes to stay current on the latest engineering processes. I recently took a class with a room full of people — most of them several years younger than me. The class lasted all day with a test at the end. When the time came for the test, I requested an MBO. I took the test and breezed through it without using any notes. We were given an hour, but I finished in thirty minutes. I could not believe how easy it was, because others were talking about what a hard time they had. I was truly amazed with the results and how quickly they worked. Thanks, Tom, for all the good advice. I only wish that I had known about MBOs when I was younger and struggling through the challenges in my life."

Tom responds: I've said the same thing myself — I wish I had discovered MBOs sooner!

Help for College Students

Bunky writes: "Mr. Moore, I've got to tell you that one of the things I am most grateful for in my life is meeting you at one of Richard Sutphen's seminars and hearing your story. This simple and most benevolent phrase has made such an enormous difference in my life and in the lives of so many with whom I have shared it.

"Most of my employees are college students, which is often a tumultuous time in a person's life. I could name countless examples of how MBOs have worked for so many of them, even in just the last few days. This includes help with final exams, job hunting, living situations, relationships, and so forth. I have complete faith in it and cannot thank you enough for sharing it. I keep feeling like your book needs to become a screenplay so it can go global!"

A Request for the MBO Community

Nancy writes: "I have a request for the MBO community. My school, like all schools, is having financial problems. We need to replace two ancient boilers. Our situation is different because we are a private Hebrew day school, but we serve the community too, and our students are happy and learn a lot. I'm not even Jewish, but I love this school and the children we teach.

"I know that there are people in the community who could offer great financial support, so please say the following BP request for my school:

> **Benevolent Prayer**
> *"I ask any and all beings for a most benevolent outcome for the Hebrew Academy's financial problems, including the immediate need for new boilers, to be solved better than can be expected or anticipated, and I thank you so much!"*

Tom responds: Thanks in advance to everyone who is willing to say this MBO to help us out.

Benevolent Work Days

Dan writes: "I just read your blog and thought I'd send a story your way that has to do with my job as a middle school principal. This was my first year in middle school in an upscale neighborhood. It's been a year of adjustments and getting to know the routines of the school and community. Before I arrived here and throughout the year, I've asked for an MBO for the school, all stakeholders, and for myself as well.

"Yesterday was the last day of class, and I had one of the senior staff members come into my office and tell me that during this year, morale was the highest that it has been for ten years. That was nice to hear. We also received our school survey results and discovered we maintained our performance in two areas and improved in eight others. This is wonderful evidence of MBOs positively affecting me and others."

MBOs and BPs in College

Marie writes: "How strange the things happening around me are! I'm not as frustrated as I used to be with college, and MBO requests give me confidence in passing my classes. The one class that's been a struggle for me is biology. I also say BPs for many others at the college. It seems to be comforting for them.

"Today I had a young lady in her twenties notice me talking with another young man in his twenties. He must have needed comforting words, because he just stopped, said hello, and then it felt like he was struggling with something. Our chat ended up with me talking about expecting great things and being positive no matter what challenges confronted me.

"When the young man left, the young woman who had seen us talking came up to me saying she needed her mom and felt I was someone she could talk to. In terms of health, she was struggling and looked very pale. After our talk, she started to feel healthier, and about a half hour later, she even helped me with an assignment I was struggling with. It seems that we are all connected more than we realize. It was such an uplifting day. Thank you for your information on MBOs and expecting great things, and a heartfelt hug to you."

MBO to Finish Class

Diane writes: "Hi, Tom. I have been requesting MBOs for six months with many successes — some small, some immediate, some big, and some still in progress! I have also specifically asked for an MBO to clearly hear my divine messages from my guardian angels. Tuesday night, I was at a class I am taking for personal growth. I have attended this course weekly on Tuesdays for the past few months, with a few Saturday daytime classes, but since I live in New Jersey and the classes are in Philadelphia, I have been questioning my commitment and whether or not I need this class. I have found some of the approaches and paperwork annoying. I requested an MBO to complete the class, and I always ask about clearly hearing the divine messages from my guardian angels as well.

"I was in the class Tuesday evening, and I was once again bored, realizing as others spoke that they were not doing the assignment or understanding the process as well as I did. Yet I did not feel annoyed as I became aware of what I was feeling, and as I sat in silence in the class, this message came from out of nowhere: *'Diane, your presence in this personal growth class is about building your courage and self-confidence!'* I just wanted to cry. I clearly heard my message, and then I realized why I was in the class. I am not annoyed at all now! I am in the right place, doing what I need to manifest what I want once I build my courage and self-confidence! Thank you, Tom. Thank you, and bless you both!"

MBOs for Learning a New Language

Jake writes: "I asked for an MBO to get assistance in improving my ability to learn a language I'm studying. I've always had trouble in the past learning languages and really wanted to find a system to help me get started. I asked for an MBO and just happened to find out about this free software that seemed like it was made just for me with regard to my learning style. (The software is called Learning with Texts, for those who are interested.) I was sure to say my three thank yous.

"Just as an addendum, I know my story may not be as exciting as one about receiving a windfall of money, but the subject of being able to learn a language has weighed heavily on my mind, as it could potentially have consequences when I seek employment later on. So you could only imagine my relief in coming across something that was so helpful to me."

Seeking Benevolent Help to Pay for College

Cary writes: "I have been asking for MBOs to help my kids pay for college right now and get jobs. My eighteen-year-old I know got a job two weeks ago. I asked for an MBO for him, and now I'm asking for MBOs to help pay for college. My twenty-six-year-old is holding her job but wants to go to graduate school and is asking for help to pay for it. I sent out an MBO request and we are waiting to see. I ask for MBOs daily for my kids' health and welfare. Thank you. I love your book. I have bought it for my family and friends."

Help on an Exam

Dan writes: "I just read your most recent newsletter and have a story to share. I've decided to begin the process of applying for an EdD degree, which requires getting a lot of things together for the application. One of them is taking the graduate record exam (GRE). Now, it's been over twenty-five years since I've been at a university, so you can imagine that having to study for the test — particularly the math portion — has been a challenge.

"Since planning for this exam, I've been requesting an MBO that I do better on it than I could ask or hope for. The day before the exam, I took two online exams and got my math score immediately. It was predictably low, but I improved on the second exam. The next day, I took the official exam and again, my math score improved. My language score was quite good; now I'm just waiting for the written score to see how I did. I am so pleased with how my MBO worked out in this area!"

16

Benevolent Outcomes for Travel

MBOs for Planning Air Travel

Tom says: We had never visited the Finger Lakes region of upstate New York, so we planned a short vacation there with our friends Frank and Candy. We booked a flight from Dallas-Fort Worth to Chicago on United Airlines on an Airbus, connecting to a regional jet to Syracuse, and returning the same way. I always request MBOs as far in advance as possible, so I requested an MBO for the flights and the whole trip.

United notified us that they had changed the flight at 1:00PM to a regional jet, but there was nothing we could do about that, as we thought we had a connecting flight at 4:00PM in Chicago and the next flight on a 737 at 2:14PM would not arrive in time.

One week before the trip, I just *happened* to check the flights, and United had changed the connecting flight to 6:00PM and had not notified us. I called our friends, and Candy, who used to work for Delta, quickly changed our reservations to the later flight. One problem remained: There were only center seats left in the back of the plane. Another problem: There were no seats available on the connecting flight for my wife and me. So I got on the phone and talked to a very nice United reservations agent who called the help desk and was able to obtain two seats for my wife and me on the bulkhead, just behind first class, and then two more seats together close to the front of the regional jet.

I called Candy, but she wanted to wait to see if things might loosen up closer to the flight date. On Tuesday morning before our Thursday departure, I received a telephone call that I was not able to get to in time. I checked the number, thinking it might be United calling with another change. It wasn't, but that prompted me to again check the flights. I discovered they had upgraded some frequent fliers from economy to first class, opening up two seats together. I quickly called Candy and she switched their seats.

When you request MBOs, you need to listen to those whispers in your ears, as your own guardian angel is trying to assist you all the time. I told everyone that it was actually my guardian angel who had called me to look at our reservations online.

MBO and BP for Emergency Trip

Lee writes: "Hi, Tom! Last week I had a family emergency in another state. I asked for an MBO for the trip to be as smooth as possible with very little traffic and good weather. We drove through Atlanta at 8:45 AM with little traffic. Because there were three of us in the car, we could use the HOV lanes. We were one of only a few cars in the lane while the other lanes were creeping along. When we made it to our destination, we went immediately to the trauma center. My sister was in very grave condition and things did not look good. I asked for any and all beings to surround her and keep her in their arms. We left to find a hotel and get some rest.

"The next morning when we went to the trauma center, she was sitting up in bed! All the nurses said that they were so grateful that I had arrived, since they thought she wasn't going to last the night. She is still in the hospital with a long rehab ahead of her, but she is definitely on the mend. I asked for an MBO for the ride home and although it rained for the last 425 miles of the trip, traffic flowed smoothly. There were no problems around us, even though we kept hearing on the radio about accidents, backups, and flooded areas all around us. Thank you, Tom, for MBOs."

A Benevolent Journey Home

Joan writes: "In the spirit of sharing stories, let me relate one that is a simple confirmation of the power of MBO requests. Up until recently, my husband and I had been living in South Korea. Last fall when we were still there, a relative I had not seen in over thirty years decided to drop in for a visit on her way back home to Canada after an Asian tour. For a day trip, I suggested we take a tour of one of the many fabulous Buddhist temples. The one I suggested is perched high on top of a mountain cliff.

"As I do not read Korean, I relied heavily on my little Garmin GPS to navigate the places we visited. It did a wonderful job of getting us to our destination. We spent a couple of hours enjoying the magnificence of both the scenery as well as the various temple features. Knowing it was at least a three-hour drive home, we left midafternoon in order to travel back in the light of day.

"About a half hour into the drive, the Garmin shut down. Nothing could restore it to functionality. The Korean map I had in the car as a backup was of no use, as the markings were all in Korean. Not a soul in the area spoke a word of English, and my meager Korean phrases would not cut the mustard in terms of getting directions. I called my husband at work to tell him to worry only if we failed to reach home before midnight. There was nothing he could do, as I could not even tell him where I was located.

"Having just completed your first book a week or so prior to this incident, I whispered an MBO request right in the middle of a rice paddy to get us to the highway before nightfall. I knew if I got to the main road, I could get us pointed in the right direction. I put on my 'internal GPS' and listened to the directions being whispered in my ear. Just as the sun was setting, we successfully reached the highway. Thank you times three!

"Our next MBO request was for a safe journey home, and our angels remained with us. In fact, they literally saved our lives. We were still on the highway driving toward home when out of the corner of my eye, I spotted an SUV two lanes over cutting lanes and coming directly toward me on the driver's side at top speed. Time slowed to a crawl. I remained calm and steady, and then I heard that whisper telling me I needed to *turn right now.*

"If I hadn't turned at exactly that moment, not only would he have hit us but we would have been spun around in rush hour traffic creating a mass pileup. Thank you times three! And yes, there was one happy camper waiting for the story back at the ranch."

Highway Accident Benevolently Avoided

Cheryl writes: "Whenever I get into a vehicle, I at least say an MBO for a safe trip. I did so on Sunday morning when I left on an hour-long drive to a family reunion. Passing through a nearby town, I moved over to let a string of traffic on at an entrance. As I was passing them, I realized that the last vehicle — a small car, fortunately — didn't see me because it just kept coming over into my lane. The only reaction I managed was to move farther left without hitting the center divider. I really thought I'd feel the car hitting my rear side and was surprised when I finally looked in the rearview mirror to see it safely behind me. I said many thank yous, caught my breath, and drove safely on. I also asked for an MBO for nice weather, since it had been storming for days and we would be outside. It was beautiful!"

Surprisingly Sunny Skies in the UK

Chrissy writes: "My husband and I returned recently from spending six weeks in England visiting family and sightseeing. We arrived the first week of October, and on the way over from Australia, I requested MBOs for getting through the security check and customs, a safe flight, and a safe landing.

"When we arrived, there were not many people in front of us for the passport check. Then we went through customs because we had bought some licorice for a friend and they waved us through. The car rental people did not take very long to pick us up compared to our visit two years ago, before I started using MBOs. On the previous visit, we waited for over half an hour to be picked up and this time only about ten minutes.

"I asked for MBOs most days for lovely weather and sunshine. But I did forget some days and it rained. We had brilliant weather all through October and November, and although the air was crisp, we had sunshine for a lot of the time. Sometimes it was for a few hours, and other days we had beautiful blue skies and sunshine all day long. People kept saying how unusual it was to have sunshine so late in the year. I just think it is not what you know but who you know. So thank you to the angels for helping us through."

MBOs to Postpone Snow and Prevent Speeding Tickets

Kelly writes: "I have an MBO for you! Last week while making a nine-hour drive from Cleveland, Ohio, to Albany, New York, I said an MBO request that we not get the foot of snow they were calling for during the drive, or even after we arrived. We didn't have any snow along our drive, and even when the snow did start falling after we got to Albany, there were only two inches — a real dud of a storm! It was all melted by noon the same day. Thank you, MBOs! I also requested an MBO before the trip that we would have a wonderful time, even better than expected, and we did!

"I said one last MBO on our return trip home too. Since my friend likes to drive fast, I said an MBO that we would be safe, as well as ignored by the state highway patrol. She ended up being pulled over for going 85 miles per hour in a 65-miles-per-hour zone, but the officer literally just warned her to slow down and told us to have a good day. I couldn't believe it, but then I remembered the MBO. Three MBOs in one weekend! I never do anything without one. I recommend them to all my friends too, and my friend who was driving is now a firm believer."

Some Heavenly Help with Travel Planning

Dan writes: "I just wanted to share a small MBO with you and your readers. I dropped into the Motor Association yesterday to book some flights. I wasn't aware that I needed to make an appointment, and since it was a Saturday, the receptionist told me that all the agents would be booked for the day. I had this funny moment during which I thought I'd try requesting an MBO but wanted to be sure the situation looked hopeless, so I let her look a bit more. Throughout that process, she remarked twice more that everyone was busy and there would be no openings.

"At that moment, I whispered an MBO request for an opening, and sure enough, she found one agent who had just come back from lunch and could see me right away. As I walked out of the office with my flight information in hand, I chuckled to myself, thinking how wonderful it is to have such heavenly help, even with such mundane things. Hope this helps your readers!"

MBO for a Safe, Short Trip Home

Tony writes: "My wife and I flew into O'Hare airport last Friday, landing around 5:30PM. It took an hour to get through customs, and I had some good conversations while in line. We got our luggage and called our transport to get us back to our car at a nearby Hyatt Hotel. I said an MBO request for a smooth and safe trip to our home, about a two-hour drive north.

"The trip to our car took about half an hour — it's usually only ten minutes — due to the seven inches of rain Chicago received the previous day. The driver of the van suggested an alternate route from the hotel to the interstate as several routes were closed due to the flooding. Traffic was snarled. It was now 7:30PM. I tried the route suggested and quickly hit a detour, then stopped at a gas station for a new set of directions. My wife went in while I waited in the car, saying another MBO request for us to find the best route to get us home quickly and safely. She returned with a set of directions that led us around the flooding and roadblocks onto the interstate, and it was smooth sailing for the entire remainder of the drive home. I said a big thank you for all the help!"

Safe Travels

Linda writes: "I doubt one day has gone by since I began to ask for MBOs that I have not done them — for myself, for family, for pets, for friends, for friends' family and friends, and for complete strangers. And sometimes I can clearly see the angels at work.

"This past weekend I suddenly felt a nudge to request an MBO for my daughter, her partner and friends, and several show dogs, all traveling via RV in the UK. They planned to cross into France via the Chunnel, by train — something they have often done. I have never felt the need to request an MBO for their frequent travels before, but I quickly responded to this feeling and emailed my MBO partner to do so as well.

"The next morning I learned that, due to a couple of uncharacteristic mistakes on my daughter's part, her RV was turned back and they missed the train that they had planned to take. They were annoyed — until they learned that the train subsequently became stuck in the Chunnel. They were at a comfortable rest stop with food, water, and an exercise area for the dogs instead of stuck under the English Channel on a train and in the RV for hours. Thank you, angels! I love it when I am given a glimpse into the angels' handiwork!"

Six Thousand Miles of MBOs

Karen writes: "In February, I had been on disability for a while, and the need to see my only grandchild, a grandson, became almost unbearable. His home is about 2,300 miles away. I have an old dog who is a wonderful traveling companion, and she was welcome at my daughter's home, so I loaded up my Saturn Vue and off we went. When we headed to connect with Highway 40, I made my request of an MBO for our trip.

"I am in my sixty-eighth year and love to travel, especially drive, so the trip was exciting for me. I was confronted with ice and snow but fared well — we got snow-stranded in Kingman, Arizona, so I took a U-turn and went through Havasu City. I spied the London Bridge and saw some of the most breathtaking sites along the Colorado River!

"I had been having a fuel tank problem with my car, and I gassed up at intervals of 150–200 miles to be sure I wouldn't run out of gas in support of the MBOs for my car running well. As we went along, I was led to gas stations whose existence I never would have guessed. It took me a whole day to drive across Texas — from El Paso to Shreveport — and MBOs kept me alert and enjoying the drive. I saw areas I never dreamed I would and enjoyed every inch of them.

"While visiting my grandson, my Vue failed, and I traded it in for a new car after requesting an MBO. I had possession of the new car with all the papers signed and such and drove to Virginia and back for a one-day excursion. The deal on the new car fell through the next day, so I was back with the Vue. I got repair help to get it well enough to drive back home, thanks to my MBO request and my son-in-law.

"I am grateful for the lesson of using MBOs. I took this nearly 6,000-mile round trip, saw new states to add to my goal of seeing all of the lower forty-eight and didn't suffer. My Vue was having ailments and couldn't face going to Virginia, so because of my MBO I was given a new car to drive there. And my Vue made the trip back to my home just fine!"

Getting Home

Laurie writes: "I really needed MBOs on my trip back home from a science-fiction convention in Atlanta. I had left my car parked at my friend's condo — we drove to Atlanta in her car — and I came back to find the battery dead. It wouldn't have been a hassle except that I live 200 miles from my friend and still had that far to travel to get home. We managed to jump-start my car, but we were worried that there wouldn't be a shop open to replace the battery, since it was Labor Day. A few MBO requests later, we discovered that the local Sears was open and could take my car immediately. The extended warranty on the battery still applied, and I got a new one for a discounted price. I drove away happy.

"Only later did I discover that I had left my credit card at Sears. More MBO requests ensued! I asked that the card would be found and put away safely, and that I would be able to get it back easily and without complication. I was a little worried the next morning when I tried to call the automotive department of Sears and kept getting a busy signal. A quick MBO request to get through swiftly resulted in the phone being answered on my very next try. And yes, they had my credit card safely in the cash register. I was able to drive there and pick it up without any difficulty. Whew!

"I've discovered that I have best success with MBOs when I frame the request positively. For example, I will say,

Most Benevolent Outcome Request
"I request a most benevolent outcome to be safe and collision-free while driving today' instead of *'I request a most benevolent outcome to not get into an accident."*

"In other words, I don't ask for something not to happen. I turn it around and ask for something positive to happen. I feel that it's all tied up with the law of attraction. By asking for something not to happen, that negative thought or image is in your mind and will actually attract the thing instead of keep it away!

"In your October 10, 2009, newsletter, you referred to Robert Shapiro's suggestion that people say, 'Things can get better for me.' I have a quote tacked to my wall that I'm pretty sure is from Shapiro too. It says, 'I'm better today than I was yesterday, and I'll be better tomorrow than I am today.' I say this out loud every day along with the 'expect great things' mantra. In that spirit, let me add my own suggestion for all your readers to say this MBO:

Most Benevolent Outcome Request
"I request the most benevolent outcome to be able to hear my guardian angel(s) better and better each day."

"It's been working for me. Good luck — or rather, most benevolent outcomes — during your travels!"

Tom responds: If you wish to print out signs to help you remember to request benevolent outcomes or the "expect great things" mantra to say each day, go to my website and click on the "signs" tab.

Benevolent Outcomes and Growth while Traveling

Daphnee writes: "As I traveled back home, I requested an MBO, and although the plane took off one hour later and could not catch up with the time, I managed to catch my connecting flight without having to run and drag my three-year-old daughter, Ninna, behind me. I was the last person to board, but I made it. I did encounter some difficulties, as there was a line to reenter the gate, but I calmed down and trusted that all would be well.

"During the transit, there was also a big staircase I had to take, and that very moment a nice man took my heavy cabin luggage for me, and I was able to hold Ninna's hand to go down the stairs. My suitcases arrived with me in Vienna, and they were among the first ones. Along with that, I passed customs without being stopped, even though I had three large suitcases. So I consider that asking for a safe and smooth trip all the way to my final destination worked perfectly, and I was even given the opportunity to learn to trust through what seemed to be small difficulties."

Benevolent Travel Preparations

Laurie writes: "Here are a few recent MBOs I'd like to share. I recently went to my local courthouse to renew my passport and requested an MBO for a great parking space close to the front door. When I arrived, it was there waiting for me — a nice end spot under the shade of a tree. I also requested an MBO for the whole process of renewing my passport to go swiftly and without complication or delay.

"Well, it had one complication: The local Walgreens that took the passport photo did it incorrectly, so it was unacceptable. But there were no delays; I was second in line. No sooner did I thank my guardian angel for the incredibly short line than the line immediately filled up behind me. Six more people walked in. So I thanked my guardian angel again. I was able to have my passport photo taken on the spot by the clerk, so I didn't have to leave and come back and waste time and energy or lose my place in line. So that also answered my MBO request for no delay!

"I experienced another MBO that had a definite 'wow!' factor. I was struggling to change hotel reservations through a convention website. I had booked one type of room and wanted to change the reservation to another type, but I couldn't do it online. I contacted the convention travel agent by phone, and even he said that the change could not be made. Well, I requested an MBO to get the room type of my choice, and literally two minutes later, the agent called me back to say that he was able to change my reservation. Wow!"

More MBOs from My Trip to Geneva

Tom says: I've already told you a few MBO stories related to our vacation to Geneva, New York, at the beginning of this chapter. Here are some more.

I requested MBOs for everything — the drive to the airport, parking the car, taking the shuttle to the airport, and a good rental car. By the time we landed in Syracuse, we were an hour late, and by the time we all claimed our bags and made our way down to the rental car counters, it was 11:00PM. Here's where an MBO I had requested for a rental car came in. The Dollar Rent a Car counter had closed. I was looking around, and a lady named Emma with whom I had had a long conversation on the plane — I always request an MBO for someone interesting to talk to — motioned for us to come over to the Alamo/National rental counter. Emma and her husband were headed to a class reunion at Cornell. She's into angels, so we had a great talk and have corresponded since.

Emma and her husband had obtained a rate of $25 per day for three days. I quickly requested an MBO, and we did even better for four days — $23 a day — and the nice rental lady chose a Durango SUV, which is normally much more expensive, with three rows of seats and a backup camera. Our total cost was $121 including tax, saving us at least $60 with a much higher-class car.

I could go on and on with MBOs, but here is one more. We went to Elmira, New York, to visit the Mark Twain exhibit at the Elmira College. We were very disappointed in it, as they had only two small rooms dedicated to one of the greatest writers of the nineteenth century. They could do so much more with maybe a full gift shop and displays of the characters from Twain's books. Afterward they gave us a puny map with directions to drive up a hill to where Twain once lived. I was looking down at it and passed through a red light a half-block before another light. Frank, who was my navigator, told me I had run the light and there was a policeman right there. I quickly pulled over to the curb, said a quick MBO, and waited for the policeman. It took him a minute to even turn on his red lights. We showed him the map, which he called "chintzy," gave us directions, and didn't give me a ticket.

Learning a Valuable Lesson on a Trip to India

Anne writes: "I've got another success story with MBO requests for you. As a seasoned traveler, you know what it is like going from continent to continent, having to deal with airports, and so on. I just returned from India and had to transfer more than once on my way there. Thinking of the way things work at O'Hare Airport — a domestic and international airport that uses a monorail to transport customers between terminals — I had assumed my suitcases would be transferred when I was in Delhi at the domestic terminal and took the bus to international.

"You can imagine my horror as we drove kilometer after kilometer and I thought of my suitcases. When we arrived and a man asked me where my suitcases were, I just about died! My Hindi is zero and his English was little better, so believe me Tom, this was one time I didn't mind asking for an MBO out loud. After about a half hour, the young man who had been making phone calls to the other terminal and to the other airline assured me my two suitcases would be transferred. I had a total ten-hour layover and it wasn't until forty-five minutes before departure that I received the confirmation that the bags had arrived.

"The ten-hour interval was also a godsend because it gave me time to reflect and resign myself to the fact that my suitcases were possibly history. After agonizing over the loss of materialistic things, I realized it was okay and that I didn't need anything in the suitcase. All of it could be replaced. What couldn't be replaced were my pictures and journal — and I had all that in my carry-on bag. Plus I had my seventeen days of memories of living with a Christian Indian family. I gave praise to God for letting me keep what was important.

"So I had time to determine and sort through what was important in my life, to be humbled by all the things I do have, and to be grateful. To be reunited with my new acquisitions was wonderful but not as important as the lesson I had learned about spiritual and materialistic belongings."

Angels and Airports

Vicki writes: "My husband Jon and I have been using MBOs daily now for about a year. We have had some really positive results, some of which I have emailed you in the past, then consequently seen in your newest book. How cool is that? We also use the 'expect great things' mantra each day with good results.

"Recently, Jon took his car in for warranty service. There was a starting problem that occurred twice, but BMW could not reproduce it and none of their computer tests indicated a fault. They won't typically repair something unless it shows up as a fault code on their system. Jon thought of a new battery — he said it just popped in his head and he attributes that to the angels. After some haggling with BMW, they did replace the battery and it fixed the problem, so now we know that angels are good at car repairs too!

"Jon had another good result from the compression of time. He was leaving the hospital in Houston. He takes an hour-long bus ride from MD Anderson in Houston to Hobby Airport, along with another twenty minutes to deal with TSA. He did not get out of his MRI and into the bus until 6:50PM. He was trying to make an 8:00PM departure. The compression of time worked so well that he got to his flight on time, and they had not even begun to board the aircraft.

"Another recent MBO that had the angels' handiwork written all over it was when I was flying home from Tyler to Dallas. My ride to the airport was delayed, so at the last minute I was scrambling to find a new ride. My new ride arrived a bit on the late side, so I was in a dead run to get to my 6:00PM flight. I arrived at 5:30PM, and I still needed to check in, since I was flying standby and had a bag to check. No one was at the ticket counter to help me. I noticed a sign that said the counter closed at 5:30PM. I went to the airline kiosk but it too rejected my check-in. A woman from the TSA came up to help me and said she would find someone for me. In about fifteen minutes, a guy came to the counter and checked me and my bag in. Without my angel's intervention, I would never have made my flight. There seems to be a pattern here for us with angels and airports!"

Benevolently Smooth Trip to New York

Laurie writes: "I recently completed a business trip to New York, and I used MBO requests for great results! Here are a few of them.

"During my flight to NYC, our plane was instructed to line up in a holding pattern over Richmond, Virginia, due to high winds at LaGuardia. The pilot announced we would be circling for thirty minutes. Well, I requested an MBO for the winds to subside at LaGuardia and for our circling time to be minimal. Ten minutes later we were back on course to LaGuardia airport. I thanked my guardian angel and added a special thanks to Gaia, whom I had asked to calm the winds.

"From previous research about my hotel in New York City, I had discovered that there were ice machines only every three floors. On this trip, it was important to have easy access to an ice machine, so I requested an MBO to be assigned a room on a floor that had one. Sure enough, the request was granted. My room was just around the corner from one.

"My trip was very successful because I had requested an MBO for helpful people to be put in my path. I was asked to do a couple of projects, one of which came totally out of the blue from an editor who had been a very hard sell in the past.

"On the drive back to the airport, I requested an MBO for a safe trip on the road and to be protected from collisions and the mistakes of other drivers. Well, it worked big time! A van driver cut off my car's driver at an exit ramp. We were exiting and the other driver decided he didn't want to exit and so swerved directly in front of us. My driver slammed on the brakes but didn't lose control. He was shaking, but I felt as cool as a cucumber. I wasn't fazed at all. My guardian angel was on my shoulder the whole time. Thinking back on the incident, if we had crashed or had even a fender bender, I would have missed my flight, and my whole schedule would have fallen apart. Thanks again, guardian angel!

"At the airport itself, I was stunned to see that the line to get through security was at least ninety minutes long. My flight left in sixty minutes. I dutifully got in line and requested an MBO for the shortest wait in line possible. The words were no sooner spoken than one of the security personnel started requesting for whoever had a flight at 3:30PM to identify themselves. I did, and he put me at the head of the line — wow! My flight arrived home thirty minutes early and just before the plane's wheels touched down, I asked for a super-smooth landing. Well, I guess you know how that went — like butter!"

Emergency Trip to Help My Mother

Sharyn writes: "I wanted everyone to know that I had to make an emergency trip to Michigan to set up care for my mother, and I used more MBO requests than I ever have before. And they all came about! She is safe and well taken care of, thanks to my angels and the love of God, who watches over us all!"

Tom responds: Notice how requesting MBOs lowered the stress factor of the emergency trip.

Narrowly Avoided Highway Disaster

Renee writes: "Once again, I'm being 'nudged' to share with you another MBO experience I had in the first week of November this year. I was on my way home to Lake Tahoe from a weekend visiting a friend who lives in the foothills of Northern California, a couple of hours from Lake Tahoe. Since I had bad tires, I was requesting MBOs the whole trip to and from. Well, I had good weather on the trip there, but I was not as fortunate on the way home. The previous night it poured down rain, and the rain continued until I started my journey home the next morning.

"In the first hour into the trip, I was following a motor home with a few cars behind me when the opportunity came to use the passing lane on a hill that ended with a sharp left turn. The section of road that I was on was damp, but it wasn't raining, and there was no standing water on the road. I accelerated to pass the motor home, and the car that was behind me was right on my tail to pass me. But the lane ended suddenly, and I used the brakes in preparation to make the turn and completely lost control. I went into a skid in the oncoming lane, about to go over an embankment. I was turning the wheel in hopes to avoid that rollover and found myself spinning 180 degrees, heading in the opposite direction.

"The next thing I knew, I was sliding toward the guard rail, which I missed by only inches. But I found that I was heading straight for the car that was behind me. Fortunately, he squeezed into the opposite lane to avoid me and we missed a head-on collision by just a hair. Then I was in the other lane going down the hill as the other motorists passed me by. I immediately pulled over and was so shaken by the experience that I knew then my guardian angel was working overtime with divine intervention. That's the only way all of that could have happened with no incident, but only we know that — wink, wink. Just think, if another car had been coming in the opposite direction at the same time. That would have been a big mess! Needless to say, I did make it home safely through the snow over the summit.

"So once again the radiant effect of saying MBOs was in effect — no one got hit in all of that. You can imagine that if I didn't use MBOs, this could have been a fatal accident for any of the drivers involved. Thank you, thank you, thank you to my guardian angel and Tom for all the great work and getting this important teaching to the world."

Benevolent Trip through the Mountains

Dawna writes: "Each and every day I request MBOs for pretty much everything. Recently on a working trip to another community, I got a confirmation that MBOs work each and every day. Getting up at 6:30AM to return home, I could see that the mountains were very foggy. I said one MBO request for less snow and fog on the highway during my four-and-a-half-hour drive home, a second for a safe trip home, a third for other drivers to stay on their side of the road, and another for courteous drivers.

"Yahoo! There was fog above or below me at times but none on the highway. There was less snow as well, for although it had snowed during the night, rain washed it all away. It rained off and on for over four hours, and the sun came out as I approached home. A lot of big trucks were going through the mountain passes and they all pulled over so I could pass safely. Everyone shared the roads nicely — another great trip home thanks to MBOs.

"So, Tom, once again thanks for sharing this empowering tool. It is nice to read about people's diverse requests. They have given me many ideas over the years. My life is so much easier because of MBOs."

Turbulence-Free Australian Flight

Chrissy writes: "Here is an MBO request that I used recently with which I had great results. My husband and I were flying back from Sydney to Brisbane recently after visiting family. Not long after takeoff, the pilot announced that there would be a lot of turbulence coming into Brisbane. I immediately requested an MBO for as little turbulence as possible and of course ended it with 'may the results be so much better than I could hope for or expect.'

"Of course, my MBO came through, and there was absolutely no turbulence whatsoever. I thanked my angels three times when we landed. I always request MBOs for a safe journey to the airport, to arrive to the airport on time, to check in without any problems, to go through the security check uneventfully, and for a smooth flight. I also add one for a very safe flight, a smooth landing, and no problems with luggage delivery. My bags generally come out in the first two minutes of the conveyer belt starting up."

Allowing Others to Go Above and Beyond

Jon writes: "I know you like to hear of travel-related MBO stories, so here you go. I had said an MBO request, as I always do when I travel, especially when I am flying standby. I was in the Houston Hobby Airport waiting to return to Dallas, and I was first on the list for the airline employee standby. Somehow I quickly moved to eleventh place and did not get on. For the next flight — which was the last flight of the night — I was second on the list, but the flight was full. I loitered a bit, and the gate agent shook his head no.

"A few minutes later, however, he said, 'Wait a minute, I may have an idea. The weight and balance is off, but I may be able to get a deadhead pilot to move to the jump seat and let you take his seat.' That American Airlines staff member ran up and down the jetway stairs a couple of times to verify things. He went to an extraordinary amount of effort to get me on that flight. Even after telling me that he could not get me on the flight, he ran around, trying to work it out for me to get me on — and he finally succeeded. My accommodation on this flight was a real long shot! I know my guardian angel had a hand in this. Thanks for sharing your information with us!"

Benevolent Horse Riding

Allan writes: "I've been requesting MBOs since your first publication in the *Sedona Journal of Emergence!* and I am always delighted.

"Now for an awesome MBO. I have horses on my farm. Outdoor riding pretty much shuts down with our New England winters, so a couple of dedicated ladies trailer their horses twenty-five miles round trip, two to three times a week, to ride in a heated indoor ring. Towing two horses and a heavy trailer in winter is something that makes me a bit edgy, so most of the time I request MBOs, as much for me as for the ladies and horses. Recently they took their trip and returned normally. I had been busy and hadn't made a request for that trip. The horses were taken care of, but when the ladies went to park the trailer, with the first touch of the brakes, the brake line blew — a total and instant loss of brakes!

"The line was so rusty and disintegrated that I don't think that trip could have been made without an accident or divine protection. I'm feeling that a request every time may not be necessary. Maybe because angels are not restricted to our timeline and work with our past, present, and future to work things out for us, our requests may also apply to times outside of our immediate focus. I am totally awed and eternally grateful. Thank you for following your path in bringing such a powerful gift to humanity. Awesome indeed!"

Smooth Air Travel for a Novice Solo Traveler

Lynn writes: "Hi, Tom. Since I found your website earlier this year, I have enjoyed it so much and have really benefited from the MBOs. Here is my best MBO story.

"In March I flew out to Phoenix to be with my mom for the last two weeks of her life. I hadn't flown in years and had to make this trip by myself. I flew out of Minneapolis, and my uncle — who had flown out earlier to say goodbye to my mom — was supposed to pick me up. I have never been to the Phoenix airport before and was slightly worried that I'd get lost and never see my family again, as I'm not good at finding my way around by myself. I said an MBO request to be able to find my uncle quickly and easily after I arrived.

"My flight arrived and I marched out of the plane and down the hallway and called him to let him know that I was there and where I was. I hemmed and hawed about what to do next before finally going down the escalators and walking over to the exit doors. Literally, as I stepped out of the doors, my uncle drove up to the curb in front of me. The timing was *perfect!* I can't tell you how relieved I was. It's too bad my uncle didn't know about MBOs. He was supposed to fly home to Wisconsin that night but missed the exit for gas and ended up being just a little too late to catch his plane — a stressful end to a very stressful and sad trip. I am a firm believer in MBOs. Thank you, Tom!"

MBOs for Lugging Luggage

Tom says: A note on this next MBO entry. Jean is referring to the reported activation on 9/9/9 of the huge crystals that lie underneath the surface of Arkansas to the southeast of Hot Springs. In the September 2009 issue of the *Sedona Journal of Emergence!*, James Tyberonn channeled Metatron, who stated the crystals would be activated on this date; I recommend reading the article. I also reported before that my family and I have dug for crystals a couple of times near Hot Springs and have brought back some really large crystals. Even these small ones have great energy.

Jean writes, "I have a double MBO for you! I was part of a group going to Arkansas for the crystal activation on 9/9/9. This necessitated two pieces of luggage plus a large cooler. I live on the third floor and was not looking forward to three trips down the stairs. As I was asking for an MBO, I heard another door being locked, so I opened mine and saw a new tenant in the hall. I asked him if he'd have time to help me with my luggage, and he very graciously carried down two pieces for me — each a separate trip — and then he told me to breathe.

"When I returned, I had the same three pieces to carry up three flights, so I started asking for an MBO as I left Windsor, where I'd left my vehicle so I could carpool with two other women. As I approached the driveway to the apartment complex, three people were walking across the street, but not in the pedestrian crosswalk, and yet cars were stopping for them. They turned into the driveway for my building, and I passed them as I pulled into a parking spot. Two of them were young men; the other was a young woman. Again, I figured that's why they were there and asked for help, and the two men carried everything up for me in one trip. Oddly enough, the earlier helper's name was Ryan, and so was one of the second helpers. Bless them all, and thank you times six!

"By the way, the owner of the other car in our caravan now closes a lot of her emails with 'believe in benevolent outcomes' after she read your column in the *Sedona Journal,* in which I wrote in describing my Seattle bus experience, and I told her it was me. I'm sure there were a lot of MBOs traveling to Arkansas."

Cat-Friendly Move across the Country

Gina writes: "I wanted to share this MBO with you. In August, we had planned to move across the country from Alabama to Arizona. Besides the truck full of furniture and personal belongings that my husband and his friend were going to drive, my daughter and I were going to haul my eight indoor-only cats in our SUV. I had meticulously planned the whole thing, from the route to the travel supplies and the pet-friendly motels. A big part of the planning process was asking for MBOs that we reach our destination safely and that the cats would handle the trip okay.

"From the moment we left the house, everything went smoothly. The cats were absolute angels, our vehicles ran fine, and we even arrived at our destination ahead of schedule. We couldn't have asked for anything more — except we forgot to ask for the furniture to arrive safely. Everything in the moving truck that wasn't packed in boxes was pretty much dinged up or broken, and I started to get a little emotional about the damage.

"Then, I realized that all of us — including the cats — had survived the trip perfectly, even better than we had imagined, and that was a lot more important than a bunch of stuff. Thanks to our angels and guides for keeping us safe and comfortable during our travels. And thank you, Tom, for your hard work in sharing so much important information!"

A Great Trip by Motorcycle

Dan writes: "Just thought I'd share my most recent MBO with you. Midweek I set out on a 1,200-kilometer — or 720-mile — roundtrip motorcycle ride. Prior to my departure, I requested an MBO for a perfect and safe ride. Halfway through my ride, I noticed my windshield was loose. Upon further inspection, I saw that one of the two windshield brackets had sheared in half, and the other bracket was just starting to show a small tear. I thought it wiser to return directly home rather than extend the trip, so I requested another MBO for a safe trip home.

"Along the entire trip home, I had a strong tailwind, which was a great help in lessening the buffeting of winds when I passed oncoming semis and buses. I also rode with another rider for about a quarter of the return trip, which was a nice reassurance, should anything have gone wrong. I arrived home safely, and on further inspection saw that the small fracture in the glass had just about doubled in size. In retrospect, I had a perfect ride with perfect weather and a perfect outcome. Also, unbeknownst to me, a close friend had sent up some BPs for me, specifically asking Gaia to provide good weather for my trip. All in all, it was a wonderful trip, thanks to that BP, my guardian angel Acme, and Gaia!"

Resolving an Airline Dispute

Karen writes: "Months ago I made a plane reservation to travel to Dallas today. I arrived at the airport today one hour early and to my surprise I was too late to check in! The itinerary in my hot little hands clearly stated that my flight didn't leave until 1:30PM — how could it be too late to check in? There wasn't a soul at the airline's counter to even check with either. I thought I was losing my mind, so I asked a United agent who was kind enough to check on it for me, and she told me the flight time had been changed to 12:40PM. I exclaimed that I was never notified of any flight time changes. She directed me to call an 800 number. I immediately asked for an MBO.

"The agent I spoke to said she was sorry but a notification had been sent to me back in July and that I should have called twenty-four hours earlier to double check. We explored my options, and she said the only thing she could do was put me on the same flight the next day but I would have to pay another $600. That was unacceptable to me. Upon further exploration, I discovered that the airline sent the notification to an email address that was ten years old — not the one my itinerary was sent to.

"The agent was still unwilling to budge and was blaming me for not calling twenty-four hours in advance. So I asked to speak to her supervisor at once. She was discouraging, saying the supervisor would tell me the same thing. I patiently waited, and when she got back on the phone she informed me that the supervisor would put me on the 6:00AM flight at no extra cost! Needless to say, I was thankful and grateful — and still am! It really is true that everything always happens for the best, even though that might not appear to be the case in the moment. When we can learn to live by this philosophy, much unnecessary stress can be avoided.

"I'm now back home and enjoying the opportunity to relax and breathe freely, knowing that I will arrive in time for all the enjoyment and festivities that await me in Dallas!"

Listen to That Still, Small Voice

Flo writes: "I had an interesting experience with a recent MBO. I was driving to Savannah with my guardian angel from New Jersey, so that morning before leaving home, I requested an MBO for a smooth trip, that my hotel room would be ready when I got there, and that I would be able to find a decent parking place in the motel's parking garage.

"All went very well until I was about an hour outside of Savannah, when I noticed that there were several motels, like the Choice and Quality Inns, that were very near the interstate. The thought popped into my head that I could stay at one of these places and save at least $50 for that night. I could call the hotel in Savannah and cancel my reservation for that one night. But instead of doing that, I passed that exit and kept on going. I passed two more exits that had several motels, and the thought kept getting stronger that I might do this instead of going on to Savannah, but since I did have the reservation for that night in Savannah and I wasn't very far away, I decided it didn't make sense to stop then. So I pressed on and soon arrived in Savannah.

"This was around 12:45PM. I couldn't get into the hotel's driveway, as there were a bunch of tour buses in it and lots of people milling around. I also needed to be registered to get a key card to enter the hotel's garage, but I couldn't register until I found a parking place. To make a long story short, I spent half an hour driving around before finally finding a place in an underground public garage near my hotel and then got lost trying to get out of there. I did finally get registered and received a key card. I also got lost trying to get out of the parking garage and had to be rescued. Then I got lost trying to find my way back to the hotel; it was cloudy and I couldn't tell directions.

"I soon found out that there was a convention of about 1,600 people spread out in all the hotels and motels in Savannah! Well, no wonder there were all these buses; this is the way these people got transported to their meeting place, which was Savannah's stadium. I got a hotel cart but didn't realize that the parking garage had elevators. I was on the second level. So I pushed and shoved the heavy cart up the car ramp. Finally I got my stuff onto the cart and then had to restrain it from rolling back down the ramp. Sometimes I think I've lost my brains and common sense!

"That evening, I remembered my MBO request and asked why I'd had such a horrid time when I'd arrived in Savannah. Then I saw those exits on the interstate in my mind's eye and realized that my guardian angel couldn't move 1,600 people out of my way, so he had tried to impress on me the idea to stop overnight before I got to Savannah — but I didn't want to do that. Had I stayed in one of those motels overnight and then showed up in Savannah the next day, it would have been smooth sailing for me. Lesson learned, maybe? Until the next time!

"All the other MBOs I've asked for have turned out to make my life go much more smoothly. Thanks, Tom, for showing us how to make our lives go more smoothly and also how to ask to help others."

Tom Responds: As I read this, I was already composing almost the exact response that Flo concluded: Her guardian angel was trying to tell her what to do, but she ignored that whisper in her ear, as we all do at times. This was a lesson to show her to pay attention in the future and to go with that inner nudging.

Benevolent Baggage Transfer

Pili writes: "I want to share an MBO with you. I was traveling yesterday, coming back from my vacation, and I was told I was only allowed to check one bag per person, and after that, I would be charged for each additional checked bag. I was with my daughter and son, so I had two bags left that I had to pay for. Because they were small, I took them with me as carry-on bags, but one bag's content was not allowed. Finally, one of the crew members let me carry on the bag with the compromise to put it down with the rest of the baggage as they used to do when there was no more room.

"Everything was perfect until I stopped to make my connection, because I had to take my bags and go through the same process all over again. I was nervous because this airport was too big, and I had a feeling that they wouldn't let me do the same thing and I would have to pay for that bag. So I did an MBO request. When I was picking up the bags to put them in the next plane, guess what? My bags were lost — the extra ones! They told me to go to another terminal to pick them up. When I got there, there was nothing — they couldn't find them. So the lady told me they would find them and send them to my city and they would be there with the other ones. So I didn't have to go through the whole process a second time. I avoided the problem, and my bags came home safely and free. Thanks, angels."

An All-Around Smooth Trip

Tom says: On a recent trip to Europe, my flight from London's Heathrow Airport to Nice was on the KLM airline with a change of planes in Amsterdam. I made the mistake of forgetting to ask for an MBO as I went through security. I was stopped by a security person and asked to put my roller bag in the metal form to see if it fit. The wheels made it too long by about an inch, and he made me run back to check the bag in at the KLM counter. I knew I had a problem because of the combined weight of the two checked bags, even though I was traveling business class.

They said I was at my limit and were going to charge me £130 overage — that's about $200. My only option was to run downstairs with my roller bag and briefcase to a store at the far end of the terminal and buy a cloth bag to throw everything into. Naturally, by now I was requesting a benevolent outcome for the problem.

I bought the cheapest bag they had, which was £15 — about $24 — and ran back upstairs and started transferring virtually everything in the bag over to the cloth bag. I then attempted to check the small roller bag and it weighed a total of 4 kilos (8.8 pounds). The supervisor said that they would have given me 2 kilos, but since it was 4, they were going to charge me £50 – about $80 — for the overage. I started taking literally everything out of the bag, including tissues, and putting it on the floor next to the bag. Then, however, the two supervisors were called away and the person at the counter told me to quickly give her the bag before they returned and she checked it.

Once back in the security line, I requested an MBO for the line. The man who had made me return to the airline counter let me up to the front of the line, even though he said KLM had not paid for "fast track." I made the flight with time to spare and had a pleasant chat with a woman on the way to Amsterdam. (Naturally, I had requested an MBO for someone interesting to talk to.)

I had a long layover in Amsterdam before taking the flight to Nice. I had requested an MBO for my bags to come out quickly in Nice, and they did come out in plenty of time to make the bus to Cannes, which was filled with people going to the TV market. I had requested an MBO to again sit next to someone interesting, and I wound up sitting next to the same British chap I had sat next to on the plane from London to Nice last March! We still may do some business. He even helped to drag one of my bags to my hotel, as he was traveling very light. I showed him where to pick up his badge on our way, as he did not have his yet, and I was able to pick up my guide that listed everyone who was attending the market, so I did not have to return back to pick it up — a very nice outcome!

I met several buyers there who were not on my list of sixty appointments

I had for the four days of the market. We had meetings either when there were no-shows for appointments or in the few remaining times I had left. Needless to say, I was exhausted each night, as I didn't leave until about 7:00PM. At the Buyers Club, I reconnected with the two young ladies from Canada I mentioned meeting in a previous column last year, and they're still requesting MBOs.

17

Benevolent Outcomes for Vacations and Holidays

A Few Thoughts about Holiday MBOs

Tom says: During the holiday season, as you're out and about attending parties, reunions, and football games and returning gifts to stores, be sure to remember to request MBOs for your driving and for the safety of yourself, your family, and your valuables during this exciting time. For example, you can say,

> **Most Benevolent Outcome Request**
> "I request a most benevolent outcome for the continued safety of those valuables I'm leaving in my car while I'm away. Thank you!"

If you are in crowded places that are known to have pickpockets and purse thieves, you can say,

> **Most Benevolent Outcome Request**
> "I request a most benevolent outcome for my safety and the safety of my possessions during this time. Thank you!"

This will lower the stress and fear factor you might otherwise have had you not requested these MBOs.

The holidays can either be a fun time for family reunions, or they can be quite stressful, depending on your family dynamics. Before any family reunion, you can say out loud,

> **Most Benevolent Outcome Request**
> "I request a most benevolent outcome for our family reunion, and may it be even better than I can hope for or expect. Thank you!"

If you're the chef, you can say,

Most Benevolent Outcome Request
"I request an MBO that this dinner will be even better than I can hope for or expect. Thank you!"

If you're having a problem with a family member — including previous physical, mental, emotional, or sexual abuse — you can say,

Most Benevolent Outcome Request
"I request an MBO to never be alone with _____ and for protection for myself and my children. Thank you!"

Benevolent Breaking and Entering

Bonnie writes: "This past week we were in Arizona for my son's wedding. We rented a house in the area. Although we were given a key for the house, we never carried it with us. Instead, we would use the keypad on the garage door and leave the door inside to the house open, entering the house this way. However, one day, in my haste to get somewhere, I forgot and locked the door inside of the garage! When we returned and went through the garage, we found the door to get into the house locked. Panic set in immediately. We walked around the house, but found no other possible way to get in. We did not have the owner's name or number with us either.

"I immediately asked for an MBO to find a way into the house. Suddenly, my husband started looking at the locked door and pulled a credit card out of his wallet. Within ten seconds of trying to get the door to open, he did it! This door was a very solid, secured door. There is no doubt my guardian angel helped him get that door open, as my husband had never done anything like this before!"

Discounted Hotel Stay

Jaye writes: "I requested an MBO for my trip to Chicago, and it went very well. I had made a reservation at a hotel because I couldn't stay with my daughter, as she has cats and I am allergic to them. I went to check out this morning and told them that the bed was a bit hard to sleep on. They are in the process of remodeling, so they gave me the $10 discount for reserving the room online plus another $64 because the bed was too hard. For three nights, with the room taxes and everything, it was only $219, as opposed to $284. My math may not be so good now, as I am fairly tired, but the upshot is that I got almost an entire night's stay for free!"

A Great Trip to Sedona Made Even Better by MBOs

Tom says: Here's a little personal MBO story. Dena and I took a long weekend trip to Sedona, Arizona, with our friends Frank and

Candi. Naturally, I was requesting MBOs from the very beginning when we first booked the trip. Both Dena and I requested MBOs for warmer-than-normal days with sunny weather over a month in advance. The results were normal cool temperatures for that time of year for the first two days, but we were indoors or in the car most of the time. The last three days were warmer and sunny — just beautiful conditions.

When I booked our airline tickets, I accidentally added an extra "n" to Dena's middle name, but we caught it just before I checked in online, so I called the reservations desk to correct it. The agent corrected it but didn't tell me that doing so wiped out the seat Dena was supposed to be in and had reassigned her to a window bulkhead seat. I requested an MBO for the situation. Since she does not like bulkhead seats, I switched with her and had more leg room on the flight to Phoenix — a nice MBO result.

The flight was ten minutes late in Phoenix, and we spent another ten to fifteen minutes sitting on the runway waiting for a gate. So by the time we loaded the car at the rental center, we were about an hour behind the time we should've left the airport for Sedona, so I requested a compression of time. We like to eat lunch at the Hideaway Restaurant overlooking Oak Creek and the red rocks, and normally the drive takes me two hours and fifteen minutes, but we arrived at the restaurant in one hour and fifty-five minutes!

We stayed at the Sky Ranch Lodge and had a room overlooking Sedona, and that evening we drove to the Enchantment Resort. I had requested an MBO for both the drive and a table right by the window. They gave us the perfect table at the corner where two windows came together. In previous times, we ate out on their patio, but it was too cool to do that in late October with the Sun sinking earlier behind the mountains than it does in the warmer seasons.

On Friday we visited Light Technology Publishing in Flagstaff, and I naturally requested an MBO for the drive on 89A — known locally as the "switchbacks," as it winds its way up from the desert to the 6,900-foot altitude of Flagstaff. We never had to sit behind a slow truck either coming or going.

On Saturday, after requesting MBOs for our upcoming drive and train trip, we drove to the old mining town of Jerome, which Frank and Candi especially liked. Then it was back to Cottonwood to take the Verde Valley train two hours up to Perkins Ranch and then two hours back. We had good seats to view out the windows of the coach car, and everyone was allowed out on the platforms to take photos of the beautiful gorge we passed through on the twenty mile ride up to the working ranch.

On Sunday we visited the Cathedral Rock vortex and I did a meditation there sitting on the side of the stream. With MBOs for the drive back to Phoenix on Monday, we arrived in plenty of time for our flight.

MBOs for a Trip to New Zealand

Cathy writes: "I just love your work with the teachings of MBOs, and I have been using your ideas after reading an article many years ago. In the past twelve months, I got connected with your website through listening to Dick Sutphen's interviews of you and have loved your encouraging stories. We recently took a trip to New Zealand, and it has been many years since we last traveled. The pace of my job as a teacher is really fast, and I didn't have much time to consider the organizational aspects of the trip. I just asked for MBOs all the way along. Everything went so smoothly; it was amazing.

"Well, nearly everything. We had one frightening experience when attempting to turn around at night on a country road, and my husband couldn't get the reverse gear. We had only just picked up the camper and we hadn't been shown how the gear stick needs to be lifted up to go into reverse. So there we were, in the middle of this dark country road with all of these cars bearing down on us, and the only gear we had was forward!

"I was so grateful when my angels sent two truck drivers who came up right behind us and generously tried to reverse the camper. When they had no success with that, they simply hooked us up and pulled us safely back to the side of the road. I was so relieved to see that no accidents had been caused by the inconvenienced traffic.

"There are so many times I thank you and my angels for helping me out. I have to tell you; your words touch so many lives, and I, along with so many others, thank God for your generosity and guidance."

Tom responds: Thanks, Cathy, for the kind words. Notice, everyone, that she was requesting MBOs during her entire trip. When a problem arose that could have resulted in an accident, two trucks "just happened" to be right behind them that were able to tow them to safety. Your guardian angels will intervene, but you have to request their assistance! That's what requesting benevolent outcomes all the time will do for you too.

Benevolent Trailer Parking

Tanya writes: "On a recent trip through the northern United States, the car in which I was a passenger was towing a small trailer. Parking hadn't been too difficult until it was time for dinner in East Grand Forks, North Dakota. The highly recommended restaurant we were going to shared a lot with a large cinema complex and several other restaurants. Parking was almost nonexistent at the dinner hour, especially since we needed two spaces, so I requested an MBO. As we pulled into the next aisle, the end car slowly backed out. Approaching the spot, we found that it was double: The car in the next aisle had parked just over the line, and no one else wanted to park there. So in we went! Thank you, thank you, thank you! And dinner was delicious too.

"My MBO request and follow-up thank you were observed by others in the car. After my explanations — and with many doubts — the driver tried it several times later in the trip. Each time, a car pulled out just as he approached his destination. I think you may have a new convert! As your other submitters say, thank you so much for this information."

Overseas Trip Made Easier with MBOs

Victoria writes: "In a recent trip back from overseas, I decided to use MBOs to expedite my passing through immigration and customs. I am a law-abiding citizen, and I understand that the searches are random, but I seem to randomly win that lottery more often than the odds would predict. As I asked for an MBO for an easy pass-through, I was not chosen for special searches at three different points. Yay!

"During this trip, I also used an MBO request to drive bees away from our food. We wanted to sit and have lunch outside, but we were quickly visited by several bees trying to taste our food. I tried to talk to the bees' spirits and ask them to go away and find some flowers, but when that didn't work and everyone was getting very frustrated with the bees, I asked for an MBO that the bees would find another source of food and let us have our lunch. Well, five minutes later, they were all gone! We had a nice lunch and were able to enjoy the outside weather. It is so nice to use MBO requests. Thank you to my guardian angel and all beings of light who are helping. And thank you to you for reminding us how to use them."

Benevolent Turkish Trip

Diana writes: "I had another amazing experience with MBOs during this summer holiday. We went to Turkey, and I requested an MBO for the city where my in-laws lived to be cooler and for life to be more bearable during the time of our visit. In the city, it started to rain a little, so the air turned cooler than it normally is at that time of year. It never rains there in the summer. Even my mother-in-law was surprised by the weather. I had a huge smile and, of course, thanked my guardian angel."

MBOs Help Create a Perfect High School Reunion

Tom says: Recently we picked up an Enterprise rental car in Plano, Texas, to drive to North Little Rock, Arkansas, for my high school reunion. I requested an MBO to (1) have a good car with good tires in good running order (since most of the cars I had rented from them in the past had at least 25,000 miles or more) and (2) that my rental car would be available when I arrived. Last time we had to wait thirty minutes for one to be delivered up front as they were sold out.

This Enterprise location had several models immediately available to choose from, and I picked a Chevy Impala with only 14,000 miles. I requested MBOs on the drive, and the state troopers were all writing tickets for other people, some going and some returning. I had also requested an MBO for light traffic, and it was easy driving both ways.

Naturally, I requested MBOs for the reunion, and it was just a great weekend in which I reconnected with many people I had not seen since high school. I also donated two books for the silent auction raising money for landscaping for the school, and they went for more than the retail price to a classmate who is interested in angels.

My brother lives in North Little Rock, and when we left the hotel where the reunion was held, I requested an MBO for the drive to his house. We arrived and noticed the left rear tire was losing air. Before long it was flat from a nail in the tire, but the MBO I requested was that my brother had an air compressor. He did, and so we pumped the tire up for the drive to Firestone. We dropped it off and returned after lunch. I had to pay $20 to for the repair, but I requested an MBO for this too. When I returned the car to Enterprise, they deducted the expense off my bill.

All in all, a *perfect* weekend!

Big Plans in Cabo Turn Out Better Than Expected

Cindy writes: "We had vacation plans for Cabo San Lucas booked with the Marina Fiesta Resort that is one of our time-share exchanges. We own a one-bedroom unit, so that is what a trade entitles us to elsewhere. Often when a resort has a two-bedroom that is not booked, they will upgrade you at no cost. Our son was going to be traveling with us for five of the seven days, so the two-bedroom would have been great — a bed for him rather than a pull-out couch. I emailed the resort and asked if they had any two-bedroom units available. They did, but it would cost $75 extra per night! I said no thank you. They wrote back and said they could offer it for $50 extra per night. Again, I said no thank you — I was just seeing if it was available at no cost. Of course, I said my regular MBO requests for our trip before we left.

"When we checked in, they 'confirmed' that our party was just two people. I said, 'No. Actually, there are three of us.' I then noticed the key cards said 127/128. I asked what that meant. They told me the keys were for two units with a lockout door in between. When we walked into our rooms, there were two queen beds with a full-size kitchen in one room and a king bed with partial kitchen in the other. Both rooms had private baths, and they shared a combined patio that overlooked the marina and offered us our own private Jacuzzi. Plus we received a bottle of champagne, chocolate-covered strawberries, and an apple carved into a swan. It was way more than we could ever have hoped for or expected. Thank you, angels!"

A Clear Vancouver Vacation

Roda writes: "I have an MBO story from when we were on vacation last year in Vancouver, British Columbia. We arrived on a Monday, and it was supposed to rain from Thursday on. Well, that would pretty well have wiped out our vacation. I started requesting MBOs every morning for a good day with no rain. It did not rain until we were getting on the bus on Sunday, our last evening. Every once in a while, the Sun even poked out. Mostly it was overcast, but they were all good or great days with no rain, thanks to the MBOs!"

Benevolent Disney World Experience

Lee writes: "I just returned from a short trip to Orlando, Florida. I had requested several MBOs before I left, starting about one month before. First, I requested good weather, as May is rather warm in Florida. The days were in the low- to mid-80s and humidity was on the low side, which was nice for walking around the parks. Second, I requested short lines at the attractions — or no lines. Only one ride had a forty-five-minute wait, and most others were under ten minutes. This is a busy time at Disney World, especially at Epcot for the flower and garden show.

"We stayed on the property and used the bus transportation system to get around. I requested that we have no wait or a short wait for the bus and that it not be too crowded. Riding the bus an average of four times each day, we had the most amazing timing. The bus was either at the bus stop when we got there or pulled up as we were walking up to the stop, and once we had the entire bus to ourselves, which is unheard of! Many more MBOs happened, and nothing is too small to ask for when requesting an MBO. Thank you for all your support of those of us learning our way in this new world."

A Great Valentine's Day Dinner

Tom says: My wife reserved a private room for our group at a local restaurant for the second Valentine's Day in a row. It's decorated in red and is adjacent to the dance floor. It has heavy glass doors so the live music is not too loud but we can at least hear it; you cannot hear the music at all in the main dining room. One of the couples had a death in their family and had to drive to Houston for the funeral, which was held on Valentine's Day. To complicate matters, my wife called to confirm the room and was told it had been given to someone else at the last minute.

We arrived early, prepared to at least give the manager our opinion regarding the unfairness of giving our room away to someone else. Naturally we requested an MBO for the results to be even better than we could hope for or expect. We went to the reception desk, and the manager was there manning it. We gave him our last name, and he immediately told us that our table in the red room was ready. When pressed, he said they knew we had reserved the room in the past, so he had asked the other group if they would like to have the black-and-white room, and they said yes, so we had our room back! The band was also late in starting, so we had plenty of time for great discussions with our friends — a nice MBO Valentine's Day.

Splendid Vacation

AG writes: "I promised that I would post at least one holiday story, so here it goes. After spending some days in Naples, my friend and I went to Ischia, an island not very far from the city. We decided to hit the beach, but it was raining. We were upset, but I still asked for an MBO to spend a great day.

"Finally, we reached a complex with thermal waters that was at the border of the city we were in. We did not have enough money to pay the entry, as we did not expect it to be so expensive, but the guy at the counter offered us a discount. We entered the complex with only three euros between us. It is interesting that this turned out to be one of the best days of my life. Due to the slight rain, there were only around twenty people in a complex that has some thirty pools with many different kinds of water. I still remember that feeling of being in the warm massaging water while slow drops of rain fell on my face.

"The only problem was that we had only three euros and we got really hungry but did not want to leave the place too early. Strangely enough, we found on the ground next to our chairs another three euros. And with six euros, we were able to buy two sandwiches and two drinks. We felt glorious as we left the complex!"

Summer Camp Update

Julie writes: "You might remember that I wrote you previously about an MBO for my daughter's camping trip. We had to change the dates to the first session because of a float trip we had planned, and even though both sessions were booked, the angels helped make that happen. Well, I now know of another MBO that came out of that situation. All the campers who were there this week — which would have been the week she would have been there, if not for the MBO and changing the dates — went home sick with what might have been swine flu! It was all over the news. I thanked my angels profusely once again."

Tom responds: This is another example of not being able to see the full extent of what takes place when you request an MBO.

Benevolent Cape Cod Vacation

Tom says: I recently had two workshops on my book, one in Braintree, Massachusetts, and one in Andover, Massachusetts. As neither I nor my wife have ever toured that section of the country, I thought it would be nice to find a place to stay on Cape Cod in between the two workshops, so I requested an MBO that we could trade one of the time-shares we own (we got it in an MBO-aided barter for the right to broadcast some movies on a Utah TV station) for a time-share on Cape Cod. There was a long waiting list on RCI.com, so I checked out Craigslist.org for Cape Cod weekly rentals, and there were quite a few. I thought it best to wait until the first of August to try to trade for a cottage on the Cape, as I thought people would want to try and rent first before trading.

In the meantime, I was attempting to license my producer's Michael Jackson documentary to a U.S. DVD company whose owner I had known for many years. He happened to mention that he was flying to Boston to spend a week at his Cape Cod house, so I naturally brought up trading him the time-share. I requested an MBO, and he came back saying that they were still going to be there on the week I needed. That proved to be fortunate, as their house is located a one-and-one-half-hour drive from Braintree, which would not have been very convenient.

Then one day last week I had the "feeling" to check Craigslist again and noticed that they had a trading section. There were a few trades listed for weekly rentals — some New Yorkers looking to trade their apartment for a week on Cape Cod, for example. Most of the posts were for permanent trades. I decided to try a listing myself and listed it at 6:20PM and requested an MBO. At 7:15 the next morning, I had an email offering me a three-bedroom cottage in West Yarmouth, only a three-minute walk to the beach and harbor and quite close to the ferries to Martha's Vineyard and Nantucket islands. There was only one major problem: This time-share trader had a specific request for a week anywhere in Hawaii for Christmas week. I found one studio listed on RCI.com, but by the time I prepared and sent a contract to him, it was already taken. I called and said I regretted we couldn't do it and resigned myself to starting my calls for another place around August 1.

The time-share trader then telephoned me the next day and said that someone wanted to rent his cottage beginning on Friday, September 4 for a week (normally trades run Saturday-to-Saturday), and he would be willing to do the deal if we could leave by noon on that Friday. He said he would wait to see if anything popped up again in Hawaii, but if not, we would find somewhere else to go next year.

We were already planning to head for Andover that morning at 8:00, as it's about a three-hour drive. I was not looking forward to checking RCI.com every two or three days until December, but then another MBO occurred when I checked the site again. A one-bedroom had opened up right on the beach on Maui and a day earlier, which was perfect for the time-share trader's travel plans. So it was benevolent for both parties, which is one of the rules of requesting MBOs — that it be benevolent for all parties concerned!

As you look at the twists and turns this took, you can see how it illustrates one of the points I mention in my workshops: It's great fun to watch the pieces come together for a benevolent outcome request as you become more aware of what is taking place around you. You can use the analogy of a chess game where pieces have to be moved around the board. In this case, it required my guardian angel to first locate someone to trade with me (instantly on their side, of course), then find someone who wanted to rent on a Friday-to-Friday basis over the Labor Day holiday, and finally someone to give up a condo in Hawaii at the same time for the Christmas holiday, just as I searched. Again, it was great fun to watch all of this unfold!

18

Benevolent Outcomes for Weather and Natural Disasters

Sunny Saturdays Update

Tom says: If you're a new reader of my work, what I'm about to say you can do might seem a little unbelievable, but I assure you that I'm getting feedback from other readers of their successes as well. In my meditations, I was told by Gaia, the soul of Earth, that we can change weather patterns. It's all part of our learning to be junior creators in training, as we're called. Requesting MBOs, my own guardian angel says, puts you on a path of higher awareness and raises your vibrational level. As a result, you feel lighter.

As an example, Gaia says that even in northern climates that might not see sun for several weeks, she will allow one day of sun a week, but we have to request it! So I pondered a little and decided on "sunny Saturdays." Most kids are out of school on those days, and people tend to be out shopping or taking part in some sports activity.

In order to request your sunny Saturday, you simply say,

> **Most Benevolent Outcome Request**
> "I request a most benevolent outcome for a sunny Saturday this week. Thank you!"

Already, my readers in the United Kingdom have been experimenting with this, and they say it works great — as long as they remember to request it. So you may have to put up a sign to that effect on the refrigerator or bathroom mirror.

I personally have had two times recently when I requested that it not rain. The first time was when my wife and I attended a block party. At first, there were some towering white clouds to the south of us. It was getting pretty dark, but the sun still lit up these clouds. There was lightning in the tops of the clouds, but that's all we saw. Then the clouds kept coming our way, and I began to see lightning strikes to the ground. I requested an MBO for the rain and lightning to remain to the south during the time we were at the block party. The woman who organized the block party checked the radar online later and said that the rain had just stayed where it was and then moved on to the west.

The second time was yesterday evening when we attended Grapefest, a festival held in Grapevine, Texas. They produce wine there, and they have several blocks of the old city town blocked off during the festival with carnival rides, numerous bands performing on each block, and loads of booths. While there, once again the clouds started darkening and lightning started striking the ground. Again I requested an MBO for the rain to stay away from Grapefest. In one of the stores we entered, a woman had been watching the radar online, and she said that the storm just divided into two parts and went around us. She said that she guessed we were just lucky.

One of my readers last year even had a tornado headed right for her house. She grabbed her two kids, requested an MBO, and ran for shelter. The tornado lifted off the ground and went back into the wall cloud. Experiment with these requests during the winter months for the Northern Hemisphere and during the summer months for the Southern Hemisphere.

Benevolent Rainstorm

Dawna writes: "A week or so before I travel, I always ask for bare road conditions and a safe and happy trip for me and my vehicle to and from my destination. One time, as I was about an hour from my departure, it started to rain — big time. Wondering what happened to my MBO, I saw a very wet young man hitchhiking. I had to pick him up. We went another mile or so up the road, and I saw another very wet young man hitchhiking. Well, I had to pick him up too. With a full truck, we carried on. Within ten minutes, it stopped raining. During the rest of the three-hour drive, the sun was shining beautifully.

"Later that evening, I asked why my MBO request wasn't effective, and this was the answer I received: 'Would you have picked up those two men had it not been raining?' I am a sixty-year-old single woman who often picks up hikers, but I had to admit that no, I would have only picked up one of them. So I suppose that the fifteen minutes of rain was so I could do a couple acts of kindness for some wet travelers!"

Tom responds: I do recommend that everyone request an MBO for safety when they pick up hitchhikers. British Columbia must be a little gentler than some portions of the United States. I used to do a lot of hitchhiking in my college days, but you don't see it as much anymore.

Welcoming Gentle Rain in Florida

Laurie writes: "Your 'welcome gentle rain' request continues to work every day and is a great stress reliever for me. The late afternoon thunderstorms in southern Florida have been locally violent and destructive in some cases, but not over my house!"

✳   ✳   ✳

Eleanore writes: "Today a big, nasty storm was forecast, and when it started, I turned to the direction it was coming from and said, *'I welcome gentle rain; I welcome gentle rain.'* And you're right: It does work perfectly! The storm never occurred, and it rained just enough to water everything that needed a drink. Don't you wish that everyone would just do it?"

Tom responds: I do wish everyone would experiment with this, as this is part of the junior creators in training work you start to do when you request MBOs. And for all of you in northern climates, don't forget to request an MBO each week for a sunny Saturday, even if the forecast is for a cloudy, miserable day. Try it out!

Laurie writes back: "Thanks for telling me what Gaia said about requesting gentle rain just before a thunderstorm. It has worked like a charm so far! Of course, I follow it up with an MBO request for protection from lightning strikes. A person can never be too cautious or ask for too many MBOs."

Working with Tornadoes

Gloria writes: "I love the newsletter. I'm still reading the back ones, and I'm only two years behind now. I just read that we were able to move the jet stream to help with the ash clouds affecting Europe during the Iceland volcano. I had no idea we could do anything that big!

"I've been working with the weather a lot. I apparently moved — or was moved! — into a small arm of the Dixie Alley tornado zone. We had two tornadoes go through my neighborhood the first two years I lived there. I kept chanting, *"Gentle winds and gentle rain."* It seemed to have worked, as my neighbors all around me had trees fall on their houses, while my tree fell the other way and hit my deck at the edge of the lake instead of my house.

"After reading your newsletter, I did the 'gentle rain' greeting to the west. It's raining now. I also watch TV when the weatherman is on showing the radar and tornado warnings. I work on calming the storm and dissipating the clouds in the warning areas. It seems to be working. I've also noticed that the severe weather seems to go north or south of me."

MBO for Snowbound Husband

Kathy writes: "I have to share an MBO experience. My husband called and said he was going to pick me up late because he was stuck in deep snow. I prayed right after the call and within ten minutes he was unstuck.

"I saw where he was stuck. There is no way he could have gotten out of there without help. God is so great and gives us so much help. I feel closer to

God after this happened because I get it now. Thank you, Tom, for letting us know about this prayer and using your gift for the greater good. It has helped me and all my loved ones."

How Can We Know?

Susie writes: "I know you are being flooded with emails concerning the earthquake in Haiti and all the suffering that is going on there. I've been asking my guardian angel and other spiritual beings to help these people, but I guess my question is: How can I be sure that my requests are being heard? I hope this is not too trivial. I really enjoy reading your newsletters."

Tom responds: When you say a BP for someone else, you don't always see the same kind of immediate feedback that you do with many of your MBO requests. In my first book, I described saying a BP for a woman on a plane who had left her purse at security and seeing the joy she felt when she returned with the purse. So when you say BPs, have faith that they do work.

In the case of the earthquake victims in Haiti, have you not read about or seen on TV the massive amount of aid coming both from governments and the general public? It is huge. So the question is whether or not you have been absorbing what I'm trying to convey with these articles — that we are junior creators in training.

Have you said a BP for these people yet? If not, say right now,

> **Benevolent Prayer**
> *"I ask that any and all beings assist the people in Haiti affected by the earthquake to be aided in recovering from this disaster, and may the results be even better than I can hope for or expect. Thank you!"*

If we have hundreds more people saying this prayer, think about the energy that will be created! Pass this along to your friends, and perhaps lead a group of people, not just you, to say this prayer.

MBO Request for Less Snow

Amy writes: "I have always been intrigued about our ability to control weather conditions. You had a discussion of it in your last newsletter, so I thought I would pass on my most recent weather MBO. We had a terrific winter storm in our part of the Northeast last week. At my home, we had an unexpected two feet of wet snow on Tuesday that broke some of my favorite lilac trees. Much more was forecast for the very next day. I asked for an MBO for the storm to give us little or no additional snow and for the result to be better than I could expect. Believe me, the forecast on local television was for several feet of snow, wind, and power outages.

"At my place of work, it snowed heavily all the next day. But there was a thin line of weather just to the east where it did nothing but rain all day. No one had predicted that rain-snow line to move down our way, but just a little bit of it did — right over my house. A mile west, it snowed. I ended up with an inch of slush and rain and not a bit of wind. Even the national radar showed a tiny blip of a rain line in a place it shouldn't have been. Later the local weatherman said that the storm had lined itself up perfectly to push a finger of warmer air right at us. I thought that was great and thanked the beings for the result.

"Like you, I am a firm believer in the ability to move and change weather systems. In fact, I'm asking for bright days of sunshine for this week. May they be even more beautiful and sunny than I could ever expect. Thank you!"

Tom responds: See what just one person was able to do? With the spring and summer storms upon us, if one is headed your way, just say,

> **Most Benevolent Outcome Request**
> *"I request a most benevolent outcome for gentle rain. Thank you!"*

Can you imagine what a hundred such requests could do, even in such northern climates as Canada and Europe? You can request MBOs for every Saturday to be sunny, even during the middle of winter. Try it!

Benevolence with Florida Storms

Laurie writes: "Here in Florida, we can get some real whoppers when it comes to thunderstorms. Just the other day, a line of storms came rolling in. I looked at the radar online, and it showed some intense activity heading in my direction. I immediately asked for an MBO that my home be protected from any harm or lightning that might occur during this storm.

"It got very dark and windy, and the rain came down in buckets, but the thunder and lightning was minimal. The best part, however, was when a literal hole in the clouds opened up and there was sunlight over my home, even while the wind whipped through the trees and the rain came down. I even saw a brilliant rainbow while all this was happening. What a beautiful answer to my MBO request!"

Tom responds: Gaia has also told me to go outside before severe storms, face in their direction, open my arms, and say, *"I welcome gentle rain. I welcome gentle rain!"* So far, it's worked perfectly. I watch the radar online, and the clouds usually begin to lessen in intensity before they reach us.

No Rain During Outing

Carol writes: "Having been a subscriber for a few years and using MBO requests pretty regularly, I thought I would take this opportunity to share my weather MBO story with you. I was helping my girlfriend move one Saturday, along with another friend of ours. The weather was looking pretty cloudy and heavy rain and thunderstorms were predicted. But we could not change our plans; we had to move her out. As the sky got to looking more and more gruesome and the clouds got blacker and blacker, we despaired of making it through the day without getting ourselves and her possessions drenched.

"It finally dawned on me that we should request an MBO for the rain, so I explained that I was going to ask my guardian angels to keep the rain at bay. My girlfriend and friend, of course, had no clue what I was talking about, so I made them repeat it after me. I asked that the rain be kept light for us and that our day would be better than we could hope for or imagine. They were skeptical, needless to say.

"As our day progressed, the rains came only a little — mostly spritzing, not even enough to wet the grass. However, it was not until Monday morning that I realized the extent of our MBO. My coworker told me about her golf game at the same time — on a course less than two miles away from where we were moving. She had to play four holes in the driving rain! That's when I gave my guardian angels a really big thank you. Needless to say, my friends are now firm believers in MBO requests and use them all the time, just like me."

Benevolent Prayer for Natural Disasters

Tom says: There have been great Earth movements in recent times, and I'm sure we can count on more coming. People are fearful and stressed. When earthquakes or other disasters happen, be sure to say a BP. It can go something like this:

> **Benevolent Prayer**
> "I ask any and all beings to assist those beings affected by this disaster in _____ in the most benevolent manner possible!"

We are all junior creators in training, and when we say BPs along with others, it creates an energy that I'm told is more than the sum of its parts. And when you request MBOs for yourself, it raises your vibrational rate and eases your ascension to the next focus.

Perfect Weather for the Fundraiser

Sunny writes: "I have been requesting MBOs for about a year now, and I have one to share with everyone. I volunteer at a dog rescue and sanctuary in Arenas Valley, New Mexico, and they were having a one-year anniversary fundraiser on August 29. All weather reports told of a return of the monsoon rains both Saturday (the setup day) and Sunday (the day of the event) that included flooding rains and fifty-miles-per-hour winds.

"I requested perfect, mild weather for both those days, with the rain waiting until after 5:00PM on Sunday. Almost to the minute, the rains waited and even stayed mild while we finished getting things broken down and everyone went home. Only then did it really pour. Everyone had a good time at the fundraiser, and it was a complete success!"

Keeping Cool and Requesting Rain

Kathy writes: "I work in a prison and work on the outside pickets, which are elevated and exposed to the elements. We have to be physically on the catwalk of the pickets for a certain amount of time, and the weather here is extremely hot. On one particular day, there was no breeze, and I simply asked Gaia to send a breeze and thanked her. Almost immediately, the most lovely breeze came and lasted for quite some time.

"On another day, I asked Gaia to keep it cool, as the previous day it had been horrendously hot, and I had become a little ill from it. She did! Gaia kept it cool, and others on the outside picket called and remarked how cool it was even though the heat index was higher than the previous day.

"Another day, as I pulled into my drive at home from work, I asked Gaia for rain, and before I stepped inside, the most gentle shower came. Now I know what it means when the Creator gave us dominion over Earth — it's simply, in my opinion, establishing a relationship with Mother Earth, asking for her assistance, and, of course, giving her gratitude abundantly. It also means taking care of her as well."

Turning Off the Rain

Rita writes: "I always read your newsletter with great interest. I ask for MBOs all the time, and the other day I was out walking without an umbrella when it started to rain quite heavily. I asked for an MBO and the rain stopped immediately. Amazing!"

Tom says: I remind all of you in the northern latitudes where you may not see the sun for weeks on end: You can request an MBO early each week for a sunny Saturday. It works!

Quelling a Terrible Tornado with MBOs

Heather writes: "Dear Tom, I just had to write and let you know one story that happened to me. And there have been many since I originally found your website. Two weeks ago, we moved to a wonderful house in the country. That itself was the result of an MBO request, but the one I wish to tell you about is the one that saved my family. We had only been here for three or four days when a huge thunderstorm kicked up. Now I love a good storm, but this one got nuts fast, and all of a sudden, I realized that we had a tornado heading straight for us. I could hear it coming and see the way the wind was blowing the debris up. I shouted for my children so we could run down to the basement, and as we were running toward it, I mentally requested an MBO for the storm to not cause damage or injury.

"Just like that, the storm slowed right down and died to a more gentle rain. To say I was completely in awe would be an understatement. I know this saved my family and the house we just moved into. Every day I say a huge thank you that I found your site, and I cannot tell you how many times I have requested an MBO and have seen it work since then. So again, thank you!"

Tom responds: That is wonderful to hear. I do recommend that you say your MBO request out loud, however. In this case, I'm sure there was such emotion and danger involved that there was an exception made.

MBO Saves Storage Building

Susie writes: "My husband and I were getting ready to leave the house, and a storm was coming up. He went to the barn, and I was in the car. I had just requested an MBO that the storm would not cause any serious damage. I heard a noise, but the sound was muffled since I was in the car. My husband motioned for me to come to where he was and I went. A huge oak tree next to a storage building had been snapped off near the bottom. The amazing thing about it all was the tree was laid over just perfectly away from the building and only a small part of the tree pushed the roof to one side a few inches. I was amazed, and you can be sure I thanked my guardian angel."

Shelter from the Storm

David writes: "This past Saturday, when tornadoes were moving through my area in northeastern North Carolina, we were right in the midst of all that unstable air. All day long the winds had been gusting up to twenty-five miles per hour. That evening, things got worse. The weather report revealed what was headed our way, and my wife and I hunkered down and doubled up, both saying our individual MBOs.

"I can tell you that the closest place a tornado touched down was about twelve miles away. But I can also tell you that when a storm like this one is bearing down on you, with tornadoes left and right, a distance of twelve miles seems like inches. This system started days earlier in Oklahoma and didn't stop taking its toll until it reached the Atlantic Ocean. It took over forty lives in the process — sixteen of them in North Carolina, where we live. Ten of those deaths happened just twelve miles from me. Thank you, Tom, for teaching me about MBOs!"

Stuck in the Snow

Kathy writes: "Hi, Tom. I went to a friend's house to check on a horse. There was snow covering the driveway, but because of the recent warmer weather, it turned out to be very slushy yet icy underneath. So I got stuck! I checked the horse, who turned out to be fine, and I got back into my car — still stuck. I didn't want to have to call my friend to leave work to pull me out, nor did I want to be a 'girl' about it. (No offense, but women are capable of doing so much more than a lot of men give us credit for.) So I requested an MBO:

> **Most Benevolent Outcome Request**
> *"Please help me to get unstuck as quickly and easily as possible. Thank you very much!"*

"It was then that I saw a shovel nearby, so I scooped out a little of the slush, but it wasn't enough. I do have tire chains, but I'd never used them before and wasn't sure how to use them correctly. A thought popped into my head: 'Put your foot out the door.' I did, and I gave a light push — and I do mean light — and the car immediately moved backward. Now, if that wasn't the quickest and easiest way to get unstuck!"

Tom responds: Hmm, maybe a slight shove from Kathy's guardian angel assisted? And notice that a shovel just happened to be nearby.

Surviving Hurricane Irene

Bob writes: "I appreciate the info on the East Coast earthquake and hurricane. I'm on the Connecticut coast, waiting for Irene and requesting my MBOs."

Tom responds: I wrote Bob back and suggested he request an MBO for less wind and rain around him.

Bob writes back: "Thanks, Tom. This worked perfectly! No major damage here. My backyard looks like a disaster area. It's covered with small branches, twigs, and leaves, but no large tree limbs came down and there was no house damage. We never lost electricity either. But within a half-mile of my house, trees are down and electricity is expected to be out for a week!"

* * *

Nancy writes: "I live in Albany, New York, and we were dead center in the path of Hurricane Irene. There have been tremendous floods and power outages in the entire Hudson Valley and higher elevations, but we have stayed free of the flooding and the loss of power that has been so prevalent now.

"I requested MBOs for us and also for everyone affected by this enormous storm. Every time I see something on the TV or the Internet that I feel could use an angelic boost, out come the MBOs! I am the kind of person who likes to take action to correct inequities or problems, and this gives me that satisfaction. Thanks so much."

Good Weather Requests

DeLeah writes: "I requested an MBO that the roads be clear and the weather decent in the morning in order for me to have a safe commute, with better results than I may expect or hope for, and I had wonderful results with this today! I said this request last night before going to bed, as there were supposed to be downright nasty conditions here last night, with rain followed by a freeze overnight along with some snow that would have made for a slippery mess. I woke up early this morning, and the temperature is above freezing and it's only wet outdoors. I love these blessings!"

MBOs During Texas Storms

Willie writes: "MBOs work! I live in Addison, a northern suburb of Dallas, and Tuesday, April 3, was a scary day. When I realized that tornadoes had formed and were wrecking things in Arlington, Texas, I said an MBO requesting protection from high winds, hail, lightning, and flooding rains.

"The sirens were going off, but because the storms had not arrived in my area, I had not taken shelter. Everything was pretty quiet, and then one of the meteorologists reported that a tornado had touched down in Addison — about 300 yards from where I live. I jumped in the closet and listened for the train-like sound of a tornado. Nothing happened. Apparently it was a false report. As a matter of fact, we had very little rain or wind and no hail. It got very dark and still, but my guardian angel kept us safe. I'm extremely thankful to know that help is always available."

Tom responds: I saw that same report, and we were plotting it right up the North Dallas Tollway, as we live in Plano. Earlier I had gone outside and said, *I welcome gentle rain* three times, as Gaia had said to do — with my arms outstretched — but when I heard that report, I added an MBO request for my house and neighborhood to remain safe. With the exception of two tornadoes a few miles west of us, all of the reported seventeen tornadoes were in the southern to eastern part of the Dallas-Fort Worth metroplex.

Request Gentle Rain for All Drought-Afflicted Areas

Eleanore writes: "I wanted to share a great MBO response with you. As you know, the country is experiencing drought conditions, and Florida hasn't been an exception — but certainly not to the extent of the Midwest. Yesterday I used the request you suggested a long time ago — '*I welcome the gentle rain*' — three times, and that's what we got! I repeated the request this morning, and we were once again blessed. It's the wonderful kind of rain that really soaks in because it isn't pouring down. The thought occurred to me to do the same for the rest of the country, so I have, and perhaps you might ask others to join in as well. My son lives in Houston, and, as you know, they're under water!"

Tom responds: I do this before every storm, as in Texas you never know what type of severe weather can crop up out of a seemingly normal thunderstorm. It works every time. For the country, you could say this BP:

> **Benevolent Prayer**
> *"I ask any and all beings to bring rain to those regions suffering drought conditions. Thank you!"*

Sunny Saturdays

Val writes: "Guess what? We had a very sunny Saturday and Sunday. It worked. We put what you suggested for a good weather MBO on the homepage of our magazine (www.aaahhh.org), so we think maybe a lot of people took part. I will give them a reminder to do it again this week, and I will keep you posted on what happens on future Saturdays. Hooray for MBOs!"

Tom responds: If you live where it's supposed to be cloudy next week, request an MBO for sun on Saturday, and see what happens. Then keep repeating the request each week.

Benevolent Prayer for Cousin in Dangerous Weather

Sandy writes: "I not only read your BP out loud when I saw your post about the storms, but I also turned on the Weather Channel and saw where it was. I have a cousin who lives in the Richardson area, and it looked to be in the thick of it also. I said an additional BP for him and his family to be safe and, even though it sounded ridiculous in my head:

> **Benevolent Prayer**
> *"I ask for any and all beings to assist my family to have the storm go around them, thereby missing them, even if the maps had it headed right for their area."*

"I texted him about an hour ago, and within the last few I minutes received this text back: 'Doesn't happen often, but we were between the really bad stuff.' Wow! I've been saying all three affirmations/prayers every single morning for two years now, and MBO requests for everything. Things are working faster and faster. Thanks again, Tom!"

Perfectly Timed Sunny Skies

Doug writes: "I learned about your work a few months ago and immediately started requesting MBOs. I've noticed after a few weeks that life has become gentler; I have less stress driving, less stress at work, and even the banks and collection agencies are more forgiving when I miss my payments. I also noticed that when I don't get what I requested, I get an explanation — or at least an idea — why I was turned down.

"My wife is a real estate agent, and last month she had a client who wanted to look at two development sites. It had been raining since the night before the tour, and when we met the client there was no indication that the rain would stop anytime soon. So, on the way to the sites, I whispered an MBO request for the rain to avoid the places we were going to.

"When we approached the gate of the first site, the rain died down to only a drizzle and completely stopped as soon as I parked the car. As we stepped out of the car, the clouds above us broke just enough to show the sun while it still rained on the surrounding area. It stayed that way for more than two hours. Just as we were leaving the site, the clouds became dark again and it started to rain.

"The same thing happened when we got to the second site. The rain stopped and the sun came out again when we arrived, and it stayed that way for a few hours. The rain didn't start again until we were already leaving. Of course I thanked my guardian angel, the Sun, and Gaia for the wonderful experience."

Surviving the Storm

Brenda writes: "I have a great MBO story! We had a horrific storm here Friday evening — most likely a tornado, judging from all the large trees that have been uprooted and how almost every block was hit. However, many of us were without electricity, phones, and Internet. I said an MBO request for the safety of my home and for no damage to occur right around my home either.

"The next day, the Internet still wasn't working, so I said an MBO request for it to work so I could watch some Roku free TV streaming (you need WiFi and Internet for it to work). Well, twenty minutes later, my Internet was working, and my electricity had only gone off for a total of fifteen minutes during the past few days. Others are still many days without power and phones. If your readers read this, we need MBOs for the whole area where the storm hit, as so many are without electricity, and there is no sign of help yet in the heat.

"Thank you again for all your help, MBO stories, and the help we all get from requesting them. Tom, your work has certainly made my life easier. I am ever so thankful for having the opportunity to read your newsletters every week. You have gotten me into the daily habit of requesting MBOs. I refer your work to everyone! Bless you and all that you do."

Be Specific in Your MBO Requests for Rain

Gerry writes: "Georgia was having a very dry spell, and the weatherman had been promising scattered showers for the metro area, but we weren't getting any in my area. I made an MBO request for a soft, gentle rain, and ten minutes later, I looked out the window and it was raining. 'Oh my God,' I thought, 'my car windows are down!' So I immediately went outside to take care of it. By the time I got outside, the rain had stopped and there were only a couple small damp spots on the driveway.

"I thought, 'Well, that was a soft, gentle rain, and somewhere my guardian angel is laughing his head off.' I then requested an MBO for a gentle, soaking rain. And sure enough, about four hours later, it started raining and rained most of the night. It makes me wonder, though, if guardian angels have a sense of humor or if that is only a human attribute. It did remind me to be a little more specific in my MBOs."

Benevolent Hurricane Sandy Outcomes

Tom says: In late October, the East Coast of the United States was struck by Hurricane Sandy and then a nor'easter a few days later. I wish to share several stories of people who were requesting MBOs and BPs for their families' safety.

∗ ∗ ∗

DeLeah writes: "We were not told Hurricane Sandy would hit West Virginia until only a day or so before the fact. We were all unprepared for a storm capable of such mass destruction. I said many MBO requests for my family and friends and our property throughout this destruction, including:

> **Most Benevolent Outcome Request**
> *"I request a most benevolent outcome that my room, the main house, and all of the families' residences around us be safe and secure, with results even better than I can expect or hope for."*

"The angels were truly with us. Our electricity went out Monday evening, but we were all up all night. The snow was so heavy on the trees that they began falling one by one, everywhere. One small tree fell on my room, but luckily it was not very big and did not do any damage. We watched a gigantic pine tree come down less than three feet from the house. I believe the angels guided it to land near the house rather than on it, because with the way it was leaning when it began to fall, it would have hit the family house and destroyed it. My sister was the one to see it start falling, and she began yelling for everyone to get to the back of the house. When we looked out afterward, it had dented in the roof of a camper but did not hit the house, though it did take down our power line and telephone line.

"The angels were truly with us on this night. In all, we had about twenty-five trees down after the storm, three feet of snow, and the whole region was out of power. Our electricity should be restored by this weekend by current estimates, but we are all thankful that the angels pushed the tree away from us. Thank you, angels. You bless us every day with your miracles!"

∗ ∗ ∗

Kathy writes: "I am in Maryland, and the eye of the storm was forecast to go right over my hometown, which is close to the Chesapeake

Bay. I too had an MBO experience. About a month ago, I bought a ticket for Orlando, Florida, because my guides insisted I needed to get away for a change of pace and some rest and relaxation. So I actually flew out last Friday as the storm was moving up the East Coast.

"Being out of the area freed me from significant anxiety and gave me the ability to request MBOs for the entire area. I never could have planned for that to happen, but I believe that my regular request for safety and protection allowed it to happen. My heart goes out to those suffering now, and I pray daily for their ability to be calm and receive all they need to be safe, warm, and dry and to fully recover in a way that is most benevolent. Miracles can happen for anyone, anytime, through MBOs."

✳ ✳ ✳

Linda writes: "Here in the Poconos, we just went through Hurricane Sandy. It was a frightening storm for so many people. I put my faith in my angels and asked for a benevolent outcome for the storm not to do damage to the property I live on, and it appears to have worked. There are renters in two other apartments as well as my landlord and his wife living here.

"It was very windy here and there were lots of power outages. People nearby lost power, and there are still lots of roads closed. Our property has lots of sticks lying on the ground, and one large tree came down, but there was no damage to any of the buildings or vehicles. I said a very grateful thank you to the angels this morning. I hope more people listen to you and get acquainted with their guardian angels. It is certainly worth it! Thanks so much."

Tom responds: For everyone, here is a BP to say out loud for all those affected by Hurricane Sandy on the East Coast:

Benevolent Prayer
"I ask any and all beings to bring aid and comfort to all those affected by Hurricane Sandy and to assist them in recovering from the trauma, loss of possessions, and any physical injuries they suffered due to the storm. Thank you!"

Serious Storm Protection

Gerry writes: "Last night, the weatherman was predicting severe storms, damaging winds, and possible tornadoes for the northern half of Georgia all night long. I watched as storm cell after storm cell rolled into Georgia from Alabama with our county in their path. I said a BP for everyone affected by the storms and requested an MBO for a circle of protection around my house and property, for protection from severe weather, and for just a gentle rain for my neighborhood.

"The worst of the storms and a tornado went through our county just above us. All we got was a little thunder and lightning and a gentle rain. I went to sleep with total peace of mind. I am so glad I discovered your website a couple years ago. I'm sure it is time-consuming, but keep up the good work."

Good Weather for Birthday Parties

Antonia writes: "Our grandson and nephew each had their own birthday parties planned for the same day, an hour apart. Rain was forecast for the day, and we were supposed to have temperatures reaching the low triple digits. That morning, I asked Gaia for good weather for the afternoon parties. The rain held off until the evening and the temperature was only in the low nineties. Thank you, Gaia, and thank you, Tom, for this great tool!"

✳ ✳ ✳

Shirley writes: "I requested an MBO for perfect weather for my son's second birthday party. Extreme high winds and rain were forecast. On the day before the party, we had almost cyclonic weather with dark rain clouds, rain, and so forth. But on the day of the birthday party, the weather was absolutely beautiful, calm, sunny, and gorgeous. I really do think MBOs work! Thanks, Tom T. Moore and the angels."

Staying Out of Sandstorm

Bill writes: "I went to Odessa, Texas, to move things from my mother's house with a friend. I requested a MBO for a safe journey back to Dallas and good weather. As we headed east, I looked up and saw the sky to the north was red and dark blue. I pointed this out to the friend who was with me, and he thought it was just pollution. I told him it was actually a sandstorm. This is a rare event at the end of June, and in all my years of living in Texas, I can't remember seeing a sandstorm at this time of year.

"As we continued to drive, the wind started blowing quite hard, and the truck and trailer were rocking from the wind. We were not in the sandstorm itself. I was relieved since I am highly allergic to the dust and end up getting asthma attacks from it.

"I looked in the rearview mirror and saw the storm crossing the road about half a mile behind us. We drove with this sandstorm at our back, but the truck and trailer were no longer affected by the wind. I could see the sand was beginning to come closer, but it remained just behind us. It was a very strange experience.

"I have lived off and on in West Texas and have never been able to skirt around a sandstorm. I felt amazed as I watched an MBO in action at how powerful these requests are in our lives. I thought, 'I have to write Tom and tell him about this and thank him for teaching us how to make our lives better by just asking.'"

The Storm-Calming Power of MBOs

Rose writes: "We have been having storms with high winds that are doing lots of damage. So far, every time an alert or warning is issued for our area, I have been requesting an MBO that the storms will be gentler than expected or predicted. So far, all the storms have been less intense here than anywhere else. We get rain, but the wind just routes itself around my area instead of blowing through it."

19

Benevolent Outcomes Involving Pets and Other Animals, Reptiles, and Insects

Benevolent Rabbit Sighting

Erika writes: "While I was out tonight walking through a green belt out behind where we live, I realized I hadn't seen any rabbits for a long time. I missed them, as I love seeing them on my walks. There were always lots of rabbits where I go walking, and I wondered if they had been killed off or something. So I requested an MBO to see one before I got home so I would know they are okay and still around. Then, just before I got home, I spotted one. I felt so happy to see it. Normally they love coming in our backyard each day, but we've had a large dog staying with us for a few months. It felt good to have my MBO happen, as I realized that I had received this as a gift from heaven and that they are really listening up there, so I said thank you, thank you.

"Here is something from *The Quiet Mind: Sayings of White Eagle* by Grace Cooke that I feel might be great for the newsletter list to read, as I appreciated it very much. It sums up MBOs and how they work very well:

Think of life as a vast whole. It is impossible for you to comprehend infinity, but this simple fact you can understand — a prayer, a thought, an aspiration to those in the heavenly world — is never lost. Instantly you make that contact by prayer or meditation angels gather to help you to fulfill your aspiration and to answer a true prayer. It may not always be answered in the way you want, but it will be answered in a very much better way, if only you will be content to leave the outworking of your prayer to God and his angels."

Tom responds: That's a wise shaman!

A Real Fish Story

Rachelle writes: "My husband and I went fishing, and we caught two catfish. They had both swallowed their hooks, and my husband had a hard time getting the hooks out. I was not feeling good about the whole experience, so I asked for an MBO that any other fish we would catch be hooked in the lip so that we could remove the hook easily and set the fish free. I didn't want more than we could eat. Lo and behold! Every single fish we caught after that had the hook in the lip or corner of the mouth so it could be removed easily, and we put the fish back in the water. It made a most benevolent fishing experience! The fish and I were happy!"

A Benevolent End to a Beloved Pet's Life

Lyn writes: "A few weeks ago, one of my cats went missing. After a few days of not seeing him, I had given up hope that he was alive. I had requested an MBO to find out what had happened to him, as I really needed closure. A couple of weeks later, I started calling him again. That night my cat appeared with half his body weight gone.

"I took him to the vet and then tried nursing him back to health at home, but he was unable to keep food and water down. Taking him back to the vet the last time, I said an MBO request to find the best treatment for him. It turned out the best treatment for him was to end his suffering, as he had pancreatic cancer that was literally making his body consume itself.

"I requested an MBO to be guided about whether to be with him or not while he was put down because I can faint from intense emotional stuff. Yet when I saw him, I knew I had to take him out into the sunlight one last time, so he was on my lap in the sunlight when the vet gave him a shot to put him to sleep before giving him the shot to put him down. I thanked my guardian angel for giving me the answers I needed to be at peace and to help my little friend. Thank you for all you do, Tom."

The Perfect Dog

Leanne writes: "This past year, my family and I decided we wanted to add a dog to our family. We decided to try to find an adult dog that needed a good home rather than a puppy, so I asked for an MBO for the perfect dog for my family. We soon found a group who housed a breed called Shar-Peis and decided that this breed suited our requirements. We viewed a male dog, but he very quickly let us know that he was not the dog for us.

"During this visit, I looked down at my feet and saw a lovely female Shar-Pei named Ava sitting under my legs, just watching all of us and waiting to join in the fun and games. She won us over that very day and came home with us the next weekend. She is a delight to have living with us and even befriended the cat as soon as they met — we viewed this as nothing short of a miracle in itself. I knew the right dog had been sent to us and remembered to thank my guardian angel for this gift."

Not-So-Bloody Benevolence

Margaret writes: "Every Memorial Day weekend, my sister and I visit the cemeteries back home to plant flowers and clean up the family graves. Both cemeteries are home to very healthy populations of mosquitoes, and the constant bites make it quite an ordeal for us. This is a perfect MBO situation, so here's the request I've used for the past few years:

Most Benevolent Outcome Request
"Angels, I respectfully request a most benevolent outcome on behalf of my sister and me for a truce with the mosquito folk while we are working outside today. If they will agree not to bother us, we agree to do everything we can to avoid accidentally harming them. And may the results be even better than I can hope for or expect. Thank you!"

"Boy, did it ever work! We saw actual clouds of mosquitoes, but neither one of us was bitten — not even once. A few mosquitoes did land on my skin, but I reminded them that we had asked for a truce and then blew a very gentle puff of air at them, and away they flew.

"One year I also asked for a truce for the whole summer so my energetic young cat and I could enjoy our daily walks. (There was a lot of concern about the West Nile Virus being carried by mosquitoes that year.) The truce worked perfectly for the next three months and ended precisely on September 15, when I got bitten!"

Diabetic Chihuahua in Bad Need of an MBO

Rebecca writes: "Hi, Tom. I have a Chihuahua that is eleven years old. He was recently diagnosed with diabetes and glaucoma. The doctor wants to remove his eye. Is there a way to request an MBO for him?"

Tom responds: You can say,

Most Benevolent Outcome Request
"I ask any and all beings to assist me in finding the best treatment for my dog, _____. Thank you!"

Then you might just get a second opinion. If you have explored all options and feel it is in the best interest of the dog to have the operation, say,

Benevolent Prayer
"I ask any and all beings to assist the veterinarian and assistants in performing a perfect operation on my dog, _____. Thank you!"

A Benevolent Prayer for Every Species

Rocky writes: "How would you rephrase the daily reminder BP to include all animals of every species, or do you feel that it already does that?"

Tom responds: Rocky — and anyone else who wishes to do so — could change the BP that I say every morning as a daily reminder (see *The Gentle Way II*, page 262) from "anyone" to "any being." In other words, you could say,

> **Benevolent Prayer**
> "*I ask that any and all beings assist and comfort any being I have ever harmed, either physically, mentally, morally, spiritually, or emotionally in any past, present, or future life.*"

Here's what my guardian angel said when I asked him whether I ever said the BP I say each morning in any other life: "No, not really. This is the first life in which you've recognized the value of saying this prayer. That's why it is so important that you continue to say this prayer on a daily basis, as it truly does erase much karma like I have explained before. So I am telling you the complete truth here, Tom. Do not doubt this statement, as I know doubt can creep into your mind. This is a true gift to you and all the other lives you've lived and will live on Earth."

The Return of a Friend's Cat

Mark writes: "An MBO I asked for was for a friend whose beloved cat, Ginger, had escaped the house and was missing. I asked for an MBO for her safe return. Three days later, when my friend was about to give up hope, Ginger timidly came up to him in his front yard, allowing him to pet her, calm her, and get her, back inside where she belonged. Thanks for this teaching. I was skeptical at first, but I am convinced now."

MBO for Dogs During Storm

Adrienne writes: "Our two dogs have always been terrified of thunderstorms; they pant, shake, and try to hide. This behavior goes on for several hours and is stressful and exhausting for all of us. It begins as soon as they hear the first thunder in the distance and lasts long after the bad weather has passed. Because of their fear of storms, they were even afraid of gentle rain with no pyrotechnics.

"Recently, however, when a thunderstorm was approaching and the dogs were showing signs of anxiety, I said an MBO request to give us all the strength to cope. The storm was an especially violent one with lots of lightning, thunder, and damaging winds, yet both dogs curled up next to me and slept through it. The following night when we had another equally bad storm, exactly the same thing happened. Even more recently, we had a shower. Instead of cowering in fear, the dogs even went outside to do their business in the rain. It may not sound like much, but this has vastly improved the quality of all our lives. Thank you so much."

Tom responds: And thank you, Adrienne, for the great idea!

The Reincarnation of a Beloved Cat

Darrell writes: "I have received both of your books on MBOs and have had great success with what I call the 'everyday items.' I also have a very special MBO story to share with you. We lost our cat several months ago, but we had finally reached the point of looking for another one. I read in one of your past newsletters that it is possible for animals to reincarnate back into the same family. So I said an MBO request that our cat Meso would reincarnate and once again be a very special part of our family. Since then, I have had very vivid dreams of our old cat for several nights.

"Today we finally went searching for a kitten, and the first place we went into, we asked to see some kittens. As we walked into the kennel, I spotted a kitten that looked exactly like our Meso. I called to it by the name Meso, and the kitten got up and came over to the kennel door. We picked it up and knew right away that it must be Meso. To make a long story short, we decided to take him.

"My wife, daughter, and I are so happy to have found this little kitten thanks to an MBO request and some great work by my guardian angel! I expect great things every day. Thanks again to you, Tom, your guardian angel, and Gaia."

A New Home for a Pet

Peggy writes: "Here is a great MBO story. My granddaughter has moved to a place that does not accept animals. She had to find a home for her two dogs and four cats. She has found homes for everyone but Elly, a cat with a big-time attitude. Next week is the deadline for her to be out of the house, but still no one wanted Elly. She tried the paper, Facebook, word of mouth — but still nothing. It looked like she may have to put her down. I said an MBO request for Elly, and lo and behold, Craigslist came to mind, and Elly found a new home just in the nick of time. Thank you, Lord."

Benevolent Help in Finding a Lost Dog

Tom says: Here is an MBO story of my own. We have two dogs in our family who have been with us for about nine years or so. I've written about them in my second book, especially Sandy, who's a beagle and dachshund mix. When we lived at our old house, we had two electric gates for the driveway, and occasionally one would, stay open because of twigs or pecans on the track. Sandy would escape, and it was a real chore to find her, especially because we lived next to a busy four-lane street. I requested lots of MBOs and tracked her down each time.

Three years ago, we decided we needed new surroundings after living in the same area for thirty-five years, so I requested an MBO for the perfect house for us, and my wife found it shortly after in the northern Dallas suburb town of Plano, Texas — the safest town in the United States, according to *Forbes* magazine. Since we moved, we have been very careful to keep the gate closed, and we have an automatic garage door we also have to watch.

On Friday of last week, my wife asked me to take a large box out to the recycle bins, and I opened the gate and placed it there. Somehow I did not close the gate all the way. Our daughter was at the house clearing out our living room because we were having friends over the next night for a New Year's Eve dinner, and she checked the garage after moving her things there from the living room to make sure Sandy was not in there. But Sandy was not there nor was she anywhere in the house. We noticed the back door was open, and then we saw the gate was open too. We all panicked.

We all went out into the neighborhood calling for Sandy. I had injured my knee carrying heavy tables, so I decided to drive around the neighborhood. I said with emotion,

> **Most Benevolent Outcome Request**
> *"I request an MBO for finding Sandy. Thank you!"*

I first tried the street behind us, but it did not feel right, so then I turned onto the busy six-lane street that we live next to and then back onto our street. My family was already down the street knocking on doors, so I turned down an alley and rolled the windows down, hoping to hear dogs barking at Sandy, but I heard nothing.

Then I turned right and came back up the street, which backed up on the alley. I stopped and knocked on a couple of doors, but no one had seen Sandy. So back in my car, I decided to try a little hand dowsing — holding your hands up to feel energy — and I told my guardian angel to point me in the right direction. I turned back onto our street and started to turn into the same alley, but I said, "I've already been down this alley." So I backed up and then turned down the other street and saw a cul-de-sac on the left. I saw a lady and her daughter washing their front porch, so I pulled up and got out of my car to talk to them. I asked if they had seen a dog passing by, and the woman responded, "Oh! The lady down at the end of the street has the dog! Her name is Rita, and she's in the last house on the block." I thanked her, jumped back in the car, and drove down to the house, which backed up on the same alley I had driven down before.

Rita and her husband have three dogs of their own, and she had carried Sandy all the way down from our street to her home, placed her in her backyard, and called animal control, which was on its way to pick up Sandy. I had arrived just in time. I thanked Rita profusely and took Sandy home. Now that's an MBO story with a great ending!

No More Bugs

Cynthia writes: "I just have to share this one with you. We live in the woods in the mountains of Tennessee. We love our land and the opportunity to share it with all of God's creatures; however, there are some that have made life a bit difficult. I'm referring to the bees and wasps. We have carpenter bees that love to drill holes in the soffits of the house and wasps that love to build their nests in the stacked stone on the front of the house, including all around the front door — our main means of ingress and egress. When the wasps start hatching out, the adults get very aggressive, and we have been chased, attacked, and stung many times, including multiple times at once. I have become extremely wary of them and the potential for anaphylactic shock setting in after one of these attacks.

"Last week I decided to begin requesting help. I wasn't sure if those requests should go to Gaia or any and all beings, so I included both:

> **Benevolent Prayer**
> "I request Gaia and any and all beings to speak to the bees and wasps and ask them to please move their activity and nesting out into the woods away from the house so that they will come to no harm and we will come to no harm. Thank you."

"Well, you already know the results — the wasps have mysteriously disappeared from around the house, and the bees, other than enjoying the nectar from a couple of trees out front, have also moved away!

"I am thrilled for all of us. Now we can come and go without threat, and I can garden without dodging skydiving wasps. I practice organic gardening and never use chemicals in or around the house or property, so this solves a serious risk we would be facing yet another season. Thank you for all your wisdom and insights."

A Calming MBO for Deer

Shannon writes: "I ask for MBOs as soon as I wake up in the morning and all day long. Everything goes my way for the most part, so I just assume that this is because I am requesting MBOs all day. The first thing out of my mouth every morning is,

> **Most Benevolent Outcome Request**
> "I request an MBO for this day. May it be better than I could ever hope for or dream of."

"I also have a lot of deer on the road to my job every day, so when I see them, I request an MBO that they stay where they are and not become frightened. It works. My husband is always amazed when he drives with me that the deer do not scatter."

Benevolent Prayers for Animal Safety

Louise writes: "I enjoy your newsletter so much! Thanks for doing such a great job with it. I recently had a situation that caused me alarm. The person who was going to look after my horses while I am away during the last two weeks in August just announced that she will be moving and that the last day she will be available will be August 26. My husband and I had already booked our flights from August 16 through 30, so I said an MBO request about it and let the universe answer. (I am getting much better at relaxing after I request MBOs, by the way.)

"The next morning I was able to find a person who could replace the one who is moving. Not only that, but a total stranger and her daughter came up to me when I was riding and asked if I needed any help. Whoopee! Now I not only have one but three helpers available. What a bonus!

"Now that I am feeling good about having people to look after my horses, is there a special MBO request that I can say from another state so that my animals are safe in the case of a hurricane, or would a normal MBO request work just the same? The safety of my animals is very important to me, so any help you can give me is greatly appreciated."

Tom responds: I suggest that Louise — and anyone with animals or pets who must be left in the care of others while on vacation — say this BP:

Benevolent Prayer
"*I ask any and all beings to keep my horses (animals, pets, and so on) safe, now and into the future. Thank you!*"

A Great Outcome in the Search for a New Kitty

Gail writes: "My story is about a benevolent outcome I asked for when looking for a new cat to add to my household. I requested just the right kitty for our family and that, when introduced to my old, huge cat and our dog, there would be none of the hissing or fighting that usually happens at first. I still marvel at how complete and wonderful the outcome was.

"We found the most loving, sweet one-year-old kitty, and she is a complete joy for us. The extent of her gentleness and congeniality is unusual for a cat, and from the first moment she met our older cat and dog, she got along splendidly with them. Anyone who has introduced a cat into a household with another cat knows what a miracle this is. *The Gentle Way* helps us in our everyday lives, reduces our anxiety, and it is a good tool for turning our life challenges, big and small, over to a higher power."

Help for an Ailing Dog with Her First Litter of Puppies

Elizabeth writes: "My puppy dog, Molly, just had her very first litter of puppies — an accident. I got up on a Friday morning and noticed that she looked really awful and was clearly not herself. I called the vet and said an MBO requesting that they were able to see her right away. Despite a busy schedule, they allowed me to drop her off. I went to work and received a call very quickly. The vet said she was bleeding internally and needed a blood transfusion immediately. It was initially touch and go, but her body accepted the transfusion and started to perk up.

"I was able to take her home the same day but was told that she would not be able to nurse her puppies after the trauma. I took her home and said daily MBOs that she would recover fully and be able to nurse her babies. By Monday, she was almost fully recovered and nursing her puppies! Thank you, thank you, thank you!"

A Safe Ending for a Kitten on the Loose

Terri writes: "Today I took my kitten to the vet. Before we left home, I made sure the carrier was secure. By the time I got to the vet, two of the latches had come loose, and when I picked up the carrier, Bella was able to dash out of the opening and hide under the car. I enlisted the help of the vet and the office manager. Needless to say, I was quite worried, especially since I have recently had foot surgery and am not steady on my feet yet. I couldn't crawl around on the ground looking for her. Bella moved around and under bushes and finally ended up under bushes that aligned with the front door. They were concerned, as was I, that once they got her to move, she might run out into the busy street instead of heading in the door. I immediately said an MBO request, asking that she be safely rescued by going in the front door. Less than two minutes later — an eternity, it seemed — here comes a very scared kitten dashing in the door and running all over. The outside door was quickly shut, and Bella was safe. Thank you, angels!"

Getting Rid of a Snake

Donna writes: "On Saturday I noticed that a black garden snake was sitting in a potted plant on my screened-in patio. I could see its head and several inches of its body standing straight up, so I used a couple of MBO requests and a BP to ask the snake to leave and move away from the house. After about fifteen minutes, it slithered out of the pot and out through a small opening in the screen that I didn't even realize was there.

"When I saw the snake leave, I realized that it was at least three feet long! I know it wasn't poisonous, but I couldn't let my kitty out while it was there, and I sure didn't feel comfortable about going out there. I honestly don't know what I would have done without the help I got from the MBOs. A friend of mine witnessed the whole thing, and she was so impressed that she's saying MBO requests for everything now. Thank you so much, Tom!"

Benevolent Break on Vet Bill

Lee writes: "I was at the vet with one of our poodles, who has a yeast infection. I requested an MBO that my dog would be okay and that the charges would be reasonable and better than I could expect. The vet started listing options, and I told her it has been a rough year and asked her what she could do to help us out. She gave me a prescription that was only $18, did one procedure for free, and gave me a discount on the office visit. Thank you, thank you, thank you!"

MBOs to Protect Dogs

Zoe writes: "My MBOs are coming before I have even cracked open my copy of your book! From your newsletter, I had an idea about how to say a particular prayer. I have been having trouble with other dogs and their owners while walking my large dog in a neighborhood that's relatively new to us. Dogs like to pounce on each other and so on. Well, I have been requesting MBOs before each walk, and each time, I know things will work out, even if we run into other dogs, although I include that in my MBO — that we not encounter them, if possible.

"Two days ago, we came up to a large man and his large dog who would not go the other way, even when I said I didn't want the dogs to jump on each other. Then, from out of nowhere, two other men came up behind me and helped me shield my dog while the stubborn man passed us. It turns out we were standing right in front of the two men's destination. I thanked them and told them that they were angels."

Tom responds: That's how MBOs work for you and your pet's safety: Something will happen, such as the intervention above. I always request an MBO for our walk with our dogs each morning.

An Owl Finds a Home

Teresa writes: "I have studied metaphysics for many, many years and was at a Kryon seminar in Dallas over a year ago where Lee introduced you to the audience. I have been using the 'expect great things' mantra and your other affirmations, and I must admit that I have been pretty astonished with the results in a fairly short time.

"As an example, we have had an owl box up in our backyard for at least four years without any success, but now we finally have a female eastern screech owl nesting in our box. I am just ecstatic about it, and I understand that this type of owl usually returns to the same nest year after year. I try to make our backyard a little current-day Garden of Eden. I am expecting great things these days. Thanks!"

My Mother, the Scottish Terrier

Tom says: We've previously covered the subject of requesting an MBO for the return of the soul fragment that was the family dog. I had not heard about the following possibility before.

Kathy writes: "I have had six Scotties over the course of thirty-five years. I now have a four-year-old wheaten and a three-year-old black Scottie. They are brother and sister by different fathers. The blonde is female; the black-haired dog is male and the younger of the two. The younger black one seems exceptionally attached to me. It is hard to describe. Is he here to guide me? Somehow, I feel my mother sent him. She passed away in my home after living with ovarian cancer in 2006. This little Scottie seems different from all my others. Why?

"By the way, I am learning to use my MBOs and tell others how wonderful they are. Thank you for coming into my life!"

Tom responds: I asked my guardian angel if Karen's black dog was here to guide her in some way, and if it was perhaps sent by her mother. "Not exactly, Tom, but certainly her mother uses the dog in that way," my angel answered. "She and the dog have been together before, so it feels like a close relationship with her. This is a little unique, since normally a person has to ask for the dog's soul fragment to be sent. In this case, however, it was the mother. So the dog senses a previous close relationship."

MBO for Dog's Health

Carol writes: "Recently I asked my guardian angel for an MBO for Feisty, my West Highland white terrier. She is eleven years old, and I noticed she had been breathing strangely, even panting when at a complete rest. I asked another connection I have to Spirit, Dr. Peebles, to scan her and give me advice. He said I should go to the vet and get an x-ray or scan. There was some problem in her lungs. Thinking the worst, I requested an MBO that whatever she had not be serious.

"After the x-rays, the vet advised me that there was no cancer or tumor but that Feisty had a diffused airway pattern with heavy infiltrates and possibly bronchitis. He put her on a bronchodilator and antibiotics, and she is much better now. My vet mentioned to me that he was relieved it wasn't something more serious, because often it is with these symptoms.

"Thank you, my guardian angel, for your help. And thank you, Tom, for introducing me to MBO requests and showing me how to use them often for the little things, a concept I learned from your teleclass. I use one or more daily now."

Benevolent Safety for Dogs

Tom says: In July of 2005 in Sedona, I learned that I was supposed to write the book *The Gentle Way*. In September of that year, my wife and I took an Alaskan cruise as part of a Kryon seminar. Lee Carroll was nice enough to let me do a quick fifteen-minute presentation to the group of sixty people about MBOs. Sue was part of this group, which I wrote about in the book.

Sue writes: "Hi Tom! I have been doing MBOs for four years now since meeting you in 2005 on the Alaskan cruise, and it's now second nature for me to quickly say one at this point. I seriously think I say at least ten a day! Here's an excellent example: Last week my dogs and I were staying at my sister's house in the country, where she has open land and no fenced yard. Her house sits back quite a ways from her dirt road. While I was in my sister's garage cleaning out her van, I lost track of time and suddenly realized I was not hearing my dogs playing nearby. I quickly ran out of the garage and looked out front to the road.

"Instant panic! There, happily playing in the road, was my two-year-old dog, Fritz, and trotting out to him — and about six feet away — was my six-year-old dog, Mason. Most horrifying of all was the sight of my ten-year-old dog, Lucas, who is losing his hearing, more than halfway down the driveway on his way to meet them. I started screaming Fritz's name and yelling, 'Come!' While running toward them and screaming their names and the command 'Come!' I also said, as fast as I possibly could,

> **Most Benevolent Outcome Request**
> *"I request an MBO for the dogs to get out of the road and be safe, be safe, be safe!"*

"Then I kept screaming and trying desperately to get my old boys' attention. It must have been quite a sight, with me running down the driveway, frantically waving my arms to get Luke's attention, since he couldn't really hear me until I got closer. Thankfully, Fritz turned and ran toward me and out of the road after the first 'Come!' command. Mason turned toward me after my MBO, and then Lucas turned and looked at me and started right to me. Well, after some very heartfelt thanks to the angels and some tears of fear and joy, I got the boys into the garage where I should have kept them in the first place. I am certain my guardian angels, along with the extremely fast MBO request I said in one breath, saved my boys!"

Loosey Goosey

Kate writes: "Here is an MBO story that is just plain beautiful. I requested an MBO as I left for work, a general one for the day. Right as I exited the house, I heard the familiar honk of what I thought was a

V-formation of Canadian geese flying north. But I looked and looked, and even though the sound was very loud, I could not find the geese. Then I spotted one lone white snow goose, twenty feet or less above the roof of my house. There were no other geese in sight! I called the Audubon Society, and the person I reached said that snow geese are common about thirty miles south of me, but that they are rarely spotted in South Burlington and that they rarely fly alone. It was pretty angelic."

MBO Saves Kitten on the Highway

Cynthia writes: "Tom, I have an incredible MBO story. I was going up the North Dallas Tollway, just passing the Keller Springs entrance, when out of the corner of my eye I saw something jump at the cement wall. I knew it was a kitten. So I got off, circled around, got back on the tollway, and saw it was indeed a kitten. It was trying to stay as close to the cement as possible. I circled about another two times and said prayers and MBOs that I could get the kitten off the highway and that it would stay alive.

"I stopped my car on the feeder that goes into the tollway, ran up on the street, and grabbed the kitten. Then I ran back to my car and got back on the tollway, and I was able to go home with the kitten. It was unhurt but very scared, dehydrated, and starving. He's about eight weeks old now and is very bonded to me because I carried him around for the first day, since he had no energy. He's doing much better now, since that was three days ago. Thank God for the MBOs that kept me and the kitten safe!"

Benevolent Prayer for an Itchy Pet

Bill writes: "I was reading your past newsletters and got your message. I met you awhile back when you spoke in Grapevine. Of all the people who have spoken there, I was most impressed with your message. Since then I have shared your stories and webpage with many. I know not everyone will accept your ideas because of their beliefs, but I seem to know when to share your message with the right people. It's amazing how that works and how I get whispers to introduce your stories at an appropriate time. I've said MBO requests and BPs even more regularly since I met you and bought your book.

"I will tell you a great answer to a prayer that just happened. For seven years of my dog's ten-year life, she has had constant skin allergies and problems. I have spent a fortune on vet bills trying to help her. Her name is Peggy Sue, and she's a very sweet West Highland terrier. This breed is prone to skin conditions, and I was told there isn't much I can do about that but keep her away from grains and bathe her multiple times a week. I said a BP for Peggy Sue last week. I don't know why I didn't think of this before! Since then, she's not scratching and miserable, and she's the best she's been in years. Thanks again, Tom, for all you do."

Lost Puppy Found

Beth writes: "My puppy, Stormy, ran away from home recently. I wanted you to know that I said my MBO requests and passed out flyers up and down my road. My neighbor from far down across the tracks called me early the next morning as she spotted my dog in the pasture next to her home. Mr. Stormy is home safe and sound now. Thank you!"

20

Benevolent Outcomes with Technology

Help with an Old Computer

Isabelle writes: "Greetings from Melbourne, Australia, and I hope this finds you and your family very well. A recent MBO I experienced in mid-April occurred when my very old but reliable computer began to have serious problems involving physical damage to the hard drive. It looked as though it had stopped working altogether or that even if I were able to get it going, it wouldn't last much longer and I would soon have to obtain another computer.

"Lack of computer access is a big deal for me, as I coordinate a support group for people living with disabilities and need to be able to receive and send emails for all matters pertaining to the group. As everyone likely knows already, these days almost all business and community communications are conducted via email. Another aspect to the loss of computer access for me is that I have disabilities myself, so obtaining a new computer isn't just a matter of going out and buying one.

"I remembered your oft-repeated advice, Tom, that MBOs can be requested for all manner of things. When my computer suddenly went on the blink, I said more MBO requests than you could count. I requested an MBO for help in obtaining a new computer, for my old computer to keep working until I had a replacement up and running, and a whole lot more.

"I also telephoned my brother-in-law, who is an IT consultant, and he gave me loads of good advice. I was able to get the old computer going again, although most of the time it wouldn't work properly. On one occasion, it slowed down over a period of thirty-five minutes and then stopped all together. Even the system clock stopped. I turned off the power switch and said, 'RIP,' as I thought that was the end. Then, a few hours later, I said an MBO for it to work, thinking I was silly to even expect it. Lo and behold, I turned it on, and it worked perfectly!

"The help continued. My sister and brother-in-law telephoned me out of the blue and said they were sending me the funds to buy a refurbished computer. I found a nonprofit organization that could sell me a good second-hand computer at a reasonable price, and I was able to pay to have it delivered at minimum inconvenience to me. So not only does my guardian angel love me and want to help me but he or she is also very skilled with technology!

"Once again, thank you, Tom, for sharing such useful life skills that bring assistance and also healing and growth. You seem to work so hard, and I look forward to the day — coming soon, I believe! — when you will be a household name and millions will be saying MBO requests for their own good and for the good of the planet."

Cable Conundrum Fixed

Lyn writes: "Just this morning I was helping a friend rearrange her office and bedroom. Everything went smoothly until it was time to turn on the computer. Nothing! We checked everything, and we had been so careful labeling cables and plugging them back in — or so we thought. We finally requested an MBO, which we should have done first! Then we took a lunch break, walked back, and immediately saw that a cable we'd plugged in earlier had come undone. Problem fixed! Thanks, angels!"

Lost Files Recovered

Tom says: The next story concerns my son, Todd. Todd has been working for us for the past couple of years, but for the past year, he's been working on a computer program that will help him buy and sell such things as money futures. He's about ready to put it into action in the next month, and over the past year, he had written twenty-one pages of detailed notes on the program.

The other night, he told his computer to save something on it, and instead, it erased all twenty-one pages of work. He had no backup on his Mac, and he said he felt absolutely ill and devastated at the thought of having lost all his work. He immediately said,

Benevolent Prayer
"I ask any and all beings to assist me in recovering my work. Thank you!"

He then got on the phone with Mac or Apple support staff and was at first told there was nothing that could be done. When he persisted, however, he was put through to a senior systems specialist who said he could probably recover the work — which my son says is unheard of.

As of yesterday evening, the Apple specialist had recovered all but the last four pages he had entered in the past week, and my son says it will all be recovered in the next couple of days or so. Naturally, he has now saved those pages on a disc. The end result of the ordeal was to lower his stress level on this challenge, since he was taught a lesson without having to start from the beginning.

MBO for a Computer Virus

Jules writes: "This is funny, Tom. I have had a very nasty virus on my computer; someone infected it very well. It was crashing every thirty to forty-five minutes for seventy-two hours. This morning, I asked for an MBO for this computer to be fixed so I could work on it. Well, I got on the computer, loaded it up, and there was nothing wrong with it other than the fact that it had no virus protection. I downloaded two protection programs, scanned the computer, found two minor things, and that was it. A computer friend of mine did a remote probe and couldn't find a thing! Now how is that for a miracle of an MBO? Thanks bunches!"

Fast Service, Coming Up!

Carmen writes: "I have a healing and hypnosis business, and I communicate over the Internet with people quite a bit. However, my Internet went down. I was informed that I needed to purchase a new modem/router. I also had a hairdresser's appointment that I had to keep, and I was running late!

"As I walked into the store to get a new modem, there were seven people in line ahead of me. I squirmed, knowing that I had a very short time to make my appointment! Not knowing what to do, I said,

Most Benevolent Outcome Request

"I ask the benevolent angels to please take care of all the customers ahead of me easily and effortlessly so that I can be served and be on my way to the hairdressers' safely. I also would like to request that the most experienced salesman easily take care of our problem and everyone else's problem. Thank you so much!"

"Within minutes, the people who had been taking so long suddenly had their problems solved, and the line quickly moved until it was magically our turn to be served. The salesman immediately knew what we needed, processed our order, and had us out the door in record time. We hit every green light on the way to the mall, and I was sitting in the hairdresser's chair right on time — a most magical day! Thank you, Tom, for making the world more aware of this gift from God and the angels. God bless you."

A Laptop That Practically Fell into My Lap

Debra writes: "Hi Tom, I found you through reading your articles in the *Sedona Journal* and have been requesting MBOs ever since. I wanted to share a recent experience. I requested an MBO for a laptop that would work well and come to me easily and quickly. I did not consider that I did not have the resources at the time to go and buy this for myself; I just trusted that my beloved angels would provide the means.

"The next day, a dear friend of mine from back home sent me a text message saying that she had a spare laptop and asking if I would like to have it. I responded that she had just answered a prayer for me! Not only that, but she took it in to have all of her material removed from the memory and shipped it straight to me. I am typing on it right now. I love you, love the angels, love the MBO requests, and love my new laptop! Thank you all so very much for the light-filled work that you do. Blessings!"

The *H* Key Is Back in Action

Nancy writes: "One evening after work, Tim was on the computer and I was reading nearby. He suddenly expressed great frustration with the computer. When I asked him what was wrong, he said that the *H* key was refusing to work. So I promptly said an MBO request for the key to work and went back to reading.

"A short time later, I looked over, and Tim was working away. I asked him if the *H* key was working, and he said it was. I asked him when he was going to tell me that, and he looked surprised and said that he had just gotten right back to his work. I laughed and told him that it wasn't as though I didn't know that it was working — all I had to do was look at him!"

Most Benevolent Wii Bowling

Ron writes: "I am really getting the gist of creating MBO requests. Since I am just starting out on this, I do see instances when it doesn't always work, but with practice requesting them every day, I am sure it gets better and better.

"Here is a success I had last Tuesday: My wife and I belong to the senior center here in our community, and on Tuesday mornings, we go there to play Wii bowling. Last week, just before entering the building, I requested an MBO for bowling some high games. Well, we bowled four games, and mine were all in the middle 200s, which I was very proud of. I hadn't bowled that well in a very long time, and I know I can thank my guardian angel for it. Not only that, but every person at my table bowled very well too. Don't you call that the 'radiant effect'? In any case, we all had a very fun time!

"I really appreciate the work you are doing, and I am going to be learning even more about angels in the next couple of months. I am looking forward to learning more, although it would have been nice to have learned this as a child as well. Be that as it may, I know more now, and I am enjoying the journey of a great relationship with my guardian angel."

Tom responds: This is an example of a "radiant effect," as I described it in my first book. When you request MBOs for yourself, others often seem to be covered as well. One example I've used before is that of a woman who wrote to tell me she had requested an MBO for her trip on a city bus in Seattle. As the bus approached the Space Needle, suddenly a truck in front stopped abruptly and the bus driver had to slam on his breaks. He stopped about six inches or so from the back of the truck. So not only was the lady not injured, but neither were any of the other people in the bus, and she was able to joke about it with the bus driver instead of being shaken by the close call.

An MBO Worth "Tweeting" About

Lyn writes: "Hi, Tom! I volunteer for a veteran's organization here in Chicago. We have been struggling with a website issue for a while. I finally asked for an MBO about this. When will I learn not to wait so long? A wonderful young woman showed up at our fundraiser meeting, stepped in, created a brand-new website, and put us on Twitter — all for free! She also showed me how to maintain the website and offered to keep us updated on Twitter. I love it!"

Help with My Xbox and Beyond

Dawna writes: "These MBOs are amazing tools. Anytime my printer or computer gets glitches, I request an MBO that it works with ease and grace. So far, it has worked every time. For example, after many unsuccessful attempts at hooking up the right wires between my modified Xbox, the computer, the TV, and another gadget, I got wise and asked for an MBO that I be able to put it all together with ease and grace. I sat in silence for a few seconds, and then, once again my request was answered. I just knew where to plug each wire so that it all worked perfectly.

"It also worked for my cousin, who was adding some new gadget on my computer. It wasn't going well, so I talked him into asking for an MBO and of course said one as well, and, as usual, it worked. He found the solution within a very short time. I was even having problems with an electric knife a few days ago; the blades would not eject, so I asked for an MBO that it come apart with ease right now, please. Well, I'll be darned if it didn't come apart on the next pull. Thanks to our wonderful workers!"

Restoring a Broken Internet Connection

Tom says: I subscribe to Google's word service that informs you of the use of specific words. The service listed a blog by Mark Ament, who writes on holistic healing and natural health. His e-book *Nature's Three Most Powerful Remedies* is available for free on his site, healingvibes .com. He gave me permission to reprint the following piece.

Mark writes: "Last week before I left the United States for the long journey across the Pacific to Bali, I stopped into a bookstore and picked up a copy of the magazine the *Sedona Journal of Emergence!* for the flight. Thumbing through the pages, a small article near the back caught my attention. The article was a compilation of stories from surprised, grateful, and very happy readers who have been using the MBO process to improve their lives. The little tool comes from Tom T. Moore, who investigates the phenomenon of angels. He's been using the process now for at least a couple of years and has seen it reduce stress and fear and make his life a lot easier — and so have a lot of his readers.

"Here's a small example of how I used this tool the other day: Back in Bali, I soon discovered — to my dismay but not my surprise — that the Internet in my office was no longer working, even though the wireless router was working fine in other parts of the house. My knee-jerk reaction was to immediately go into fixing mode and try to get it repaired right way, but the concept of MBOs was fresh in my mind. I decided to give it a try. I stopped what I was doing and asked out loud:

> **Most Benevolent Outcome Request**
> *"I'm not sure why the Internet is not working, and I request a most benevolent outcome for repairing the Internet. Thanks!"*

"With that simple phrase, I noticed that I felt better and less stressed about the situation. A little while later, I decided to leave the office and go into town to take care of some other business. On my way home, I happened to pass my favorite computer store and found myself stopping my motorbike at the front door. I explained the situation to one of the technicians, who then offered to come to my house and see if he could fix it himself. He said he'd be there in about forty-five minutes.

"Now, if you've never been to Bali, you probably don't know about the concept of 'rubber time.' It basically means that forty-five minutes could be an hour or maybe even two or three — and quite possibly never. Living here, you quickly learn to make sure you have other things to do when waiting for an appointment. So I was surprised when the tech pulled up in front of the house less than forty-five minutes after we met in the store! We spent the next half-hour together trying to get the connection working. After eliminating everything else, he determined that it must be that the cable I had running to my office was bad. I agreed, and he started packing his tool kit. As he was walking out to the door, I asked him how much I owed him, and he said, 'Don't worry about it.'

"Heading back to the office, my first thought was to rush down to the computer store and buy thirty meters of outdoor cable this time. (My office is detached from the house, and the current cable runs through a jungle of plants.) Instead, I changed directions and went to the kitchen and had a drink. While I was drinking, I remembered that we had another long run of Internet cable leftover from a previous company we had used. It was an outdoor cable, and since it wasn't being used, I decided to pull it off the house and use it for the office.

"I wrestled the cable off of the walls and out from under the roof tiles, and about twenty minutes later, I had it on the ground. Stretching it toward the office, I was sure I had my problem solved, but the cable came up too short. Now, I know myself, and normally that would have upset me, so I was surprised when it didn't. I rolled the cable up and tossed it aside and then found myself observing the wireless router and looking for some other solution. I noticed that it had an extra ten meters of cable on it or so. I simply moved it closer to my office and looked to see if the wireless connection would work. It did, and presto! I had an Internet connection again. The total cost to me was a little bit of sweat and labor and absolutely zero dollars.

"This is a small example of a larger principle. I know that it's a pretty insignificant example, but restoring my Internet and actually making it work better than before for no cost certainly was an MBO. I think what grabbed my attention the most was how I behaved so differently than I might have normally — which most likely would have involved buying a new cable and spending a few irritated hours running it.

"Since then, I've been requesting MBOs for lots of things in my life. Not everything is coming out exactly how I had envisioned it beforehand, but it does seem that things are really working out for the best and that the practical details of life are getting easier. For me, just like for Tom T. Moore, the tool of requesting MBOs is reducing fear and stress and lightening things up a lot. Thanks, Tom, and thanks all you guys out there working on this. If this article resonates with you, I hope that you give MBOs or your version of them a try. There may just be someone out there just waiting for the chance to help!"

Tom adds: I've been requesting MBOs for fourteen years now, so I know these requests really do work perfectly. In order for the requests to work for you, you need to request them yourself from your own knowledge and experience.

Video Game Triumph via MBO-Awakened Third Eye

Carlos writes: "Monday I requested this MBO:

Most Benevolent Outcome Request
"I request the most benevolent outcome of being able to awaken, stimulate, and sharpen my third eye. Thank you."

"As soon as I finished the MBO request, I got this tingling sensation in my third-eye area that lasted for about ten minutes. Yesterday morning I repeated that MBO request, and the same thing happened. I even got the tingling sensation hours later all on its own! It happened late last night when I was playing a video game. A couple of times while I was playing, a few things happened that I knew I didn't do or couldn't have done myself. I casually looked at my ring count for the stage I was doing, and the amount was 444!"

21

Benevolent Outcomes for Games of Chance

Most Benevolent Quilting Outcomes

Denise writes: "I thought I'd share a really fun series of MBO stories that occurred earlier this year. I am a quilter and found I had the opportunity to attend what is called a long arm quilt show in March. This was not too long before the show, and the hotels supporting the show get booked up almost a year in advance. I was able to get a hotel room for the three nights but not at the hotel where the show was being held. As I was traveling by myself, I knew I would feel more comfortable in the show hotel. I asked for an MBO and called the show hotel back a few weeks before I was to go, and lo and behold, a room had opened up and I was able to book it for all three nights!

"I took part in a number of classes and noticed that the teachers generally would hold a raffle to give away a prize or two at the end of the class. So at the beginning of my last class, I asked for an MBO to win a prize — and I did! (I don't win many things, either.) To top it all off, the show itself was having a raffle to win a huge basket full of quilting items. As I dropped my entry into the box, I of course requested an MBO to win the raffle, went on my way, and forgot all about it. I received a phone call two days after I came home informing me I had won the raffle basket! The box came, and it contained almost $1,000 worth of items, all of which are very useful. I still can't believe all of the wonderful occurrences during my trip. MBOs certainly make life more fun!"

Tom responds: Yes, everyone, you will have more fun in life when you begin requesting MBOs!

Luck Be a Lady Tonight

Deb writes: "I have a thirty-one-year-old son with Asperger's Syndrome named Jesse. He lives at home with his dad and me and is able to work. He is a great kid (he will always be a kid to me). My therapist is also Jesse's life coach; his name is Rick.

"We all request the MBOs. Jesse likes to do the scratch-off lottery tickets, and before he scratches them off, he always says,

Most Benevolent Outcome Request
"I am asking for a benevolent outcome of cash. Thank you."

"Sometimes he wins really big and sometimes he loses, but he just loves to play them. He never forgets to request his MBO. I thought you would enjoy that. Jesse is a sheer delight. As I always say, I wouldn't take anything for him, but then on some days I would give him to you. He keeps me busy!"

Tom responds: Folks, just a reminder that requesting MBOs to win the lottery will not work if it's not in your soul contract for sudden wealth. Jesse probably does okay because the amounts are not huge on scratch-offs. In my book, I mentioned a lady who worked at the drugstore near where I used to live who seemed to consistently win — not the big million-dollar ones, but smaller prizes in the thousands. She was just tuned in to the numbers, it seems. Her guardian angel was whispering in her ear.

MBO for Bingo Victory

Deb writes: "I have to tell you, I had an MBO. I asked for a win at bingo, and I won $500; that was on October 25, 2010."

Tom responds: Incidentally, Mary recently wrote again to say she won another $350!

Betting on MBOs

Sue writes: "The gambling chapter in your book *The Gentle Way* was interesting. Like you, I have had this presumption that I would have to do physical labor for my prosperity. But if there's magic in the ethers — magic with your guardian angel or guides — would it not be possible to win big enough to get caught up and be comfortable for the remainder of this life?"

Tom responds: Regarding games of chance, my guardian angel told me it was not in my soul contract to become suddenly enormously wealthy — whether through the lottery, an inheritance, or otherwise. It does seem to work better if you request an MBO to pay off a specific debt or for a specific purpose. So I would recommend going for the smaller amounts, and then if your soul contract calls for sudden wealth, you'll be happily surprised.

Make Mine a Plasma

Sue writes: "I just wanted to tell you that I love both your books! They have been so helpful in my life and in my kids' lives too. We all request MBOs all the time. I wanted to tell you of one MBO that was the best so far. My youngest daughter and I were at my place of employment's biggest fundraiser auction of the year, and I bought three raffle tickets for $25. The largest prize was a 42-inch plasma TV.

"Just before the numbers were drawn, I said an MBO request to win the TV — and guess what? We did! My daughter was so excited; she couldn't wait to tell her oldest sister! I have requested MBOs for parking or good days at work, but nothing really substantial until now; how this has reinforced my faith! My kids and I have been going through a rough time — I am in the process of getting a divorce — so this was a really nice surprise."

Lotto Win

Sisi writes: "I just received an MBO. I just got in and went to do some posting and check my lottery results. Standing in the cue, I internally asked my ancestor and guide to provide me with a little lotto win. Guess what? I won $74 .11! Thank you!"

Benevolent Bingo!

Ron writes: "I have been working with my MBOs and having some success with some small things as well. I have been sharing your website with all of my friends and relatives too.

"I am in charge of our bingo program here where I live in a senior living apartment building. One of the ladies who attends our bingo games weekly recently told me she was upset because she wasn't winning any games. So last night I shared your story with her about your bingo success on that Alaskan cruise, and she was excited by that. I also told her how to make a request to her angel for winning a round in our bingo game. So she made her request before the games started, and she won the very first game we played! She was so very excited, and I could see the gleam in her eyes as she looked at me. I was so happy for her too. She is now very interested in learning more about MBOs.

"I also had another lady who overheard me talking about angels, and she asked if it would work for her too. I told her I was sure it would work. So I told her how to make her MBO request, and she won a bingo game too. None of these ladies had won games in a very long time, so they were both very thankful and wanted to learn more. I told them both about your books and also told them again how to request their MBOs. I am so happy to be able to share this information and your books with everyone I know."

Tom responds: If you wish to read more about requesting MBOs for bingo, I wrote an article for a bingo newspaper about my own successes and the successes of others. You can read it on my website.

Ron writes back: "Thanks, Tom. It just so happens that I had your article with me last night to show my two friends after the bingo games. They were both very excited about this. I have a question for you: What if several people ask for help during a bingo game like this? Will all of them win or just a small amount of them?"

Tom responds: One of the rules of requesting an MBO is that it must be benevolent for everyone involved in the request. So winning every game would not be. But winning a game showed each of those ladies that requesting MBOs works. Hopefully they will start requesting MBOs for all the other things going on in their lives. Notice how happy it made them. Can you imagine what requesting MBOs all the time will do?

The Winning Raffle Ticket

Lee writes: "Tom, I have a great MBO story to tell. A website, SignsOf Angels.com, had a month-long contest to win a salt lamp — a contest you can enter as often as you like. I said an MBO prior to entering the first time to win this lamp. I entered several times during the month, but most times I forgot to say an MBO request. But you only really need to say it once, right? Well, today I found out that I won! I am such a believer in MBOs and the joy they bring! Thank you!"

A Little Help on Gaming Nights

Carlos writes: "A couple of nights ago, I was playing Spades with my mom, niece, and cousin. It was my cousin and me against my mom and my niece. About a quarter of the way into our game, I said an MBO request to have a great hand for that round. My mom laughed and said that wasn't fair, so she requested an MBO for the same thing. At the end of that round, both teams achieved the exact number of books that we each bid (that was the only time that both teams hit our bids exactly in the same round without going over or under). Throughout the game, we said a few more similar MBO requests, and we had a lot of fun saying that our guardian angels were probably watching us and putting bets on us."

Tom responds: Something similar happened to us on Thanksgiving Day. We were playing "Chickenfoot," a domino game, after stuffing ourselves. I requested an MBO to win one of the games and my son said, "Hey, no fair asking for outside assistance!"

Winning Olympics Tickets

Lois writes: "Last summer I was visiting with friends of my older son in London. They mentioned that they were trying to get tickets for the Olympics, which are only available by lottery. These are highly coveted and in very high demand; not everyone who wants to go will get to go. I knew that my son and his girlfriend were already planning to come to London to visit friends during the Olympics this summer. So I said a BP for Lou, my son, to win one of the lotteries, with a *'may the outcome be better…'*

supercharge at the end. I just heard that when the last of several drawings was held, Lou got tickets for them all to the opening day's ceremony, which was the one they wanted to go to the most. I was quite pleased. They were all jumping up and down with glee!"

Winning a Radio Contest

Kristy writes: "Yesterday, a local radio station was having a special 'thanks to our listeners' day, and every hour they were giving away $300. It was early in the morning, and I was getting ready for work, so when they announced the contest, I said an immediate MBO request that I would win the money before I went to work. I'm sure you can guess what happened: Five minutes later they announced that the tenth caller would win, so I called. It rang, which is unusual in a radio contest. Usually, a busy signal is all I hear. I almost hung up because I couldn't believe they'd already taken nine other calls. Lo and behold, I won! That was the first time I'd ever asked for an MBO for a contest."

22

Benevolent Outcomes for Entertainment

Theater Ticket MBO

Delores writes: "Tom, I have begun to request MBOs to see how it feels. Last night, I requested an MBO to see a sold-out play at a very small local theater with only about fifty seats where some friends were performing. I arrived early and was put on a waiting list — there were five people ahead of me — and the staff told me that it was unlikely I'd get in. To my delight, my name was called, and I was able to see the show.

"It turns out that there were last-minute cancellations, which I was told were pretty rare for that theater. My angels were working for me as, due to my schedule, it really was the one and only time I could see the play and support my friends. And it was great! Thanks for letting me share this with you!"

A Great Day at the Park

Lee writes: "Yesterday my husband and I took our grandson to a theme park. We asked for MBOs before we left and also throughout the day. We had a great time despite the park being almost filled to capacity. The longest we waited in line was fifteen minutes. We left to eat dinner before the two-and-a-half-hour ride home. While at dinner, I asked for an MBO that the ride be shorter than we could imagine, the traffic be light and flow smoothly, and that we stay out of radar range.

"Off we set, and although we passed several troopers with cars pulled over, we were not one of them. I must add that we only drove seven miles over the posted speed limit. We left the restaurant at 8:20PM and arrived home at 10:25PM — a full half-hour sooner than usual. Thank you."

A Swift MBO Solution for a Double Birthday Present

Nancy writes: "In October 2009, my daughter Angela and her girlfriend Maddie wanted to see Taylor Swift in concert really, really badly. Maddie's mom Debbie and I talked and agreed to let them go to the concert for their sixteenth birthday presents. The concert was already sold out, but I told Deb not to worry and that we would get tickets for the girls. Deb searched eBay and Craigslist for tickets while I requested the following MBO:

> **Most Benevolent Outcome Request**
> *"I ask for a most benevolent outcome for getting good tickets to Taylor Swift's concert at an affordable price. May the outcome be better than I could hope for or expect."*

"Deb searched and conferred with me about the location of this set of tickets or that set. She even bid on a set here and there but lost to other bidders. I assured her these sets were not the right tickets for the girls. Two nights before the concert, Deb found a pair of tickets on eBay that were in a pretty good seating location and a decent price. Deb bought the tickets from a man whose daughter lost the privilege of going to the concert because she had to pay for a broken cell phone due to her own carelessness.

"Deb picked up the tickets the day before the concert and told the girls they were going. I then said,

> **Benevolent Prayer**
> *"I ask any and all beings to be with Angela and Maddie as they go to the Taylor Swift concert tomorrow night and that they have a fantastic night and awesome first concert experience. May the outcome be better than they could hope for or expect."*

"While the girls were at the concert, Deb and I had dinner at a restaurant nearby. Deb received a text from Maddie stating that they just hugged Taylor. I was in disbelief because they were nowhere near the stage. We found out later that after the first song, Taylor and her entourage showed up at the top of the girls' aisle with her acoustic guitar singing. When she finished the song, she handed her guitar off and walked down the aisle hugging everyone on the ends of the rows. It was an MBO that I will always remember — and so will Angela, Maddie, and Deb!"

A Benevolent Day at the Ballpark

Tom says: My friend Frank had expressed interest in attending a Texas Christian University (TCU) baseball game a couple of months ago, so when I received an invitation from my alumni association for a game ticket and lunch on the patio overlooking third base, I called him, and we went on a Saturday.

As I had not been on the campus since 2001, I knew it had changed, so we went over a little early so that I could view the changes. Naturally, I requested an MBO for the hour-plus drive to Fort Worth and for an enjoyable time "even better than I could hope for or expect." We drove around the campus eyeing all the new buildings, plus construction on even more buildings. What a campus this has become! As I was not sure exactly where they had relocated the baseball field, we headed for the southwest corner of the campus and found it. There were two guys there manning the parking lot. They said they would take care of us after the tour and would give us a good parking spot — a nice MBO for a short walk to the stadium!

We went to the new student union building that was easily three or four times larger than the one that existed when I attended TCU many years ago. We were given a map at the information counter and walked around where I pointed out to my friend Frank the old buildings, which had wound up behind many new ones. I was amazed how the architects had fit them all in without it feeling crowded.

At the baseball game, we had a nice lunch and then were allowed to go down below into the stands where there were unoccupied seats. It was an 80-degree day and my fair skin was cooking, so in the sixth inning, we returned to the cool, covered patio to watch the rest of the game. TCU was losing 2–0 all the way up to the bottom of the ninth inning, when they loaded the bases and a pinch hitter from Plano (where I live) hit the ball over the left fielder's head all the way to the wall, scoring all three runners. It was one of those rare walk-off hits, and it won the game. All the pinch hitter's teammates mobbed him on second base. This was truly a better experience than I could have hoped for or expected.

After the game, I requested another MBO for the drive back home, which ended up being uneventful. A very enjoyable day!

Might I also recommend here that if you play any sport, request an MBO that your performance be even better than you can hope for or expect. You'll find you are much calmer and less stressed; perhaps you'll even win the game for your team!

An Incredible Evening with Dennis DeYoung

Marie writes: "Hi, Mr. Moore. I'm a big fan! I have been buying your two books for family and friends, I read your weekly newsletter, and I can't wait for the latest one in my email. I have been reading a lot of angel books, but I find MBO requests to be the most effective. I've been meaning to chime in on your Facebook page but was too shy because English is not my first language. I sure do have a lot of stories to tell about what requesting MBOs has done for me, though.

"The latest one was last night at the concert of Dennis DeYoung, former lead singer of Styx. I love music and going to concerts just like you do. In *The Gentle Way*, I believe you wrote that you requested an MBO for front-row tickets for a concert you wanted to see, and I have been doing the same myself for all of my entertainment activities.

"Anyway, it was rainy here all day yesterday in California, and the concert was supposed to start at 7:30PM. Naturally, I requested an MBO to have a good time at the concert and for the weather to clear and to stop raining, at least on my way to the venue. Of course it did not rain, so even though the ground was very wet, I was smiling as I entered the venue. I did not thank my guardian angel yet, though. I was waiting for the part I had requested about having a good time at the concert.

"The concert begins. No Dennis DeYoung yet, but here comes a Journey tribute band opening the show, which was not announced on the ticket. I'm a huge Journey fan and I never miss their concerts, but I haven't seen them since their last U.S. concert in 2009. Anyhow, the Journey tribute band rocked for one hour, and I danced like a maniac and sang along to every song that Steve Perry sings. At the end of their show, they thanked Dennis DeYoung for letting them play and open for him.

"Then, it was Dennis DeYoung's turn, and the whole show was purely awesome. He sang mostly Styx rockers and few ballads. My guardian angel knows I love rock music. DeYoung is sixty-three, but man, he still sounds the same as he did in the 1970s, and he can still rock! No, I did not get the first-row ticket I'd hoped for because I bought the ticket at a later date, but it was not a bad seat at all. Of course, as always, I thanked my guardian angel, not thanking him three times but saying, 'Thank you very much, dear angel' with a lot of emotion."

23

Benevolent Outcomes for Shopping

Great Buy on a Tractor

Shannon writes: "Yesterday my husband drove from Fredericksburg, Texas, to Floresville, Texas — about 100 miles — to buy a tractor. When he got there, the guy had already sold it — even though he knew my husband was on his way. So my husband called me and was quite upset, and I made a quick MBO request that he would find the right tractor at the right price for the job. When he got home, he went to a neighbor's house that always had different tractors on trailers, and he was able to buy a better one for a much cheaper price. I love those angels! And my husband is ever so slowly becoming a believer in MBOs."

Deluxe Walker for an Aging Aunt

Pam writes: "Blessings to you, Tom. I say MBOs every morning, and I want to tell you about one of them. My aunt was coming from Michigan for a visit. She has problems with her back and with walking, so I was looking for a walker to buy for her to use while she was here.

"I saw in the paper an estate sale very close to me that weekend. I thought I should really go to that. Well, I've been busy and didn't go right away. I passed the sign, thought about going again, and made it a point to go when I was through with whatever it was I was doing at the time. Well, as I was walking up the driveway, what do I see but a walker with wheels, handbrakes, and the seat in the middle! This type of walker costs just over $100 at the store.

"When I say my MBO requests, I always add that I would like to find just what I need at the very best possible price. Well, to my great surprise, the walker was marked at five dollars. My aunt was so thrilled that I found it for her. So I'm keeping it in case anyone else comes to visit and needs it."

A New Washing Machine

Kathy writes: "Here's a fabulous MBO that I experienced yesterday. Our washing machine recently began making a horrid sound, and last week, the washer technician confirmed that it was time to go shopping for a new one. This was very distressing news, because right now my husband is unemployed, and we surely don't need to spend hundreds of dollars on a new appliance. In addition, our machine was only seven years old and was an expensive one.

"We decided to go shopping for a new washer yesterday, and in the morning before we left, I requested an MBO that we find a good-quality washer that would cost less than $700. I also requested that our salesperson be knowledgeable, helpful, and friendly.

"When we got to the store, there was a waiting line to talk to the only salesperson, so we wandered around looking at the washers. After a few minutes, a different salesman walked up to us, and when I asked him if he knew anything about washing machines, he said he'd been selling them for eleven years. He was very knowledgeable and helpful, explaining such things as the typical lifespan of different types of washers and how much water each type uses on average. We ended up buying a very good-quality machine for only $611. Thank you, guardian angels, and thank you, Tom, for sharing the technique of MBOs with us."

A Nightgown and Robe for My Mother

Lynn writes: "Hi, Tom! I got my friend Debbie in Cedar Rapids, Iowa, to start requesting MBOs. I sent her your book and am now sending her your new one, which I also got and love! That could, of course, be partly because I am in it. Anyway, here is an MBO adventure that Debbie sent me, and I thought you might share. Maxine is her eighty-five-year-old mother."

Debbie writes: "I have to tell you my MBO tale from yesterday. I gave my mom a nightgown. It was too big, so I went back to the store myself to exchange it. As I pulled into the parking lot, I asked for MBOs for the whole experience of returning it. I found a perfect parking spot, even in the season rush, and it was a good spot on the end, so I didn't get my car dinged. I had a most favorable outcome in the lingerie department, where I found a better nightgown in the proper size. To top that off, a woman in line ahead of me turned and asked if I could use a coupon for ten dollars off of a purchase.

"As I walked out to leave, I saw a robe that had 'Maxine' written all over it — well, not literally! I was able to use another lesser-amount coupon for the robe purchase and then had an extra coupon I offered to the person behind me. Upon delivery, everything fit perfectly and my mother excitedly modeled it all for me. Mission accomplished!"

Tom responds: In another note to me, Lynn added that she loved the "pass it on" coupon element to Debbie's story; I loved that part too.

Sweet Music to My Ears

Marsha writes: "I want to share something with you that happened to me yesterday. I've been wanting to start playing the violin again at age sixty, but I realized that my old violin, a full-sized instrument, was now rather uncomfortable for me to play because of my arthritis and the way my joints were being 'encouraged' into radical positions and so on.

"I tried a three-quarter-sized violin in a store and discovered that it was exactly the right size for me and was much more comfortable to play. Since I'm on a shoestring — nearly barefoot! — budget, the only three-quarter-sized violin I could afford was priced at around $75. I bought it, figuring that I could learn on anything. I was wrong. The violin had structural problems that were so bad that a repair person said it would take around $1,000 to get it into acceptable shape. I called the store where I'd bought it and told them I was returning it for a refund or an exchange, figuring they might have another of the same model in better condition. All the way to the store, I requested an MBO in finding an affordable violin that was in better shape.

"When I got there, I discovered that they had a beautiful German-made violin priced at $400 that had somehow slipped through the cracks in their inventory. They couldn't sell it; the computer kept kicking back the transaction because it didn't think the violin existed. So they traded this lovely violin for the $75 one I was returning — a straight-up swap! Thanks to my guardian angel, I now have the kind of violin I thought I could only dream of. MBOs work!"

Miraculous Price on Singing Bowl

Lois writes: "I went to a birthday party about a month ago, and on the way, I asked for an MBO for a good experience that evening, adding, 'May the outcome be better than I could hope for or expect.' I arrived at the restaurant about twenty minutes early, as I had never been there before and had left early. I decided to look around the neighborhood and spotted an antique shop. While wandering around in there, I found a very large antique Tibetan singing bowl. In a miracle of miracles, I got it for $40. After checking later online, I found it was worth at least ten times as much. The rest of the evening went well too!"

Most Benevolent Designer Handbag

Lois writes: "I have been experiencing a difficult time lately where money is concerned. My budget has not been this lean for over twenty years. I see so many other entrepreneurs experiencing this as well that I know it is not just me.

"Last Saturday I felt I really needed a new purse that was a neutral color and the right size — big enough to hold my stuff but small enough not to hurt my back by weighing me down on one side. It needed a strap or handle long enough to put over one shoulder so I could carry things in my hands while also carrying the purse. I asked for an MBO to find a beautiful purse with all the features I needed for under twenty-five dollars and then went into one of my favorite discount designer stores. I was in the parking lot when I asked for the MBO. I did not find the purse, so I left the store and forgot all about it.

"The next day I was running errands prior to meeting a friend. It hit me that I should browse a different designer discount store while killing time waiting for our meeting time. I usually do not go into this particular store. When I went in, the purses were really picked over. There were not many there. I looked anyway, and what I found blew me away. There were two identical, gorgeous, well-known designer's bags of the perfect size in a neutral color with a strap. They had all the features I had asked for. The price was under twenty-five dollars including the tax. I am still in awe. I have never seen a leather bag by this designer under seventy dollars in any discount store, and I bought one of the bags. Every time I look at my miracle bag, I am reminded that miracles can and do happen.

"This may sound like a small event in the grand scheme of things. But it is a huge reminder I will carry with me daily that miracles are possible even when we are not expecting them!"

Tom responds: The past two years were the worst in the twenty-seven years I've been doing international film and TV program distribution. But I am seeing definite signs of recovery, including the fact that last week we made the largest sale we've had in over two years. So keep requesting MBOs in your business and work, folks!

Ninety-Nine-Cent MBO

John writes: "I think requesting MBOs while we're shopping is a great way to have small miracles happen on a daily basis. I've had dozens of amazing things happen in stores. Just recently I had been looking for sunglasses in very nice stores and had planned to pay twenty-five dollars or more for them; that's not a lot, but I don't like to spend too much.

"Anyhow, I asked for an MBO before I went into a ninety-nine-cent store; all I said was,

> **Most Benevolent Outcome Request**
> "I request the most benevolent outcome to have a great time in this store, and may this outcome be even better than I could hope for or expect."

"As soon as I walked in, I was drawn to the sunglasses and found a really nice pair for ninety-nine cents. I couldn't believe it, since I know these stores generally have very shabby sunglasses. Well, I bought them, and so far they are as good as a very expensive pair, as far as I can tell. I'm very happy.

"I was so surprised by this find. It never happens with something like sunglasses. It's fantastic how our guardian angels always seem to find just the right item not only to make us happy but to kind of make our jaws drop at the same time."

The Perfect House at the Perfect Price

Sunny writes: "I just want to share that just yesterday one of my biggest MBOs came true. We signed the deed on the perfect house in the perfect neighborhood with nice neighbors, and we did it at the perfect price. I am over the moon!"

Tom responds: If you're searching for a home, say,

Most Benevolent Outcome Request
"I request a most benevolent outcome for the perfect home for me, and may the results be even better than I can hope for or expect. Thank you!"

Doggie Deal Delivered

Cheryl writes: "I had been searching for almost a year trying to acquire a dog kennel. At first, getting a kennel may not seem like that big of a deal until you realize you don't have the transportation required to get it home. This week, it was down to the wire. My ability to travel for work became dependent on getting this item.

"After encountering disappointment with yet another business I was trying to buy a kennel from, I drove out of their parking lot saying,

Most Benevolent Outcome Request
"I request a most benevolent outcome in finding a dog kennel and not only that but also at a better price! Thank you!"

"(One tends to get dramatic with disappointment, but the sincerity is still there.) Within ten minutes, I found another business that sold kennels tucked away on a side street. They not only sold the kennel I wanted for $100 less than others, but they also offered free delivery! At times like these, the simple words 'thank you' to the angels feel so inadequate.

"Tom, I just want you to know that it's been about three or four years since I picked up one of the most blessed books of my life. It was yours. I generally use MBOs like I'm breathing because they work! Why I hadn't requested an MBO for the dog kennel, I'm not sure — perhaps it just wasn't that important until this week. I went from requesting the MBO to purchasing the new kennel in ten minutes flat! I would like to thank you for following the path you chose and passing this blessing on to so many. You could have said no, but you didn't. Thank you!"

MBO for the Shopping Channel

Barbara writes: "Tom, I have a wonderful MBO story for you. I made a purchase on a well-known television shopping channel, but when it arrived, it was too large. I packed it up and put it out in the foyer of my condo for the mailman to pick up for return. It was stolen before the mailman arrived. There was no one else at home in our building at the time. I reported the theft to the Postmaster and the local police department, obtaining case numbers in each instance.

"I decided to call the shopping channel and report the incident to them, just so it would be on record should it turn up there. I thought, 'Who knows?' I said my MBO and spoke with a very nice lady who took all my information and placed me on hold. When she returned, she stated that they were returning my money and there would be no further payments due on the order. That absolutely blew me away. MBOs are the best! Thank you so much for bringing light and ease into our lives."

Shopping Directions from My Guardian Angel

Marie writes: "Last Friday, I went shopping. I was looking for a good, inexpensive vacuum cleaner. I said,

> **Most Benevolent Outcome Request**
> *"Guardian angel, I request an MBO to find an inexpensive and good vacuum. Guide me where to go. Thank you!"*

"Boom! I heard my guardian angel tell me to go to Target, and guess what? The vacuums were on sale! I found a good, inexpensive vacuum. Next, my guardian angel guided me to go to Best Buy, and I found my canister vacuum on sale. Not only that, Tom, but I bought other stuff I needed, and I had money left over."

Martha Stewart Brand MBO

Michelle writes: "I needed paint for the exterior of my house because of issues with my insurance company. I am on a very tight budget and had to borrow twenty dollars for paint. I requested an MBO to find paint within my budget to fit my needs. (I specifically wanted flat black exterior paint.) We ended up at Home Depot — not my normal home improvement store — where I shared my request with the paint department manager. I emphasized my tight budget. He said something about a certain brand of paint being on sale. Well, that paint — Martha Stewart's brand — was on sale for eleven dollars a gallon, and I got two cans of it. He also found the exact type that he could add the black tint to without any issues. Hurray for my angels! I was so ecstatic that I laughed all the way home. Thanks!"

MBOs Help in Multiple Ways with a Big Move

DeLeah writes: "Hey, Tom. We are so blessed to have these MBOs. I am moving to the East Coast this summer, and so I said,

> ### Most Benevolent Outcome Request
> *"I request a most benevolent outcome that I find a wonderful trailer at a great price to assist me with my move, with results even better than I could expect or hope for."*

"The next day I was on Craigslist, and the first trailer I saw there was the perfect size and shape. Whereas all other trailers were a minimum of $200 or $300, I paid $80. Fantastic! I love working with the angels as much as I do, and I am continually amazed by the miracles sent to me every day."

DeLeah writes again: "I am getting ready to relocate to the East Coast this week, and for the past month I have been garage sale-ing my little heart out for a pet carrier but have been unable to find one. I am leaving this weekend, so I said the following MBO request this morning before leaving for work:

> ### Most Benevolent Outcome Request
> *"I request a most benevolent outcome that I find the perfect pet carrier for my cat at a great price with results even better than I can expect or hope for!"*

"After work, I went to my local Goodwill store, and they had one that was the perfect size. Thank you, angels!"

Motorcycle MBO

Dan writes: "I was just having my morning read of your newsletter and thought I'd share my most recent MBO. A while back, I took motorcycle lessons and was prepared to buy a bike and start riding. A few weeks ago, I found what I considered a good used bike at a good price, and I was going to pursue it when I returned home from a business trip. Of course, I bathed the whole issue in MBO requests.

"Shortly thereafter I got a message from my son informing me his father-in-law was planning on selling his bike, which was virtually identical to the one I was looking at, for about $1,000 less. And, because I was considered family, he also knocked another $500 off the price. Just yesterday I met him halfway from where we both live to pick up the bike. En route, the weather was windy, gray, and raining — not exactly ideal bike-riding weather. After we completed the exchange, I began the 240-mile ride home. Not surprisingly, the weather cleared, and I had nothing but blue skies and sunshine for my inaugural ride home with absolutely zero incidents or even close calls. Another wonderful MBO!"

The Perfect Set of Wheels

Kelly writes: "Just to update you, I have been requesting an MBO for the perfect car. I thought the car I initially wanted was perfect for me, but I have struggled to get financing for it. Then I requested an MBO for financing, purely because my bank does not finance freelancers like me. After gathering information, they contacted me to tell me I qualify for quite a significant amount of money, so I bought a car that's slightly less. Thank you for teaching about MBOs and BPs. Starting tomorrow, I am going to be requesting an MBO for paying the loan within the year."

Black Feathers for a Benevolent House Purchase

Doreen writes: "My husband and I have been looking for a house or cottage on the ocean for quite a while, but we gave up on finding one in our price range and the area we want. Then three different properties came up for sale that satisfied our conditions, so we decided to take a look. One in particular caught my eye, so I said an MBO request for a sign as to whether to buy it or not. When we looked at the first one, we both loved it, but we decided to look at the others. Just before we left the first one, I looked down, and there was a large black feather on my path. I picked it up and felt that this was the sign I was looking for, as I had heard that feathers are a sign from the angels.

"We looked at the second one and didn't care for it, so we decided to go back to the realty office and put in an offer for the first one. We had originally thought that we would just find land to build something on, but this came with a mobile home — completely furnished — with drilled water, septic, and electricity. Plus it's in a cottage area with over one acre of land and had just been reduced by $10,000! Not only did we find what we wanted after looking for two years, but we got all the extras thrown in. Plus, the price was the same for just the land in all the other cases, and it's just a one-and-a-half-hour drive away from where we live. Our offer was accepted, and the closing is August 13. I also found another small black feather this morning.

"Since then, I have Google-searched black feathers and have read that they mean there is a change coming and the angels are there for comfort and to help. Tom, could you ask your guardian angel if I got the correct message to purchase this place or if I misinterpreted it, thinking it was a sign to buy when it may have been a warning not to instead? Thanks so much for the newsletter. I love getting it each week."

Tom responds: No need to check. Our guardian angels choose signs we will recognize, just as you did, Doreen. Naturally, this week I looked down, and there was a black feather right by my feet!

Steal of a Deal on a Ceiling Fan

Lee writes: "I was at a big-box home improvement store pricing a ceiling fan for my vacation home. I found one that I liked, but it was

$138. I wasn't buying that day, so I made note of the fan's information and left. The next day my husband and I went to the same store in our hometown to return some things we didn't need. Before I left the house, I said an MBO request to find a fan at a price far cheaper and better than I could imagine. After returning our items, we started to browse the store and ended up in the fan department. The identical fan I had seen the day before was marked down for clearance at $69.99! You can bet I snatched it up and thanked my angels for fulfilling this MBO. Thank you, Tom, for spreading the word on MBOs."

MBO for Line in Grocery Store

Sunny writes: "I had a funny experience today with an MBO, which showed me you have to be very precise in your wording. I went grocery shopping, and when I was done, I saw the long lines. I joined one of them even though I was the third customer in that line. The first guy in line had loads and loads of groceries, so I requested an MBO for another cashier to open. About two minutes later, just when I started to put my groceries on the belt, I heard a lady saying, "Come over here, I will open this cash register." My MBO was answered in no time, but I should have made my request for 'another cashier to open so I can be first in line and get out quickly.' Here you go: Be precise!"

A Great New Camera

Rick writes: "I went to a retailer today to do my normal shopping, but I have also wanted to get a digital camera for some time. There is a certain brand that I like and trust, and I had done some comparison shopping before deciding on this particular model. As I walked into the store, I asked for an MBO for purchasing the perfect camera and that it would be an easy purchase.

"I walked into the electronics department and had a sales associate help me. He pointed out that the model I wanted was out of stock, even though there was nothing on the display model that indicated this. He said it would be in within a week, but he checked the storage case below the display just in case. He pulled out a slightly more advanced model and compared the features between the two cameras. The one in stock was $70 more expensive. But because I decided not to wait and purchased that one instead, the salesman gave me a 10 percent discount for my inconvenience, as well as for the display model not being marked 'out of stock.' So in the end, I got a better camera for $225 instead of $250. I tried it out, and it's pretty good; I just have to play with it more to get used to the features."

Benevolent Smartphone Outcome

Siobhan writes: "In July, I am embarking on a cycle ride from Devon, UK, to Northern Ireland. It's a bit of a pilgrimage, really, as it's the twentieth anniversary year of my dad's passing, and I haven't visited his grave in nineteen years. I have also used this adventure to raise money for a local hospice. I want to raise a minimum of £1 per mile. I have said MBO requests, and my fundraising has gotten off to a good start. I would really appreciate the weight of the MBO world community, and I ask for all your readers to say a BP to help me reach my target.

"Also, for my trip I have invested in a smartphone to replace the need for a netbook, camera, maps, books, and so on. I said an MBO request to help me choose the best mobile provider and get the best price. With all the information available, I decided that eBay was my best bet, and the phone I chose was going between £70 and £110. Well, I won the second phone I bid on for the bargain price of £54. Awesome, I love MBOs! Thank you so very much, Tom, and your guides, for creating this community and spreading such a wonderful life tool. Love and light to all."

Resolving an Online Dispute

DeLeah writes: "I have been an active member for a few years now on Listia. com, an auction site that uses a credit system rather than money. The only money involved is the shipping cost of items. Well, I found a seller and won five of her auctions — very small items. She wanted $16 to ship these items when I know it would not cost more than $3.50. I tried to reason with her and did everything I could to make it smooth. She ended up leaving me negative feedback for all five auctions and then denied my request to give me back my credits, which made this into a dispute in which a moderator looks over everything and makes a fair decision.

"I was a little upset at this point, as this particular website has a policy in place that if you refuse to pay the shipping the seller may keep the items and your credits. So I said an MBO request:

> **Most Benevolent Outcome Request**
> *"I request a most benevolent outcome that a fair decision be made in this situation on Listia with results even better than I could expect or hope for."*

"I left it at that; I did not think about it and just released it to the angels and my guides. I received guidance the next day to write Listia and explain everything that had happened, so I did this as well. Today I received a message letting me know that not only were all my credits refunded, but they also took away all negative feedback from this lady and made it neutral. Thank you, angels! I love MBOs and don't know what I would do without them in my life. We are truly blessed to have Tom and his system of MBOs and BPs."

A Nice New Pair of Western Boots

Bonnie writes: "Yesterday I needed to follow my daughter back to the car rental place to return the car after her vacation. We had talked about it the night before, and she had asked me about it before she went on vacation, so I knew about it ahead of time. She also wanted to stop at the Mall of America to drop off my granddaughter's ring she had bought in Denver that needed to be sized. So I did my daily MBO meditation ahead of time, requesting a safe journey and asking that the mall would have a Western shop where I could find a pair of boots that wasn't too expensive so I could start country-western dancing again.

"So the journey went really well. We dropped off the car and headed over to the mall, about three miles away. I told my daughter I wanted to look for a pair of boots if there was a store there, so we went to the directory to find out where Zales was. I found a Western store — RCC — and then tried to figure out which way to go from where we were. We went to Zales first, then to find RCC.

"We walked into RCC, and I said to the salesman that I wanted a pair of black men's boots, size 8, for under $70. The boots also needed to have a leather foot but a rubber heel. We had already looked at a few and they were all over $120, but the salesman went looking and I kept trying on boots. They either didn't fit right or cost more than I wanted to pay.

"So we finally went over to the women's section, and the salesman found some boots that were wide enough — that's why I was looking at men's in the first place. In the end, I walked out of there with a pair of black ladies boots that fit me perfectly, spun great on the carpet, and cost $69.95. I said, 'Thank you, thank you, thank you!' Now how is that for getting exactly what you want? I just totally *love* expecting great things! And thanks, Tom, for everything you do."

The Perfect Rental House

Beverly writes: "We are due to relocate, and we are currently here house-hunting. I made an MBO request to find the perfect house — with an ocean view and really nice furnishings, as we would be leaving all this behind in Texas. We also have two dogs, which can be a tall order, as people are reluctant to lease to pet owners.

"The very first house we saw — which I had previously viewed on a website only, where I had seen that it specifically stated 'no dogs' — was just perfect! The owner had already turned down four prospective tenants too. The minute we stepped inside the house, I knew it was perfect, and she liked us enough to allow both my dogs. Astonishingly enough, she even turned down a bigger deposit.

"So once again, MBO requests and trusting in the universal outcome of the situation has been a winner. I can't believe my luck, to be honest. It is half the rental price that we have in our allowance as well. Now we are due to fly back to Houston on Saturday and then set off twelve days later, driving up here. Needless to say, another MBO is in order. It is an eight-day journey involving a ferry crossing with both of our dogs in tow!"

MBO at Grocery Store

John writes: "Recently I've used MBO requests for helping me remember things. Just the other day I went out to do some grocery shopping and left my list of what I wanted to buy at home. I didn't realize I had forgotten the list until I got to the store. So I made a quick MBO request to remember what was on the list, and little by little, it all came back to me in a seemingly effortless fashion. I've never had my memory come back to me so easily, without much effort on my part. It was another wonderful revelation as to other things I could use MBO requests for.

"I've also done this with items I've misplaced around my home, and it works almost 100 percent of the time. The only times it didn't seem to work were when I was upset or worried about something. If I could calm my mind, just relax, and not give it a second thought after I said the MBO, then my request always worked."

Benevolent Accessorizing

Sharon writes: "I go through my routine MBOs in the morning, and depending on the situation, during the day I might add a couple more. Being the skeptic that I am, or the tester of all things, I consistently test myself and the spirit world. I test the theories I come across. One day when I had time to kill, I was in a shop waiting for a photo collage that I had wanted to print out for my sister's birthday.

"While I was there, I was looking for things for a tablet that I had recently bought. One of the items I looked at was a bag to store the tablet in. The bags ranged from $10–25 depending on the brand you selected. The one I selected had no price tag on it, so I had no clue how much it was, but I requested an MBO for the bag I had picked out to be on special and to get a couple of dollars off the full price.

"After a little synchronicity that my grandfather had organized to let me know he was around — which is another story — and much trouble getting a code for the bag, I finally got the price, and next thing, I heard this man say, "Well look, this bag is on special! You get $2 off the original price." I smiled, knowing that the MBO was in play."

Earth Angel Sells Vacuum Cleaners Door to Door

Carole writes: "Just read your great blog. First, I should say that my college-age daughter has always complained I don't have enough junk food in the house — specifically Oreos — and that I didn't put them in her lunches when she was little either. I have been doing general MBO requests and your 'expect great things' affirmations daily. I have also been requesting MBOs for a better relationship with her.

"I have also been doing angel exercises from Doreen Virtue's book *Angel Visions*. One chapter in that book mentions stories of people who have visitors from "Earth angels" — strangers who appear out of nowhere to help with a specific task, then don't hang around. Most of these angels are said to be very tall. She also has a chapter in another of her books about Archangel Michael and vacuuming techniques. You can visualize this angel attaching a tube at the top of your head to your energy field, turning on the vacuum, and taking out any negative energy you may have acquired during the day from others.

"I had a run-in with a very negative person in the school where I was working as a substitute teacher. That night I tried the angel exercise and was not sure if it did anything or not, but I requested an MBO anyway. The next day an event happened, and I wish I had been more alert; after fifteen minutes, I realized the synchronicity and the effects of the MBO. I was busy with a project and pressed for time. This experience taught me to expect the unexpected, and it could be a great thing.

"The doorbell rang and I answered it. There was a young, nice-looking, very tall man smiling and holding a huge box of Oreos. It was the type you would get at Costco — the equivalent of five regular boxes. He said, 'This is for you. I am doing home product demonstrations. I like to give something in return for this, since my boss requires I do this for a certain number of people each day.' I laughed when I saw the box and thanked him. I mentioned to him that my daughter loves them. But since I was alone, I didn't feel comfortable having him come in. I said, 'Go get your appliance, and I will meet you in the hallway. Do you have a business card? I don't know who you are.'

"I got my coat and locked the door while he went to his car. When I got out to the hallway, there were two huge boxes containing a vacuum and a rug shampooer. I looked at his card and the business name on it was Chittenden County Kirby — a name I had never heard of. He also showed me his Vermont driving license. He said his name was Patrick — the name of my neighbor upstairs who looks nothing like him — and that I probably would not have heard of the company since they do not advertise.

"I said, 'You know, I get our rugs shampooed by a friend of mine — he doesn't charge much, and I already have a vacuum. Good luck; there are 200 people in the development, so you should find somebody. Here, you should take back your Oreos, but thank you so much anyway." I tried to be as nice as I could, but I didn't realize then that he was probably an Earth angel. If I had, I would have looked back to see where he went afterward!

"P.S. I think it's pretty clear who his 'boss' is, don't you think?"

An Unbelieable Deal on Tiles

Ann Marie writes: "Tom, I have to tell you about my friend's MBO. She is redoing her bathroom and wanted real marble tiles. Well, a 12" x 12" square normally goes for anywhere from ten to fifteen dollars. So on Sunday, after doing an MBO in church, she drove to Lowe's. As she was walking toward the tile aisle, she saw boxes of tiles on the end of the aisle with a sign: 'Marble — only $1.42 each tile.' She was speechless — it must've been a mistake.

"Then the salesman showed up and told her they were overstocked in those tiles. They were not selling, and his boss had said, 'Mark 'em down.' My friend told the salesman that at that price, she could do both bathrooms and that she had measurements requiring twenty boxes. He told her that if she bought them right then, he would discount the price down to $1.00 per square. Now *that* is an MBO for the best possible deal, yeah!"

Tom responds: That was a good MBO! I'm sure her guardian angel was pleased as punch.

The Perfect Dress

Annie writes: "Here is an MBO for you. Yesterday, my daughter told me about a banquet that she will be attending in September and how she needs to find a dress to wear that day, followed by, 'Mom, can we go shopping today?'

"I was tired and not in the mood, so I asked my guardian angel for help. I said,

> **Most Benevolent Outcome Request**
> "*I request an MBO that we find a dress that she adores fast, effortlessly, in the first store she chooses, and at a reasonable price.*"

"Before leaving, I was inspired to look for printable in-store coupons for one particular kind of high-end store I assumed we would be close to in that mall.

"Once we got there, I let her lead the way. She entered the store in question — not knowing I had a $30 rebate — and picked four dresses. We went into a large and airy dressing room where I could sit and watch (usually these places are small and smelly), and she fell in love with one lovely dress. She was beaming, which is a rarity. I presented my coupon, we paid, and we were done in record time! Today, I am still stunned at how fast and easy it was. I know a lot of mothers can relate."

Fast Delivery of Purchase

Lee writes: "I ordered something online on June 13 and said an MBO for fast delivery. The estimated delivery was between June 21 and June 25, and I received my package on June 17. That was fast! Thank you!"

24

Benevolent Outcomes for Lost Items

Finding Lost Keys

Jim writes: "A young waitress where I eat lunch frequently complained to me a couple of days ago that she had lost the keys to her car and was desperate to find them. I explained to her about MBO requests and even suggested one she might use. Today she said she found her keys in her girlfriend's car — a car she had previously searched — within two hours of requesting the MBO. She is now a believer."

Tom responds: See how much stress this young person was under until she found her keys? Requesting MBOs just makes life easier!

Benevolently Rediscovered Glasses

Janet writes: "I thought I would share my recent MBO with you. I went for an energy session with a local acupuncturist last Monday. As I was making another appointment, I checked to see that my glasses were in the holder of my pocketbook. I left the office, and on arriving home — with no stops in between — found that my glasses were missing. I called the office to see if by chance I had dropped them there, and I went back the next day to look in the hallway and the parking lot — no glasses. I was upset, as I had purchased them only a week before. Anyway, I requested an MBO.

"Tuesday passed, and then Wednesday went by, and still no glasses. On Thursday I went to check the mailbox. I had my pocketbook in one hand and took out the mail with my free hand and heard a clink. I looked down, and there were the missing glasses. I had been to the mailbox the previous days also, so where had they come from? I can only credit my guardian angel for that. Thanks for sharing how to use MBOs."

A Wandering Wallet Returns

Kahriana writes: "A family member recently moved to a new job in Ontario, and thanks to MBOs, everything transpired very smoothly: excellent airfares, no charge for overweight luggage, a smooth flight, a timely landing, so on and so forth. We are most grateful. However, the night before departure, her wallet was nowhere to be found. I asked for an MBO for the 'immediate reappearance of her wallet,' and within minutes, she was guided to a very odd spot in our residence where neither of us puts anything. I touched the wallet, and it was very cold — too cold to have been inside the house. Thank you, angels!"

Lost Social Security Card

Pili writes: "Hi, Tom. This is an MBO story about finding a document. A few weeks ago I needed my daughter's Social Security number and I looked for it everywhere, starting in the place I have always kept it. But I couldn't find it, so I used another document that had the number on it. Yesterday I needed it again, but the number was not enough this time because I required the actual card. I knew finding it was going to be a difficult task, so I requested an MBO and my intuition told me to look where I always keep it, which made me laugh because I knew it wasn't there. But as soon as I started looking for it, to my surprise, the card was right there, in the same place where it has always been. Thanks, angels."

Benevolent Key Replacement

AJ writes: "After procrastinating about getting my car repaired, I finally dropped it off early one morning, the day before an extended holiday. Hoping to save time, I took a taxi back home. As soon as the taxi drove away, I realized I'd dropped my house keys on the seat. Immediately I asked for the MBO to find my keys. I have to admit, I was in a bit of a panic. After walking around my apartment building, I found a contractor working on site who was able to let me into my flat with his master key. This was the first part of my MBO.

"I telephoned the taxi company several times, and they were unable to locate the cab that had brought me home. (I was informed that there are over 2,000 taxi drivers in my city.) I had not asked for a receipt and did not know the taxi number. So I kept asking out loud for an MBO to find my keys. I asked the contractor if he could find me an extra key for my door, since I had so many errands to run that day. After twenty minutes, he came with a box of keys and located the only spare key for my door. This was my MBO."

Glasses Lost and Found

Diane writes: "I just wanted to share an MBO with you and your readers. This proves that sometimes the results of a benevolent outcome request might not be instant but that the request still works. My husband has to take his glasses off when he is taking pictures with the camera. He was at this event and took his glasses off. He put them down someplace, but when he went to pick them up afterward, he could not find them. So he had to drive home without them. Good thing he can see the road without them.

"This happened last week, September 9. I quickly requested an MBO to find the glasses or for someone else to find them. I requested my MBOs a couple of times. Today, September 17, he went back to one of the places he had been last week, and the owner of the restaurant handed him his glasses! I quickly thanked my angels and his. This has proven to me that it might take a few days, but the angels are always at work, helping us out."

Benevolent Rubbermaid Recovery

DeLeah writes: "I recently moved from the West Coast to the East Coast, and on the drive over, I had a few large Rubbermaid plastic containers tied down on the back of my trailer. Well, I lost one about five miles back in Wyoming, and I pulled over to secure everything before going back to find it. I said this:

> **Most Benevolent Outcome Request**
> *"I request a most benevolent outcome that my container be returned to me safely."*

"Forty-five minutes later, I was at the exit to return to the next exit going the opposite direction when I noticed a police car behind me with its lights on. I pulled over, and the police officers returned my container to me! They were very nice and helpful. The lid was not recovered, so I stuffed everything I could into my car and they disposed of the garbage that was not salvageable. Thank you once again, angels!"

Locating a Lost Ring

Richard writes: "I really enjoy the newsletters and I have just about finished reading your book, which has really opened my eyes about guardian angels.

"Yesterday my wife and I were raking leaves at our home, and later on that night, I noticed that I had lost my wedding band. We went outside and searched the entire yard and then searched again with a metal detector; the ring was nowhere to be found.

"My wife and I finally decided to go back into the house and try to look the next day. On the way into the house, I remembered to say the request to my guardian angel. When I finished the request, I walked on the other side of the yard, reached down, and there was my wedding band! To beat it all, the ring was lying in a spot that we had both gone over with the metal detector. The requests really do work, if you only believe.

"Thanks for your book and making us aware of what is going on around us each day. I could almost hear the wings of my guardian angel going off to deliver my request when I said the prayer."

Lost Credit Card

Lucy writes: "Tom, here is an MBO story that happened just now. I went into the grocery store with the intention of buying something and getting some cash. When I got to the next place in the checkout line, I discovered my bank card was nowhere to be found. I put my purchase down and went to my vehicle, looking for the card along the way. I opened the car door and searched in all the usual places with no luck. Then I said a quick MBO request for finding the card immediately. I looked down at my feet, and there it was on the ground. It had not been there before! You guys are so good!"

Finding a Doubting Daughter's Diary

Martha writes: "Wow, talk about an instant benevolent outcome! My daughter misplaced her diary in the house a few days ago. In it she keeps records of her work shifts, her university assignments, her address book, and so on, so it is her lifeline. She prefers to write things down rather than keep an electronic record. She told me about the loss when it happened, but I didn't really pay much attention, just saying it would turn up.

"Today I was talking to her in her room when she mentioned it again, and she was getting quite flustered in the process. She said she had searched absolutely everywhere. She's a neat freak, so it would be obvious if it were there. I asked her if she had asked her angels for help. She said she had. I hadn't told her about MBOs and told her to repeat after me,

> **Most Benevolent Outcome Request**
> *"I request a most benevolent outcome that I find my diary quickly and easily, and may the result be even better …"*

"I hadn't even gotten the full sentence out — and she wasn't even saying it with me — when I turned to start walking out of the room and for some reason looked down. Something caught my eye that was wedged at the end of her bed behind a chest of drawers. I don't even know how I saw it, as it is about half the size of an A4 sheet of paper and was in the shadows. It was as if it was illuminated for me. I practically pounced on it with all confidence, and there it was — her diary!

"I started laughing and told her to thank her angels wholeheartedly. How was that for immediate results? She just sat there holding the book with a stunned look on her face, knowing she'd already checked all under and around her bed. The angels really were on the ball with this one."

I Can See Clearly Now

Diane writes: "I have to tell you an amazing MBO that happened to me this week. Some time ago I had made an MBO request about my contact lenses so that I would never lose one. I wear the old-style hard contacts. Since requesting MBO protection for my lenses, I have had some near misses but none that prove MBOs work more than this one.

"In the UK, we have had an unprecedented snowfall this week that has caused chaos. One very early morning, I struggled into the station just as the train was just pulling in, for which I was extremely grateful. Just then the peak of my hat fell down and knocked a lens out — and I was standing knee deep in snow!

"My daughter thought she spotted it; however, I was highly dubious, as everywhere was glistening like a billion possible contact lenses. Anyway she gave this handful of snow to my son-in-law, and we sat on the train while the snow thawed in his hand. Sure enough, nestling in his palm was my contact lens. I was so grateful — and I am so grateful to you and to MBOs, Tom."

Tom responds: I finally requested an MBO too for not losing my glasses, as I was constantly forgetting where I left them and had to return to a restaurant a couple of times to retrieve them. So far, so good.

Amazing Computer Recovery at the Airport

Katherine writes: "I recently traveled to visit my sister out of state. I went through security with my laptop and was walking around the airport when I realized my computer was missing. All my business information is on that computer! I went to security to see if someone had turned it in. They had not seen it, but they took my cell-phone number. I walked away feeling anxious and very concerned.

"Then I smiled to myself as I remembered requesting an MBO for a successful trip. It was as if all my anxiety was swept away. I knew I didn't have to ask how it would be returned; deep inside of me, I trusted that I would get it back. Within minutes of that recollection, security called me to tell me that the women who cleaned the restrooms had found it. As I walked out of the restroom, a few of the security men I had spoken to earlier were on a cart cheering for me as I left the bathroom with my computer. They raised their hands and shouted, 'Success!' Can you imagine? I was elated and so grateful.

"I teach all of my clients about MBO requests. Thank you, Tom!"

Lost Smart Phone Comes to Light

Sallie writes: "I realized one day that my smart phone was AWOL. I don't use it like some people use theirs, so it took me a long time to miss it. Looking everywhere and thinking back, I realized it must have gone missing two days prior. In my mind, I could trace back to using it then. I called Verizon and inquired whether it had been used since then. After finding that it had not, I decided to have the service turned off until I could replace it.

"The logical thing to do at that point was to say an MBO request. I did so, and my husband backed me up with an additional BP. Approximately ninety minutes later, the phone rang with someone claiming to have found my phone.

I say that because I actually think he saw me drop it. My guardian angel must've gotten with his guardian angel forthwith, and I heard from him quickly.

"You might consider me a little silly for this: Although I thought that he really stole it, I went straight to the ATM, got a twenty, and paid him for his kindness as he handed me my phone. Tom, this MBO stuff rocks! I've learned about such things through my husband. Thank you so much for your teachings."

Sunglasses Miraculously Stay on Truck Bumper

Lindsay writes: "I was gardening alongside the driveway on a super-hot day a couple of weeks ago, working up a sweat. My expensive prescription sunglasses were sliding off my sweaty nose, so I took them off and set them on the back bumper of my husband's truck. An hour later, he came out and told me he was going to do a bunch of errands. Off he went, and about forty-five minutes later, it dawned on me that he had driven off with my glasses. I ran down the street and looked for them without any luck. I felt foolish but said an MBO and called my husband. He was driving and said he'd check and let me know when he stopped. Much to my amazement and joy, they were still there. I repeatedly thanked my angels."

MBO-Driven Movement of Missing Package

Brenda writes: "I'm writing to let you know I greatly appreciate your work. Since receiving your book a year ago, I've signed up for your weekly email. It is very informative and a constant reminder of how we must remember to say our MBOs. I recently had an issue in which I had a valuable package get misplaced and sent to Puerto Rico.

"After ten days, I decided to request an MBO for it to be found in Puerto Rico, have it move back into the main United States, and be shipped to my home in New Jersey, safe and sound. Within an hour of requesting the MBO, the package started to move. I am thankful for you getting this beautiful work out to all of us. It truly helps."

Two Lost Keys Found

Dawn writes: "My scenario is interesting. I have a storage unit piled high with half the furnishings from a four-bedroom house. I recently rented another unit so I could haul old boxes to the new unit and review, repack, and donate its contents. One of my sons helped to haul several pieces of furniture to a donation place with a rental truck, and then he was going to finish emptying his apartment and bring his boxes to his girlfriend's condo, where he was now living.

"Somewhere along the way, he lost the keys for both storage units; they were both on one key ring. When he discovered the keys were missing, he had a complete meltdown. He turned the truck inside out searching for them, and then he searched the condo to no avail. He was in the process of returning to his apartment to see if they were there when I told him I was going to text him a message and that he was to follow the instructions. I then texted him the MBO request to find the storage keys to read out loud.

"In the meantime, my son was ranting like a lunatic about having to get a locksmith or one of those tools to cut the locks. I called him back and asked him if he received my text. He replied that he had but that he didn't have time to do it. I told him to literally shut up and read the text message and to follow the instructions. I told him he would be talking directly to his guardian angel and that if he would just say what I texted him, he would find the keys. Guess what? He found the keys at the old apartment."

MBO Turns Up Missing Hubcap

Ron writes: "The other day my wife and I were out shopping. When I returned home from our trip, I noticed that my right front hubcap was missing. I was really upset about it. I also mentioned it to one of the men living in our complex. The next morning I had to go out to the store again, so I made an MBO request:

> **Most Benevolent Outcome Request**
> *"I request a most benevolent outcome that my hubcap be returned to me. Thank you."*

"Then yesterday a man came to our door with my hubcap in his hand. He said he found it not far from our place leaning up against a trash can and he knew right away it was mine. I thank my angel for wonderful help too. And thank you, Tom, for all the work you are doing in teaching people about how to use MBOs."

A Lost Purse Finds Its Owner

Penny writes: "My son and I were at Cincinnati Zoo in the jungle trails area. It is really a packed dirt path through the woods and is fairly secluded. When we came up to the lemur exhibit, there was a bag sitting on the ground. I didn't want to move it because my intuition was telling me loud and clear that the person who left it was probably nearby. So I asked for an MBO for the person who left the bag to notice right away that it was missing and come back for it, and for no one else to pick it up in the meantime.

"We walked a short distance to the next building, and about two or three minutes after I said the MBO request, a woman came tearing around the corner with her small daughter in a stroller. She was looking panicked, so I asked her if she was looking for a bag. She said yes, and I was able to tell her it was just around the corner. That was a very quick answer for a very important need! I made sure to tell my skeptical son what I had done."

Tape Measure Recovered

Kellye writes: "A couple of days ago, I was working on creating a floor plan for an upcoming event that I am to host. I desperately needed a ruler or tape measure to create the floor plan because I needed to make sure of the space that I needed to allow for our vendors. It was the end of the day, and I had to have it completed soon. When I went to search for the tape measure, it was not in the place where I normally keep it. At first I freaked out, but then I thought, 'Just say an MBO request,' so I did. I requested an MBO 'to find either a ruler or my tape measure now. Thank you.' Then I paused. My head slowly turned to the left, and there it was — hiding behind a candle on my desk. I am so grateful for this knowledge, as it was very important that I found that at that exact time. Thank you!"

MBO for a Missing Debit Card

Rose writes: "I went out of state for a week to spoil my youngest grandchild and took one of my two debit cards with me. After I came home, when I was reorganizing my purse and billfold, I started to look for the card I did not take and could not find it. After a few hours, I said an MBO request to have it returned to me sooner than I could hope for or expect. Since this was on a Sunday, I knew it wouldn't do any good to call the credit union until Monday morning to report it missing, so I continued to unpack. I began to dump a bag of laundry I brought back with me, and my missing debit card surfaced from the pile of dirty clothes. Someone has a sense of humor!"

Finding a Key and a Flashlight

Jean writes: "I'm still asking for MBOs, although some of them seem to be taking an unbearably long time. The one I requested earlier this week didn't. I attended a meeting out of town and carpooled. I always put my spare key, which I keep on a ring with a small LED flashlight, in the watch pocket of my jeans. When we got back, I reached for my key, but it was gone. And I know I put it there before we left.

"After asking for a fast MBO, I checked the car I'd been riding in, plus my own car, my other pockets, and my purse — no key. Fortunately, I had another car key on the same ring as my residence keys, so I could get home and inside. I emailed the hotel where the event was held because the flashlight had the name of the restaurant I got it from on it, which was in the States (I live in Canada), and I had visions of the hotel mailing it back to them! But they replied that it hadn't been turned in and told me to check with them the next day.

"I had just read their reply when the phone rang. It was the driver of our carpool. She had reached in her slacks pocket on the left side and found my key with the flashlight. We have discussed this several times and cannot figure out how my key got into her pocket! (She always puts her keys on her desk.) Needless to say, I was very grateful to retrieve my key the next day.

"The angels certainly came through rapidly for me in this case. Thank you, thank you, thank you. And thank you to you, Tom, for getting the word out about MBOs and how to use them through your books, blogs, and newsletter."

MBO for Lost Sunglasses

John writes: "Just recently I was in a big department store looking at many different things, and as I left after at least an hour (I was really tired too), I realized I left my sunglasses somewhere in the store. From a logical point of view, trying to find these sunglasses would have been nightmare, so I decided to take the easy route and ask my guardian angel to help me find them.

"I said an MBO request to find my sunglasses and then just let my guardian angel lead me to them; I did this by wandering around aimlessly and not using my logical mind at all. I even managed to calm myself down enough from all the anger I felt after I realized I lost my sunglasses. After about five minutes of wandering around, I walked right up to them in the back of the store as they were waiting for me to return. They were on a table next to a chair I was thinking about buying.

"Anyway, this little exercise was a real eye-opener for me, since it allowed me just step back and let my guardian angel lead the way, and it also helped me find my sunglasses in a very easy and effortless manner. It's little things like this that make working with my guardian angel such a pleasure. I'm always amazed at the results. And it's interesting to see what you can accomplish when you have trust and faith in your guardian angel!"

Tom responds: I had a problem with leaving my reading glasses in restaurants and having to return to pick them up. I requested an MBO to never leave them anywhere again. Plus I purchased an expensive pair of sunglasses as a present to myself the first time I returned to Cannes, France, for a TV market after I had recovered from congestive heart failure. I've said a similar MBO for my sunglasses too. Both requests are working perfectly!

MBOs Guide a Beloved Pet Back Home

Patti writes: "My cat was missing three weeks once. I copied a photo of her and posted it everywhere and kept one on the fridge. Then I wrote her a letter expressing all my emotions about her and thanking her for her friendship. I also wrote you, Tom, about how to request an MBO asking for her return home and for all beings to assist her safe return. I also visualized light around her at all times and a beam of light from my apartment so she could find it. She returned home safe and sound, as if she had been visiting someone for three weeks. She had no injuries and wasn't even hungry!"

Missing Medical Supplies Recovered

Meredith writes: "I worked at a medical supply store and was in charge of shipping medical pieces to doctors or distributors. These pieces are used in surgery, so their delivery is often urgent. I sent some pieces to Mexico, and when the client received them, he said sixteen pieces were missing! Of course I was responsible for this matter, so I started tracking and investigating, but I got no results this way. I then said an MBO request that the pieces would be found — otherwise I would have to pay for them, and they are very expensive.

"We had been searching for the pieces all morning. A matter of minutes after I said the MBO request, I talked to the client and he told me he had made an error in counting. Can you believe that? He did a recount and found out everything was perfect. Thank you, dear angels! And thank you, Tom, for doing this great work."

Tom responds: This has happened several times to me in our film distribution business. We would send a box of video masters to a TV station or network and be told there was one or more missing, even though we were extremely careful in checking and rechecking our shipments. We would request an MBO and the station or network would call back and say, "Oh, we found the missing masters."

MBO to Find a Lost Necklace

Brenda writes: "The other night I lost a valuable twenty-four-karat gold necklace with a Quan Yin pendant. I had shopped at four stores that day, and I thought for sure it was lost forever. Twenty-four-karat gold is very soft, so I assumed the necklace had broken or that I hadn't pushed the clasp closed correctly. Right away, I requested an MBO for it to be found by an honest person so that it could be returned safely to me.

"I started calling the stores yesterday morning, and with the second phone call I got to speak to the woman who found it. She assured me that she had locked it up immediately and that both the necklace and Quan Yin pendant were together. Thankfully, both my pendant and necklace are now back in my possession. I know the MBO request to my guardian angel helped me to find such an honest person. It also gives me hope that there are many honest people in the world, even in such difficult economic times."

Recovering My Grandson's Beloved Toy

Lee writes: "Hi, Tom. I have an MBO story for you. My grandson has a 'comfort' stuffed animal that we call his 'woobie.' He was getting ready for bed and we couldn't find it anywhere. We looked high and low. Finally I remembered MBOs and requested one immediately for help in locating his most sacred possession. Within three seconds, a thought popped into my head and I asked my husband if it was still in his truck from when he picked the baby up at his nursery school. He went outside and looked, and there it was in the car seat. Tragedy was averted — and very quickly! I said thank you, thank you, thank you!"

MBO for Lost Marriage Certificate

Ann writes: "I have an MBO story here for you that just happened, and I felt that I had to write it to you, as I've been a bit lazy sending you other MBOs that have happened over the past few months.

"Well, this evening I asked my husband to search for our marriage certificate, since he was the one who kept it after we got married three months ago. I needed to use it the next day to go change my surname at the doctor's (I'm currently heavily pregnant) and at my bank (they wouldn't do it unless they saw the certificate).

"My husband forgets things easily — even telling me the same stories over and over again weeks apart without realizing he's already told them to me — but he's not losing his mind; it's just his nature. Anyway, he couldn't remember where he kept it but reluctantly went to look for it and came back fifteen minutes later saying he couldn't find it.

"I was really mad at my husband for (1) not wanting to look for the certificate in the first place, and (2) not having been careful enough to keep it safe. Mind you, while he was searching for it, he asked me to leave him to do it on his own, so for him to spend a mere fifteen minutes searching and later tell me he couldn't find it just made me want to explode. All he could say while lying on the sofa at that point was, 'We'll just order another one,' which could've taken weeks.

"I just walked away and went to bed. I was so angry at him that I couldn't even sleep, so I decided to say an MBO request to help me find the original certificate without having to order a new one the next day. Deep down I knew the certificate was in the room he was searching in, but I just didn't know where. My anger and anxiety over finding it were quite high, so I made a decision that as long as I was in that bed, all I should be doing is sleeping and not thinking about how angry or anxious I was. So I kept repeating, 'It's okay. The angels will find it.'

"A few minutes later, all the anger and anxiety had suddenly disappeared. I was even okay with the thought of ordering a new copy of the certificate the next morning. After a few minutes, I calmly got up and went into the room where my husband had searched for the certificate. I looked through the first drawer — nothing. I opened the second drawer, and there it was on top of his clothes. How he could have missed it, I don't know. I'm guessing that he didn't even bother looking through the second drawer, as it had clothes in it while the others had all paperwork. I said thanks to my angels for helping me find the certificate and teaching me a good lesson of completely handing over control and letting them guide me through anxious times.

"Also, in the process of searching for the certificate, I found a makeup brush I lost three months ago on my wedding day. Again, deep down I knew it was in that room, but I just didn't know where. I had asked my husband, and he said he hadn't seen it. I asked for an MBO when I lost it, and today is when I found it. I wasn't actively looking for it but always wished I had it whenever I did my makeup. Maybe having my husband not find the certificate was a way for my angels to get me to finally properly look for the makeup brush I lost.

"I hope you have a lovely day, and I will try to write my other success stories soon."

MBO for Lost Gift Cards

Laurie writes: "My work gives movie tickets, Starbucks gift cards, and gas cards as incentives. I normally save up these cards in a plastic bag in my purse, and a couple of times a year will treat myself when I am having a tight money week. Well, I used one of the gas cards and remember putting them back in the bottom of my purse.

"A few days later I decided to treat myself to Starbucks, but I couldn't find my gift cards. I was upset, but I said an MBO request for the return of the gift cards. Then I felt bad and said another MBO request, stating that I hoped whoever had found the gift cards at the gas station really needed them.

"A few days later I went to visit my mother, and lo and behold, she had found the bag of gift cards on the floor. It must have fallen out of my purse. Needless to say, I was very happy to have them returned to me after I had assumed they had been found and used up."

Missing Earring Comes to Light

Daphnee writes: "Here's a little story I'd like to share that involves my four-year-old girl who was given some expensive earrings by my sister and her godmother. This morning, she lost the back of the earring, which is very tiny. I requested an MBO to find it, and I had not even started to look when the angel directed me straight to the place where it had fallen. Nobody was laughing at me anymore as I said my thank you three times. I am now going to request an MBO to request more MBOs every day."

Tom responds: That was a nice MBO find!

MBOs Guide Me Right to Lost Items

Marie writes: "One of my friends had another friend trying to help her find a craft book, so I said a request for an MBO and then walked straight to where it was. They had already looked through that box so I doubt they would have looked again. The funny thing is that when I lost something else that was a gift from my son, I went straight to it as well, and it wasn't in an area that I normally kept it in. I always say thank you to my angels after requesting an MBO. Thank you, angels, and thank you, Tom."

25

Most Benevolent Time Compressions

Getting to Church on Time

Liamona writes: "I decided to try to go to a service at a Unity church. I hadn't gone before, because it's at least a forty-five-minute drive from my home. The Sunday I decided to go, I got caught up in some projects and lost track of the time. I started driving thirty-five minutes before the service was supposed to start, and I needed to get gas for my car on top of that. So I requested a compression of time, and I didn't look at the clock the whole time I was driving. Somehow I ended up at the church with five minutes to spare!"

Tom responds: For those not familiar with being able to bend time a little, you simply say,

> **Most Benevolent Outcome Request**
> *"I request a compression of time until _____. Thank you!"*

Then don't look at your watch or clock! This works great for getting to appointments on time and for having more time to finish a project.

Compressing Time and Avoiding Speeding Tickets

Darlene writes: "I always request an MBO for divine protection, keen awareness, defensive drivers all around me, and a safe, uneventful trip to work each morning before I back out of my driveway. If I'm running late, I always request an MBO for a compression of time so that I can arrive at work and punch the time clock at the precise time I am supposed to. This has worked for me each and every time I have requested it. Sometimes, in my mind, I just know I'm going to be late but I never voice it, and my guardian angel always gets me there.

"Last week, I went to see my parents, who live six hours away. As I was returning home, I went through a small town and, in my haste to get back home, was pulled over for speeding. Despite the fact that I was stopped for going forty-eight miles per hour in a thirty-five zone, I only received a warning. Thank you for enlightening me on MBOs. I use them all the time!"

Making an Important Appointment

Sandy writes: "I want to thank you for your generosity in all you share. I have been reading and enjoying your articles in the *Sedona Journal*, which I buy monthly. It wasn't until earlier this week that I finally visited your website and signed up for your newsletter and blog; that I did was due to the following story.

"Two weeks ago today, I was finally getting around to reading your MBO column in the latest issue of the *Sedona Journal*, and I read the entry about time compression. It interested me because there have been many times recently when I've attempted something similar but more along the lines of requesting for time to stand still — usually when I'm running late, which is my norm!

"The following day, I had made plans to take our new kitten in for shots. I was going to the veterinarian's office to meet my friend who had rescued the kitten we'd adopted — he still had two more of our cat's littermates. I was familiar with how to get there, although I'd never been to that veterinarian's office before, but I checked the map anyway — no problem there. I was trying very diligently to keep an eye on the clock so that I left on time to make it for the 2:30PM appointment.

"I loaded the kitten in his crate, got in the car, and looked at my watch; it was 1:54PM. I told myself, 'It's okay, Sandy; you'll make it. Just keep breathing and you'll keep moving.' Meanwhile, I thought I'd request an MBO for the kitten so that he would have an easy, stress-free experience and not be scared or suffer any ill effects from the shot. I was about four miles into my eight- to ten-mile, one-way trip when I looked at the car clock and thought, 'Wow — I'm making pretty good time!' I came to a stoplight that I know to be a rather long one since it crosses one of the busier main thoroughfares through the city. I looked at the clock once more and began to get a wee bit nervous.

"My mind wandered back to what I'd read about time compression, although I couldn't remember the right name and instead called it 'time folding' in my mind. I remembered the steps, though, and thought it was definitely worth a try. So I said,

> **Most Benevolent Outcome Request**
> *"I would like to request a time folding. No matter how many red or green lights I come to, I will safely and securely reach my destination on time, and I won't just pull up into the parking lot at 2:35 and say it's okay to be a few minutes late."*

"Then I followed the final and most important instruction: Do not look at the car clock or your watch!

"Here's what happened: The traffic light I was sitting at skipped a cycle. My light never turned green until the next go around! Then I hit a multitude of red lights, took one wrong turn and had to backtrack approximately one block. When I finally pulled up in front of the vet's, I turned the car off and took the key out, simultaneously looking at the car clock: It was 2:29PM. Wow! I was so thrilled. I got out of the car and told my friend 'I did it! I did it! I folded time!'

"Of course I explained what I'd done, all the while offering thanks to all my guides and angels for assisting me. It was truly a wonderful experience. And the kitten did wonderfully too, relaxing on the ride home like I'd never thought possible. Another reason this is so incredible is that this kitten had been found feral and had received no human contact until five weeks before this vet trip."

Impossible On-Time Arrival

Billy writes: "Here is another interesting example in the use of time compression. I was on my way with a delivery to a printing company. I got stuck in traffic and found myself running quite late. Against all odds, I made a request for an MBO to arrive at the printing company on time. Traffic started to flow and time seemed to slow. It was amazing! Driving that distance at that hour would normally be physically impossible, yet I arrived on time. The only thing that could explain the phenomenon is that somehow time was delayed or otherwise put on hold. Thanks again to you and the others you work with."

Time Compression

Rick writes: "I have a compression of time story for you. I had a follow-up appointment to see my orthopedic doctor. It's a ten-mile drive up the highway. There was major construction going on, so I left my place a little early, as a fifteen-minute ride can easily turn into twenty minutes or more. I said an MBO request for arriving on or before my appointment time and that I get on the highway in a safe manner. On-ramps now have stop signs during construction, which makes driving hazardous with the lane changes.

"I got onto the highway in a safe manner, all right: There was a jackknifed tractor trailer three miles up the highway. Traffic in all three lanes was at a crawl. I specifically asked for a compression of time to get to my doctor's appointment on or before my scheduled appointment. I then sat in traffic for what seemed like an eternity, doing my best not to look at the clock. Once I got past the accident, it was smooth sailing on the highway, but once I got off the highway, I had the secondary roads to contend with, which meant traffic lights. But every traffic light that I passed through was green. I never had to stop for a red light! Well, this has never happened to me before, and I take this route often. There are seven lights on this route, and all stayed green or turned to yellow once I got to the intersection.

"Although I did not arrive on or before my scheduled appointment, I did get there only two minutes late and explained to them about the accident. I barely had time to sign in before they were ready for me. I went back to the exam room immediately. My wait time in the exam room to see the doctor was less than five minutes, and I was in the office no more than ten minutes. On top of that, I received a clean bill of health and was released from his care.

"I use compressions of time quite a bit for this trip and usually arrive five to ten minutes early. Sitting in traffic like that raised some doubts, but the end result — including the doctor's exam itself — cleared all those doubts. I'll take it!"

Tom responds: As I explained in my first book, if you appear to be running late for an appointment as Rick was, you simply say,

> **Most Benevolent Outcome Request**
> "*I request a compression of time until _____. Thank you!*"

Or you can say, as Rick said, "*... on or before my appointment time. Thank you!*" You'll typically arrive a couple of minutes early. We are now able to manipulate time a little, and this is a good way to do it. But remember, just as Rick did: Don't look at a clock!

Getting to a Seminar on Time

Iris writes: "I left home on time to attend a seminar. I then noticed I had left my wallet on the coffee table and had to go back. I was trying to drive thirty-five miles at the tail end of rush hour, and once I retrieved the wallet, it was 6:17PM. I know it takes at least an hour to get to my destination. I repeated an MBO request that specified that time be compressed. I did not look at the clock. I miraculously arrived at 6:55PM! Thank you, angels, for altering time so that I was not late!"

Time Compression Helps Two Friends Make Flight

Nancy writes: "Tom, here's something that happened on Sunday while a friend and I were traveling. We were visiting friends in San Antonio last week and heading back to our home in North Carolina on Sunday morning. We left the resort early to get to the airport at least two hours before our flight, since we had a car to drop off and luggage to check.

"Well, somehow we passed the airport exit. I pulled into a gas station to ask for directions. Sure enough, we drove past where we were supposed to turn off. I asked the manager how long it would take us to get there, and he said, 'About thirty minutes.' I looked at my watch and noticed that our flight was scheduled to leave in one hour. So I asked for an MBO that time would stop for a few minutes and that we would arrive at the airport with at least twenty minutes to spare.

"We turned around, got back on the freeway, found the right exit, and headed to the rental car drop-off. Of course, we had trouble finding this location too and ended up stopping at another gas station. We were about five blocks away. I looked at my watch and found it had taken us only ten minutes to get to that point!

"Pulling into the rental car stop, we were met immediately by an attendant and finished checking in in less than a minute. As we were walking to the airport shuttle stop, a bus pulled right up to the curb and we left almost immediately. When we got to the airport, most people headed inside toward the counter, but my friend and I headed to the curbside check-in. There were two people ahead of us with only one attendant. Of course, just then, another attendant returned from his break and we walked right up to the counter.

"Going into the airport, we immediately checked our gate location and headed for security. There were about ten people ahead of us with three stations open, but the line was moving pretty quickly. Then a fourth station opened, and we went through this station with no complications — only five minutes total in that line!

"But that wasn't the final surprise. Our gate was about a third of the way in from security, and we quickly walked to it, getting there about fifteen minutes before the flight was scheduled to take off. Stopping by the gate and taking a deep breath, we heard an announcement coming across the loudspeaker. The connecting flight had been delayed and the plane was just arriving then. Boarding wouldn't start until the plane was serviced, in about twenty minutes! So not only did we make our flight with ease, but we were able to get a cup of coffee and sit down for a few minutes. Many thanks to the angels of time travel."

Most Benevolent Timing

Nancy writes: "Driving home from the hospital after visiting a friend, I realized that I was going to be late for an appointment. So I sent up an MBO request for a time collapse or something so my client wouldn't be standing outside waiting for me in the rain. When I got to the office, I found all the lights on and my client inside. Turns out my business partner 'just happened' to stop by on her day off at the same time my client showed up! I arrived ten minutes later, right on time for the appointment."

26

Small but Satisfying Benevolent Outcomes

The Benevolent Actions of Others Make Life Easier

Jo writes: "I have noticed some great blessings from my MBO requests immediately after making them, such as when I asked for a benevolent drive home from Texas to Canada and drivers were literally moving out of my way. Then other nice things were happening too, like doors being opened when I had my hands full. So I am seeing some wonderful results, and many thanks again."

Just a Simple Cup of Joe

Mark writes: "I have been enjoying your newsletter very much and have been using requests for benevolent outcomes for a couple of months now. In one of your past newsletters, you mentioned the importance of asking for MBOs for anything — especially the small stuff — so we remember to ask for MBOs for the big stuff.

"Less than an hour ago, I really wanted a cup of coffee, but I am providing phone coverage and could not leave my desk. I whispered my request to my guardian angel,

> **Most Benevolent Outcome Request**
> *"I request a most benevolent outcome for someone to buy and bring me a cup of coffee. Thank you!"*

"Soon after that, a coworker sent me an email offering to get coffee and another from a coworker who offered to buy mine."

Tom responds: Now there's an MBO I never thought of requesting!

A Snowy Promise Kept

Ruthie writes: "I ordered pizza from a local shop, along with bread, cinnamon sticks, and sodas. Despite our three and a half feet of snow, the order was delivered as promised, except for sodas. The driver said, 'I'll be back.' I doubted that, so I asked for an MBO that the driver would really bring back our soda. Much to our surprise, he came back and gave us two liters of soda. MBOs work."

Tom responds: As I wrote to Ruthie, MBOs make even the more mundane parts of life easier.

Pleasant Lunch MBOs

Carolyn writes: "Thanks for all you do, and a big thanks to your guardian angel and Gaia too! Last Sunday, some friends and I went to eat lunch around noon. I asked for an MBO for perfect parking and a perfect meal experience with friends — even better than I could hope for and expect! As the first place we went to was filled with the after-church crowd, we went to a nearby Panera Bread café. It was a relaxed and fun lunch. Besides that, the soda fountain wasn't working, so everyone in the place got free cookies! How's that for a benevolent outcome?

"The next day, another friend and I decided to go to lunch, so I asked for another MBO for a perfect lunch and afternoon. We went to the local restaurant called Pastry Expo, and after we sat eating our quiet and relaxing lunch, the owner brought us European chocolates as an extra — another greater-than-expected MBO! We then had a beautiful afternoon at a nearby plant nursery and enjoyed the beautiful flowers, and my friend had no problems finding what she was looking for to buy. Thanks so very much!"

Help in All Kinds of Little Ways

Helena writes: "Happy New Year to you. I have made it my New Year's resolution to tell as many people about MBOs as I can. I am really promoting all your good work. I am also concentrating on requesting MBOs for myself a lot more.

"Now let me tell you what happened to me at Christmas. I spend Christmas with my sister and brother-in-law. Every year on the evening of Christmas Day, all nieces, nephews, wives, boyfriends, girlfriends, and friends come around and we act silly playing games and things. We end up having a giggle, and there is a lot of noise, as you can imagine. Well, Tom, we play these silly games and we put in twenty pence per game, or if we get overexcited, we play for a pound per game. Each time before we played the game, I kept saying,

> **Most Benevolent Outcome Request**
> *"I request an MBO for winning this game."*

"And guest what Tom? I won the games each time; it caused so much laughter. When I decided to stop playing, and I had already requested the MBO before pulling out, my winning number came up still. It was hilarious!

There was so much laughter in our house that evening. Wouldn't it be nice if I could get a large win in the lottery?

"Last night, I went out to supper with a friend and I asked for an MBO for the 219 bus to come as quickly as possible to get me to my friend's house, and it turned up just like that — and this bus usually takes ages to arrive. I got to my friend's house in no time. I am doing all kinds of MBOs now because I just love doing them."

Retrieving a Lost PIN

Diana writes: "I have an MBO story about finding and remembering a lost PIN and account number. My husband had forgotten which account goes with which PIN number for Internet banking. I asked him to say and write:

> **Most Benevolent Outcome Request**
> *"I request a most benevolent outcome for finding my account and PIN number and for the Internet banking to work. Thank you."*

"It worked within one day, and the whole thing was solved soon enough."

Smooth Sailing with Surround Sound System

Dana writes: "I wanted to share something that happened this morning. We have a surround sound system that was bought for us as a gift. We have had it for almost a year, and I have never figured out how to use it. It has a Blu-ray player in it. It is often difficult for me to figure out how to switch the TV from satellite to DVD player. There are a million buttons, and if you hit one wrong button it messes everything up. The entire thing has been one big headache, and honestly I really dislike it. It makes everything so much more complicated. I prefer simplicity.

"In any case, I wanted to watch a DVD today, so I thought I would try my luck at making it work. I did everything I was 'supposed' to do, but no luck. I started to get rather frustrated, and then it hit me: request an MBO! Well, I turned the player off and calmly said my MBO request, and as soon as I turned it back on, it worked! Coincidence? I don't think so!

"I know it sounds like a small accomplishment, but it really boosted my confidence. Saying that MBO request saved me a whole lot of frustration. Normally I freak out and want to break the thing, but today I was able to simply request an MBO and enjoy my movie!"

MBO for Hiccups

Philip writes: "Hi Tom! I was reading your book and started getting the hiccups. I then requested an MBO for curing my hiccups, and to my surprise, this prayer worked immediately. This is a cure I haven't heard about! Thank you, thank you, thank you!"

Tom responds: I guess Philip became too excited reading the book!

Small Serendipities

Wendy writes: "I wanted to share with you two things that have happened since Sunday. First, I was at the mall, which was of course packed on Mother's Day. The traffic in the parking lot was horrendous. I started to say an MBO request for a parking spot, and I barely had one word out of my mouth when an empty space appeared two cars down.

"Then, this evening, I was looking for a new blouse that I had purchased, as I wanted to wear it for a job interview tomorrow. I searched for about twenty minutes before I decided to say an MBO request, and again, I had barely said one or two words, and there was my blouse — still in the shopping bag!"

An Answer in Music

Diana writes: "Yesterday I was on my way home from paying my water bill and said an MBO request for my finances. The next song on the radio was 'Everything's Gonna Be All Right.' Talk about quick responses! Thanks."

Tom responds: I've received messages like that many times in music!

Using MBOs Every Day

Dawna writes: "I have been using MBOs for a few years now, thanks to your column in the *Sedona Journal*, and they work wonderfully. I am ever so grateful to have learned this easy tool to guide us in our journey on this wonderful planet. Anytime I feel low, I request an MBO for the angels of love or peace or joy — or harmony, balance, prosperity, or wisdom — to please walk with me and raise my vibrations. And yes, sir, within seconds, I feel a difference! Since I am a healing practitioner, I ask for MBOs for my clients as well. It is amazing to see the results when you ask for this extra assistance. I request the sun to shine on days I'm going out, and voilà! There it is, shining ever so brightly. Anytime I go to town, I request MBOs for parking spaces, and there they are too.

"Thanks to you for your uplifting, free newsletter each week. It's enjoyable to read others' experiences with MBOs, and I have gotten much inspiration from them. I am ever so grateful to you for bringing this powerful tool to humanity."

Quieting Bothersome Bread Machine Racket

Patricia writes: "Today I baked bread with the bread machine. It usually makes such a banging noise that I stopped using it for a while, but I decided to ask for an MBO for a quietly running machine and, lo and behold, it was very quiet. My son — who'd been amazed at other MBO results he'd seen me get before — asked me what I had done, and I said that my guardian angel had quieted it for me. He then said, 'That's it. I didn't believe it before, but that did it.' He didn't say if he would use MBO requests, but I'm sure he will now. I ask for MBOs for everything. My life is so much easier now. Thanks, Tom. God bless you."

The Concentrated Solution to a Small Problem

Carlos writes: "Sunday night, I requested an MBO for my retainers to be cleaner than they've been in a while (they're the Invisalign-type retainers). My specific MBO request was,

> **Most Benevolent Outcome Request**
> *"I request the most benevolent outcome that my retainers be cleaner than they have been recently — as clean as new. Thank you."*

"Just as I had filled up the glass with water and dropped in the retainer cleaning tablet, my mom asked me, 'Why don't you put less water in the glass? That way, the solution would be more concentrated.' I couldn't believe it. I'd been using the tablets for a week by then, and that was the first time that the idea had come up. The MBO request worked!"

Speedy Book Delivery

Carlos writes: "Before I went to sleep last night (at 4:30AM), I requested two MBOs. The first was for my books to arrive soon:

> **Most Benevolent Outcome Request**
> *"I request the most benevolent outcome of my books arriving as soon as possible. Thank you."*

"I had ordered *The Gentle Way* and *The Gentle Way II*, along with Doreen Virtue's *How to Hear Your Angels*. They were scheduled to arrive between today and Friday, but they arrived today! I'm so glad I'm having luck with MBO requests already. I know it can only go up from here now that the books have arrived."

27

MBO Combination Platters

Benevolent Outcomes in Britain

Annie writes: "Although it's late, I just had to tell you about the most amazing MBOs that happened today. As I wrote to you a while ago, my hubby doesn't believe in anything spiritual or out of the ordinary, so I just putter along on my own, regardless. Today he had bid on an eBay auction and was the highest bidder, but then he read the small print about the item and realized he had bid on the wrong thing. There wasn't much time left before the bidding would be closed, and he was panicked that he would end up with something he didn't want, so I silently said an MBO request. Within two minutes, someone else bid. He was so pleased! Naturally, I kept quiet about it, and he is none the wiser for it.

"The most amazing MBO result, however, happened when our heating system suddenly stopped working at about ten o'clock at night. We are going through a very bad winter in England at the moment, and as it's New Year's Eve tomorrow, we wouldn't have a hope in hell of getting anyone out to fix it. The heating systems in the UK are usually with boilers, and if that fails, you are looking at a hefty repair bill. After numerous attempts at switching it off and on, my husband decided the pilot light or something like that had gone, and he had no hope of getting anything to work. So I silently said an MBO request again and asked him to try again. It worked! We are so happy about this, as we were so cold and at our wits' end about what to do.

"You know, every time I request an MBO, I amaze myself, because it's so thrilling when it works. Besides, it reminds me that there are always invisible forces at work, helping us whenever we want, if we just ask. So thank you for your weekly newsletter. Anyway, I will stop rambling on now and hope you have a very happy New Year and a most benevolent 2010!"

Tom responds: It's stories like these that remind you just how magical requesting MBOs can be in your life. No one else might have bid on eBay with your MBO request, but someone did. The boiler, for all intents and purposes, was as dead as the proverbial doornail, but it sprang back to life with the request of an MBO. If you haven't done so already, make a New Year's resolution to request MBOs in your life throughout the year. It will make 2010 a good year for you!

Dissolving Anger and Granting Provision

Stella writes: "I have thought about writing to you many times, but I promised myself last evening that I would finally do it. First, I want to thank you for all you do. It is unusual for me to find spiritual guidance that really resonates with me. My heart has always told me that miracles and wishes should be received by simply asking, not by performing complicated rituals. Although those can be fulfilling for some, I don't want nor need the pomp and circumstance. So finding your site, newsletter, articles, and books has been not only reaffirming but enlightening and it has helped me see miracle after miracle!

"I was introduced to the concept of MBO requests through your column in the *Sedona Journal* and thought it was too good to be true. So I started to test it out on little things like parking, as you suggested, and of course I quickly became a believer! I now request MBOs several times a day and expect positive results each time — mostly. I have so many success stories, but I will share the two that have affected me the most.

"First, these requests were effective in dissolving anger: I was with my two-year-old son visiting his father — we are no longer together — in another country over Christmas for about three months. I was extremely anxious about this extended trip, because — without getting into too many details — his father has a very frightening temper that can come on with little warning. Every morning, I requested an MBO for our communications to be based on love, respect, understanding, patience, kindness, compassion, loyalty, support, and joy. I would repeat this to myself whenever I felt his mood change, and his face and voice would change instantly. This was miraculous! I had spent seven years in a very bad and painful relationship with him and had never seen him stop once he began his dark moments, yet here I was with this little yet very powerful phrase, creating positivity and peace for all three of us. Thank you!

"Second, MBOs helped with scholarships and finances: My sister and her family have been having a very difficult time financially, so they had not been able to have their children return to the private school they had always attended. This year, however — armed with MBO requests — my sister decided to apply for scholarships for both her kids, and both were awarded scholarships!

"There still remained the item of the outstanding balance from the year before, however, so another MBO request later, the school agreed to apply the awarded funds to the previous year's tuition. That still left quite a hefty balance to be brought up to date for the beginning of the school year, so together, we requested an MBO for free and clear money to be able to put toward the school fees. Well, you will never guess: An inheritance from a distant relative came in just in time to help pay down the fees! The idea was to not borrow the money but instead have it for free — and voilà!

"So I know MBO requests work, and I know my angels are with me always. I can ask for a hug, and I get the warmest and most loving physical hug around my heart. But why can I not find a job? I have been requesting this for months now. I ask for the perfect job, better than I could possibly imagine. As a single mother, I really need to provide for my son, plus I know my ego has taken a big hit. Can you perhaps ask your guardian angel why I am not having any luck? I have sent résumé after résumé — even for jobs I really didn't want and I was overqualified for. Please, is there hope? Why won't this MBO happen for me?"

Tom responds: Perhaps your own guardian angel is whispering in your ear to take a course or two in management? Each time you go out, you might also request an MBO to meet someone who needs to fill a job. And if you apply for a job you're overqualified for, drop off or reduce your qualifications. Once in the new job, you might then be quickly promoted from within, which is how a lot of companies like to work.

Have you considered going to garage sales and buying at five cents on the dollar and selling at twenty-five cents? Many people do that and make a very decent living. They had a story on TV recently about a person in Dallas who would go to a liquidator store and buy new electronic stuff and resell at a nice profit on eBay. I hope this gives you some ideas!

MBOs Help on Many Levels

Dan writes: "I just wanted to write to share some MBO successes. I was referred to your work by a friend and have read both of your books. At first, I started with MBO requests very tentatively — looking for a good parking spot or asking that the coffee shop have my flavor of coffee available. With those consistent successes in hand, I stepped up and asked for MBOs in my professional and financial arenas.

"Professionally, my career has literally gone international with notoriety and acclaims from my immediate higher-ups as well as on a governmental level. On a financial level, an obscure stock I bought has jumped 400 percent in value, which will soon enable me to pay off my mortgage! And I should say that I have also shared your work with a colleague who has used it to good advantage in her own career and has shared it with her children, who have also had startling results."

A Fantastic Weekend in London

Dan writes: "Last weekend I went to London, England, to compete in the Mind Sports Olympiad, which is like an Olympics for the mind. It's a weeklong event that has competitions in everything from mental calculations to chess to backgammon and many other events. I went to compete in the creative thinking category. Before I left, I asked for an MBO and requested that I win the gold or finish in the top three. I tied the three-time world champion from South Africa for the gold in this category. The fellow who came in second was last year's gold medal winner, who was from Spain. Yes, a result better than I could've hoped for or expected!

"As a matter of fact, the whole London weekend went better than I could've hoped for or expected. The hotel gave me a room upgrade as soon as I arrived — thank you! My exam result was perfect too. They even had a film crew doing a documentary, which resulted in a lot of screen time for me. I'm not sure if or where it will air, but it was fun nonetheless.

"My best story of the whole weekend occurred after the exam when I went to the Savoy bar and had a drink. The bartender was showing some old bottles of liquor to some other patrons and asked if I wanted some of the pre-Fidel regime rum. At 25 GBP a shot, I thought I'd treat myself to two drinks. Nice stuff, I thought.

"When I checked out in the morning, I noticed what I thought was an anomaly on the bar bill. As I made my way down to check out, I hurriedly sent out an MBO request that it all be resolved well. I then inquired of the manager why I was being charged 450 GBP for the two drinks. He informed me that, yes, the price of 225 GBP per drink was correct for a 1932 pre-Castro rum — eek! After much blustering, embarrassment, and a few more under-my-breath MBO requests, he graciously forgave the 400 GBP and charged me for what I thought I heard: 25 GBP per drink! Thanks to my guardian angel for the whole weekend!"

Most Benevolent Bird Care and Car Care

Sheila writes: "I can't recall how I was led to your website, but I am so glad I was! I was impressed by it and immediately ordered both your books. My first two MBOs happened quickly, and I posted on your Facebook page about them. The next three also happened quickly. This was all within the space of two days. Today was my third day using MBOs and the most amazing. I have been both a student and teacher of metaphysics for thirty-five years and haven't ever had such consistently phenomenal results.

"This morning I took my car to the repair shop. I requested an MBO before I left home. I had to wait about five minutes for my son to pick me up at the shop, so I sat and chatted with a lady waiting there who was considerably younger than me. She mentioned that she rescues animals: dogs, cats, and birds. I have a pet bird and have been concerned what would happen to her when I pass. All my family and friends have dogs or cats; there is no one who could take my bird.

"So I asked this young lady if she would be able to care for my bird. She said she would definitely take her and gave me her phone number, which I passed on to my family. I mentioned to her that there are no accidents in the universe;

I was meant to meet her. She said she guessed so, because she had brought her car in the day before and they had been too busy to help her and told her to come back today. As I left, she said, 'Don't worry, I've got you covered.'

"As I floated out of there, happy as could be, I requested another MBO that my car would be ready around 1:00PM. This busy shop was loaded with cars that were there ahead of me. At 1:00PM I got the call that my car was ready. Thank you for sharing this with the world and for all the good you do!"

MBOs for Mate, Career, and Prosperity

Dan writes: "I hardly know where to begin. At the end of June, I was reveling in how well the year ended at the school where I work. We had great results for the year, which have garnered positive comments from my superintendent. When the holidays began in July, I asked for three specific MBOs over the next three months: one that I would be led to my perfect life partner, a second that I would experience financial prosperity, and a third that I would have clarity surrounding the best career for me. How's that for asking big?

"On the relationship front, I finally got to the point where I was able to end a relationship that wasn't going in the direction I wanted. This is significant because for years we were both content with an on-again, off-again type of arrangement, and this was the first time I was able to deal with this in an objective manner. What a relief!

"On the career front, after decompressing from school and experiencing the start-up of a new school year, I realized my career in education really is the best place for me. It fulfills me on so many levels and enables me to make a contribution, which is very important to me.

"On the prosperity side of things, I think fulfillment for me was more of a realization that I am already blessed and can just enjoy the moment rather than tie my happiness only to a multimillion-dollar win in the lottery. I have all my material needs met, can enjoy some travel, and have some cash left over at the end of the month for some personal spending.

"Did my MBOs work? Yes, although perhaps not in the way I expected. But I am at peace and continue to request personal MBOs and BPs for those around me. Thanks, Tom. This summer has been a real blessing and an eye-opener for me. Thank you for this work."

MBOs Every Day

John writes: "Well, I use MBO requests for everything. When I go to the store, I request an MBO before I go in, and I have all sorts of interesting things happen, from finding things I thought I'd never find or finding perfect gifts for friends — for birthdays and things like that — to having shorter lines at the checkout.

"I often request MBOs for small things: Whenever I drive, I request an

MBO to arrive safely at my destination. I use MBO requests at work to have a great day and to get more done, or sometimes I ask only to have a little work that day if I don't feel so well. Amazing synchronicities happen every day. Of course, just like all the others who write in to your newsletter, Tom, I use them for parking spaces as well, and I find the most amazing spaces where there were none before.

"I also did an MBO request recently when I started to choke on a bagel I was eating. I did everything I could think of to stop choking, and then finally in desperation I remembered to request an MBO. In something like five seconds, the choking just stopped. I was amazed. The same thing happened again a week later, and I also had it stop in about five seconds or less. It was like magic; I couldn't tell exactly how it was done, but it felt like a small miracle.

"I also consult with my guardian angel for big things like finding a new job or having new friends show up, and things just drop right in my lap. Tom, you recommended also requesting MBOs for impossible things, like having large sums of money come to you. It might not happen, but you can give it a shot, after all!

"It's also a very good idea to request an MBO to pay off a specific bill rather than asking for a large sum of money. Working on specific bills seems to work much better. You can ask to have your car insurance bill reduced or ask to have your credit card bill paid in some miraculous way — or maybe to simply get some help with it. I also request MBOs before I go anywhere I have to pay a bill in person, and sometimes I get discounts, even for things that seem impossible. I got a big break on my car insurance once after requesting an MBO before I went to go see the agent, and that had never happened before in my entire life!

"I also do an amazing MBO request before I go to bed, something like,

Most Benevolent Outcome Request
"I now request the most benevolent outcome to have a wonderful and restful sleep tonight and to wake up in the morning refreshed, rejuvenated, and healed. Thank you."

"When I say that before bed, I wake up feeling so great that it's amazing! On days when I forget to say it, I wake feeling so-so and then realize that I forgot my MBO request. It really does make a big difference.

"Asking for healing for myself using MBO requests works really well. You can even ask to have your psychic abilities be increased, your intuition awakened, or your third eye stimulated. And things really will get done: I feel this incredible energy in my forehead when I do that. You can request an MBO for clearer communication with your guides and angels. The list goes on and on; whatever you can think of, you can request an MBO for it.

"As for communication with my guardian angel, I get it in the form of intense 'knowings.' I've gotten to the point now that my communication channels are becoming very open. Lately I've noticed that I can ask for directions while driving my car and get the most amazing 'impulses' about where to turn and where to go. I never get lost anymore, and I don't need a map or GPS. It's really great! You could take me, put me in the middle of a strange forest with no idea of where I'm going, and I could get myself out in no time by asking my guardian angel and guides for help. I've grown in confidence now, and I feel so protected and loved. It's really fantastic! I hope more people get into MBO requests; it's worth the time and effort, and your spiritual development will grow by leaps and bounds as well!"

Make MBO Requests a Daily Habit

Sandy writes: "I got up in the morning and said the three affirmations from your site, as I've done every day for over two years now. I had to drive over to the auto shop because my husband needed to drop off his car to get some work done and he needed a ride back home. I had a meeting with a friend, and it was going to be tight scheduling, so to speak. Here's what happened for me the rest of the day.

"First, I got in my car and said my regular MBO request. I was leading the way over to the auto shop, and I came to this stoplight where we go over a railroad crossing. I saw the red of the traffic light and beyond that, the blinking red of the railroad gate, indicating a train was coming. I was like, 'Oh, rats, just figures — the one morning I'm in a bit of a hurry.' So I quickly said an MBO request, and these were the exact words:

> **Most Benevolent Outcome Request**
> *"I request a most benevolent outcome for this to either be the crew working on the track or a really short train."*

"I heard the whistle, and within a minute, the train came into view. I kid you not, it consisted of an engine, a car, and a caboose. That was it. I laughed all the way to the shop and couldn't help but tell my husband all about MBOs and what had happened — a leap of faith, there!

"Second, I drove my husband back home, dropped him off, and quickly said another MBO request for my trip downtown to meet my friend. It's a routine drive, and as I exited the highway and went into the city, I expected there to be a place available where I usually — due to an MBO — park on the street for free. But there wasn't. I thought, 'I will drive around the block, give someone a chance to leave, and try again.' As I was sitting at the red light, waiting to make a left turn out of a one-way street, my attention wandered for just a split second and the light turned green. I slowly pulled out, and because of a truck or van parked to my left at that corner, my view was completely blocked and I did not see the older white sedan barreling through a red light at thirty miles per hour or more. It never even slowed, but I slammed on my brakes and he missed me by all of two feet. I had a small meltdown, but it was over and I was back to center in less than thirty seconds. I went on and made my final turns, and sure enough, a car was just pulling out, and there I was with my parking space.

"Third, later that day, my husband was trying to call about his car and kept getting put on hold. He tried waiting twice, to no avail. He hung up the phone and was getting really agitated. It was 3:55PM. I said out loud — because hey, my cover was blown about MBOs from this morning:

> **Most Benevolent Outcome Request**
> *"I request a most benevolent outcome that the auto shop calls here in the next five minutes to let us know about the car."*

"They called three minutes later. If you think all of that is great, which I do, in the following week and a half I have told more people about MBOs than in nearly the two years since I found out about them. And I'm hearing back from those people that they are using them! I truly feel like I've raised my own vibration once again, and I simply wish to thank you for your efforts, Tom, and both of us for having 'set it up' to meet each other way back whenever."

MBOs for Daughter, Husband, and Trip

Peggy writes: "I said an MBO request for my daughter, who is having a back operation. She is home now, and while not out of the woods yet, she's doing better every day. I also requested an MBO for my husband, and he said this has been one of the best years he has had. Then I asked for an MBO on our trip, and we had no problems. Every day I say a BP for all those who are in misery or want to ascend, including the animals and all on Earth, so that they may get whatever they need to survive and enough to share as well. Peace and love."

MBOs for Money, a New Job, and the Perfect Mate

Cheri writes: "Your guardian angel says that if we say an MBO request for the lottery and winning it is not in our soul contract, it won't happen. What if we say an MBO request for a certain amount of money? If we say an MBO for money and it's not in our soul contract, how do we know that? And if we said an MBO request, shouldn't we get the money because of the MBO? Does this make sense?

"Also, I've emailed you before about my job being cut and you gave me MBO requests to say. Thank you again for that. But if I said an MBO for finding the perfect mate, does that play into the part about the job? If that is the case, I'll do without the mate because I'm four years from an early retirement, and this job cut messes up my plans.

"Thank you, Tom, for teaching us and spreading your knowledge of MBOs. They do work, but I'm stuck on this job thing right now."

Tom responds: In my books, blogs, and newsletters, I've said that you can request an MBO for a specific amount of money to, say, pay off a specific bill. If you've set up a challenge for yourself in this life to come up with a creative way to take care of an obligation, then you will somehow take care of the debt in a way you have not thought of yet.

If you've requested an MBO for the perfect mate, that person could meet you through friends, at a party, online, or even at a new job or through your search for a new job. Whatever the outcome, it will be an MBO for you. You just have to be patient and watch events unfold. My guardian angel says humans are very impatient — but he says it with humor!

Guidance for Several MBO Requests

MJ writes: "I am in the process of selling my home. It is time I moved on. My boys are graduated, I am in a situation where I need to sell due to money issues, and the property is too hard to keep up. I recently read how someone was given a suggestion for how to ask for an MBO properly to get the best outcome as she was selling her home. I didn't read what phrasing she used for this request, though.

"I am also wondering how to ask for an MBO for both my sons, who will not be moving with me, as I am moving down south. My oldest is autistic and in a group home, and my other son will be getting on with his life, living on his own for the first time. I want the best outcome for both. They do have their dad — my ex-husband — here, so they won't be totally alone, and I am taking steps to make sure I am reachable all the time. Can you help me? I would be very grateful, as I am new to all this. Thank you."

Tom responds: MBO requests are for when you want to ask for specific things for yourself; BPs are what you say when you wish MBOs for other people. You can say,

> **Most Benevolent Outcome Request**
> *"I request a most benevolent outcome for the quick sale of my house, and may the amount I receive be even better than I can hope for or expect. Thank you!"*

For your sons, you can say this BP:

> **Benevolent Prayer**
> *"I ask any and all beings to assist in taking care of my sons and leading them to many successes in each of their lives. Thank you!"*

You could even request an MBO to be led to even better treatments for your son's autism that will allow him to live an even better life than you can hope for or expect at this time. You can also request an MBO for the perfect home for you in your new town.

Looking for a New Job and a New Romantic Partner

Maureen writes: "Hi, Tom. This is personal, but I want to ask you about something I did once before. I broke up with someone I was in love with a year ago, by his choice. I had a terrible time getting over it and have found myself lonely and still thinking of him sometimes, although I have worked through most of it. I really want to find the right partner and have prayed about it almost daily since. Could you ask your guardian angel why I cannot meet my partner and why I have many job interviews but no job? It brings me down, but I am trying hard to be positive and grateful for what I have. I would so appreciate this. Thank you."

Tom responds: I asked my guardian angel when Maureen would find a new love and a new job, and this was his response: "Tell Maureen that both her own guardian angel and I tell her to keep requesting MBOs when she meets new people and when she applies for jobs and has interviews. She is in a difficult situation, but if she requests MBOs, it will soon become much easier for her — although perhaps not as soon as she would wish. Her guardian angel says to hang in there and to not be discouraged, as this time will pass and she will find new employment and someone to share her life with."

Maureen replies: "Tom, guess what? The day you sent this, I went to a breakfast meeting of friends who meet once a month to discuss spiritual topics. At the meeting, a man and his wife mentioned they had their assistant leave their investment firm and needed someone. I said I was interested, and they called me in for an interview. Two days ago, I got the job! This is after looking for two years. They run their business from a spiritual perspective, and that is exactly what my belief system is. I am a nurse with a business degree. Thank you so much, and I will keep saying the MBO requests and waiting for the right partner to show up."

Tom responds: So as a reminder, if you are looking for a job, remember to say,

> **Most Benevolent Outcome Request**
> *"I request a most benevolent outcome for the perfect job for me. Thank you."*

With each job interview, you can say,

Most Benevolent Outcome Request
"*I request a most benevolent outcome for the results of this interview to be even better than I can hope for or expect. Thank you.*"

And of course if you are looking for that person to share your life with, you can say,

Most Benevolent Outcome Request
"*I request a most benevolent outcome for the perfect mate for me. Thank you.*"

28

Miscellaneous MBOs

A Benevolently Smooth Move

Catherine writes: "Tom, thanks so much for all you do! I am a new subscriber and I just read my first issue of your newsletter. I used the MBO requests on my very recent move — my first experience with MBOs — and the results were stupendous! They were very efficient and effective, and best outcomes were definitely achieved. Physical issues such as back pain were minimal, and I cleared out and settled in a very satisfactory way. Next time, I will ask for it to be fun as well! God bless."

MBO Brings Favorable Legal Outcome

Emily writes: "Thank you for all you do to get us the information you give us. I have been reading your newsletters regularly for a while now. I think it might be about a year. I have also been using the MBO requests as much as I remember to. Of course I am getting better at it — over the past few months, I have been making a practice of almost using it daily.

"There has been one particular issue in my life that I said many MBO requests for. It was a legal matter that had been going on for almost three years. Whenever the thought came to me, I would say an MBO request for that legal matter. About a month ago, I asked Carol, a great friend, to say a BP on my behalf for this legal matter to be solved. The case went to trial on April 16 and 17, and on April 18 the judge ruled in my favor. This ruling is a major relief on my life as well as a wonderful blessing.

"Needless to say, I now don't leave the house without saying an MBO request for anything and everything I may encounter while I am out and about. Thank you again for all you share and teach us."

MBOs Complete the Puzzle

Dan writes: "You often ask for blog submissions, so I thought I'd send this one in. I don't have a great story to tell, but rather I would like to share a different view. I've spent a good part of my life searching for answers to life's big questions, even to the point of going to a Bible college for a few years. I thought, if anything, that would be the place to figure out the big questions about God in my life and how I should live. Unfortunately, I never got that answer there.

"When I was introduced to your MBOs, I found a tangible and easy way to connect with that spiritual part that I knew existed but was somehow unattainable. Since then, I've come to the point in my life where saying MBO requests to start the day, even before I leave my bed, and using them throughout the day is as essential to me as breathing and just as natural. I now find I get stressed far less — almost not at all. It's not that challenges don't arise, but I truly worry far, far less about them and leave them to my guardian angel.

"I also use BPs for things I can see coming for family and friends, and I use them on the spot, such as when I'm passing an accident scene and see emergency responders on site. I can also say my life definitely seems to be blessed in virtually every way, from good health to career success to prosperity. I've shared my story with many friends and family members, many of whom also use MBO requests in their lives with positive results.

"I guess in closing, I can only say that MBOs were the literal missing piece in the puzzle of my life and have helped to provide the direction and connection I needed. Thanks, Tom. I hope this helps your readers in using MBOs in their own lives."

Learning to Separate Visions and Daydreams

DeLeah writes: "I requested an MBO to be able to differentiate between daydreams and true medium visions with results even better than I could expect or hope for. It was answered for me this week in a very unique way — when I have true medium visions now, I see myself observing the vision from outside my body, kind of like a spirit watching the entertainment below. If it's a daydream, I am in my body playing out a role. I love the angels' creativity!"

A Message from an Old Friend and a Smooth Zoning Meeting

Robin writes: "There is a lot going on. I forwarded this email to you because it's a strange and interesting situation. To start with, I received an email yesterday from my friend Jean — who died last December! I have no idea how this could have happened. On top of that, the email contained a link to your blog post. I don't think my eighty-two-year-old friend Jean would even know how to send a Facebook-linked article to anyone when she was alive. She only set up a Facebook account so she could see the photos and stories her niece was posting. So that's interesting — an email from Spirit with your message attached!

"I also had an MBO last night I wanted to tell you about. I'm on the Zoning Board of Adjustment, and we had a meeting last night. I asked for an MBO because these meetings can be quite contentious. There was one case before us: an ice cream and chocolate shop looking for a parking variance to open up in the downtown area. I made a joke that they should have brought some chocolates that night; it could persuade us to pass the variance. In fact, we did pass the variance on its merits. After the vote, the owner came up and presented me with a large box of chocolates wrapped up as a gift, and everyone laughed. I opened the box and shared them with everyone on the board, which changed the mood. So it was win-win for all concerned in a most unlikely way."

MBOs for Boy Scouts and More

Marian writes: "I regularly say several MBO requests and BPs — for safe trips, perfect weather, a great time, and so on — and ask my son and grandson to indulge me and request MBOs for his Boy Scout activities. The troop attended canoe races the weekend before last, and they all won first or second place in their events and had a great time and a safe trip."

Be Careful What You Ask For

Diane writes: "I have been saying my MBO requests for a while now, and they truly manifest. I ask for many types of things, although I rarely ask for money for anything. Just the other day, however, I realized that having $10,000 would be very helpful to me to pay off a loan that had been weighing me down. When I requested the MBO, all I asked for was that amount of money.

"The day after I requested the MBO for that specific amount, I was reminded to be careful what you ask for, because you surely will get it. My father called me to let me know that he had bought a $10,000 life insurance policy for me, along with a plot for my grave, and that he had named my sister the beneficiary so she would be able to handle my affairs whenever the time came, as he would be gone himself by then.

"I don't believe much else can be said, other than the fact that the next time I ask, I am going to be much more specific! I surely hope you enjoyed this. Please feel free to share; I feel your audience will get a big chuckle."

Great Results in One Week

Christa Marie writes: "Recently you asked your guides about asking for frequent MBOs. I asked for one repeatedly but felt that there were blocks or that I was missing something important about the process. You explained that better results are achieved by asking for an MBO for every facet of the issue at hand, especially for complex situations. I started doing this with incredible results! To identify issues, I pay close attention to the thoughts or emotions that pop up after I've asked for the first MBO. I work at these until I feel peaceful or get the sense that I've covered all the bases. It really works for me! I even use my dreams to guide me in the process.

"Since I started using the *Gentle Way* method only a week ago, I have experienced an enormous shift in myself. Emotionally, I am much more peaceful. Spiritually, no other technique has helped raise my awareness of and connection to my guides and angels. My whole life is changing for the better in a big way, as well as in everyday ways. Thank you so much for being the teacher of this wonderful, gentle way and also for introducing it to as many people as possible."

MBOs Working Better Than Hoped For

Ruth writes: "I very much enjoyed using MBO requests all day yesterday. One thing I noticed is that the 'benevolent' part of them satisfies my need to remember 'thy will, not mine.' That concept has often gotten in my way when I think of asking for some small thing — like parking spaces — for myself: 'I need a parking spot quickly, Lord — but really, however you think best.' Usually, by the time I say this, the positive energy and expectation has seeped away.

"With the request for 'a most benevolent outcome on a parking space, please!' you've let me know that I am asking and trusting my guides, angels, and Spirit to look out for everyone's best outcome as they help me in small and large ways throughout the day. Let me just say that I've now used it for relationships, schedule snarls, and much more than parking spaces. I have found it a delight and a personal, easy all-day boost and cleanse. Well, off to another day of fun MBOs! Love and gratitude to you."

Keep Asking for MBOs

Lynn writes: "I so enjoy your newsletters and reading about MBOs, and I just wanted to let you know that MBOs now fill my life, even when I don't ask for them! Yesterday, my friend Diane and I drove to Portland, an hour trip over the coast range. I always ask for a safe, expedient, and smooth journey when I do this. She says that she forgets but feels like they happen anyway. And as we talked, I realized I feel the same way. Now that I've got my angels in action, I think they are just there. I still tend to ask, but I don't worry as much if I forget. I am just wondering if you think this happens once we have put our angels into action."

Tom responds: My guardian angel has told me that, even with as long as I have been requesting MBOs — around fourteen years now — if I were to stop requesting them tomorrow, it wouldn't be too long before I would be just like everyone else: simply reacting to events and not being protected and guided.

Remember, one of the major benefits of requesting MBOs is that the act of requesting them keeps you on the soul contract or life path that you yourself laid out prior to your birth for the purpose of gaining the most knowledge and having the most experiences that this life can provide you.

Two Star-Sighting MBOs

Laurie writes: "Recently I had two MBOs that can be described as 'star sightings.' The first one was being able to see the International Space Station zip by overhead like a very fast-moving star. I wasn't certain I was going to be able to see its transit because of hazy local cloud cover and the low angle of passage in the night sky, so I asked for an MBO to catch even a glimpse. I watched diligently for the few minutes the space station was supposed to be visible — nothing. But then my glance strayed to a whole other quarter of the sky, and there it was! I had been looking for it in the wrong place. I never would have seen it if not for the MBO.

"The second one was a star sighting of the celebrity kind. I recently attended a major sci-fi convention in Atlanta, and one of the guests was a famous *Star Trek* actor. I knew he was going to be there, so before I left for the convention, I asked for a little MBO that maybe I could meet him in passing — maybe in a restaurant or some other casual setting.

"Well, at the awards banquet, I ended up sitting two tables away from this celebrity — this was completely random, as there was no reserved or assigned seating — thus fulfilling the 'restaurant setting' part of the request. Then, as he was escorted to his table, he turned his head and looked straight at me! There was no reason for him to do that except for my little MBO. I met his gaze and gave him a thumbs-up gesture of thanks and approval, and then he winked at me in acknowledgment. As soon as it happened, I knew that was the 'meeting in passing' part of my MBO. That small encounter meant a lot to me.

"So thank you, guides and guardians! MBOs happen all the time. All you have to do is ask."

Tom responds: Laurie has been requesting MBOs for some time, so she has had many benevolent outcomes.

Requesting MBOs for Reiki Sessions

Annette writes: "I start each Reiki session by requesting an MBO from my Reiki guides followed by a BP for the client, and I close each healing by thanking my guides and all benevolent beings who attended and assisted in the healing. I also request an MBO for my day each morning and then throughout the day for more specific outcomes — like a safe drive to my destination and so on. I also find that I do a lot more living prayer and 'I hope' requests during the day. The more I do, the more naturally the doing becomes."

Tom responds: Keep in mind, everyone, that you can go to my website and click on the "signs" tab, where you can print out the "Request Benevolent Outcomes Today!" sign as many times as you need. Place them on the refrigerator, in the bathroom, and even in your car to help you remember to make requesting MBOs a habit.

Benevolent Legal Settlement

Diane writes: "We had a court date this past Monday, and of course I made an MBO request a few days before and again that morning. Well, we went to court and did not have to go in front of the judge, and we settled on a lower price. Oh, how I love my MBOs!"

Raising the Good Vibrations

Eleanore writes: "Initially, just the name of your books spoke to me. For me, *The Gentle Way* was so very appealing. Within the past two days, it has been an essential part of my life. I have encountered the bitterest, nastiest, and meanest humans ever. I'm sure that abject fear is at the base of it. The changes occurring in the U.S. on a governmental level right now apparently are not being received well by some, and I find that I have moved into a complex where a great many of these souls reside. I understand that it is one of my lessons, but my sensitivities have been so assaulted that I have kind of lost my way. My heart actually feels like it's crying.

"Seeing people being homophobic, racist, and downright cruel has upset me to a degree that has surprised even me! I have been requesting MBOs, and I was answered yesterday when I took myself to the beach to recharge some joy and positive energy. When I'm upset, I crawl into my shell. I met an angel in the personage of a very delightful black gentleman who very graciously talked me down from my angst. I'm still not quite back to my wonderful, positive self, but knowing the problem is half the battle. I am meditating and conversing and asking for help and a more enlightened understanding.

"Without the tools and knowledge I learned from you and your material, I certainly don't think I would have handled things as I did. I am telling you this to let you know how invaluable your materials are to me and to just say thanks for being there."

Tom responds: Here is some advice for everyone if you live in similar circumstances: You're supposed to be the candle in the darkness for those people. Each day, send the whole complex white light. That will soften them up. Just breathe in white light from the Central Sun through your nose and your crown chakra, and hold it for at least a count of eight, then send the white light out from your heart chakra. Imagine it enveloping the whole complex and permeating each person there.

You can also say a BP each day:

Benevolent Prayer
"I ask that any and all beings help everyone in this complex to come to love and respect all people of different races and beliefs. Thank you!"

I think if you do this for a while, those who can't stand the light — a lightness of feeling — will move away and slowly be replaced by others who vibrate at higher levels. You can also request an MBO for that to happen. Those who are supposed to leave will, and those who are there for your learning and challenges will not.

Using MBOs Daily

Khiloni writes: "I was in touch with you last year regarding MBO requests to improve my career prospects. After getting promoted, hugely thanks to MBOs, I started using them every day in every part of my life, and I can't remember the last time I was this content and relaxed with the way things are going in my life."

Honoring Our Earth Mother

Amy writes: "I have a question for you to ask Gaia. With the fortieth anniversary of Earth Day this week, is there anything else a single person or small group can do to help the planet's health, other than being a good steward in what we buy, do, and eat? It seems as if the average person has so little concern about the health of the planet, so I was wondering if we can make inroads with MBO requests and other kinds of actions that can be taken by anyone. Will it really help?

"I also teach high school students and want them to understand the issues facing our planet today, especially those brought about by human beings. Does our focus on these negative aspects only serve to make them worse by attraction? If so, how can we inform children and create people who want to help Earth without schooling them in so many negative aspects? Thank you for sharing this gift with all of us."

Tom responds: I asked Gaia what people might do to assist and make the planet better.

Gaia says: "That is a nice thought and question by your reader, Tom. You can honor me and Earth in many ways, but especially by being good stewards of the planet. You are moving in that direction, Tom. Each individual can do his or her part to make the planet better, whether it's picking up trash on the side of a roadway, assisting the animals of this planet, or planting trees where forests have been cut down. There are many ways to make a difference; you just have to get out of your chairs, stop watching so much TV, and be proactive.

"Ask yourself what appeals to you, and then find out how you can accomplish it. Your part might be with other people in an organization, or it might be something you do on your own. Perhaps other people will see you and join with you or start to do what you're doing on their own, too. Don't forget to send lots of white light to me. This is another way to honor me and assist me with my work as well."

MBO Request for the Highest Expression of Your Soul

Jeff writes: "I have an MBO idea for your subscribers to try. It came to me yesterday that I should mention this one to you:

Most Benevolent Outcome Request

"Guardian angel, I request a most benevolent outcome that I be fully open to all possibilities that lead me to the highest and most divine expression of my soul and all of the experiences my beautiful soul chooses in this lifetime. Thank you, thank you, thank you!"

"If you find value in it, please feel free to share it; if not, then that's cool as well. Just thought I'd pass it on."

Tom responds: That should keep everyone on their soul paths!

What to Do about a Stalker

Valerie writes: "Hello, Tom. I wanted to know if you could send me some of that beautiful, spiritual angel help my way. I think that the more people who help make these requests in a time of need, the better. It can only help.

"I have been having a problem with a stalker following me around and doing things toward me in the spirit world that are not of our father in heaven. I need to know exactly what I can say to help myself out of the turmoil this person has been putting me through. I am requesting that this person leave me alone, and I need some immediate help from law enforcement. Thanks for your help."

Tom responds: For Valerie — and anyone else having this problem — each time you go out, I suggest you say,

Most Benevolent Outcome Request

"I request a most benevolent outcome for my drive to _____ and for my complete safety during the time I am away from my home. Thank you."

I would also suggest you surround yourself with white light. If you haven't done this before, just imagine a beautiful, brilliant white light coming down from above and completely enveloping you. Then, if you know the stalker is around, imagine sending him beautiful white light, too. Lower-vibrational people cannot stand this light for too long. One woman who was having a terrible time with a very mean boss did that all the time, and he just lost his job.

If you have to contact the police or other authorities, say,

Most Benevolent Outcome Request
"I request a most benevolent outcome for my meeting with the police, and may the results be even better than I can hope for or expect. Thank you."

You can even say a BP for the stalker:

Benevolent Prayer
"I ask any and all beings to assist in bringing help to this man with his obsessive behavior and that this help will be the most benevolent for him. Thank you!"

MBO-Enhanced Psychic Abilities

DeLeah writes: "Tom, here is an MBO story: I requested an MBO to come into my full psychic abilities in the best way possible for me and my higher self, with results even better than I could expect or hope for. Since I've been saying that request off and on for a few weeks, I have started seeing more spirits and feeling more paranormal things. I also find it easier to channel the angels, spirits, and my guides. Thank you once again for this beautiful system. It never ceases to amaze me."

I Am Ageless

Joan writes: "Hi, Tom. I seem to remember that you had a great anti-aging philosophy, but I can't find it. Would you please reacquaint me with the concept? Thanks. Cheers and blessings."

Tom responds: When someone asks me my age, I say, "I'm ageless." This seems to work in a couple of ways: Psychologically, everyone has a mental idea of what people are supposed to act and look like at ages thirty, forty, fifty, sixty, seventy, and eighty. If you say, "I'm ageless" every time someone asks you your age, you mentally erase that concept.

The other reason is metaphysical (beyond physics). It will be proven one day that our cells are cognizant and actually able to communicate with each other. When we tell them we are ageless, I believe it actually slows down the aging process. If you continue to say this, you might even find within a short time that you'll forget how old you actually are. I've had to stop and count from my birth date when I've had to fill out forms that ask me to list my age!

MBOs and BPs at the End of the Day

Marc writes: "Hi, Tom! I've actually been a long-time follower of your newsletters and of course *The Gentle Way*. Thanks so much for your message and all that you do! Here's a thought or two that might be of interest: I like to give a thank you to my guardian angel and all the benevolent beings out there at the end of the day. Since I use MBO requests daily, that little extra thought just seems right to me; it lets them know that the love really does go both ways! Also, whenever I watch the evening news — as we know, it's not all positive — or just whenever I see something that touches me, I just start lining up the BPs. I think that it's just a part of gratitude and love to make a habit of spreading more light into the world. Cheers!"

1-800 MBO

Laurie writes: "Here's an instant MBO for you. I was struggling with confirming a hotel reservation. I called the 800 phone number, went through all the prompts, and was informed by a recording that all representatives were busy. I hung up, waited a bit, and then dialed again. In the middle of dialing the 800 number, I requested an MBO for a representative to answer immediately. Well, one picked up right away, and I mean immediately. It was only a few seconds after my MBO request. I've used my '1-800 MBO' on all such calls ever since and have had terrific results."

Tom responds: Thanks, Laurie! I'm sure I'll not be the only one using this from now on.

Is This Your MBO?

Sandy writes: "I've been saying the BPs, affirmations, and MBO requests daily for over four months now. What a wonderful direction my life goes in these days! When I'm pulling out of a great parking spot and I see someone waiting for it, I begin to chuckle at myself, because I keep getting this urge to roll down my window and excitedly ask them, 'Is this the parking space MBO you requested?' It would be so neat to connect with someone if that was indeed what it was! And I am very thankful for connecting with the messages that you, your guardian angel, and Gaia bring us."

Life Is Easier with MBOs and BPs

Mary writes: "I look forward to getting your newsletter and blog each week. Keep up the good work. I use MBO requests all the time and tell others about them. My two children use them; they are four and nine years of age. I don't worry as much as I used to. I now notice when I start to get fearful thoughts, and I make a conscious choice to stop; MBOs and BPs help a lot with this. Thank you, Tom."

A Peaceful Passing

Cheri writes: "I had to share this. My mother finally lost her battle with breast cancer on July 23. I've had a very hard time with it because it was unexpected. My family and I prayed and prayed. I gave my aunt your website address, and she started requesting MBOs immediately. We both said one about surrounding my mom with loving pink light.

"This is the interesting part: On the evening of her passing, she was encased in pink light. We couldn't figure it out. The blinds were closed. The rest of the family thinks part of it was the dimmed lights, but my aunt and I know that it was our MBO request. She also had white light coming from the top of her head. I couldn't see it, so I moved to the end of the bed, and I saw three lights that reminded me of a crown.

"Since this happened, I continuously request MBOs. Thank you for all you do. I hope one day to be able to communicate with my guardian angel or hear my angels, because I talk to them all the time."

MBOs in Prison

Jill writes: "Requesting MBOs has become such a way of life that it's become a normal part of my routine, which I surmise might be the reason some of us fail to send in our MBO stories. I am a correctional officer at a prison. I sense that certain offenders regret their crimes and want to do better. I have given the MBO statement to a couple of such offenders. I told them about your books as well. What I would love to give them is a BP; however, as a correctional officer, it's against policy. Hopefully, once the few who I tell begin using MBOs, they will spread the word."

Tom responds: In my first book I suggested MBO requests for both correctional officers — I used the old term "prison guards" — and inmates. A correctional officer could say each day,

> **Most Benevolent Outcome Request**
> *"I request a most benevolent outcome for remaining safe in my job today and to assist the inmates in their rehabilitation. Thank you!"*

An inmate could say,

> **Most Benevolent Outcome Request**
> *"I request a most benevolent outcome for remaining safe today. Thank you!"*

Both inmates and officers can also request MBOs each time they leave their area and are headed to prison work, the cafeteria, the exercise area, and so on.

Phone Home!

Diane writes: "I want to share this with all parents — especially moms. You know how sometimes your kids who live far away from you just don't seem to have the time to call? Well, when I don't hear from my son for at least four days, I request an MBO to have him call me. And you know what happens? He does call later that evening! Thank God for MBO requests just for those little important things in life, and thanks, Tom, for sharing as always!"

Go with the Flow and Smile

Jenny writes: "Has anyone tried asking for a benevolent outcome for when you audition for plays or musicals? I have auditions next week, and I am nervous and frightened that I will have a failed audition and just do a horrible job and never be considered for a part. I used a benevolent outcome request for an earlier audition that was held in August, but I guess I was so nervous and frightened that I was continuously asking for guidance from my angels, which I suppose was a no-no, because I held that fear that I was not going to get a part."

Tom responds: I have been doing international film distribution for twenty-nine years and have been listed as an executive producer on several films, so I have a little experience in this area. Before you go to the audition, say,

> **Most Benevolent Outcome Request**
> *"I request a most benevolent outcome for this audition, and may the results be even better than I can hope for or expect. Thank you!"*

Then, while waiting at the audition, I want you to put your thumbs and forefingers together and then breathe in through your nose and out through your mouth. This will calm you, and you'll feel your heart rate drop.

Keep in mind that the producers and director have someone specific in mind for the part you are auditioning for. Even if you might not fit their vision, if you do a good audition, they'll remember you in the future when their vision fits your appearance and personality. So just go with the flow. Smile and enjoy the moment!

Teaching Others How to Fish

Tse writes: "I would like to share this with the readers. I have found MBO requests to be a good tool to teach others 'how to fish.' I have a long-time friend who is inept at managing money. In the past, she has called me with her money woes, and I would come to her aid by gifting her with money — until I learned that I was not the only 'gifter' in her life and realized I was being used.

"A few months ago, she was unable to make her rent payment, and instead of giving her money, I shared how to request an MBO. She called me a few days later, relating how her rent money manifested after she requested the MBO. This week she again related a situation regarding lack of money, and I reminded her to request an MBO for the situation. In the past when I've been unable to help others, especially those close to me, I would sometimes feel responsible. Now when I share with others how to request an MBO, knowing that our guardian angels are there to help us, I no longer feel responsible, as I've shared with each of them how to be a cocreator with the Creator."

Tom responds: Our guardian angels are always giving us those little "wink moments." When you start requesting MBOs and saying BPs, you become more aware and begin noticing them more.

MBOs Are a Little Slow, but They Work!

Jackie writes: "I have found that some of my MBOs come sometime later. A few days after I have forgotten about it, something great will happen. Then I will remember I had made the request for an MBO for it to happen."

Beyond Language and Culture

Billy writes: "I feel the desire to tell everyone about your MBO method. I should mention that MBO requests work for Japanese people who ask in the Japanese language as well. I told a physician about it, and he's been using it regularly. He started with asking for a parking space just as you suggested and is now expanding his requests. I also told a secretary at the legal office I work at part time maintaining their computers and teaching the staff, and she got the same results. It smoothly goes beyond languages and cultures."

Public Perception of Muslims

Eleanore writes: "You know the adage 'when the student is ready, the teacher appears.' Well, I have been wrestling with the social climate today that involves people's perception of the Muslim community. It is very difficult for many of us. While struggling with no small amount of confusion as to how to address this issue, I came across your article entitled 'Changing the Future.' Therein I found my answer.

"I don't know about others, but often I forget that you can request an MBO for anything. Your efforts have a definite impact on me and most certainly on anyone who takes advantage of the knowledge you are sharing."

Tom responds: For Eleanore and anyone else interested in improving the world, you could say this BP:

> **Benevolent Prayer**
> *"I ask any and all beings to assist those who wish to bring peace to the world —
> no matter what religion they practice. Thank you!"*

Regent Street MBO

Arthur writes: "Hi, Tom. Thank you for making me aware of how important angels are in our lives. I have been requesting MBOs for a while and have always had positive results — finding parking in difficult situations, getting transportation when I really need it, and so many others.

"Recently I went to London for three months and took a jacket that was missing three buttons. As it was made in the UK, I took it to one of the manufacturer's shops; the manager took it and promised to have it back as soon as he could. After a month, I called to see if it was ready, only to be told they could not get the buttons, but they would try another tailor. I then said an MBO that everything would work out even better than I expected.

"After two months, I was near the shop and decided to pop in to see how things were going. To my surprise, the manager said he was so embarrassed that he would make sure it was ready the following Friday. In addition, I could choose a shirt as a way of saying sorry for the delay. The jacket was ready as promised, and I collected my free shirt. Not bad, since the repair was only being done as a favor."

The Best Outcome for Everyone around Me

Nicolette writes: "I have been using MBO requests even when I go shopping or to visit someone. I have received smiles from people becoming more aware of me, and people have even told me things that people normally do not just share. I feel that I can use MBO requests for the best outcome for everyone involved with me. Thank you for sharing MBOs; it works straight away."

MBOs for Artistic Inspiration

Rob writes: "I have been requesting MBOs since I bought your books a couple of years ago, and I have seen firsthand that they do work. I have many stories to share with you, but I will share one today about my band that is completely over the top. We originally formed the band about eleven years ago, but after recording a demo, we lost our steam and broke up. Because I have always had so much confidence in this band, I have tried to get the guys to agree to regroup for the past six years or so, but I have had no success.

"A few months after reading *The Gentle Way*, I said an MBO request that I would be able to record music with my brother, who was in this band. About a week and a half later, I got a call from him asking me if I would have any interest in re-forming. I immediately said yes, and I thanked my guardian angels. I then emailed our drummer/singer, with whom none of us had had any recent contact, and within a day, he responded with great enthusiasm. The astonishing thing is that I emailed him using an email address that he had not checked in a couple of years; he told me he just checked it on a whim. None of us had any of his other contact info. Our other guitar player was very enthusiastic about re-forming as well, and I immediately started to practice because I had not picked up my bass in about five years.

"Fast-forward one year, and we are now signed to a record label and recording our debut full-length album. When I recorded my bass tracks, I was a little nervous because our music is very difficult to play, and I was going to use a Music Man Sting Ray bass, which is harder to play than my Washburn but sounds amazing. When I picked it up from the rental store, I noticed that it was fitted with heavy strings, which also put me behind the eight ball, because I am used to playing with medium-light gauge strings. Every night before I went to the studio I said,

> **Most Benevolent Outcome Request**
> *"I request a most benevolent outcome that the result of my bass playing on our album will be better than I can ever have expected and that I play on a level that far surpasses my ability."*

"Now, I have always considered myself to be a good bass player. However, since our music is so technical, in the past, I was forced to simplify some of the bass lines because they were just much too difficult for me to play, and I was unable to pull them off. When I went into the recording studio, I felt a confidence that I had never felt before, and I asked my brother to teach me all of the parts that I could not play in the past. I was able to learn these very difficult bass lines very quickly, and I found myself playing on a level that was far beyond my normal ability without any practice. The guys in my band were floored because they had no idea I was capable of playing at this level. I was even able to perform the parts I knew in a much better way, and I even jazzed them up a bit. I almost felt that my hands were on autopilot!

"Another thing I want to note is that I am a pick player. I have tried plucking the strings with my fingers in the past, but due to the technical nature of our music, I played much more skillfully while using a pick. During the recording sessions, I played most of the album using my fingers, which gave my bass tracks a whole new feel and sound. Keep in mind I had not used my fingers to play in years, and I was playing on heavy strings, which is very difficult, especially since I had no calluses on the fingers of my right hand. This was by far the most profound MBO I have ever experienced. Tom, if you can please ask your guardian angel for his comments about this, I would really appreciate it. Also can you please script an MBO request that we can use for record sales? Thank you so much, Tom, for introducing MBOs to the world. You are a very special person."

Tom responds: Rob, that's one of the best MBO stories I have received in a while. You're doing pretty well with your MBO requests yourself, but here's one:

> **Most Benevolent Outcome Request**
> *"I request a most benevolent outcome for our band to be led to the best ways to promote, market, and sell our album. Thank you!"*

Laurie replies: "I read Rob's story about recording his album on your blog — how his guardian angel helped with his bass playing — and it reminded me of how MBO requests and my guardian angel have helped with my own creative efforts. In the past four months, I was assigned to write two children's books. Each day I requested an MBO for 'any creative and helpful beings to whisper in my ear and inspire me' while I was writing that day.

"The words and ideas flowed almost effortlessly! There were times that I swore I could actually hear a voice in my head suggesting a word or an idea that moved the story along. I was on such a roll that I finished the second book three weeks ahead of my deadline. Oh, and I got that second book assignment because the original writer just happened to drop out of the project and I was just lucky enough to contact the editor in charge when I did. But as Obi-Wan once said: 'There's no such thing as luck.' I agree with him!"

Keeping My MBOs Organized

Dan writes: "This message is all about my MBOs. I've been using them now for the past few years and have been nothing but impressed. Just recently, though, I thought I would write them down as a way of organizing my requests and ensure I didn't forget anything that I needed some help or direction with. Since the last week in November, I have written down about thirty-five different MBOs relating to everything from a safe trip to a good meeting with staff and clients to renewed contact with friends. In every case, things have turned out better than I could have hoped for or expected, thanks to Acme, my guardian angel!"

Prayers for a Benevolent Life

Lois writes: "Just like it is important to ask the right questions to find out what you really want to know, it is equally important to say the right MBO requests and BPs. Thinking of them is the challenge, because it involves realizing what it is that we truly want. I have had a breakthrough in this arena; I am now asking for things I would never have dreamed of asking for in the past.

"I started doing these prayers over two years ago, and it is just now occurring to me to ask for things like seeing the humor in everything, laughing, and helping others to laugh (I saw a major shift the next day!), feeling joy all the time (I'm not there yet, but getting closer), not judging others (I'm getting better at this), and effortlessly forgiving everyone I need to forgive. I have also been asking for healing in my core issues at the soul level and the fulfillment of my soul's destiny on Earth. Be careful asking for this one — the healing process can kick your hiney, but it's worth it.

"I just thought I would let you know about how well these requests are working. It is becoming quite the joyous ride. I did a new-moon drumming last night with two friends, and we did the group MBO requests and BPs. I will let you know how those turn out. I send gratitude your way, dear Tom."

Great New Housemate

Kate writes: "Here's one that happened fifteen minutes ago: I made an MBO request earlier this week for the perfect housemate because my current one bought a house out of the blue. I advertised on Craigslist, and a young nurse named Emily called. It turns out she knows my stepdaughter and remembers her talking about my daughter twelve years ago, not to mention she has a sister named Kate, which is also my name, and I have a sister named Emily, which is her name. She hasn't signed the lease yet, but it seems pretty good. Whew, only one week to spare till the deadline. Thanks, angels!"

MBO for Design Inspiration

Rhonda writes: "My husband and I use MBO requests and BPs constantly and with great effect. I can't tell you how many times I have found things using MBO requests. This weekend, I was putting together the twenty-five- to thirty-page newsletter that I do each month, and I was having trouble coming up with a visual format that pleased me. I was grumbling about it to myself, saying things like, 'This sucks. This doesn't work. I hate this.'

"Finally, I realized I hadn't requested an MBO, and while I was fixing myself a cup of coffee, I promptly said something like,

> **Most Benevolent Outcome Request**
> *"I request the most benevolent outcome for inspiration for the newsletter format. Thank you, thank you, thank you."*

"I immediately thought of something, went back to the computer, and came up with a stunning visual format. That made me happy the rest of the day! Thank you, Tom, for bringing this to so many people's attention. Our angels rock!"

A Nice, Reliable New Renter

Delores writes: "I have been using MBO requests for a wonderful tenant who is easy to get along with and pays the rent on time. Last Saturday, a young lady came by with her mother and fell in love with the studio apartment and signed the lease. Thank you!"

Speedy Delivery via Angel's Wings

Janet writes: "Hi, Tom. I have a nice story for you. Last week I decided to mail a small parcel to my son. It wasn't tiny; the box was a cube of around ten inches or so on all sides. I live in Toronto, Canada, and my son lives in Bend, Oregon.

"The postal outlet told me that if I paid an extra twenty dollars, the parcel could be there within three business days. I didn't want to spend so much money; the contents were nice, but it wasn't so important that he get the parcel quickly. So I opted for the cheapest delivery selection, which was around two weeks from the time of pickup. I was there after the daily pickup on Friday afternoon, so it wouldn't have been picked up until Monday. As I was leaving the outlet, I made an MBO request for the safe and quick delivery of the package to my son.

"You can imagine my surprise and delight when my son informed me that the parcel had arrived yesterday — within the three business days of the expensive option I had shunned. Even better, the subject line of the message he sent to tell me about it read 'Angel Wings,' which referred to the fact that I had sent him a small porcelain angel that I had made in a ceramics class last year. I haven't told him about MBOs, so he didn't know his message actually had a double meaning. Thanks again, Tom, for all these wonderful 'embroideries' onto regular, ordinary life!"

A Benevolently Quick Lift

Ryan writes: "The first day that I used MBO requests, I was walking to my corporate job in my suit asking for an MBO for a wonderful, easy day at work. My office was on the twelfth floor, and there were six lifts that I could use to get up. Every time I went up or came down, an elevator door would automatically open for me. I didn't have to press any buttons. The lift would just be waiting for me. The first time, I thought, 'Oh, how cute,' but then by around the sixth time in a row in the same day, I was thinking, 'MBOs work!' And I've trusted the process ever since. It's great to have connected with you, and thanks for helping me make my life that little bit easier."

MBOs and BPs Every Day

Sandy writes: "I am ever so grateful for the MBO information provided by you. As I've written before, I've purchased a few sets of your *Gentle Way* books and have given them to others. I use MBO requests all the time, as well as the BPs for the family and for the weather every day and every time I am in a car, and it really works.

"For instance, every night I ask for all my family — my immediate family, my extended family, and my husband's family — to be safe. A few days ago, my husband's sister-in-law's car was hit head-on on the driver's side by a woman driving the wrong way. The car turned upside-down, but she and the five children in the car survived. Now that is a benevolent outcome! Thanks again, Tom, for your accessibility as well as your sharing. God bless you!"

Increasing Psychic Abilities

Leah writes: "I say MBO requests all of the time now, so remembering a specific one is quite hard. The other day, out of the blue — funny enough, while in the shower — I had this inspired request, so I said it:

Most Benevolent Outcome Request
"I request a most benevolent outcome to see, feel, and hear clarity, truth, and my inner beings' and guides' voices clearly and loudly in every situation that I am faced with today, and may the results be greater than I could've expected or those around me could have expected."

"Well, I have been hearing and speaking to my guides and occasional spirit passersby now for about five years. A friend came to my house last week, and I was inspired to hold the ring that she had on. I held it tightly in my hand. All of a sudden, I started getting all of this information. I have only recently started to get to know this lady, so I didn't really know her background or anything. Anyway, her mother, who had passed away seven years ago, came through to me and gave me some information to prove that it was really her — you know, memories that only she and her daughter would know. Brilliant! My friend was a bit spooked but is feeling very happy and relieved to hear from her mother. I feel so glad that I helped bring some comfort to my friend!"

* * *

DeLeah writes: "Lately I have been requesting many MBOs about increasing all of my abilities so that I may help more people in a variety of ways, and this week I am seeing lots of results. I have predicted three different events in my friends' lives accurately, and I have also developed a very unique empathic premonition ability.

"The most recent event to come from this was when I woke up last Tuesday — my whole right arm throbbed and radiated pain. It hurt so much I could barely use it. After three days, the pain passed and my arm was fine. Exactly one week from that time, my boyfriend was in a car accident where he rolled his car three times and miraculously came out with only his right arm broken!

"Working with the angels is such a blessing, and I encourage everyone to do this throughout all of their days. Thank you so much, Tom!"

Tom responds: That's a great idea! Say,

Most Benevolent Outcome Request
"I request a most benevolent outcome for increasing my psychic abilities. Thank you!"

* * *

John writes: "I have a tip for those who wish to increase their intuition. I often request an MBO such as:

> **Most Benevolent Outcomes**
> *"I request the most benevolent outcome to have my intuition increased ten times and for this increase to be permanent. May this outcome be even better than I could hope for or expect. Thank you."*

"When I say this MBO, I always feel energy start to move through my body. This energy starts to work inside and at the top of my head, and I can feel it. If you were to say this MBO request every other day and keep saying it for months, your intuition could be greatly enhanced. This has got to be one of the easiest ways to increase intuition. I often request this MBO while sitting at my computer reading forums, watching TV, or doing some other activity in which I'm just sitting still. I hope others try this; it's fantastic how helpful this can be. You could turn yourself into an expert intuitive as time goes by."

Greasing the Wheels of Video Production

Rick writes: "I made a trip to San Francisco this weekend for a video production shoot. It looked like it was going to get ultra-expensive, but I said some MBO requests, so some money was donated, and other things like transportation and lodging were complimentary or nominal. Also, we needed a baseball uniform made pretty darn quickly for this video shoot. Several companies told us they couldn't turn the job around and ship it in time, but we found one that not only could do it but could do it for half the price the other companies quoted us. Now I'm requesting MBOs for air travel, safe transportation, and the video shoot itself."

Chakra Activation and More

Bobby writes: "Tom: I request MBOs daily for various purposes, including activation of my chakras. Requesting MBOs really helped me solve some of my problems and those of some people I helped with and achieving certain goals."

Tom's Benevolent Radio Interviews

Tom says: Here's an MBO that happened for me this past month. In the space of one week, I was scheduled to speak at the EPIC Voyagers group in the DFW metroplex on Sunday afternoon about my communications with my "brother on another planet," Antura. He's a member of my soul group or "cluster," as my guardian angel calls the group of fragments that our souls dispatched to have these lives on Earth for our souls' learning purposes. (Since writing this response, I have published a book of my conversations with Antura, *First Contact: Conversations with an ET*, available from Light Technology Publishing.)

I had also scheduled three radio interviews during the week — one on Monday evening as the premier guest on the new Epic Voyagers radio show on the Inception Radio Network, then Wednesday evening with Coaches Café, and Thursday morning with the Spiritually Raw radio show. On Friday I received a call from Dave Schrader of Darkness Radio in Minneapolis. He was going on vacation and wanted to record an interview from 7 to 8 on Monday evening. I was already scheduled at 8PM for the Epic show, so we changed it to 6:30PM.

The talk I gave on Sunday afternoon was enthusiastically received, and instead of one and a half hours, I wound up speaking and answering questions for two hours. My voice almost gave out, as the air in the DFW area has been quite dry with 100 degree temperatures. I was concerned that two and a half hours of talking on Monday night would result in the same situation and had four throat lozenges lined up on my desk. But I did request an MBO. I said,

> **Most Benevolent Outcome Request**
> *"I request a most benevolent outcome for my voice to hold during these radio interviews tonight. Thank you!"*

I had no problems during the interviews and had no need for the throat lozenges — just my normal water during breaks. This is just another example of applying the request of MBOs during your daily lives to assist you in whatever tasks you are doing.

MBO for Video Camera

Peter writes: "I drove for five hours to do an angelic music healing concert, and I forgot my video camera. I prayed so that some people would come for the healing. Finally, ten minutes before it started, someone came with a professional video camera and asked me if I would like him to film the music concert. I thanked the spirit guides for answering my MBO request so quickly. Oh yes, it helped those who came to the little concert."

Hard Times Are When MBO Requests Shine

Beverly writes: "We are scheduled to fly back to the UK tomorrow; we were supposed to be off to Dubai to spend a week with our son and daughter-in-law. We usually always fly British Airways, but last time we came to Houston through Amsterdam, so we are returning that way tomorrow.

"My daughter-in-law's mother has been suffering from colon cancer for two years, but she had just visited them from Germany for two weeks, so it was very unexpected that she died on Sunday, although we all knew her condition was terminal. Her funeral is at 10AM Saturday on the Dutch-German border, which means that we can be there, as it's only a two-hour drive from Amsterdam's Schiphol Airport.

"We can then spend six days with our son, daughter-in-law, and grandchildren in Amsterdam instead of going to Dubai. This was the MBO for all of us and means we can support our daughter-in-law during this time of sadness. This just shows that an MBO can happen even during a very sad occasion."

Tom responds: I have seen numerous times that someone's passing is set up so that family and relatives can be there.

Benevolent Songwriting and Song Marketing

Rodger writes: "My personal path seems to be songwriting and creating. I've asked for MBOs for my songs to become popular, to win a Grammy, and to get awarded gold records. It's a big request. Is one request enough? Should I follow up?"

Tom responds: I would suggest each time you submit a song to an artist or recording company, you request an MBO for the results of submitting the song to be even better than you can hope for or expect.

MBOs Keep a Big Move Going Smoothly

Beverly writes: "I have just been in the process of selling my main home in the UK and buying another that was suitable for Mike and I plus our daughter and two teenage grandchildren. We will only be back there for two weeks every three months. I said an MBO request for the whole thing and for individual processes as they came along.

"First, we found a buyer within two weeks. In fact, we found two buyers, which meant we achieved $35,000 above the asking price. The buyers had nothing to sell, and the sellers of the house we are buying are going into rented accommodations. We put an offer on the first house we viewed, as it was a perfect match for us. No bedroom walls are touching and there is a downstairs bedroom large enough for a sitting area for our daughter with her own patio, plus four bathrooms, which is a miracle!

"I traveled to the UK last week to move out of the main house and put my furniture into storage until we can move into the new house. The mover let me down at the last minute, which meant it all could have fallen down. I said an MBO request, and I found a better mover who could do it a day earlier and, as I forgot about cleaning the property, I had a day to arrange this! Also, on the day I would have moved, it rained all day, so I was glad it all changed.

"Then on the moving day, the buyers' solicitor emailed for a copy of the original planning application for our extension. As they already had the completion certificate, I had boxed it and thought it was long gone. I was very frustrated, as I have bent over backward to accommodate the buyers. The movers heard me telling my friend who was helping me, and it transpired that the box with the papers in it was still in the garage because they could not fit it in the container!

"So more MBO requests than I can put down happened, and on the way home a very kind friend upgraded me to business class, which, as it is OTC in Houston, was another miracle. I trust you're doing great, and much love to you and yours."

MBO Makes Painting Easier

David writes: "My wife and I went to Tiffin, Ohio, this weekend. My cousin, Sister Jane, the nun, had some painting projects for us. She is building a straw bale house as an environmental project, and she is about six months and $15,000 short. So anyway, since at seventy my eyesight isn't what it used to be, and I am a reluctant painter anyway, I agreed to prime the closets. There were three, and they were very tight, so it was very hard to maneuver. One sidewall closet was only three feet high but ran the length of a fifteen-foot room, and it had an opening just wide enough to get into. I asked for an MBO, and here I am, scooting around with a roller on the floor trying to paint some very hard-to-reach places. I painted until I ran out of paint.

"Today I would normally be so stiff and sore I could hardly walk, but I never even got the start of a single cramp through this whole process, which lasted over four hours. I guess it is the combination of serving others and requesting an MBO."

MBOs Work Great!

Charlotte writes: "Tom, every time I have requested an MBO for anything, it has come to pass. They work so well. Some people laugh at me when I ask them if they believe in angels and have them request an MBO, but it works for me. Oh, by the way, I collect angels. Thank you also for your books; I have both of them, and I love them."

MBO for New Hairdresser

Judi writes: "I've been asking for MBOs and BPs for three years now. I've had so many unbelievable outcomes that I guess I just take them for granted now. But I felt I should share. These are simple things really, but there are some big ones too.

"The way my hair looks and feels is very important to me. Recently, my hairdresser raised his rates, and I had to look elsewhere. I'd been going to him for four years and was very satisfied, so it was daunting to find someone else. However, I had Tom Moore and my guardian angel on my side. I said an MBO request for finding someone who would be a great hairdresser with reasonable rates.

"Not only did I get a kindred soul but someone who was just as good as my old hairdresser, but also funny and blessed with spiritual gifts. It made my day, for sure. I, of course, gave thanks for all the wonderful blessings given to me through the work of my guardian angel and his or her cohorts."

Speedy Book Delivery

Lee writes: "Hi, Tom! Once again, thank you for making my life easier. I ordered a book from Amazon on May 3. It was due to ship the week of May 17–22. I had planned a short-notice trip and would not be home until after the book was delivered, but I really wanted to read this book, and it was not available on Kindle yet.

"When I found out about the trip, I said an MBO request that I would receive the book by May 12, before we were leaving. I got an email saying I would receive the book by May 14. I didn't worry. I just said, 'If I am to receive it in time, then I will.' Today, May 9, I got up and was reading my emails and had one from Amazon. Guess what? My book has shipped, and I should have it by May 11! Thank you!"

The King of Pop's MBO

Jan writes: "I recently heard a spot in which Michael Jackson told a reporter that he asked for a really good song to come to him, one with a great beat. A few days later, he said, he was driving down Ventura Boulevard and the beat of 'Thriller' came to him."

Tom responds: Speaking of Michael Jackson, right after his unexpected death, one of my producers called me and said he was going to do a quick documentary on the pop star, as he already had several hours of footage and was filming more interviews and buying more footage. Since then I have sold this documentary to several countries at good prices with good commissions, and more sales are on the way. This was quite benevolent for my company in an extremely slow period for business. This was truly something that I could not have anticipated or requested an MBO for.

29

Benevolent Prayers

Remember to Send Light Out to Others

Tom says: Benevolent prayers (BPs) are what you say for other people, while MBOs are specifically for you. BPs are often said for people in peril. As an example, by the time you read this, the people in Haiti will hopefully be starting to recover from the earthquake, but you can still take just a minute to say,

> **Benevolent Prayer**
> *"I ask that any and all beings assist the Haitian people in recovering from the earthquakes, and may the results be even better than we can hope for or expect. Thank you!"*

Also, when was the last time you sent love and light to this planet? One time in meditation, I asked my guardian angel how many people who read the *Sedona Journal* send light, and he said only about 10 percent. Now, that's a terrible percentage for those of you who claim to be lightworkers. It's so easy! Just imagine sending love and light completely around the planet, and then release it to go where it's needed most. Put this on your schedule at least once a week!

Benevolent Prayer Lightwork in a Hospital

Kevin writes: "Hello, Tom. I am writing in hopes that you can shed more light on this subject. I am currently working at a local hospital as a security person. For some, this could be looked at as a hotbed for the practice of living prayers. In the past week or so, I have been focusing a lot of time and energy on working with MBO requests and living prayers. My question to you or your guardian angel is whether, since I am working a lot around the sick and injured, it would be wrong to use the hospital as a practice ground.

"On one level, I feel as if I could be interfering with someone's karma if they don't ask for healing. However, on another level, I feel if I am able to help people, then who am I to question? There are times when people in the hospital come up to me and discuss their illness or injury, or they discuss a problem that a loved one is undergoing. There are times I have a desire to say a living prayer for these people, but I am dealing with this inner conflict. There is also a part of me that doesn't want to seem like a madman, running around the hospital practicing my living prayer skills on everyone, but I feel if the opportunity presents itself, then I maybe should say a prayer. Can you shed some light on this matter or offer some suggestions? Thank you."

Tom responds: For Kevin and anyone else in a similar situation, I think you're among the lights to shine brightly where you work. Keep in mind that when you say a BP for someone else, it is answered in a most benevolent way for that person. Perhaps the most benevolent way for them is not to recover but not to suffer before they transition.

Remember that you can say prayers by yourself, without calling attention to yourself, as this is your lightworker work. One suggestion would be,

> **Benevolent Prayer**
> "I ask any and all beings to bring aid and assistance to _____ that will be the most benevolent outcome for him or her. Thank you!"

These BPs are answered instantly by a whole cadre of whole souls we call angels. You can write this down to say until you have said it so many times that you can say it from memory.

Then if people wish to talk to you about either their illness or their loved one's illness, you can suggest they request an MBO such as,

> **Most Benevolent Outcome Request**
> "I request a most benevolent outcome for recovering from this disease (or injury). Thank you!"

If they feel despondent, you can ask them if you could say a BP for them or their loved one. Some people will welcome it and be comforted, and some people will not. If they don't welcome it, drop it and say the BP later by yourself. This might be the case most of the time, but that's your work — to create good energy in the hospital. You are dealing with every religion and atheist imaginable in that place, so don't proselytize. Just know that you're doing good work!

Benevolent Prayer Brings a Benevolent Party

Krista writes: "Here's a short BP story. I said a BP and asked Archangel Michael to clear the energies in my home. I asked that anyone who wanted to feel the high vibrations, happiness, and spiritual/healing energies of my home come this weekend. And to my surprise, about sixty students started a party in my tiny apartment of forty-eight square meters (516 square feet). It was great, and so is your book! Thank you!"

Retrieving Lost Information and the Power of Collective Prayer

David writes: "I am new to your newsletter. I signed up last Saturday, and after looking at your latest channeling, I began looking around, checking into your archives. I believe in angels and can think of no better knowledge to have than to learn to use that which we have been given. I'd like to thank you for your kindness.

"Just last night my wife was becoming frustrated looking for the exact name of a continuing education course she took about a year ago. She needed the exact wording in order to obtain credit from her employer. Anyway, she couldn't find it, so I suggested your approach of a simple MBO request. She followed my lead, and voilà! Within two or three minutes, there it was! How cool is that?

"I also believe in the power of common prayer. With the collective efforts of many — for example, wherever two or more gather in his name — there has to be a resulting benefit, even if we cannot always see it right away.

"It must be rewarding to be able to share this kind of information with others. I understand that you have people from all over this planet interested in your work and subscribing to your newsletter. In the name of increasing the power behind the intent, I can't help but wonder if you might consider designating two — or maybe even more — specific times for people to be able to offer your BPs together. I am certain there is a shift in consciousness under way on Earth, and now might be the right time to pursue transmitting this kind of collective thinking."

Tom responds: My guardian angel says that due to the great differences in time around the world, saying BPs that I suggest in my column, blog, and newsletter act in a crescendo in which the whole is greater than the sum of the parts.

Tangible Response to Daily Prayer

Jackie writes: "I just had an interesting experience that I attribute to your daily BP, which I say as often as I remember. I said the prayer this morning before I had a chat with someone I've had difficulties with recently. I've tried to help him see what causes his current troubles, but the words are not being heard, and I may have unintentionally caused him harm.

"After we stopped talking, he sent a message to me saying he felt a lot of energy come to him afterward. He thought it was just me sending the light, but I didn't know what he was talking about. Then I remembered the BP that asks for beings to assist and comfort anyone I have harmed. I mentioned this and he expanded on his statement, saying he felt healing light, very strong and dazzlingly bright.

"To me, this definitely sounded like a response to my prayer! I may not have been in the head space to consciously send nice energy to him, but my guardian angel knew I had asked and responded for me. This is my first confirmed response to this daily prayer. What a powerful response it was."

Hot Water Heater Repaired

Silvia writes: "Hi, Tom! I wanted to share a BP that is linked to Europe. My mom lives in Switzerland and told me that her hot water heater was not working anymore; it just suddenly stopped. So I mentioned to her to call on Archangel Michael, and I said a BP. I asked any and all beings to help my mom in Switzerland to get her hot water heater working, ending with 'and may the result be better than what she expects or hopes for.' A day or two later, Mom said she had hot water again. Thank you, universe! Isn't it great? Thank you, Tom, for all you do."

Benevolent Colorado Trip for Boy Scouts

Marian writes: "My son is a Boy Scout leader in Texas, and my grandson is a scout. They spent this past week at summer camp in Colorado. I requested many BPs for them and sent them an email the day they left, asking them to humor me and say out loud the MBOs I sent to them. Temperatures were forecast to be in the lower thirties at night with highs in the upper fifties. With temps over one hundred at my home for over twenty-five days, that sounds like a bit of heaven to me but not to them.

"I said this BP a week or so before they left:

> **Benevolent Prayer**
> *"I ask any and all beings to ensure _____ and _____ have optimum clear picture-taking weather wherever they physically go on their way to, from, and during their Boy Scout summer camp week, July 23 through August 1, 2011, and may the results and benefits be even more than they expect or can anticipate. Thank you!"*

"The high and low temperatures in Colorado were in the low fifties and upper seventies, respectively, all week — much better! To quote my son, 'the weather was perfect.'

"I said other BPs for their safe travel and benefit during their Boy Scout trip, asking for results and benefits even better than they could expect or anticipate. There were four troops traveling together. On the way to Colorado, a truck carrying scout leaders from another troop had an unplanned meeting with a deer. Everyone and everything was safe except the deer and truck.

"Quickly I went back to the BPs and reworded them, always including a thank you:

Benevolent Prayers

"I ask any and all beings to assist the Boy Scouts in their travel to have a safe and smooth ride. May they be ignored by the highway patrol unless they choose to contact the highway patrol, and may they return home safely. Thank you!"

"I ask any and all beings to ensure the Boy Scouts and leaders have an exciting, fantastically positive, memorable adventure during their white water rafting excursion down the Royal Gorge and during their Boy Scout summer camp week. May they return home safely, and may the results and benefits be even greater than they expect or can anticipate. Thank you!"

"I ask any and all beings to ensure all animals along the roads traveled by the Boy Scouts and leaders stay where they are off the road and not be frightened. Thank you!"

"I ask any and all beings to ensure the prompt, perfect repair of the truck belonging to the scout leader involved in an accident during the Boy Scout trip to Colorado, and may the outcome be better than anything he could have hoped for or expected. Thank you!"

"I ask any and all beings to ensure the optimum good health of the Boy Scouts and leaders, especially during their camping trip in Colorado. Thank you!"

"Every one of these BPs had a positive outcome. They had a great, memorable experience that was in many ways better than they anticipated. Now if only my BP asking for cooler temperatures and gentle rain here at home would hurry up in being fulfilled!

"I have one question, though: How do I word a BP for my grandson who does not turn in his homework and is seemingly always one step from failing in classes where he should be an A student? I suspect most parents and grandparents would appreciate some BPs for improved achievement during the school year. Thanks so much."

Tom responds: Great story of MBOs and BPs. I was in charge of setting up the summer trips for my son's scout troop, and we went the first year to a scout ranch in southern Colorado that was poorly run at that time. The next two years we went to Camp Alexander near Colorado Springs and had a fantastic time. Naturally, I requested MBOs for the trip up and back in our fifteen-passenger vans. We even had snow one night there, but that was because we were attending the first week of the season in June. I even learned to mountain bike there.

Try this BP for students:

Helping Relatives in Trouble

Patricia writes: "I had an almost instantaneous BP recently. I have a granddaughter who was in jail for a short time, and I requested a BP for her that things would turn out better than expected when she went to court. Well, less than an hour later, she was released, and then when she went back to court a few days later, I again requested a BP that it would turn out better than expected. She doesn't have to go back, as the case is closed. It is over with and she is completely free. I am grateful."

A Prayer for Forgiveness

Fredricka writes: "I am so happy to hear your surgery went so well, Tom — just more evidence of the validity of all our MBOs! In the latest newsletter, Donna wrote about requesting an MBO for helping with forgiveness. I too have an issue with that, and I'd like to know how she worded her request. Or if you have a suggestion for me, I would appreciate it."

Tom responds: When I received Fredericka's email, I heard a little whisper in my ear to suggest the BP I have on my website under the "signs" tab. This is actually a prayer for forgiveness, as I was gently reminded. It goes like this:

My guardian angel responded to this: "Yes, the living prayer that you say each day benevolently affects all the others, Tom, and it affects them more than you can imagine. As I told you before, this erases much karma — more than you can imagine, as I said, so that you do not have to do so much balancing elsewhere, even in the lives where you were one of the 'bad people,' as they would be defined today. So that is certainly one major thing that you should continue to do and encourage others to do.

"Beyond that, there are those times when you assist or help others just out of the goodness of your heart. These times also erase karma in your other lives, as it is a balancing that must eventually take place. You've become very good at balancing these things over many, many lives. You're much more open to doing these things and realize on a subconscious level that leaving tips for waiters and other seemingly small courtesies you do for people help to balance lives. It helps to raise you to another level faster. The more that people do things for other people out of the goodness of their hearts and not for financial remuneration, the higher the level that you will all vibrate on."

I next asked my angel, "Have I ever said the benevolent living prayer I say each morning in any other life?"

His response: "No, not really. This is your first life to recognize the value of saying this prayer. That's why it is so important that you continue to say this prayer on a daily basis, as it truly does erase much karma, as I have explained before. So I am telling you the complete truth here, Tom. Do not doubt this statement, as I know doubt can creep into your mind. This is a true gift to yourself and all the other lives you've lived and will live on Earth."

You can also send white light each day to the person you wish forgiveness from, but the above BP does it best, I think.

Protection from Bullies

Lana writes: "Can you suggest a BP that I can do for bullying behavior? I have a colleague who really bullies other coworkers and gets away with it often. She does not bully me, though, because I would not accept it. I know I'm not responsible for defending other people, as they have their own lessons to learn and so on. I do, however, have to constantly remind myself not to think nasty thoughts about my bullying coworker. I looked for something on the blog but didn't find anything specific. Can you help?"

Tom responds: Let's try this one:

> **Benevolent Prayer**
> "I ask any and all beings to assist and protect all those who come in contact with _____ from any verbal, physical, or sexual abuse. Thank you!"

You never know why some people are forced to put up with bullying, so I threw in the kitchen sink here. You can also send white light each day to this person. Some people can't live with so much light and will leave for another job.

New Wheels

Eleanore writes: "There is a young woman where I live who is confined to a wheelchair — the kind you must propel by hand. I asked her one day why she didn't have a motorized scooter, and she said they would not authorize one for her. I said a BP to ask that she be motorized so she wouldn't have to work so hard to get around.

"Three days later, I met her. To my amazement, she was driving a motorized scooter! I told her how delighted I was for her and asked her what happened. She told me that one of the other women she knew got a new scooter and didn't need this one, so she gave it to her. I was completely blown away, and you can be sure I sent much gratitude to those angels who managed that gift."

Benevolence for Others

Christine writes: "I say BPs all the time for everybody — even people I don't know but who are exhibiting distress or even for difficult news on TV. In those situations, I have no idea of the prayers' effect, but I do know they make me feel better, connected, helpful, and at peace. My granddaughter has raised her grades thanks to a BP and now has a social life because she was allowed to have her phone back. It took a few weeks. Coincidence? I don't think so; she had not had her phone for over a year! That's one happy teenager!"

30

Expect Great Things

Tom says: I have mentioned several times in previous columns that each morning I say,

Expect Great Things Mantra
"I expect great things today, great things tomorrow, and great things all the rest of this week. Thank you!"

My guardian angel tells me in my meditations that this acts very similarly to an MBO request and can really make a difference in your life after you start to say it each day. You can print out a sign from my website (www.TheGentle WayBook.com) to help you remember to say it each day.

An Angelic Sense of Humor

Katherine writes: "I was taking my morning walk, thinking about a long list of frustrations and issues I had going around and around in my head and feeling pretty stuck, when I remembered to say an MBO prayer. I looked up toward the sky and said something like,

Most Benevolent Outcome Request
"I request an MBO for resolving all these issues, and may the results be even better than I can imagine or expect."

"When I looked down again, I saw a huge horse trailer with a sign that said, 'The Gentle Way.' I kid you not! A horse trailer parked on a city street in a very upscale neighborhood. What are the odds of that, and then to have it say, 'The Gentle Way'? The side of the truck read, 'Horsemanship Seminars.' I had to laugh! My angels sure do have a sense of humor!"

Tom responds: Our guardian angels do have a sense of humor, and they are always trying to let us know they're around. It might be a love song that pops into your mind that you had not thought of in a long time, a song you hear on the radio, a series of numbers, or any number of other things. When you begin requesting MBOs, you see how they work for you each day.

Expecting Exceptional Financial Progress

Dan writes: "I'm still trying to wrap my head around my latest MBO event, so I'll just share it with you and let you and other readers decide. Yesterday afternoon I was sitting on my deck, reflecting on how effective MBOs have been in my life. Having said that, I also was of the opinion that I had been playing it somewhat safe in my requests: good parking spots, preferential seating, good meetings, and the like.

"I decided it was time to ask for MBOs that were exceptional. Then I went on to not only describe the three areas I was looking for exceptional improvement in — career, finances, and finding my perfect mate — but I also identified all those related thoughts and beliefs that were holding me back: in particular, beliefs of being not worthy, not good enough, and so on. I specifically asked for these to be removed so that I could make that exceptional progress I was looking for.

"Once finished, I remained in my chair, feeling that quiet calm and thankfulness from knowing my MBO had been heard. No more than two minutes later, I received an email from a distant cousin, informing me that about two weeks earlier he had received a request from a land agent who was working on behalf of a junior mining company. The company wanted to do some exploratory drilling to determine if the land that belonged to my maternal grandparents — to which my three cousins and I still own the mineral rights — had sufficient quality and quantity of minerals to warrant further mining.

"After doing some quick online checking of mineral maps for the area, I discovered that the farm is right in the middle of one of the most concentrated and richest deposits for that mineral in the world. If developed, the future income potential could be very significant."

Expect Great Things You Never Thought to Ask For

Renee writes: "I wanted to share with you that a couple of weeks ago I was anticipating my unemployment check in the mail that, because of a hiccup in the process, was late. Instead I received a check for $470 from a civil action claim that I don't even remember filing for back in 2007. Boy, that was really expecting great things! Thanks again, Tom. I really do expect great things on a daily basis."

Tom responds: My guardian angel says the "expect great things" mantra is an MBO request that allows your own guardian angel to bring you things you never thought to ask for each week.

Expecting Great Things in All Areas of My Life

Margaret writes: "I have very happily been requesting MBOs for some time now. I just saw your 'expect great things' mantra, and I started saying it out loud last week. I first used it because it quelled my anxiety about my friend's upcoming induced labor, which resulted in an underweight baby with a bad heart condition. But now my friend, her baby, and her husband are all doing well.

"It just quells my anxiety in general. I have so many things to attend to in my day-to-day life. Saying it in addition to specific MBOs truly helps. Life is so much more delightful. This enables me to send out higher vibrations to the etheric atmosphere rather than lower ones. It reminds me that I am creating my reality in cooperation with All and that I am not a victim of fate. The new energies are all about creating!

"This past Monday evening, the phrasing manifested in grand fashion. I had just left my dental appointment. It was sunny in Chicago at that time. Driving home, I suddenly got a surge of energy to go all the way out to Whole Foods to buy salad mixes for my diet. Off I went.

"As I approached the store, a strong black wall of clouds suddenly arose from the west. I thought I needed to turn around now and head back home. Then I decided I could get to the store before the wall clouds hit in all their fury, and by the time I finished shopping, the first blast would be over and gentle rain would be falling.

"My thoughts and timing were right on. The fierce winds and rain hit while I shopped. I left the store with gentle rains falling and power knocked out all over the area because of downed trees. Going home, it occurred to me my electricity would be out, and it was. Unable to get into my garage, I parked in my driveway. The electricity wouldn't be turned on for another sixteen hours.

"If I had turned around to go straight home when I first saw the clouds, my car would have been stuck in the garage for the following day, and I would have missed the last day of the school year. I woke up with the dawn and arrived at school earlier than I had arrived all year. I was ever so happy with your phrase: 'I am expecting great things today.'

"Now I'm using it, along with specific MBOs, to take care of a mix-up with my state's income tax bureau. They owe me returns for the three previous years, but due to their incorrect reading of my accountant-prepared tax forms, they keep insisting it is I who owe them money. It will all be cleared up in the morning, and soon I will get back the three years of returns they owe me."

MBOs and BPs in Prague

Galimir writes: "Thank you, Tom, for providing such a cool tool for all of us! I have been diligently requesting MBOs for the day, for myself, for my wife and our relationship, plus your 'expecting great things' mantra. I have also been requesting different MBOs throughout the day that are specific and purpose-oriented to every single day of my life for almost a year now, and I must say that these requests are now one of my major tools for transformation. Thank you!"

MBO for a Good Week

Kate writes: "Tom, I made a general MBO request for the week. The sun came out when I went for a walk after a dismal week of cold wind and gray. It went back to cloudy within a minute of me getting back from the walk. That is not an exciting one, but it made me take notice. I also found myself face-to-face with Senator Bernie Sanders of Vermont yesterday in our co-op market. I turned around, and there he was next to me, his face only inches away, so I had the opportunity to thank him for being practically the only sane voice in Congress."

Tom responds: I normally suggest saying the "expect great things" MBO request each day.

31

Guardian Angels

What's My Guardian Angel's Name?

Thelma writes: "Blessings. I must convey to you that I certainly enjoy and look forward to your weekly newsletters, and I have been vocally requesting MBOs and BPs daily. I also keep a daily gratitude journal, and in it I include my MBOs and BPs for others. Most of my requests have been fulfilled, especially since I have been adding: 'And may the results be better than I can hope for or expect.' I always remember to say thank you ever since you introduced me to MBOs in your first book.

"My main concern is to make contact with my guardian angel and know his or her name. I know there must be some contact, as I do have most of my requests answered. Can you offer any advice or ask your guardian angel if he has any suggestions for my own contact? I need help."

Tom responds: I do receive these requests quite often. I recommend that you — or a friend or family member — perform an Internet search using the words "contact my spirit guide" or "contact my guardian angel." You will have many options to choose from. Go with what feels right to you.

Keep in mind that I do not call my guardian angel by his actual name. He told me that my vocal cords are not constructed to pronounce it. I would only be frustrated in trying. He said I could call him Tom, Dick, or Harry, but that Tom would be a little difficult in my meditations. (He has a sense of humor, you see!) So if you just relax and ask, "What should I call you?" you might get a name out of the air as I did.

When Your Guardian Angel Whispers

Carol writes: "How can I know my angel is connecting with me?"

Tom responds: Your guardian angel whispers in your ear all the time. The trick is to become more aware so that when a thought comes to you to do something — perhaps something you hadn't thought about before

— you recognize its origin. Requesting MBOs all the time heightens this awareness, as you start to see events take place to bring you the MBO.

My Angel Is Always by My Side

Debbi writes: "Well, I know people like to hear positive stories, so I have one about MBO requests. I asked my angel to give me some sign so that I know he is always by my side and I can always feel safe, and here's what happened.

"I got a call from a friend I hadn't heard from in a long time because she had something she wanted to share with me. After the initial conversation ended, she suddenly started talking about how she had gotten a strange sign from an angel and how she strongly believes in them. She said she knows that the angels see everything in a much bigger picture, so now she understands some things in her life.

"We talked a lot about that subject, but the point is that we had never talked about angels before nor about anything like that in general, and I definitely didn't start the topic because I don't like discussing that with other people. She even said she had been praying to angels for years and that she now has something she thought was impossible: She has basically gotten everything she's asked for and much more! Trust me, I was so shocked that I started laughing really hard in the middle of the conversation; it was incredible. And now I feel so calm and relaxed, because I know that was the sign I requested and my angel is by my side."

Learning to Trust the Angels

Chrissy writes: "If some people are having trouble allowing the angels to do what they need to do — in other words, if they are not sure that MBOs will work — they can do and say the following, which has worked for me in the past. Hold your hand over your heart, breathe in, and say, 'I trust.' As you let the breath go, release from inside all your worries. Trust that the angels have only your best intentions in mind and will never let you down. I hope this helps some people. God bless, and keep up the brilliant work you do."

Tom responds: Great suggestions from Chrissy, everyone!

Building My Relationship with My Angel

Ishh writes: "I recently discovered that I really do have a guardian angel. I asked for some help, and he or she helped me; I am so grateful! I have decided to acknowledge and nurture my relationship with my angel from now on. Today I started a book in honor of our relationship and called it *Me and My Guardian Angel*. I apologized to my angel for not recognizing him or her before and expressed my gratitude that he or she is with me. I made a